Social Change and Human Development

Social Change and Human Development
Concept and Results

Edited by
Rainer K. Silbereisen
and Xinyin Chen

Los Angeles | London | New Delhi
Singapore | Washington DC

Introduction and editorial arrangement © Rainer K. Silbereisen and Xinyin Chen 2010

Chapter 1 © Steffen Schmidt 2010
Chapter 2 © Jochen Brandtstädter 2010
Chapter 3 © Ross Macmillan and Arturo Baiocchi 2010
Chapter 4 © Dirk Hofäcker, Sandra Buchholz and Hans-Peter Blossfeld 2010
Chapter 5 © Rainer K. Silbereisen, Martin Pinquart and Martin J. Tomasik 2010
Chapter 6 © Jutta Heckhausen 2010
Chapter 7 © Reinhold Sackmann 2010
Chapter 8 © Melvin L. Kohn 2010
Chapter 9 © Xinyin Chen and Huichang Chen 2010
Chapter 10 © Rukmalie Jayakody, Jessica Heckert and Dang Nguyen Anh 2010
Chapter 11 © Ingrid Schoon 2010
Chapter 12 © Jacek Wasilewski 2010

First published 2010

Apart from any fair dealing for the purposes of research or private study, or criticism or review, as permitted under the Copyright, Designs and Patents Act, 1988, this publication may be reproduced, stored or transmitted in any form, or by any means, only with the prior permission in writing of the publishers, or in the case of reprographic reproduction, in accordance with the terms of licences issued by the Copyright Licensing Agency. Enquiries concerning reproduction outside those terms should be sent to the publishers.

SAGE Publications Ltd
1 Oliver's Yard
55 City Road
London EC1Y 1SP

SAGE Publications Inc.
2455 Teller Road
Thousand Oaks, California 91320

SAGE Publications India Pvt Ltd
B 1/I 1 Mohan Cooperative Industrial Area
Mathura Road
New Delhi 110 044

SAGE Publications Asia-Pacific Pte Ltd
33 Pekin Street #02-01
Far East Square
Singapore 048763

Library of Congress Control Number: 2009932310

British Library Cataloguing in Publication data

A catalogue record for this book is available from the British Library

ISBN 978-1-84920-019-6

Typeset by Glyph International, Bangalore, India
Printed by the MPG Books Group, Bodmin and King's Lynn
Printed on paper from sustainable resources

CONTENTS

Notes on contributors   vii

Introduction: How social change affects individual adaptation   1
Rainer K. Silbereisen and *Xinyin Chen*

Part I   Dynamic of social change and individual responses   29

1   A Challenge-Response-Model in research on social change   31
Steffen Schmidt

2   Life management in developmental settings of modernity: Challenges to the adaptive self   50
Jochen Brandtstädter

3   Conceptualizing the dynamics of lives and historical times: Life course phenomena, institutional dynamics and sociohistorical change   73
Ross Macmillan and *Arturo Baiocchi*

Part II   Determinants on the individual level   99

4   Globalization, institutional filters and changing life course. Patterns in modern societies: A summary of the results from the GLOBALIFE-Project   101
Dirk Hofäcker, Sandra Buchholz, and *Hans-Peter Blossfeld*

5   Demands of social change and psychosocial adjustment: Results from the Jena study   125
Rainer K. Silbereisen, Martin Pinquart, and *Martin J. Tomasik*

6   Globalization, social inequality, and individual agency in human development: Social change for better or worse?   148
Jutta Heckhausen

Part III Transitions and transformations in international perspective — 165

7 Institutional responses to social change in comparative perspective: Germany and Poland — 167
Reinhold Sackmann

8 Class, stratification, and personality under conditions of apparent social stability and of radical social change: A multi-nation comparison — 190
Melvin L. Kohn

9 Children's socioemotional functioning and adjustment in the changing Chinese society — 209
Xinyin Chen and Hiuchang Chen

10 Social change and premarital sexual behavior and attitudes in Vietnam — 227
Rukmalie Jayakody, Jessica Heckert, and Dang Nguyen Anh

11 Social change and transition experiences among young adults in Britain — 245
Ingrid Schoon

12 Political elites as an agent of social change: The Polish perspective — 271
Jacek Wasilewski

Index — 289

CONTRIBUTORS

Dang Nguyen Anh is the Vice Director for International Research Cooperation for the Vietnam Academy of Social Sciences. Prior to assuming this position, he was the Director of the Center for Population at the Institute of Sociology in Hanoi. Anh's research focuses on the determinants and consequences of migration in Vietnam.

Arturo Baiocchi is a Sociology doctoral candidate at the University of Minnesota. His past and ongoing work examines how notions of mental health are understood and used by different social groups. Arturo is currently a training fellow sponsored by the National Institute of Mental Health and the American Sociological Association.

Hans-Peter Blossfeld holds the Chair of Sociology I at Bamberg University and is the Director of the State Institute for Family Research at Bamberg University. He has published 20 books and over 150 articles on social inequality, youth, family, and educational sociology, labor market research, demography, social stratification and mobility, the modern methods of quantitative social research and statistical methods for longitudinal data analysis. He has directed several international comparative projects on demography, family, work and education, among them the GLOBALIFE project. Currently, he is interested in the flexibilization of work in modern societies, the division of domestic work in the family, and the development of individual competences and the formation of educational decisions in early school careers. Address: Lehrstuhl für Soziologie I, Otto-Friedrich-Universität Bamberg, Postfach 1549, D-96045 Bamberg, Germany. [e-mail: soziologie1@sowi.uni-bamberg.de]

Jochen Brandtstädter is Professor of Psychology at the University of Trier, Germany. Substantive topics in his research include adult development, action theory, theoretical psychology, development in partnership relations, self-regulatory processes, dynamics of goal commitment and disengagement across adulthood and later life. He was Fellow at the Institute for Advanced Study (Wissenschaftskolleg) Berlin (1983–84) and at the Center for Advanced Study in the Behavioral Sciences, Stanford (1998–99);

his memberships include the European Academy of Sciences (Academia Europaea) und the German Academy of Sciences Leopoldina.

Sandra Buchholz is a research scientist at the University of Bamberg, Chair of Sociology I. She holds a Ph.D. in Sociology from Bamberg University (Dr rer. pol.). From 2003 to 2005, Buchholz served as a research scientist in the international comparative GLOBALIFE project at the Otto-Friedrich-University Bamberg. From 2005 to 2007, she was working in the DFG-project 'Flexibility Forms at Labor Market Entry and in the Early Career' (flexCAREER) at the State Institute for Family Research at the University of Bamberg. She is interested in labor market research, international comparison, life course research, industrial relations, and quantitative methods. Address: Lehrstuhl für Soziologie I, Otto-Friedrich-Universität Bamberg, Postfach 1549, D-96045 Bamberg, Germany. [e-mail: sandra.buchholz@uni-bamberg.de]

Huichang Chen graduated from Shanghai Normal University with a MA. He is currently a Professor at the Institute of Developmental Psychology, Beijing Normal University. He is a Regional Coordinator of the International Society for the Study of Behavioral Development (ISSBD) and a Member of the Executive Committee of Chinese Psychological Society. His research interests are mainly in children and adolescents' social and emotional development.

Xinyin Chen is Professor of Psychology at University of Western Ontario. He received a William T. Grant Scholars Award and several other academic awards. He is interested in children's socioemotional functioning and relationships, with a focus on cross-cultural issues. He has edited or co-edited several books (e.g., *Peer Relationships in Cultural Context*, *Socioemotional Development in Cultural Context*) and published over 100 journal articles and book chapters about culture and development.

Jessica Heckert is a graduate student in the dual-degree program in Human Development and Family Studies and Demography at the Pennsylvania State University, where her current research examines the experiences of children and youth in developing countries. Prior to pursuing graduate studies, she worked as a youth and community development specialist in the Dominican Republic and Haiti.

Jutta Heckhausen is Professor at the Department of Psychology and Social Behavior. Her research addresses the role of motivation and control striving in life-span development. She has published several books and her numerous research articles are published in the premier journals of developmental and personality psychology such as *Developmental Psychology, Psychology and Aging, Journal of Research on Adolescence, Journal of Gerontology, Journal of Personality and Social Psychology, Psychological Review*. From 1984 until 2000, Jutta Heckhausen was a researcher at the Center for Life-Span Psychology at the Max-Planck-Institute for Human Development in Berlin. In 1995/96, she was a fellow at the Center for Social and Behavioral Science at Stanford. In 2000, Jutta Heckhausen joined the Department of Psychology and Social Behavior at UC Irvine.

Dirk Hofäcker is a research scientist at the University of Bamberg, Chair of Sociology I and at the Institute for Family Research at the University of Bamberg (ifb). From 2002 to 2005, Hofäcker served as a research scientist in the international comparative GLOBALIFE project at the Otto-Friedrich-University Bamberg. Since 2006 he holds a position as a researcher at the ifb and is also the coordinator of the ESF-funded Research network 'TransEurope.' His interests are in family sociology, comparative labor market research, life course research, attitudinal research and quantitative methods in the social sciences. Address: [e-mail: dirk.hofaecker@uni-bamberg.de]

Rukmalie Jayakody is the Associate Director of the Population Research Institute and Associate Professor of Human Development at Pennsylvania State University. Her research focuses broadly on the impacts of social changes and the impacts of public policies. She has published widely on public policy changes and family well-being in the U.S., as well as social changes and their impacts on families in Vietnam.

Melvin L. Kohn is Professor of Sociology at the Johns Hopkins University, USA. His research has mainly been in the field of social structure and personality. In recent decades, this work has been almost entirely cross-nationally comparative and collaborative. His principal books in English are Class and Conformity: A Study in Values (1969); Work and Personality: An Inquiry into the Impact of Social Stratification (1983, co-authored with Carmi Schooler); Social Structure and Self-Direction: A Comparative Analysis of the United States and Poland (1990, co- authored with Kazimierz M. Slomczynski); and Change and Stability: A Cross-National Analysis of Social Structure and Personality (2006). These books and collections of his papers have been translated into and published in Chinese, German, Italian, Polish, and Ukrainian. Kohn is a past-President of the American Sociological Association and a former member of the Executive Committee of the International Sociological Association. A fellow or honorary member of learned societies in several countries, he was awarded an honorary doctorate by The National University of 'Kyiv-Mohyla Academy' (Ukraine) in 2008.

Ross Macmillan is an Associate Professor of Sociology and Director of the Life Course Center at the University of Minnesota. He has published widely on theory and methods for life course research, pathways in the transition to adulthood, and life course criminology. Most recently he co-authored 'Biography and the Sociological Imagination: Contexts and Contingencies' with Michael Shanahan and has edited two volumes of Advances in Life Course research entitled 'The Structure of the Life Course: Standardized? Individualized? Differentiated?' and 'Constructing Adulthood: Agency and Subjectivity in the Life Course.'

Martin Pinquart is Professor of Developmental Psychology at Philipps University, Marburg, Germany. He has published widely on the effects of social change on human development, effects of critical life events, developmental regulation, and geropsychology. Most recently, he has published Individuum und sozialer Wandel [individual and social change], edited with Rainer K. Silbereisen (Juventa, 2008).

Reinhold Sackmann is Professor of Sociology (Social Structure of Modern Societies) at Martin-Luther-University Halle-Wittenberg, Germany. He has published widely on life course sociology – most recently, *Life Course Analysis and Biographic Research* (Verlag fuer Sozialwissenschaften, 2007). He has written on topics such as coping with low fertility in comparative perspective, the transformation generation, and the internationalization of education policy. Dr Sackmann is member of the Network of Experts in the Social Sciences of Education and Training (NESSE) of the Directorate General for Education & Culture of the European Union.

Dr Steffen Schmidt is a philosopher, currently working at the University of Jena, Departement of Sociology. His main research interests include theory of social change, sociology of knowledge, philosophy of culture, social philosophy. A new interdisciplinary project focusses on the legacy of Hegel's philosophy, especially for the social sciences. An assortment of main and current publications: Hegel's *System der Sittlichkeit* (2007); 'Génération Précaire – Ambivalenz und Reichweite einer neuen Selbstzuschreibung', 'in: Michael Busch/Jan Jeskow/Rüdiger Stutz (Hg.), Zwischen Prekarisierung und Protest. Die Lebenslagen und Generationsbilder von Jugendlichen in Ost und West (2009), S. 77–101; 'Die Weltgeschichte ist das Weltgericht' – 'Hegels Konzeption der Weltgeschichte,' in: Walter Pauly (Hg.), Hegel's Staatsverständnis (2009), S. 199–217.

Ingrid Schoon is Professor of Human Development and Social Policy at the Institute of Education, University of London. Her research interests lie with the study of human development in context, in particular the transition from dependent childhood to independent adulthood in changing and varying socio-historical contexts. She is the author of more than 100 scholarly articles, book chapters, and reports. Her recent publications include a monograph on risk and resilience and an edited volume on transitions from school to work (co-edited with Rainer K. Silbereisen), both published by Cambridge University Press.

Rainer K. Silbereisen is Chair of Developmental Psychology and Director of the Center for Applied Developmental Science at the University of Jena, Germany, and Adjunct Professor of Human Development at the Pennsylvania State University, USA. He has published widely on contextual influences on human behavior and development, and in particular on the role of social and political change for adjustment. Recent publications are *Approaches to Positive Youth Development* (Sage, 2007; edited with Richard M. Lerner) and *Transitions from School to Work. Globalisation, Individualization, and Patterns of Diversity* (Cambridge, 2009; edited with Ingrid Schoon). He is Fellow of the American Psychological Association and a Member of the Academia Europaea, London; UK.

Martin Tomasik is a post-doctoral research fellow at the Center for Applied Developmental Science in Jena, Germany. His research focuses on adaptive psychosocial adjustment to life-course transitions and contextual change. His doctoral thesis was about 'Developmental Barriers and the Benefits of Disengagement' (Friedrich Schiller University Jena, 2008). Recent publications comprise a journal article on 'Demands of Social Change as a Function of the Political Context, Institutional Filters, and Psychosocial Resources' (Social Indicators Research, 2009; together with R. K. Silbereisen) and an article on 'Adaptive Adjustment of Vocational Aspirations among German Youth During the Transition from School to Work' (Journal of Vocational Behavior, 2009; together with S. A. Hardy, C. M. Haase, and J. Heckhausen).

Jacek Wasilewski is professor of sociology and dean of the Faculty of Humanities and Social Sciences at the Warsaw School of Social Psychology, Poland. He is also a head of a research team on political elites in the Polish Academy of Sciences, and editor-in-chief of the quarterly *Studia Socjologiczne*. He has written on political elites, including parliamentarians and local elites, and on social stratification in Poland. Recently he has edited *Political Leadership in Polish Counties* (Institute of Political Studies, Warsaw, 2009), and co-authored with Jan Pakulski a paper 'Circulation of Political Elites: From Foxes to Lions' which was published in Polish (*Studia Socjologiczne* 2006) and in Russian (*Politicheskije Isledovanija* 2009).

INTRODUCTION: HOW SOCIAL CHANGE AFFECTS INDIVIDUAL ADAPTATION

Rainer K. Silbereisen and *Xinyin Chen*

This book deals with the role of rapid social change for human adaptation and development. Our case in point is the fusion of the consequences of political transition following the fall of socialism with crises related to the negative effects of globalization. The aftermath of this fusion was wide-reaching. It affected ideologies and belief systems, central societal institutions (from political representation to economic activities and welfare), the structure of community life and neighborhoods, as well as conditions for families. In the chapters that make up this volume, we ask what these changes meant for people's adjustment and well-being. We are especially interested in how people deal with changes of the economic and social contexts they were used to relying upon, and in what activities are likely to improve their situation, which is often characterized by a devaluing of resources accumulated before the period of transition.

A historical prototype of research on individual consequences of macro-level change is Glen Elder's (1974) landmark study on the Great Depression of the late 1920s. This worldwide financial crisis resulted in economic hardship for many families, primarily through unemployment, and subsequently led to attempts by family members to close the mismatch between resources and claims. The concomitant and often painful adjustment of the household economy, typically by reducing expenditure for essential commodities, resulted in psychological and even physical tension between couples that ultimately damaged the socialization function of the family, with negative consequences for children's psychosocial adjustment. As some of the chapters testify, Elder's research also provided a blueprint for many social and behavioral scientists who became interested in more recent societal changes related to the end of the bipolar world system in existence since World War Two (e.g., Silbereisen & Tomasik, 2008).

Social change and individual adaptation

In the following, our understanding of the nexus between social change on the macro-level and consequences for individual adaptation will be delineated in a series of steps. This process provided the rationale for the selection of contributions appearing in this book.

Types of social change

Social Change and Human Development: Concepts and Results brings together research on the longer-term consequences of a particular type of social change. It is connected with the break-up in the late 1980s of the former socialist countries in Central-Eastern Europe, signified by the opening of the East-West border in Hungary and by the subsequent demolition of the Berlin Wall in 1989. It also considers the consequences of the dissolution of the former Soviet Union and the evolution of successor states, with the sometimes radical turnaround, as seen in Hungary and Germany, or the hesitant political reforms towards a representative democracy and free market economy, as in the Ukraine. Moreover, the economic liberalization and opening up to world markets in countries such as Vietnam and China that were taking place at about the same time are included as an example of massive societal change with a revision, rather than a complete breakdown, of the political system.

The common denominator of the social change addressed by the contributions to this volume is the radical transition from the founding ideological principles to new values, such as freedom of expression and movement across borders, which made the old political system and its institutions obsolete. As is to be expected from the logic of such transitions (e.g., the fall of the Berlin Wall and its short-term consequence of the dissolving of established institutions of power), they were followed by a longer period of transformation that included the re-establishing of institutions in line with the new political system, such as those related to the economy, education, and welfare. As in the case of Germany, the high aspirations of the initial transformation period were complicated by the effects of another type of social change, typically characterized by the catchphrase 'globalization,' which heralded rapid technological change, worldwide information access, and global markets for goods and labor.

Although at face value globalization seems to match many of the ideological changes towards a liberal model of political and economic action in the transition countries, in effect it interfered with attempts to restructure the formerly state-owned and centrally managed industries, with an unprecedented increase in unemployment and a widening gap between social strata as prime manifestations. Typically, the merging of evolving transformation and growing tensions related to globalization resulted in what some have called 'post-transformation' – what was meant to form the solid political and economic base for the new societies needed to be corrected again, because unintended consequences became overwhelming. A case in point is the high debt German municipalities accumulated in order to meet the aspirations nourished by the political transition, which subsequently made them and their service provision especially vulnerable when their income from taxes on enterprises declined due to the economic uncertainty (Sackmann, Chapter 7 this volume).

Although the above characterization seems to apply basically to all examples of the countries and transitions included in this book, upon closer examination there are differences in how political transition and transformation was brought about, and in how the transformation of the economic system was handled. Both had consequences that percolated down from the macro-level via institution-building to the level of individual adaptation. In contrast to the other countries mentioned, Germany seems to represent a special case with regard to the type of political transformation process utilized. After the fall of the Berlin Wall and the formation of a transition government in the East (the former German Democratic Republic – GDR), unification of the country and transformation of society in the East was thought to be accomplishable simply by the transfer of West German institutions and functional elites (Zapf, 1996). This 'incorporation model' (the unification of Vietnam shows some resemblance) differs from an 'autonomy model' (see Wasilewski, Chapter 12 this volume), whereby the transition was accomplished either by agreement between opposing elites within the country, as in the case of Poland, or by top-down reforms that maintained old structures and basically transformed political capital gained in the old system into economic capital under the new circumstances, as in the case of the Ukraine.

Another typology by King and Szelenyi (2005) focuses on the role of elites in forming the new economic systems. They distinguish between different types of influences. China and Vietnam are instances of 'capitalism from below' where, as a consequence of pivotal political decision-making, a market system starts with small businesses and evolves in parallel to the maintained state economy: both are controlled by the established political system. In contrast, 'capitalism from above,' as characterized by Russia and the Ukraine, is where a state-run economy is transformed into a privatized system, but where, due to the lack of democratic control, it results in the concentration of capital among members of privileged political networks rooted in the past. Finally, 'capitalism from without' refers to a situation, as exemplified by Poland, where elite consensus and political integration into Europe leads to the establishment of an open economic system with high levels of foreign investment. In this regard,

Germany is probably closer to Poland than any of the other countries mentioned.

In sum, the countries covered in this book, and thus the type of social change addressed, share a more or less pronounced political hiatus followed by a longer period of political and economic transformation. In terms of the economic system, they differ in their dependency on the old political system and in the related logic of how economic reforms were brought about. As, according to Elder (2003), social change should be seen against time and place, these differences and commonalities have to be considered when investigating the consequences for individual adaptation.

Comparison across countries and samples

The book includes chapters dealing with countries characterized by transformation plus globalization, and naturally we are interested in comparisons among them, but for a particular purpose. Two approaches can be distinguished in utilizing the structural heterogeneity of change just described. First, one can utilize such differences in order to study the role of a particular element in the process by exploiting its systematic variation across many, carefully chosen countries, as exemplified by the Globalife project on differences and commonalities in the reaction to structural uncertainty due to globalization (Hofäcker, Buchholz, & Blossfeld, Chapter 4 this volume). The element in question is the role of protective regulations for individuals' welfare which differ across countries.

Second, one can use the variation to find out about the generalizability of a well-established model across a number of conditions that have not been analyzed previously or which formerly did not exist. For the latter, we have an exemplary case in the landmark series of studies by Kohn and his colleagues (Kohn, Chapter 8 this volume). They found that the relationship between the substantive complexity of work and intellectual flexibility applied not only to industrial workers in the USA but also to those in Poland, which was still socialist at the time of the study. The only difference was that it was the workers in the American sample and the managers in the Polish sample that reported higher stress levels, in the latter case probably due to the close supervision and control from higher up. The political and economic redirection in Poland challenged this interpretation – would the 'new' Poland now show a relationship between complexity of work and intellectual flexibility similar to the USA? The answer was, 'yes.' This formed the starting point for a series of studies on the Ukraine, an instance of capitalism from above, and on China, representing capitalism from below. By and large the answer again was, 'yes,' thereby demonstrating that the relationship between particular work experiences and intellectual flexibility is robust across various societal and economic conditions, as far as they provide the theory-adequate variation of work experiences and offer opportunities to choose or to be selected for complex jobs based on intellectual capability; obviously change on the political and economic level had left this regularity intact.

In the past, social change of the kind entailed in this book has often been studied with similar approaches – comparing samples from different countries that differ in the quality or level of change achieved, or samples from the same country gathered at different periods of the transition and transformation process. As a matter of fact, many investigations of German unification followed this model, by combining a comparison of East and West Germany with comparisons across time during the period of the change (Silbereisen, Pinquart, & Tomasik, Chapter 5 this volume; Tomasik & Silbereisen, 2009). Given the strains related to the breakdown of social institutions and to tensions in the labor markets, the widely held hypothesis was that people in the East would reveal poorer mental health compared to those in the West. The results were equivocal, and it took a while for it to become clear that the assumption of homogeneously high levels of strains was too simplistic (Pinquart & Silbereisen, 2004). This observation was the incentive to assess differences in exposure to manifestations of the societal challenges, and against this backdrop to think about the psychological mechanisms that link the strains experienced with adjustments achieved.

A conceptual model

The book is organized with such a conceptual model of the relationship between social change and individual adaptation in mind. It describes which aspects of change on the macro-level represent the starting point for individuals' actions and reactions, and thereby clarifies the point that comparisons at a highly aggregated level (such as countries or periods) necessarily underestimate the large variation in psychosocial outcomes.

Had one only taken Elder's model more seriously – as the level of hardship during the Great Depression varied, so did the strains related to political and social changes addressed in this book. The level of strain depended on conditions, such as an individual's stage in the life course or education, or as a function of the particular kind of macro-level change. For our own research agenda (Silbereisen et al., Chapter 5 this volume) this process became clear when a new generation of studies started from the sociological challenge-response model proffered by Best (2007) and developed further by Rosa and Schmidt (2007) and Schmidt (Chapter 1 this volume). The basic tenet of this model is that changes in the ideological base and the subordinate social institutions of a society should be conceived as challenges that lead to a response, which may in turn be the origin of a new challenge. The quality and direction of responses can vary depending on a large set of circumstances, and take the form of adaptation, resistance, resignation or innovation. Against this backdrop, the linear model of modernization sometimes used to describe the case of the transition and the course of transformation in Germany (Zapf, 1996) was deemed way too simple, although its apparently straightforward explanations (the old system lacked the 'modern' bottom-up planning needed for an economy under the strains of globalization) had some appeal.

The notion of challenge and response reminded psychologists interested in socio-political change of the various approaches that differentiate processes of coping as mediating mechanism between strains and outcomes – the model of Lazarus (Lazarus & Folkman, 1984) being the most prominent example. So the task was clear: to determine and assess manifestations of challenges at the individual level. We called these challenges 'demands' (Tomasik & Silbereisen, 2009), and understood individuals' dealing with them as an instance of either engagement, i.e., active attempts at resolving demands by direct action or by seeking support in facing the problem, or as disengagement, i.e., in the case of insurmountable obstacles, quitting the field in order to preserve the potential for future attempts at resolution. Our reference for this distinction was the model of primary and secondary control by Heckhausen (Chapter 6 this volume). Other approaches in studying the individual consequences of the transition from communism, however, have not focused on coping attempts but instead centered on the loss of economic, human, and social resources (Shteyn, Schumm, Vodopianova, Hobfoll, & Lilly, 2003). According to Hobfoll (1989, 2001) such loss of resources is more relevant for mental health than the gain of resources. This can explain why the obvious gains in terms of individual freedom cannot outweigh the negative effects of resource loss, such as uncertainties concerning people's occupational career.

The model of the linkage between social change and individual adaptation shown in Figure 1, drawn from Pinquart and Silbereisen (2004) and amended slightly for this work, helped in the selection of contributions for this book. We wanted to have chapters that illustrate the role of the various conditions and their interplay. The demands represent the perceived mismatch between claims and resources induced by challenges on the macro-level, conceived as discrepancies between the ideological base of a society and the reality of social institutions. An example of this is the proclaimed humanistic orientation of the socialist countries that stood in sharp contrast to the reality of systematic suppression of politically nonconformist positions. Depending on the type and stage in the transition and transformation, different challenges may be dominant,

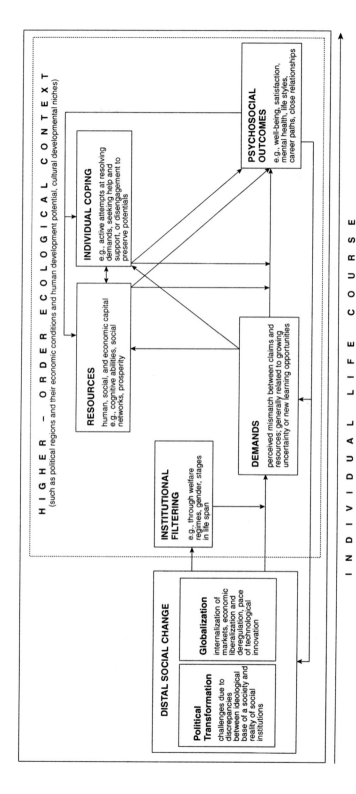

Figure 1 Model of the linkage between social change and individual adaptation.

such as the dissolution of justice and welfare institutions, the emergence of a new system of education and qualifications, or changes in the job market due to globalization. Between these challenges on the macro-level and the micro contexts of individuals are 'filters' that diminish or aggravate the challenges (Hofäcker et al., Chapter 4 this volume). In fact, Elder had already shown that the stage in the lifespan represents such a filter – when the Great Depression hit, due to their socialization in stable times, those in adolescence were better off than those who were confronted by the challenges in childhood (Elder, 1974). Instances of other institutionalized filters are 'welfare regimes' (Esping-Anderson, 1990) that reflect a society's understanding of what risks individuals have to bear, and what should be the responsibility of the state and the community, such as who is eligible for protection against redundancy, or who is eligible for unemployment benefits. Such welfare regimes differ across Europe, as does people's understanding of fairness related to the allocation of responsibility (Hofäcker et al., Chapter 4 this volume).

Action is required in order to find a balance between the new claims implicated in the demands and existing accustomed ways of living and behaving. Examples of such demands in the domain of work during the transformation period in Germany and other European countries include growing uncertainty concerning job security, increasingly demanding qualification requirements, and fears about the sufficiency of pension funds. Uncertainties in the domain of family refer to concerns such as the growing instability of partnerships, ambiguity about the right timing for family formation, and the obsolescence of the older generations' model of how to negotiate one's development. Finally, there are uncertainties concerning public life, such as the increasing complexity of cultural orientations due to immigration or threats by extremism.

According to the model, the actions potentially changing the accustomed ways of living and behaving are conceived as a particular pattern of various forms of engagement and disengagement that is also influenced by several kinds of resources, such as economic, social, and human capital. Some resources typically become obsolete during political and economic transition and transformation, whereas others may be exhausted by attempts to resolve the demands. The model is deliberately unspecific with regard to particular psychosocial outcomes. Well-being and life satisfaction, however, are of particular importance, due to their universal role in improving people's resilience against otherwise overwhelming challenges and in enabling them to take innovative and constructive action (Diener, 2000). This example also demonstrates the repercussive feature of the model. Similar to the macro-level, where responses not only resolve challenges but often also result in new ones, at the individual level, psychosocial outcomes resulting from coping with demands may ultimately change the demands for better or worse. This may then lead to new adaptive cycles, or even end in collective action to ultimately change the challenges on the macro-level. One of the chapters (Macmillan & Baiocchi, Chapter 3 this volume) deals explicitly with potential antecedents of social change, rather than taking social change as input for individual adaptation, as is the standard case throughout this book.

Types of samples

The samples of individuals addressed in the chapters of this book vary in size from small convenience to large nationally representative samples. At the one extreme are small groups of Chinese school children (Chen & Chen, Chapter 9 this volume), at the other, entire cohorts born at a specific time in the United Kingdom (Schoon, Chapter 11 this volume). Both examples also illuminate another feature of the book: We were especially interested in studies that compare across historical periods. Both the Chinese and British studies compare periods of particular relevance to the processes of social change, such as before and after the economic reforms in China, and growing up during economic 'boom and bust' in the case of the British study. Rather than comparing historical periods, other chapters compare individual samples from groups of countries characterized by different exposure to social change, such as Chapter 4 by Hofäcker and colleagues (this volume) that contrasts the effects of uncertainties linked to globalization across institutional regimes differing in how to protect people affected.

As made explicit by the model in Figure 1, an individual's life is embedded in various ecological contexts, such as the larger administrative regions where they reside or the communities where they live, and is influenced by how they deal with political and economic change. In the chapter by Sackmann (Chapter 7 this volume) the behavior of a number of municipalities as institutional actors is at stake, and following a theoretical rationale, a comparison is made including units from both parts of Germany and from Poland. Silbereisen and colleagues (Chapter 5 this volume) took care that their samples were organized by a multitude of large administrative regions within a number of federal States of Germany, thereby relating individual data on demands and coping to data on the level of economic and social prosperity. At any rate, it is clear that all the samples studied have been adequately chosen for the purpose. For instance, when studying the validity of the public view that the political and economic changes in Vietnam are responsible for a growing share of premarital sexual activities, then a comparison of rural and urban samples is just right to correct this view (Jayakody, Heckert, & Anh, Chapter 10 this volume), and no more elaborate sampling scheme is required.

Psychosocial outcomes

The chapters of the book also entail a broad array of outcomes, in part related to institutional actors, such as the municipalities studied by Sackmann (Chapter 7 this volume), but in all other cases concerning individual behavior and adaptation. In a number of chapters the focus is on education, work and volunteering, and family, and in particular on the differences and changes related to transitions within and between these domains (Kohn, Chapter 8 this volume; Hofäcker et al., Chapter 4 this volume; Heckhausen, Chapter 6 this volume; Schoon, Chapter 11 this volume; Silbereisen et al., Chapter 5 this volume). This emphasis comes as no surprise given the prominence of uncertainties concerning life-course decisions and the greater role of individual agency characteristic of modernity and the current political and economic transformation period (Brandtstädter, Chapter 2 this volume). Further, we have chapters that concentrate on personal capabilities and orientations, such as intellectual flexibility (Kohn, Chapter 8 this volume) and personal lifestyles (Macmillan & Baiocchi, Chapter 3 this volume). Finally, there is a set of chapters that refer mainly to differences and changes in socio-emotional functioning (Chen & Chen, Chapter 9 this volume; Jayakody et al., Chapter 10 this volume) and well-being (Silbereisen et al., Chapter 5 this volume). We take the research outcomes addressed in this book as representative for the range of consequences of social change for life-course organization (a typical research field of sociologists); for psychosocial functioning in terms of cognitive capabilities, action orientations and close relationships (a core of psychological research); and finally for mental health as an overall index of adjustment (of interest for all other disciplines involved, i.e., anthropology, demography, and political philosophy). The age range studied in the chapters overall encompasses childhood, adolescence, adulthood, and also ageing, with emphasis on adulthood.

Organization and content

The book is organized in three sections, starting with chapters concerning more general concepts about current social change, followed by those addressing various components of the model shown in Figure 1, and concluding with country-based chapters representing major variants of societies in transformation.

Dynamic of social change and individual responses

Schmidt. This chapter takes the concept of challenge and response discussed earlier as a structural blueprint for psychological research and provides clarification of what is actually meant by challenges in the context of social change and of how responses evolve. Societies are comprised of social institutions and practices on the one hand, and of the superordinate belief systems characteristic of a society on the other hand. On the microlevel there is a similar distinction between the attitudes and behaviors of the actors, and the values and beliefs guiding these habits. Challenges are tensions between any of these levels of social reality. They are conceived as resulting in partial incompatibilities of action plans, and as requiring responses beyond routine efforts. Challenges between the two aspects on the societal level form the prototype most often studied, of which the challenges behind German unification are a good example. The ideological promises of a humanitarian system were at odds with restrictions on individual freedom imposed by the political institutions, which resulted in a growing tension with the expectations of the population at large. The breakdown of the system in 1989 is testimony to the lack of a solution, and the response was the replacement of the macro-structures following the Western mould, that is, representative democracy and market economy were established (Zapf, 1996). Such a change on the macro-level is, of course, no guarantee that people would adjust quickly and develop beliefs and habits commensurable with the new macro-structures. Moreover, many action orientations that had served well in the old system could still be used, thereby producing new challenges to the recently established political system.

The author exemplifies the dynamic in the challenge-response approach with three results conducted at a major German research center on unification (Best, 2004). First, despite the downturn of industries, entrepreneurs, managers, and workers maintained the old habits of loyalty to the firm in exchange for job protection, even at the expense of extended working hours and insecure wages. In the long term, however, this was an inadequate response as the new economy required reductions of the work force, particularly in full-time permanent positions. This led to differentiation between workers in secure core positions and those in precarious employment. Second, although the changed macro-structure ultimately resulted in changes in individual orientations and habits, a new cleft emerged between elites and the population. Whereas the pace of adaptation was rather quick among those better educated and more accustomed to capitalist economics, a growing share of ordinary people became reluctant to adapt and rather began to entertain a renaissance of traditional socialist ideals of justice. Third, even among East German elites, in the years after unification a split emerged between their private convictions and public behavior. Further, almost two decades after German unification and the accompanying political change, they still did not take the sustainability of the new institutions for granted, and rather referred to values and action orientations of humanitarian egalitarianism reminiscent of the old socialist belief systems.

Brandtstädter. The current challenges of transformation just described need to be seen as located in time and space. For example, even before the breakdown of political and economic systems seen in many East European countries in the late 1980s, people in Western countries had experienced accelerating trends in cultural innovations, in the globalization of production and communication, and in the pluralization of life concepts. Given the pace of change, individuals can no longer live their lives by following scripts valid for past generations. Rather, in line with societal expectations, they are expected to regulate their strivings by exploring options, pursuing them with passion, and always being aware of the need to adapt to difficulties without losing self-worth. All of this has to be accomplished in spite of marked uncertainty about rewards for such behavior, of difficulties in planning ahead, of being confronted with more options than an individual could ever use, and despite the demise of meanings shared by an entire population.

Earlier research following this line of thought has addressed how people deal with the growing competence-loss characteristic of ageing, and the creative plea of this chapter is to see the parallel in reactions to social change. Both entail situations of irreversible losses and constraints, and accommodative modes of coping are important for finding new meaning and satisfaction under personally adverse circumstances. Such modes of action correspond to a more open-minded form of information processing and involve greater satisfaction with what has been achieved. The obstacles experienced ultimately turn out to be a source of pride rather than rumination and even depression due to chances missed.

A healthy balance between tenacity in pursuing goals and flexibility in adjusting to waning opportunities is not only a key to successful life management in ageing, but is also a crucial personal resource in dealing with tensions between levels of social reality prominent in the political transitions and economic transformations dealt with in this book.

Macmillan and Baiocchi. The social change underpinning this book began with strong political tension; it was followed by a dynamic propelled by the change of social institutions, and resulted in uncertainty for individuals who had to adapt to new orientations and behaviors. One area where this has been particularly evident is the growing hesitancy concerning marriage and family formation in transformation countries (Hofäcker et al., Chapter 4 this volume). Such trends themselves can seed further social change on all levels, such as new strategies to improve the work–family balance as a political reaction to the declining birth rates.

This example depicts the reverse direction of the link between social change and individual adaptation mentioned in our model (see Figure 1) and conceptual clarification and an empirical demonstration of how this might function is provided in this chapter. It gives a glimpse of the mutual dynamic of challenges and responses on all levels, 'macro-to-micro-to-macro' (Coleman, 1987; Esser, 1993), and of the possible processes involved. The case in point is the decline of marriage as a trigger for social change in other domains. Marriage is no longer the normative constellation for adults' heterosexual relationships and family making. Rather, living single over extended periods of time, for instance as a consequence of divorce or living in cohabitation, increased in prevalence. The authors' claim is that the new demography concerning family constellations weakened the normative power of marriage and its related belief systems and thereby paved the way for a more liberal stance towards homosexuality. Given the strength of past traditions and prejudice, this is obviously an instance of social change in the cultural realm.

How could this be? The idea is that a life course status, such as marriage, is actually a rather broad 'schema' comprised of rules, examples, and templates, rather than an exactly circumscribed and permanently stable prescription for how to act in a given life course role. Due to their rather abstract definition, schemata can be interpreted individually and be transposed to new contexts, thus also allowing new resource accumulation. An unintended consequence of schemata applied to new contexts, however, may be their solidification due to unexpected success in terms of resources. The resources themselves can have different values depending on the wider context, and thus a newly extended schema may also result in a fresh valuation of resources. The experience of new actions and social relations may change belief systems or other aspects of the social fabric of a community. As all of the above occurs under the influence of broader social structures, the fluidity of the schema-resource nexus provides the potential for social and cultural innovation.

The chapters discussed thus far provide an illustration of how, in principle, one can conceive the interplay between change at the level of societies and change in individuals' beliefs and behaviors. The chapters of the following section refer to the several concepts shown in our heuristic model (see Figure 1), and provide insights into their relationships at the individual level.

Determinants on the individual level

Hofäcker, Buchholz, and Blossfeld. This chapter reports the framework, design and selected results of a research program (GLOBALIFE) that compares various OECD countries concerning the effects of globalization on individual life course decisions. Under globalization uncertainties of the world markets have increased remarkably. For instance, the internationalization of markets, characterized by rising competition among unequal economies, resulted in deregulation and other related measures; both increased the pace of technological innovation and accelerated social and economic change. Increasing worldwide connectedness through developments in information technology propelled the change further, but at the same time – as we have all seen by the financial shock in 2008 – the volatility of the markets also increased tremendously. One reaction by enterprises to such structural uncertainties is the increase in precarious forms of employment. These particularly affect young people and do not promote steady job experience or establish strong ties to business networks. A consequence on the individual level is to postpone long-term commitments, and instead to establish less binding forms of work or partnership. This has further consequences for family formation and declining birth rates, making youth and young adults the 'losers' of globalization.

At closer look, the uncertainties do not impact directly on individuals, but are experienced via 'institutional filters' representing the divergent ideologies and practices of the employment, educational, and welfare systems (Esping-Andersen, 1990). In traditionally family-oriented societies (e.g., Italy and Spain) the decline in the birth rate has been most pronounced, whereas in Scandinavian countries it is still comparatively high. This is most likely due to economic uncertainties being more pro-actively dealt with in Scandinavia, and because there is greater compatibility between work roles and the family obligations of both partners through better childcare facilities. Other periods of the life course are also discussed, namely, mid-career transitions among women and men, and the transition to retirement in later life. As it turns out, the divergent economic and welfare regimes often produce more variation than globalization as such, and in spite of pressures from challenges they seem to be rather stable characteristics of the societies, deeply rooted in cultural beliefs, such as a common standard of what constitutes a fair load of global risks an individual could be expected to carry.

The construct of uncertainties is conceptually located on the macro-level, but obviously it is their perception by individuals that results ultimately in certain ways of coping with a given situation, such as postponing life course transitions.

Silbereisen, Pinquart, and Tomasik. This chapter, in contrast, addresses the actual variation in individual manifestations of such uncertainties. Such 'demands' are conceived as the endorsement of retrospective comparisons concerning a negative trend in chances to resolve age-typical developmental tasks in the domain of work and family. As expected, those without a job or those who are single or divorced, reported a higher load of difficulties in planning their occupational career, or in deciding to have a child. Moreover, those living in East Germany (former GDR) revealed a higher accumulation of demands. Residing in the East made work-related demands of the unemployed worse, due to the more precarious economic situation and a lack of recognized qualifications, whereas living in the West corresponded to higher loads among those divorced or widowed, because family break-up was less common than in the East. The demands also reflect vulnerabilities accumulated throughout life. Premature autonomy during adolescence increased the risk of cumulated negative demands, probably due to less persistent efforts in school and further education, and subsequently to a lack of human- and other capital known to be helpful for overcoming strains (Haase, Tomasik, & Silbereisen, 2008).

As shown in the previous section, political transformation cannot be understood without embedding it in the larger context of globalization and other changes on the macro-level. In a similar fashion, dealing with demands related to the transformation cannot be understood without considering the narrower context of where people live.

This chapter provides evidence that the process of dealing with demands was indeed conditioned by differences in context-related economic opportunities. On average, and as expected, individual level data showed that higher demands in the work domain corresponded to lower well-being, assessed as a positive effect experienced over the month prior to data collection. However, when variation in unemployment and welfare benefits across a large number of administrative regions in both parts of Germany were included in a multilevel analysis, it became obvious that the closeness of the relationship was weakened (reduced in negativity) in regions characterized by economic hardships. The authors see this conditioning happening in two ways. First, because individuals tend to compare themselves with others of a similar fate, the demands become more normative in economically depressed regions, and thus less harmful for well-being. Second, living in such a region allows an individual to attribute their situation to the dire circumstances rather than to personal deeds; this also makes the demands less problematic for well-being. The plausibility of the interpretation is supported by the converse result that living in more affluent regions corresponded to a closer relationship between engagement with the demands and well-being, probably due to the fact that in such regions not only are resources better in general, but also role models of how to solve work-related demands are more visible. The softening role of resource-poor contexts for the association between demands and well-being may be less advantageous **longer-term, as it may** also undercut personal activities to improve the situation.

Heckhausen. The engagement just mentioned is part of a conceptual distinction introduced by Heckhausen (1999) in her model of developmental regulation that we deem especially suited for research on social change. The core notion is that, in order to resolve a developmental task, individuals negotiate focal goals, such as finding a first job after school, and that this can be distinguished as strategies of goal engagement and strategies of goal disengagement. The first entails the investment of time and effort towards achieving the chosen goal (selective primary control) and often includes motivational activities to maintain commitment to goal achievement in spite of difficulties (selective secondary control). In this case, individuals typically rely on support and advice from more experienced others (compensatory primary control). Naturally, not all goals can be achieved by everybody, and so goal disengagement (compensatory secondary control) is often inevitable. In order to avoid self-blame in this situation various strategies may be utilized, such as comparing oneself with lower achievers or by refocusing on possible success in other fields. Although, on average, engagement is the better strategy – as, for instance, in the case of well-being – under some circumstances, such as when resources are fully depleted, disengagement may lead to positive outcomes (Tomasik, Silbereisen, & Heckhausen, 2009).

The pivot of this chapter is to relate the process of developmental regulation to the societal opportunity structures and their possible change under conditions of globalization, which make developmental regulation more complicated when compared to the past. The chapter draws on Esping-Anderson (1990) in order to specify hypotheses about strategies used in pursuing career related goals during the transition out of school. In the case of a 'liberal' regime (permeability between career paths is high, as is individual responsibility and possibilities for upward mobility) such as the school system in the USA (California), Heckhausen expects and finds that high aspirations, relatively independent of actual school achievement, will result in many students achieving a BA after high school. In contrast, in the 'conservative' system represented by the schools in Germany (Berlin), a close calibration between occupational aspirations and school achievement is better for success. Moreover, the two settings can also be distinguished by the type of developmental regulation that is most adequate, namely, selective primary and secondary control in California, and compensatory primary control in Berlin, thereby achieving a better fit to an environment less sympathetic to personal agency. Taken together, the concepts and results presented here can serve as a model of what might be expected if the societal changes addressed in this book would ultimately change the established welfare regime and related practice towards more or less liberalism.

Transitions and transformations in international perspective

This section reports studies on political transitions and social and economic transformations in a number of select countries. The studies use comparisons within and across countries, and these comparisons are made such that the samples chosen index different periods of the political, social, and economic transformation process under scrutiny. The countries covered represent the Anglo-Saxon background (USA, United Kingdom), Central-Eastern Europe (Poland, Ukraine), and Asia (Vietnam, China). Although the particular structural uncertainties and individual demands resulting from the macro-level changes were not assessed directly, by arranging comparisons across time and space in a particular way, the role of the exposure to social change and its consequences become clear.

Sackmann. The book thus far has addressed individual responses to the change of social structures, but obviously there are also institutional actors involved that are of particular interest for the fate of individuals. This chapter is unique as it addresses responses of municipalities in Germany and Poland to the decline in the birth rate that followed the post-communist political transition. This certainly unintended precipitation of the break-up of the socialist order reduced the budget allocated for institutions in charge of education. One way to close the mismatch between shrinking financial resources and citizens' educational aspirations would be a reduction of teachers and other personnel in charge of the young. Interestingly enough, this was not the case in Poland compared to Germany, and this reflects bigger differences in how the political and economic transformation after 1990 was handled.

First, whereas former East Germany was incorporated into West Germany and its institutions and elites, Poland followed an autonomous way of transformation, requiring the negotiation of a new institutional order without a guiding blueprint. This basic juxtaposition was hypothesized as resulting in differences concerning aspirations for the 'new life.' In Germany, as a reflection of the high standards held in the West that the East would want to match and the remarkable West to East transfer of financial and other resources, a fast increase in aspirations was expected. In Poland, because there was a more protracted increase of resources that had to be provided from within the country, a slow rise in aspirations was foreseen. In other words, and referring to Elder (Elder & Caspi, 1988), as the mismatch between new aspirations and existing financial resources had to be resolved, the expectation, which was confirmed, was that municipalities in the former East Germany would accumulate a much higher debt than otherwise comparable municipalities in Poland.

Second, Sackmann also expected that the action by municipalities in Germany would show a lower level of innovation in terms of institution building. In Germany the autonomy of municipalities and school principals remained small, as was common in the West. In Poland, however, responsibility was transferred to local authorities, and the structure of schools was changed so that the amount of schooling per student was increased. This also meant that, unlike in Germany, the number of teachers was upheld or even increased and that, in particular, school and schooling became a model case for the building of autonomous institutions. Both types of transformation to a democratic society are flexible enough to handle the unexpected, such as the decline in the birth rates, but the ways of institutional coping and their probably long-term effects differ.

Kohn. This chapter is a wonderful testimony to the success of a life-long striving to challenge one's own theory by investigating disruptions of social structures crucial to the approach. It starts with the landmark study on the relationship between social structure and personality Kohn conducted in the 1980s together with his colleagues (e.g., Kohn, Miller, Miller, Schoenbach, & Schoenberg, 1983; Kohn, Slomczynski, & Schoenbach, 1990). For employed men in the USA, they found that higher positions in social stratification and social class corresponded to greater intellectual flexibility, self-directedness and sense of well-being. This was explained by the substantive complexity of the job and the relative freedom from supervision. Employees in a higher position in the social structure had better work conditions in terms of high complexity and low supervision, and this experience mediated the effects on personality.

In the chapter, Kohn leads readers on a journey to various populations in various countries at different points in recent history. In the former socialist Poland, few differences were found in the sample of employed men when compared to the USA, however with one intriguing exception. Whereas in the USA it was those low in the social hierarchy who revealed higher distress, in Poland it was more senior managers. This was explained by differences between the capitalist and the socialist systems. After the political transformation in Poland it became clear that, irrespective of the economic and political model, it was indeed the position in the social hierarchy that counted for the impact on personality. A further study on another transformation country, the Ukraine, followed. Here the general approach was again confirmed, although the strength of the association was weaker, probably reflecting the situation when the market economy was first established. For those believing in a rapid translation of macro-level change into individual orientations and behavior, the results thus far throw a somewhat disappointing light on the power of social transformation. However radical the changes may have been, they did not apparently affect the basic stratification of the societies and their structuring role for the influence of work experience on individuals' capabilities, at least not during the periods studied.

The last way-station of the journey addresses changes leading to the establishment of a market economy in China. Basically the same pattern of results as in the transformation Poland and Ukraine were found concerning the relationship between social structure and personality. However, other than as expected, no moderation by the degree to which the urban regions in China studied differed in terms of privatization was found. This is an issue of concern for the approach as similar comparisons were never made in the other transformation countries, justified by the apparent homogeneity of experiences. Interestingly enough, problems also turned up concerning the postulated mediating role of work complexity. As in the other countries, this was similarly related to social structure, but not to personality. Kohn discusses other life conditions that may impinge more on personality, such as the experience of uncertainty and new demands under the pressure of social change, which is well-known from Hofäcker and colleagues as well as Silbereisen and colleagues (this volume).

Chen and Chen. This chapter also concerns China and the rapid change of its command economy to a market economy. To succeed in such a new system requires attitudes and behaviors, such as preferring individual autonomy over fitting in with family interests, which goes against traditional Chinese values that were maintained under the past economic and political system. Changes on the level of the economic system should be paralleled by changes in the goals and practices of family socialization, such as taking the initiative to explore opportunities rather than waiting for parental encouragement or consent. When comparing samples of school children representing different periods in the recent process of economic reforms in urban centers of China, the authors can indeed confirm that between 1998 and 2002 there was a trend towards setting a higher premium on warmth and support of autonomy, and less endorsement of power assertion. These attitudes are known from Western research as creating the kind of situations that enable individuals to explore opportunities and to learn how to take the initiative.

Research on change in the traditional Chinese appreciation of children's shy-inhibited behavior is crucial for this book. In contrast to the West, such behaviors are known to have been associated with positive adjustment in terms of peer acceptance and academic achievement in China. Again, using samples representing different periods during the reforms to a market economy, Chen and colleagues found that by 2002 shy-inhibited behavior corresponded to rejection by peers and depressive mood, whereas in 1998 the picture was mixed, and in 1990 it was exactly as predicted by Chinese tradition. It would seem that a decade or so was enough to establish a rather radical change in a fundamental aspect of young people's behavioral repertoire and preferences concerning social relationships. Unfortunately the research thus far does not support an individual assessment of the degree to which the families and the children were indeed confronted with the manifestations of the economic reforms in terms of incentives to change their life goals and behaviors. Nevertheless, in the future data from rural areas, which are still almost unaffected by the economic reforms, could be compared with data from rural-urban migrant children. Overall, the chapter demonstrates that changes in central goals of socialization can be achieved not only over the passage of several decades (see Kagitcibasi & Ataca, 2005), but within a decade or shorter if the pressure for change is high and uniform, and if various institutions, such as school and family, act in alignment.

Jayakody, Heckert, and Anh. This chapter refers to Vietnam, another 'capitalism from below' country (King & Szelenyi, 2005) that from the 1990s onwards has undergone a breathtaking reform toward a market economy and opening to the world. As in the case of China, the question is whether attitudes and behavior have also changed in a comparable fashion. The chosen example of extramarital sexual activities is at the core of heated public debates as to whether there is a rapid increase towards the high figures known from other Asian countries (that have long had capitalist economies). The short answer is, 'no' – the figures still belong to the lowest of all Asian countries, but they are remarkably higher for people living in urban centers. An upward trend can be seen, but this starts much earlier than the economic reforms of the 1990s.

This result sheds light on possible mechanisms by which changes at the individual level were related to the societal changes, more broadly speaking. One potential antecedent of course is economic growth and liberalization, including issues such as a shift from the predominance of agriculture to service industries, moves from rural areas to urban centers, and increases in income. However, this possibly only reflects enabling factors. Consequently, the authors underscore the role of ideational changes in world views, knowledge about preferences in the outside world, and subsequent changes in values. A prominent role in this regard is played by Western-style TV and its contents that favor a libertine orientation towards sexuality. Field experiments of introducing TV into remote tribal areas of Vietnam revealed its high attraction for young people, especially due to its ascribed role of modeling flirtation and other intimate adult behaviors.

Schoon. Readers may wonder why we put a study referring to the United Kingdom after the chapters on Asia. The reason is that in this chapter the focus is also on economic change without a radical political transition and transformation, as well as again including a comparison across historical periods. The British Birth Cohort Studies refer to a total of 20,000 individuals who were born in 1958 and 1970. Although only about a decade apart, the cohort members experienced remarkably different conditions for psychosocial development. When the older cohort approached the school-to-work transition, a period of economic growth came to an end, but they had completed their full-time education in a boom time. The younger cohort, in contrast, was born and achieved its education during an extraordinary recession period between 1970 and 1980. They were affected by high unemployment rates and other manifestations of an economic bust. The author utilizes this representative data set to put conceptions of overarching changes in the life-course regime and its origins to test. By 'de-standardization' she understands the claim that the role of traditional demographic differentials, such as social class or gender, lost power in distinguishing the course and quality of career and family development. 'Individualization' is indicated by a higher role of individual agency compared to demographics, such as cognitive capabilities and school motivation, when it comes to decisions which career path to choose, and how to combine work and family.

The claim concerning de-standardization does not receive much support. Although there was a hint that parental social status and education were somewhat less relevant for the school-leaving age of the later born cohort, entry into full-time employment and into parenthood revealed the traditional social differentiation; the same applied to the sequencing of employment careers. Concerning individualization a somewhat different picture was seen. As far as career trajectories are concerned, the relative strength of social background factors and aspects of agency was almost alike between the cohorts, and definitely not in the direction of higher individualization among the younger cohort. A strong individualization effect turned up, however, with regard to linkages between work and family. Here there was a clear trend towards a higher share of childless singles and a lower share of couples with children, indicating a higher prevalence of transitory intimate relationships. Whereas among the later born participants, high school motivation and a return to full-time education seemed to be relevant, among the earlier born cohort these agency variables did not play a role.

Concerning the processes that translate the changing economic prosperity into a lifestyle change, the data as such cannot go much beyond speculation. In accordance with Hofäcker and colleagues (Chapter 4 this volume), one explanation could be that the growing uncertainty about one's economic fate results in attempts to regain control, and one way to do this is to postpone family transitions or to make them less permanent. At any rate, the crucial element is probably not greater individual freedom in decision making, but the growing incompatibility between traditional life arrangements and the need to adapt to labor market constraints, such as growing qualification requirements. This position is in discord with the belief that increased chances for personal agency are driving lifestyle changes.

Wasilewski. The last chapter represents a piece of scholarly thought about the role of elites in the transition and transformation of societies, an aspect not addressed in the other chapters, and exemplified by the political changes in Central-Eastern Europe, even before the 1990s. The author's crucial claim is that the course and result of elite influence always revealed the path dependency of social change, and also changed across the process.

In some post-socialist societies, transition from the old to the new system was organized by the old elite who had become wary of the weakness of the communist doctrine, and gave in to younger, less orthodox and more technocratic leaders – i.e., the masses had basically no influence. The Polish case was different as the more open segment of the old communist elite was confronted with a mass movement for universal human values (Solidarność) and its leaders. No one side could overthrow the other, and therefore a negotiated 'elite settlement,' which included all major players, had a high likelihood of installing a democratic regime.

During the long-lasting and perhaps not yet finalized transformation, elites played three different roles. The 'breakthrough elite' supplied the vision, appealed to emotions, provided the first answer to a new identity, propagated readiness for change, and gained moral legitimacy. However, it was not yet involved in policymaking proper, and rather appealed more to symbolic politics. The 'institution-building elites' subsequently replaced symbolic politics by concrete policies, rules, and institutions. Naturally they were confronted with conflicting interests, and their legitimacy rests on efficacy in establishing democratic systems, not on moral superiority. Finally, the 'consolidation elite' is charged with stimulating the economic growth and with providing stability as a background for the establishment of democratic habits.

In the elite settlement mode of transition and transformation, the reform-minded part of the old elite becomes part of the new system. In particular, and concerning the institution-building and consolidation phase, it is only fair to say that they were able to translate past political capital into economic capital of the future, but basically not at the expense of the new democracy. This situation was rather different in those former socialist countries where factions of the old elite initiated the transition without any opposing or settling partner from other corners of the society.

Conclusion

An important conclusion we can draw from the evidence presented in this book is the need for an interdisciplinary approach. Social change as addressed here represents the merger of societal transformations following a cataclysmic transition, with tensions originating in the globalization of economic activities. It is also influenced by demographic shifts that in part predate the transitions, like the ageing of populations, and which in part result from people's reactions to uncertainty, such as the decline in birth rates. Without an understanding of the particular type of transition and transformation, such as the juxtaposition between the incorporation and the autonomy mode of political and economic transformation, particularities in the building of new social institutions would be difficult to comprehend and their scaffolding function for individual behavior and developmental regulation would be overlooked. One can even claim that the changes to institutions drive individual adaptation.

By way of example, changes to the school system in East Germany (former GDR) were followed relatively quickly by a change in the timing of first vocational interests to match that common in the West, whereas the timing of romantic involvement did not change, in spite of the new leisure opportunities (Silbereisen, Reitzle, & Juang, 2002). Only an interdisciplinary view brings such complex relationships into focus.

Irrespective of the apparently radical change of the entire fabric of the transformation societies, continuity rather than discontinuity is probably more pronounced than one might expect. As the cross-national studies on the relationship between work experience and intellectual flexibility revealed, the connection between social stratification and complexity of work remained basically intact, and thus the social changes studied in this book revealed more continuity in public discourse than expected. Other research on countries of the former Soviet Union showed that this conservative element in social change may not apply equally to early phases of transitions, which are usually characterized by turmoil. As Titma and Tuma (2005) reported, it was only after consolidation of the new political system that the well-known advantage of education for life success applied, whereas in the early transition period, such credentials had lost their value relative to the advantage of personality attributes like self-efficacy.

Social change of the type studied in this book does not affect individuals in any direct way. Rather, what reaches people's doorsteps as new demands have undergone various transformations through the influence of other conditions. One is filters, such as welfare regimes, which protect some at the expense of others and follow a logic rooted in the beliefs of the respective culture. Interestingly enough, these regimes also seem to be rather stable in spite of the profound changes surrounding them, and their influence seems to be larger than that of globalization and transformation per se.

Demands are rooted in social change, although they are not the proximal cause. They represent the strains (or the opportunities) that require action in order to find a new balance between claims and resources. Beyond the usual 'capitals,' such as social support and cognitive capabilities, a type of 'accommodative' regulation seems to be important as a dispositional resource. Similar to the societal challenges that are filtered via institutional regimes, at the individual level the ecological contexts play a role. It seems that the same load of demands concerning work and family makes people differently vulnerable to reductions in well-being, dependent on the level of economic prosperity and social welfare (Silbereisen et al., Chapter 5 this volume). If many other people are affected by the same hazards, individuals seem to see their own fate in relation to them, so that the negative effects of the hazards can be discounted. In a similar vein, Hofäcker and colleagues (Chapter 4 this volume) refer to the 'relative uncertainty' as the actual strain, conceived as the uncertainty experienced relative to what one is used to expect within a country or culture. It is also likely that the attribution of the causes of one's problems, either failed own activities or systemic failures, is important when it comes to protection from challenges at the macro-level. The ecology itself is, of course, affected by the societal transformation. Thus, neighborhoods or entire regions may become depleted of the resources people need to counter the new demands. In the study by Silbereisen and colleagues (Chapter 5 this volume) the positive effects of engagement coping were stronger in affluent regions.

The chapters have shown that the prevalent type of research on societal transformation needs correction. When comparing across countries that differ in the level of transformation, or within countries between periods of social change, the range of challenges varies, but it is not at all clear that this corresponds to equivalent variation in individual demands or in the processes of dealing with them that condition the psychosocial outcomes. With few exceptions, even psychologically inspired research on the transformation countries is still mute with regard to the translation of challenges to individual adjustment. Given that the blueprint for such more elaborate research dates back to the 1970s (Elder, 1974), this comes as a surprise. But note that even Kohn's (Chapter 8 this volume) amazing series of studies on the continuity of the role of social stratification across countries and transformations was finally confronted with speculations about how people cope with the new economic opportunities in China. Did differences in uncertainties and demands experienced actually play a role, although differences in the regions' level of privatization were just too remote to index variation in exposure to the economic changes?

Another observation in reading the chapters concerns the time scale of the changes studied. When the unification of Germany happened, politicians talked about perhaps a decade or less for the transformation to be complete on all levels, from institutions to individuals. Reality taught a different lesson, not only because the tensions from globalization and the unintended side effects such as the decline of birth rates, superimposed the challenges from transformation. The 'syntax' of a transformation actually has no finite end – the negative after effects of some responses represent second order challenges, as some have called them (Best, 2007), and this requires new responses. Years ago, and referring to the 'migration' of institutions from West to East in Germany, one of us used insights from research on acculturation among immigrants as a time scale (Silbereisen, 2000). Whereas it takes little time to adapt to new habits dictated by the pragmatics of life, like the adjustment of timetables for first occupational interests, it may take many years, if not a generation, to change basic values and their full penetration into the fabric of a society as well as its scaffolding function for human adaptation and development. Seen against this backdrop, the results by Chen and Chen (Chapter 9 this volume) on the apparently quick adaptation of interpersonal styles are amazing. Probably it means that the incentives for adaptation were strong, but it remains an open question whether the changed behavior generalizes as quickly beyond the realm of school and achievement.

The ideal for future research would entail both directions – from change on the macro-level to individual adaptation, and from there to new changes on the macro-level. What circumstances drive people to collective action is actually known, such as the perception of disadvantages for one's own group, and the weakness of opponents (Wright, 2002), and the inherent flexibility of some institutions may also contribute (Macmillan & Baiocchi, Chapter 3 this volume). However, research that combines both branches of social change as cause and consequence, so to speak, will obviously require new collaborative efforts and interdisciplinary research designs.

This book is the outcome of such an endeavor on a smaller scale. The authors met on the occasion of an international workshop sponsored by the German National Science Foundation (DFG), organized by two impressive young investigators, Martin Tomasik and Claudia Haase, together with one of the editors of this book (RKS). The sessions took place in secluded rooms of an old monastery in the vibrant city of Würzburg in Germany, thereby illuminating the issues of continuity and discontinuity so important for this book. In addition to the authors, we had international discussants (Andy Dawes, Suman Verma, and Fred Vondracek). We also hosted a group of PhD students from the Pennsylvania State University and the University of Jena, who presented their research on social change inspired by the work of the contributors. In the spirit of the discussions all chapter drafts were revised, and we want to thank all involved for their openness and patience.

We appreciate the assistance of two students, Astrid Körner and Louisa Arnold, who helped to organize the workshop and took care of all participants. Annett Weise and Verona Christmas-Best gave us the pleasure of their support in putting together the book. Our thanks also go to Michael Carmichael of Sage Publishers who has been very supportive in making it all possible.

References

Best, H. (Ed.). (2004). *Challenge und Response. Das Forschungsprogram des SFB 580 in den Jahren 2004 bis 2008* (SFB Mitteilungen, Heft 15). Jena/Halle: Sonderforschungsbereich 580.

Best, H. (2007). Der Challenge-Response-Ansatz als forschungsleitende Perspektive für die Transformationsforschung [The challenge-response-approach as a leading perspective for research on transformation]. In D. de Nève, M. Reiser, & K.-U. Schnapp (Eds.), *Herausforderung-Akteur-Reaktion: Diskontinuierlicher sozialer Wandel aus theoretischer und empirischer Perspektive* (pp. 11–24). Baden-Baden: Nomos.

Coleman, J.S. (1987). Microfoundations of macrosocial behavior. In J.C. Alexander, B. Giesen, R. Münch, & N.J. Smelser (Eds.), *The micro-macro-link* (pp. 153–173). Berkeley, CA: University of California Press.

Diener, E. (2000). Subjective well-being: The science of happiness, and a proposal for a national index. *American Psychologist, 55*, 34–43.

Elder, G.H., Jr. (1974). *Children of the Great Depression: Social change of life experience.* Chicago: University of Chicago Press.

Elder, G.H., Jr. (2003). The life course in time and place. In W. R. Heinz and V. W. Marshall (Eds.), *Sequences, institutions and interrelations over the life course* (pp. 57–71). New York: Aldine de Gruyter.

Elder, G.H. & Caspi, A. (1988). Human development and social change: An emerging perspective on the life course. In N. Bolger, A. Caspi, G. Downey, & M. Moorehouse (Eds.), *Persons in context. Developmental processes* (pp. 77–113). Cambridge: Cambridge University Press.

Esping-Andersen, G. (1990). *The three worlds of welfare capitalism.* Cambridge: Polity Press.

Esser, H. (1993). *Soziologie: Allgemeine Grundlagen* [Sociology: General fundamentals]. Frankfurt a.M.: Campus.

Haase, C.M., Tomasik, M.J., & Silbereisen, R.K. (2008). Premature behavioral autonomy: Correlates in late adolescence and young adulthood. *European Psychologist, 13*, 255–266.

Heckhausen, J. (1999). *Developmental regulation in adulthood: Age-normative and sociostructural constraints as adaptive challenges.* New York: Cambridge University Press.

Hobfoll, S.E. (1989). Conservation of resources: A new attempt at conceptualizing stress. *American Psychologist, 44*, 513–524.

Hobfoll, S.E. (2001). The influence of culture, community, and the nested-self in the stress process: Advancing conservation of resources theory. *Applied Psychology: An International Review, 50*, 337–421.

Kagitcibasi, C. & Ataca, B. (2005). Value of children and family change: A three-decade portrait from Turkey. *Applied Psychology, 54*, 317–337.

King, L. & Szelenyi, I. (2005). The new capitalism of Eastern Europe. In N. Smelser & R. Swedberg (Eds.), *Handbook of Economic Sociology.* Princeton, NJ: Princeton University Press.

Kohn, M.L., Miller, J., Miller, K.A., Schoenbach, C., & Schoenberg, R. (1983). *Work and personality: An inquiry into the impact of social stratification.* Norwood, NJ: Ablex.

Kohn, M.L., Slomczynski, K.M., & Schoenbach, C. (1990). *Social structure and self-direction: A comparative analysis of the United States and Poland.* Oxford: Basil Blackwell.

Lazarus, R.S. & Folkman, S. (1984). *Stress, appraisal and coping.* New York: Springer.

Pinquart, M. & Silbereisen, R.K. (2004). Human development in times of social change: Theoretical considerations and research needs. *International Journal of Behavioral Development, 28*, 289–298.

Rosa, H. & Schmidt, S. (2007). Which challenge, whose response? Ein Vier-Felder-Modell der Challenge-Response-Analyse sozialen Wandels [which challenge, whose response? A four-field model for challenge – response analysis of social change]. In D. de Nève, M. Reiser, & K.-U. Schnapp (Eds.), *Herausforderung – Akteur – Reaktion. Diskontinuierlicher Wandel aus theoretischer und empirischer Perspektive* (pp. 53–72). Nomos: Baden-Baden.

Shteyn, M., Schumm, J.A., Vodopianova, N., Hobfall, S.E., & Lilly, R. (2003). The impact of the Russian transition on psychosocial resources and psychological distress. *Journal of Community Psychology, 31*, 113–127.

Silbereisen, R.K. (2000). German unification and adolescents' developmental timetables: Continuities and discontinuities. In L. Crockett & R.K. Silbereisen (Eds.), *Negotiating adolescence in times of social change* (pp. 104–122). Cambridge, MA: Cambridge University Press.

Silbereisen, R.K., Reitzle, M., & Juang, L. (2002). Time and change: Psychosocial transitions in German young adults 1991 and 1996. In L. Pulkkinen & A. Caspi (Eds.), *Paths to successful development: Personality in the life course* (pp. 227–254). Cambridge: Cambridge University Press.

Silbereisen, R.K. & Tomasik, M.J. (2008). Berlin – Warsaw – Jena: A journey with Glen H. Elder through sites of social change. *Research in Human Development, 5*, 244–258.

Titma, M. & Tuma, N.B. (2005). Human agency in the transition from communism: Perspectives on the life course and aging. In K.W. Schaie & G.H. Elder Jr. (Eds.), *Historical influences on lives and aging* (pp. 108–143). New York: Springer.

Tomasik, M.J. & Silbereisen, R.K. (2009). Demands of social change as a function of the political context, institutional filters, and psychosocial resources. *Social Indicators Research, 94*, 13–28.

Tomasik, M.J., Silbereisen, R.K., & Heckhausen, J. (2009). *Is it adaptive to disengage from demands of social change? Adjustment to developmental barriers in opportunity-deprived regions.* Manuscript submitted for publication.

Wright, S.C. (2002). Collective action in response to disadvantage: Intergroup perceptions, social identification and social change. In I. Walker & H.J. Smith (Eds.), *Relative deprivation: Specification, development, and integration* (pp. 200–236). New York, NY: Cambridge University Press.

Zapf, W. (1996). Zwei Geschwindigkeiten in Ost- und Westdeutschland [Two paces in Eastern and Western Germany]. In M. Diewald & K.U. Mayer (Eds.), *Zwischenbilanz der Wiedervereinigung: Strukturwandel und Mobilität im Transformationsprozess* (pp. 317–328). Opladen: Leske + Budrich.

Part I

DYNAMIC OF SOCIAL CHANGE AND INDIVIDUAL RESPONSES

1

A CHALLENGE-RESPONSE-MODEL IN RESEARCH ON SOCIAL CHANGE

Steffen Schmidt

The starting point of developing the model presented here was the theoretical and practical situation for social scientists (for some years) after the breakdown of the communist rule. There was on the one hand a great requirement to describe and explain the enormous social change which took place in Eastern and Middle Eastern Europe. On the other hand, of course, there had already been several theories. But nevertheless, the well-known old or newly adopted theories had significant difficulties in explaining the ongoing process of change in a proper way, too.[1] It is impossible here to assess the specific advantages and disadvantages of the several theories themselves. Summarizing the situation, one could say that there was (and still is) a plurality of theories on social change and at the same time a widespread conviction that we do not have any 'gold standard' for explaining transformation processes. Regardless of this situation, social scientists continued working on and even enforced their efforts to understand the unique, incomparable and mostly unexpected change of the former socialist states into capitalist societies. At the Universities of Jena and Halle, a Collaborative Research Center (SFB 580) was established which aims at investigating the social developments after the structural change by focussing on discontinuity, tradition and structure formation. This center is an interdisciplinary network of sociologists, political scientists, psychologists, historians, jurists, economists and health scientists. The interdisciplinary arrangement of the center allows a multifaceted approach to the most important problem areas in the process of change after 1989, namely the economy, politics and the social sector.[2] The *Challenge-Response-Model* presented here is based mainly on an idea of Hartmut Rosa (Rosa, 2004) and was developed by him and myself over the last two years in order to have a heuristic tool for research on social change within and for it to be useful for this Collaborative Research Center. That is the reason why we had to take into account several given prerequirements and assumptions when we joined the Center: *First.* The transformation process is understood as a progressive series of challenges and responses.[3] *Second.* Social change arises from the strains between institutional structure and the actors' orientations. *Third.* There was an agreement to focus on the actors' perspectives and roles in the process of social change. Under these conditions we started to elaborate our model.[4] With the help of this model, we hope, social ruptures, conflicts and potential pathologies can be adequately understood and identified, and hence criticized.[5] As we try to demonstrate in our research project on theory of transformation (a project in the SFB 580), the model might well provide a convincing explanation of why the eastern socialist states crumbled at the end of the twentieth century and why the post-socialist transformation is an ongoing process.

In the following article, I will introduce the model (1.), then, I will switch briefly and exemplarily to the interpretation of the breakdown of the GDR and Germany's reunification in general terms of our model (2.). I will add some remarks on the practical appliance of the model in the SFB 580 (3.) and towards the end, a short outlook on the following process will be given (4.).

Sketch of the model

As already mentioned, we had to estimate not only the given situation in the Collaborative Research Center, but the actual state of affairs of theories on social change and specific transformation theories respectively had to be estimated, too. In the model proposed, we intend to synthesize the advantages of recognized theories by avoiding to overtake their known partialities and other deficiencies.[6] Thus, we suggest a model which intends to integrate a plurality of theoretical insights and comes up with a great variety of empirical findings. The designed scheme already allows the badly wanted systematization and integration of the findings which systematically and dynamically combine several levels of society (cf. Kaase & Lepius, 2001: 353). Moreover, the interim heuristic matrix[7] permits the connection of different transformation theories: perspectives of culturalism and structuralism as well as actor centered approaches; modernization theory and the power resources approach are represented. Thus, we tried to develop a model[8] that will show in which modes social change can occur and at the same time can explain that and why this change takes place substantially more diverse and open-ended than suggested for example by the modernization theories.[9] Concerning the general problems of transformation research it was essential to find a universal pattern of the analysis of social change, by which the transformation process before,

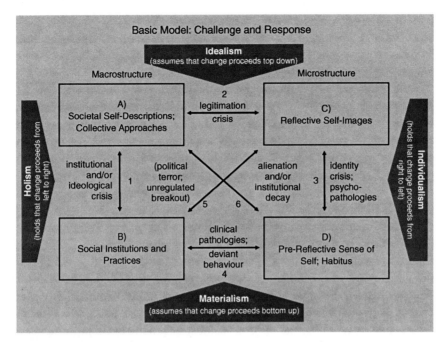

Figure 1.1 Challenge and Response model.

during and after 1989 can be represented.[10] The model above (Figure 1.1) is proposed to be such a pattern of analysis. It concerns the representation of structural and procedural relations.[11]

We suggest the model shown in Figure 1.1 (cf. Rosa, 2004; Rosa & Schmidt, 2007) whereby potential divergences and crises result from unsolved challenges; divergences which lead to incompatible impulses for action present challenges; adaptive reactions are interpreted as responses.

We distinguish four levels or domains of social dynamics of change which form a relationship of mutual interdependence as well as partial autonomy. *Social institutions and practices* (level B) form the initial point as they are a self-evident object of research in sociology. Inquiring for their functional preconditions, societal beliefs or patterns of meaning and (normative) expectancies represent themselves, by which they are sustained. Whereas such beliefs and generally the self-concept of a culture are an explicit theme in *societal self-descriptions and collective approaches* (level A), behavior expectancies, rules and demands are usually implicit in social institutions and practices. Explicit and implicit rules and expectancies do not have to correspond with each other. In institutions, the applied rules and the modes of behavior that are put in practice can collide with the current self-description of a society. Also, there are 'sedimented' or objectified societal beliefs in social institutions and practices that are likely to get into tension or contradiction with leading cultural discourses. Thereby, both levels interact with each other. Explicit collective self-descriptions go into social institutions and practices as well as e.g. modified social practices open out into new self-descriptions.

Analogical, on the side of the individual actor, two levels can be distinguished: In the *reflective self-image* of an actor his values and beliefs, aspirations and expectations can be found in explicit form (level C). In contrast, the *individual habitus* creates a domain of expectancies, attitudes and so on which are implicit and often at pre- or unconscious (level D). Between these two levels an interaction occurs, too.

None of these domains exist unaffected by the others, and the relations between them are unequally more differentiated than can be put on record here. Still, the interim simplification allows a categorical location of the central theoretical positions concerning social change. Theories that take the 'right side,' which is the actor's domain with the levels C and D, for the initial point of social change, we can call a bit simplified *individualistic theories*. Approaches that suggest the other way around and suppose that change happens through processes and events at the collective domain can be described as *holistic theories*. Concepts which regard social change as beginning with the factual living conditions, actual institutions, social practices, bodily needs and so forth (levels B and D) and postulate that being determines consciousness (and accordingly the self-descriptions in A and C), are commonly called *materialistic*. In contrast, theories that conversely take A and/or C as an initial point of any kind of change and its effects concerning B and D are typically assigned to *idealism*. Thus, regarding the variety of historic transformation processes, our proposal is that actual social change can take every one of the directions mentioned in the model.[12] Which direction it factually takes in a single case depends on the respectively given historic and cultural conditions.

This model of social analysis is intimately connected with the *Challenge-Response-Approach*, by which it gains considerable explanatory power concerning the analysis of transformation processes.[13] At first, the events and conditions which are to be interpreted as challenges in the model must be identified. Challenges are created at every point where there are ongoing tensions and incompatibilities between two or more levels of social reality (which we described here as levels A to D), that is where the level divergences in concrete situations are connected with incompatible impulses of action. These levels or domains are interacting with each other, they are 'semiautonomous' and at the same time elastically linked to one another. Tensions are inevitable as all four levels are dynamic and create independent tendencies of change. A common response to these tensions or frictions is a reciprocal and flexible adaptation due to which is a continuing 'micro change.' However, if these tensions or frictions grow into severe conflicts which signal permanent incompatibility and divergence, if the *challenge* is not as easily accomplished and the *responses* fail, they amount to a *crisis*.[14] A crisis arises when two levels have grown so far apart that the routine adaptation efforts fail and the levels seem constitutively disparate. In consequence a crisis indicates the need of revision. It is not to be resolved without making serious alterations. From this situation (potentially) disruptive change emerges concerning at least one level.[15] This change is a response to the crisis and constitutes itself categorically a new challenge for the other levels. Our proposal for modeling challenges in the form of crises is shown in the same Figure 1.1. Thus, in this model a challenge is not an exception but the rule. It normally is the inducement for flexible adaptation between the different levels of social reality, quasi a motor of permanent change and in consequence can be understood as chance for development. It must be explicitly stated that a challenge does not need to be a hazard for society.[16] Only in the absence of a response, or if it fails, does the challenge escalate into a crisis (with hazardous or system-upsetting consequences). So it is obvious that our model is far from being a theory of crises (as Figure 1.1 might possibly suggest).[17] Once again, we do not consider discrepancies, inconsistencies or challenges to be pathological per se – quite to the contrary, they are inevitable and function as a creative, innovative force of social change. They do not have to open out automatically into crises. Social change sometimes happens as well without any crises. Crises and pathologies (which we take as always entailing some form of human suffering) only arise when the discrepancies have grown beyond the horizon of possible reintegration via mutual, creative adaptations and partial, context-dependent reconciliations or compromises and when they lead to consistently contradictory impulses on the level of action. The model shows that a resulting disruptive change might take every direction, that is, from top to bottom as well as from left to right and respectively vice versa.[18] In consequence, different types of social revolutions can be described with this model, such as political revolutions (levels A and B), institutional revolutions (level B), ideological (level A), mental (level C) or habitual (level D) overthrows. The following exemplary *Challenge-Situations* are to be distinguished (cf. the six numbered arrows in Figure 1.1), which potentially can (not: must) escalate into types of crises:

1 If there are tensions between the levels A and B, if societal self-descriptions come into conflict with social institutions and practices and cannot be balanced, an institutional (level B appears pathological) and/or ideological crisis (level A seems problematic) might emerge. Outrun these tensions between A and B the limits of elasticity and creativity of the routine adaptations, but the dominant collective beliefs stay uncontroversial, an institutional crisis arises. If, for example, a society comprehends itself as free and equal and in consequence it generates the obligatory expectation of equal treatment of all people, the existence of institutions that serve securing privileges of individuals constitutes a challenge. According to the severity of the conflict (and the actual conditions of power) the aforesaid institution will come under pressure.

This pressure can be absorbed by a modification of the collective self-descriptions in so far as it is able to legitimate the partial unequal treatment in the horizon of the asserted cultural beliefs.

In contrast, an ideological crisis occurs when the dominant ideology or the established legitimation discourses lose their binding character and persuasiveness by perhaps not being able to describe appropriately the new establishing institutional reality and in consequence are regarded as being outdated and unrealistic.

2. Between the levels A and C reciprocal influences and dependencies take place, too. The individual reflective self-image can be modified by collective discourses and self-descriptions, i.e. new emancipation theories might change the individual self-image. Vice versa new emerging actor's beliefs can affect the public discourse and the propagated values, for instance when religious beliefs procure public attention. If the tensions between the levels A and C are not to be dissolved, a legitimation crisis is imminent: The validity seeking collective self-descriptions lose their credibility and the individual assent is detracted.

3. Individual reflective self-images and the connected beliefs, desires and schemes of life (level C) are placed in a strained relation to the individual, pre-reflective incorporated habits, expectancies and modes of behavior (level D). If the tensions grow too strong between the levels C and D and there is no appropriate answer to be found, the result can be either an identity crisis (level C seems doubtable) or some classic psychological pathology (level D develops pathological traits). Thus, an actor might comprehend himself as a good family father and get on with this role perfectly well until he suddenly discovers homosexual affections in himself. Who is he, who does he want to be? Should and can he abandon his previous self-image or should he oppress his sentiments? In the latter case, a disruptive change in form of a crisis seems a likely consequence.

4. Tensions between institutional practices (level B) and individual habitus (level D) that exceed the bearable degree and cannot be dissolved by routine *Responses*, create potentially *clinical pathologies*. Thus, a child who is used to romp and by its entering school suddenly is forced to sit still for a long time can suffer severely and develop symptoms of a serious illness. In contrast, it is also feasible that the child rebels and attracts attention by *deviant behavior*. Another example is the disease deriving from monotonous and hard factory work that is contradictory to natural needs.

5. If social practices and institutions (level B) do not accord with the individual self-image (level C) it amounts potentially to *alienation and/or institutional decay*. In the first case the actor continues to 'function' appropriately concerning the institutional demands, but is not able to actively acquire the institutions and practices and to assign a value and meaning to them in the context of his own living, anymore. In the second case the actor undermines the institutional expectancies concerning the behavior consciously. However, a practice or institution that is not supported by the actors anymore will decay in the long run as it is dependent on engagement and support from level C. The rapid decline of the 'Freie Deutsche Jugend' (official political youth organization of the GDR) might serve as an example. At the same time institutional decay is an expression for an ideological crisis. The self-descriptions do not convince anymore; instead, beliefs and practices are in conflict with one another. People do not find themselves in their institutions (cf. Taylor, 1985).

6   Tensions between A and D are also feasible and it might be the case that they result in *political terror*. If a society is not accepting certain modes of life (level D) concerning its self-description, then this can end in social exclusion and in extreme cases lead to the persecution of the respective population group. Conversely, individuals whose bodily practices, emotional world and habitus are in extreme contrast to the societal self-interpretations might develop an affinity to violent rebellion as it is expressed by a rampage. Tensions can also always be created through one-sided change: Thus, Chen et al. (2005) report about the current transformations in China that reserved, shy pupils, which was once the societal favored ideal of a pupil, are now increasingly 'handicapped'[19] since the self-description of the Chinese society (level A) has changed. The same modes of habitus are now assessed rather negative. For the new self-description of China as a modern and dynamic society, the former highly appraised reserve does not fit as well as an active, self-confident appearance as the embodiment of a successful person. Of course the habitus cannot change as fast as the expectations, and consequently tensions between A and D arise.

Exemplary appliance of the model to the transformation process in the former GDR

According to our heuristic matrix, we interpret the climacteric period ('Wende,' the breakdown of communist rule in the former GDR) of 1989, itself a response to previously unresolved challenges, as a special historic case in which a society (the Eastern one) dispersed at once from the left side of the model. In a very short time, the old levels A and B were changed and substituted by new ones. The main self-descriptions (level A) moved from the image of a socialist state of workers and farmers to the image of representative parliamentary democracy and the social market economy. At the same time, there was a great transfer in economy, politics, the welfare state, education, justice, and so on (that is in level B). Of course, such a change does not take place easily or smoothly. At least in domain A, there was a competing interpretation dispute, and so in domain B some institutions left and continued working. Nevertheless and indisputably, a wide exchange took place. In the other Eastern and Central European socialist countries, this exchange was hardly slower. Many realities were transformed in a dramatically short time. Acceleration appears to be characteristic of this transformation process in almost the same manner.

In our project, we concentrate mainly on research results related to East Germany, knowing that this is a special case of transformation. But we believe that this is still just a case of transformation of society, and should be studied not only as a mere consequence of the two German states' reunification. Surely, in this case, the left side hardly transformed itself but was exchanged by a transfer from the West (of Germany), and even new personnel to the functioning of the new institutions were supplied and transplanted. These are some reasons why one speaks of a 'Westernization of the East,' and certainly this (ultimately extremely successful) approach is one of the reasons why sometimes one spoke of a colonization of the GDR and the feeling of being a 'second-class German' could occur.

From our general assumption of the breakdown and replacement of the left side of the model, some conclusions directly follow. Through the rapid import of Western self-descriptions and institutions, there necessarily had to emerge new tensions and challenges for the dominant East German orientations and habitual dispositions (domains C and D). Thus, we have to ask in which way these new tensions and challenges were and are solved or handled. By gradual adjustment of the actor's orientations, beliefs and dispositions, by a progressive variation of adopted self-descriptions and institutional modes of operating, by mutual movements of adoption or by unbridgeable rigidifications? A first evaluation and combination of the material findings and results of the Collaborative Research Center 580 shows that there will be opportunities for all these examples; furthermore, that the actual course of social development (or transformation) is characterized by a variety of interventional *Challenge-Response-Chains* on all four levels.[20]

Practical appliance of the model in the SFB 580 concerning the ongoing transformation process in the former GDR

In this short contribution, it is not possible to spell out the entire process of our research. But we can present some first results of the effectual research collaboration and appliance of our model in the SFB 580 which we summarize in the following generalized outcomes:

1 There is an extreme persistence of habitual dispositions and convictions/beliefs of actors.
2 We find a growing gap between elites and population (in response to the divergences between the left and the right side of our model).
3 There is a divergence between the reflexive over-adoption and institutional insistence (that is divergence between C and B) that is often associated with tensions between Mission-Radicalism (Leitbild-Radikalismus) and institutional conservatism (that is divergence A and B, C and B). We identify a widespread critical distance between the actors and the institutional and ideological conditions.

On the one hand, these three research findings describe in retrospect the responses to the challenges arising from the collaps of the GDR-system and from the decisions which were made in the beginning of reunification, that means responses to the challenges arising from the process of new structure-building. On the other hand, these theses are reflecting the present development and they can serve as hypotheses for the future direction in the next few years, too. In the following I explain these three theses with examples from the empirical projects.

1 Strength of persistence or relative rigidity of the actor's convictions and habitual dispositions (domains C and D)

The strength of persistence or relative rigidity of the actor's convictions and habitual dispositions is virtually stated in all projects. This is, one could say, not surprising, since individual self-descriptions (domain C) cannot be altered convincingly overnight (we want to refrain here from eventful experiences of conversion). And habits (domain D) are clearly only constricted and hardly accessible for an intentional alternation: after the loss of the left side (domains A and B), the relative rigidity of the right side initially allowed for a certain security and stability – albeit a limited one ('residual value measures' and beliefs of 'what is right').

For us, it is certainly interesting to reconstruct how it eventually causes the movement of the right side as well as extended transformation processes. Particularly revealing for this purpose are, for example, the findings of the research project area 'Employment and Labour Market.' After the 'turning point' (Wende), which on their part was also a response to the lack of competitiveness of the GDR economy, there were great and rapid changes on the left side (domains A and B): the altered judicial and institutional framework, inevitable company restructurings (and the adopted employment political externalization strategy) created a massive challenge for employers and employees. In their individual action orientations and socio-moral beliefs (domains C and D), the entrepreneurs and managers, as well as the employees of East German companies, in the first instance orientated themselves on the experiences and value measures which they had gained before, in the context of East German companies. These were marked by absolute predominance of interior labor markets and closed company employment systems, often in combination. This led to the experience of unquestionable affiliation to the company as well as common destiny.

The actors reacted to the shock of the employment system's break-up with strategies which seemed obvious regarding their socio-moral orientations and experiences (domains C and D of the model): with an anew closure of the remaining staff which virtually united them to a company allying for survival ('Schicksals- und Überlebensgemeinschaften').

The predominant number of surviving or newly founded East German companies started with strategies of personnel policy aimed at stabilization and security. Therewith, it was tied up to the tradition of internal labor markets of the GDR, under entirely new parameters. This was consistent with the predominant socio-moral orientations of employers and employees.

The injury or disregard of this leading motive would have caused massive problems of legitimation concerning the company's authority. The strategy consisted of making advances to the 'constraints of capitalism' through low wages, high willingness to perform and long working hours. This obligingness was rewarded with the protection against the rigors of the labor markets.

This was, at first, quite in the tradition of the company's socialistic-paternalistic community. In the case studies of the research projects of the SFB 580, a multitude of hints can be found that security was demanded and accepted also against economic calculus. The staff's responsible decision-makers tried to avoid cancellations against all calculations of profitable efficiency (e.g. the legendary example of the blind man who was employed in quality control with the knowledge and the accordance of all others). Conversely, in many manufacturing companies employees waited for their wages for weeks or even renounced it temporarily in order to secure the survival of the company and their place of employment. It reveals that actors' 'old' orientations and dispositions (domains C and D) rule actions (initially) also under new institutional conditions (domain B).

But what happened next? With an increasing instability of the markets and order situations, the staff's responsible decision-makers must recognize the problems and costs of closed employment systems and employment security. Often, they were forced to reduce staff with high costs. This resulted in uncertainty of the continued employed and in backlashes of the dismissed staff who tried to mobilize the works' councils, the courts and labor unions. Thereby, the employment relations differentiated increasingly in a relatively closed, secured and steady core and a precarious edge-group (changes in domain B). By that, the action orientations and socio-moral beliefs of the actors get into motion (domains C and also A) and new legitimation strategies develop: the 'survival alliances' of employees and employers legitimate their security of employment through performances that are suitable for the market now and not any longer through the employer's social responsibility.

If we regard the proceeding approximation and the partial overtaking of West German patterns as a didactic play for the relationship of actors and institutions in the process of social change, it becomes obvious that East German staff officers at first interpreted the new institutions on the ground of the actors' orientations which were grown in the GDR (high security of employment for as many as possible) (and politically, so to speak, 'from left'). In the course of time, staff officers overtake the Western patterns and institutions by the accelerated assumption of concurring capitalistic models and adaptation of the new economic, political and labor-law provisions 'from right' (through the extensive use of possibilities of flexibilization in personnel policy). The virtual turning away from the old models of the company's community – and that is essential for us – does not happen until painful and in part traumatic economic experiences of crises have been made. The peremptory pressure to act, it seems, 'facilitates' grave cuts, provokes (and legitimates at the same time) new replies, supports or creates a change of attitudes. But certainly there are counter-examples, too. The pressure can also cause a paralysis of the persons concerned as well as a rigidification of divergences or even a 'drop out' (establishing subcultures). Whether pressure is experienced and used as chance or as menace depends on the individual expectations of self-efficiency and the available resources, as the psychological research project of Rainer Silbereisen and colleagues shows.[21] Above, it has been 'predicted' by the theoretical model that the occurring tensions can be answered by different modes. The replies are thus by no means determined; a failure of the 'adaptation process' is just possible.

We want to mention another example that once again analyses tensions between the left and the right side of our model, yet is distinctly not restricted to the transformation society of the former GDR. The research project of Klaus Dörre and colleagues[22] follows up a notably interesting case of divergence of habitus (domain D) and institutionalized expectations (domain B): the demands of the labor market and of the welfare state's institutions towards the so-called members of the 'underclass' (or the 'clients' of the 'precariate'), following the thesis of the project, are often not congruent with their actors' dispositions. Agencies for labor and institutions of education aim at active, self-dependent clients who work as 'entrepreneurs of labor-power' at the commercialization of themselves and in doing so are convinced of their self-efficiency, whilst at least one group of persons concerned follows completely different patterns, regarding their practices of time, future planning, ascription of responsibility and lifestyle. This 'mismatch' occurs likewise in the West and the East. The high number of unemployed who are not compatible with the self-description of the labor society (domain A) and just as little with the operating mode of the social security systems (domain B), here occurs at first as a social challenge. Then, the reform of unemployment benefit can be regarded as an institutional response which again includes an enormous challenge for the recipients of unemployment benefit, due to the demands towards the actors, whereupon they produce different replies: habitual approximation in the sense of a planned 'activation' displays an adaptation of domain D towards domain B (the dispositions change according to the institutional requirements); in contrast to this, the creation of a disconnected sub-society or reactions which open out into clinical depressions of the concerned, describe pathologic-critical modes of response which produce new challenges. However, the reforms of the labor market, analysed by the research project, show further unintended effects that can be interpreted as a consequence of an institutionalized practice of action which is not orientated on the formulated political models (domain A) but on 'hardheaded' patterns of action. Thus, it happens that the created One-Euro-Jobs[23] are no 'stepping stones' that lead to a regular employment relationship but that they lead to a far-reaching substitution.

2 Growing gap between elites and population

The research programs of the projects of the Collaborative Research Center 580, especially those focusing on elites, show that in response to the challenge of exchange of the left side, an increasing divergence between elites and population emerged in many spheres. This divergence consists basically in the adaptation of the functioning elites to the macro-social requirements regarding their action orientations, whereas great groups of the population are skeptical towards the institutional modes of operation and efforts as well as towards their legitimating models. At this level of attitude, there is on the one hand a tendency of horizontal convergence in German-German elite formation, but on the other hand, a double vertical difference between elites and population is visible as well. Both directions of development are crucial for the analysis of a 'post-transformation' society. The vertical distance between elites and non-elites is detectable for East and West Germany in general, though it is especially distinct in the East. The East German population is additionally pervaded by a line of conflict which separates insiders (winners) and outsiders (losers). That elites and population dissent from one another concerning their assessment, can be accounted for in general terms by the reactions of the persons concerned on the occasion of the decision-maker's positional priority of action. The people concerned individually are not under the pressure of developing engaging collective problem-solving strategies or to enforce them against resistance. Numerous research projects affirmed the observation that it comes to a growing gap between elites who are willing and able to adapt and who try to overcome the differences between the domains A and C in favor of A, and the broad population which clings to the grown socio-moral beliefs in reaction towards the new models and institutional practices. Moreover, the research project of Rudi Schmidt, Katharina Bluhm, and colleagues[24] has found distinct indications that not only the 'cleft' between neoliberal (economic) elites and the population which is still orientated on socialist ideals of justice is deepening, but also that these elites themselves in their 'private' orientations of action (domain C), question their own economic acting. Here, the tensions between domains A and C seem to continue – which brings us to the third and last thesis.

3 Taking distance

Detectable and revealing are especially the deviances from the arrangement of the elite-non-elite-relations. These particularities become comprehensible through the differences of 'we-sense' ('Wir-Sinn') which were elaborated through an East-West comparison by another research project of Hartmut Rosa, Michael Corsten and collegues[25] can be found within elites and non-elites in equal measure. This gives reason to the assumption that there is, in regard to the elites, no simple adjustment of East German socio-cultural measures of value and patterns of interpretation to West German standards. Whereas West German actors in their patterns of action and interpretation palpably orientate on collective practices and norms that have grown in local-political institutions, so that a tight interlocking or co-evolution between practice of action and orientation of values (between domains B and C) emerges, East German citizens tend to abstract universal principles, since they encounter the new institutional reality with a certain skepticism and without the long-term practice. West Germans usually consider the given institutional rules as taken for granted and in consequence as being unquestionable. The change of the system, which East German citizens – elites and non-elites – experienced as a break, however, causes that they neither stick to the old institutions ('ostalgisch') nor do they unreservedly adapt to the new rules. They answer with abstract-idealistic patterns of the collective, with beliefs of a universal human, for instance with an orientation on humanitarian equalitarianism which reaches into the depth of the (at domains C and D enrooted) social structure. Thus it appears that East German elites and population likewise possess 'residual' value measures, patterns of interpretation and action orientations, which on the one hand secure them the capacity to act in contexts of rapid and unpredictable change and which they on the other hand might use against the new practices and relations. These patterns especially contain latent common beliefs about 'what is right' and 'what needs to be.' Such socio-moral orientations (domains C and D) may work as resources, as obstacles or as assessment factors for coping with the system upheaval or generally for social change. In all three respects though – that is our third main thesis – they introduce a critical distance between the actors and the institutional and ideological relations, which still marks a powerful difference between East and West Germany.

Conclusion and prospects

It is apparent that the material research findings of the SFB 580 actually can be arranged systematically and be related to one another with the help of our heuristic model and by this can be fructified for the holistic interpretation of transformation processes. Nevertheless, a couple of questions remain. One problem for the practical appliance is still the adequate empiric identification of challenge-situations: From which accurant moment on does a 'normal' tension turn into a challenge and how is it empirically determinable if incompatible action impulses emerge respectively? Should or must we distinguish between 'normal' and 'serious' (more dramatic) challenges? This is not only a question of determination but must be carefully examined in successful empiric appliance and cooperation. Anyway, our approach shall enable to avoid premature constrictions to certain lines of conflict or challenge-situations, as it often happens that the six crucial conflicts of the model do not appear isolated, but in multiple modes of interactions. For an adequate examination of the responses the joint solving of different questions is required: Why are there, for example, not only different, but possibly not any responses at all to seemingly identical challenges? What influence do cultural (or national) factors have? How big is the scope of configuration concerning the responses and what does it depend on? That there is a scope of configuration does not mean that the actors control the situation, but still their behavior is relevant for further developments.[26] The ability for answering is thus not to be confounded with 'control of the situation' or 'autonomy.' Which responses establish themselves, grow dominant and 'system constituent,' which others step back (and why?) and stay without any effect? What are the constituents of lasting success of certain solutions and whereby are they distinguished? It is thus essential to develop criteria for the quality and appropriateness of responses.[27] Here we assume in general that a response is appropriate and successful when it eliminates or declines an existing divergence. In contrast, a response is considered a failure when the divergence and incompatibility persists or grows. Thereby the question is very interesting, why the transfer of seemingly exemplary problem solutions occasionally fails.[28] Likewise, the reasons as well as the intermediate- and long-term consequences of absent and failed responses are interesting to us in regard to persistent tensions, not realized challenges or even crises. Is it feasible to define a cause profile for failure?

Our search aims at the feasibility to identify representative progress profiles of transformation processes which prove to be valid under certain historical contexts.[29] However, this does not say that there are a priori laws of societal development. In regard to the model, social change happens when there are tensions between two or more of the four levels of social reality and in reaction to these attempts towards adaptation are made. Thereby we assume, firstly, that adaptation (therefore change) is fundamentally possible into every direction, secondly, that there are de facto very different tempi, modes and abilities of adaptation, and thirdly, that under specific historic circumstances and resource conditions some progresses are more probable than others and are (almost) predictable.

Thereby our model is based on a central decision which requires a lot and which is not without problems. We assume that specific domain-divergences, as far as they lead to incompatible impulses of action or decision, induce balancing respectively adaptation motions that aim at reconcilability ('compatibilization'). According to this meaning our model can be understood as an 'equilibrium model.'[30] However, we do not postulate a self-dynamic societal tendency or movement towards states of balance. In fact we only argue that the respective divergences act as challenges which cause (different) responses. Because tensions and divergences can be created by the semi-autonomous 'interior developments' of the domains, which we comprehend as 'elastically linked,' and constitute the societal normal case, the social dynamic is preserved. There is nothing said about the direction of the adaptation movements as our model does not suggest any particular predetermined tendency or direction of development.

Therefore our theoretical work will emphasize the identification of those factors that create a response-demanding challenge out of a simple divergence or tension. Our current answer – incompatible action impulses – seems to be too unspecific. Hence we will check our transformation theoretical findings particularly with regard to aspects which help in explaining under which conditions existing field-divergences create genuine 'transformation energy.' Furthermore, the belief that there is no representative progress scheme of social change is one of our basic assumptions. There is no universal dominance of the material level over the symbolic or actor-level compared to the institutions, or vice versa. But it does not exclude that propositions can be made concerning in which direction, under certain historical circumstances, specific conflicts dissolve preferably. There is nothing to be said a priori against the assumption that the change of economic approaches in the twentieth century can be explained in terms of consequences of the structural necessities and changed methods of production, which in turn had characteristic consequences concerning the dominant modes of subjectification.

Notes

1 Several transformation theories were developed or modified, but a lot of unsolved questions and innertheoretial problems remained. Cf. e.g. Linz & Stepan, 1996; Merkel, 1999; Zapf, 2000; Kaase & Lepsius, 2001; Dittrich, 2001; Hopfmann & Wolf, 2001; Lutz, 2003; Kollmorgen & Schrader, 2003; Kollmorgen, 2005.
2 For further information see: http://www.sfb580.uni-jena.de.
3 Cf. Best, 2004. Since the actors' responses to the massive problems of the transformation process create new action requirements ('challenges of the

second order'), the complexity of the actor-institution-constellations increases in the course of time. In this respect, relatively strong structures do not originate from single responses to single definable challenges but they develop in the course of an entire set of challenges, whereas every response produces new challenges and problems. For the history and central importance of the *Challenge-Response-Approach* in the SFB 580 cf. Best 2007 and other contributions in de Nève et al. 2007.

4   Without going into details, let me refer to the main objectives of our theoretical research project: *First*. As a cross-section project, it collects and integrates the findings of the empirical projects of the SFB 580 into a generalized interpretation of the transformation process. *Second*. On the basis of these results, the project aims at producing a solid foundation for transformation theory, which is still missing. *Third* and finally, it seeks a new conceptualization of social change as a contribution to general social theory.

5   An important social science's problem is to decide what could provide non-arbitrary grounds to identify pressures (or needs), directions and agents for social change in a given historic situation and, possibly, to distinguish desirable forms of change from dysfunctional or harmful ones.

6   Cf. e.g. Coleman, 1990; Haverkamp & Smelser, 1992; Booth, 1994; Esser, 1999; Schelkle et al., 2000; Joas & Knöbl, 2004; Costa et al., 2006.

7   We are still at the very beginning and it is a long way to develop a scientific model. That's why we prefer to call our proposal a heuristic matrix or scheme. Anyhow, in this chapter we sometimes name it model, already.

8   For a detailed discussion of the initial idea cf. Rosa, 2004.

9   The teleological bias of modernization theories decreases its ability for explanation of social change in general. Also, these theories give little information about the continuing change even in Western societies. Cf. e.g. Eisenstadt, 2000; Therborn, 2000a and 2000b; Knöbl, 2001; Inglehart & Welzel, 2005; Rosa, 2006.

10 The project serves the foundation research insofar as it tries to provide the conceptual equipment that is capable of describing social change precisely at different levels at the same time. This ground terminological reservoir will be available to application-orientated researchers.

11 Thereby we are conscious of the fact that every modelling is necessarily a stereotyping simplification (cf. Esser, 1991).

12 What does not follow from the approach presented here, therefore, is a general theory of social change that locates the source of social evolution on one particular level (as idealistic, materialistic, individualistic or holistic approaches usually do).

13 As an advancement of the *Challenge-Response-Approach* our initial thesis is that the system breakdown is not only a challenge but is itself already a response.

14 For the difference of everyday challenges and transformative crises cf. Cioffi-Revilla, 2005. Cioffi-Revilla leaves a lot of space for a possible failure of the reactions to them (cf. ibid., 144); in general he assumes: 'A society that always succeeds in responding to situational changes will grow in complexity, especially if the situational changes present increasing challenges' (ibid., 148).

15 The genuine pressure for adaptation emerges usually not until conflicting, incompatible impulses of action arise out of the factual divergence.

16 Concerning the *Challenge-Response-Approach* cf. de Nève et al. 2007. In our model the challenge is not taken normatively. It is a stimulus for a response.

Whether the challenge is realized or not and if a response follows is not predestined.

17 But it can serve as a heuristic tool for the social analyst in his attempt to identify distortions and potential social pathologies and to point out possible ways of overcoming them.

18 Changes can have extra-social or purely field internal reasons. Society exogenous factors are continuously operant as well (cf. Smelser, 1992). However, the view held here is that these exogenous factors unfold their transformative effect *not until and only if* they open out into manifest contradictions between the four levels. Concerning endogenous and exogenous change, especially exogenous events, cf. Esser, 1999, 351 et seq.

19 The effects of being reserved and shy on the development of pupils were tested. In the evaluation of teachers concerning the psychic adaptation of pupils in 1990 the shy pupils were considered better and promising whereas ten years later this evaluation reversed. We owe this information about the survey to Martin Pinquard and Rainer Silbereisen.

20 In our project, we try to reconstruct systematically and accurately the logic of transformation, specific characteristics, inherent mechanisms and process-chains of social transformation since 1989 in the light of our newly developed matrix.

21 The title of the project is *Psychosocial resources and coping with social change*. Cf. for details of the research projects and resulting publications: http://www.sfb580.uni-jena.de.

22 Title of this project is *'Difficult' Customers: The influence of strict regulations on the labour market orientations of the unemployed and those in insecure employment.*

23 That means jobs in which welfare recipients are working (without adequate pay, but they get approximately one euro per hour additionally) and which are very cheap for employers.

24 Title of the project: *Change of generations in the management. Persistence or change of the management strategies in East and West Germany.*

25 This project focuses on *Civic engagement*.

26 The adequate conceptual consideration of exogenous influencing factors and so-called 'constraints' to individual acting and especially the functional modes of operation is necessary, too.

27 Thereto is an intensive discussion, cf. de Nève et al., 2007 and especially Reiser & Schnapp, 2007b and Reiser & Schnapp, 2007a: 46 et seq.

28 Concerning the failing transfer, as an extra academic example the transfer of players in international football business might serve, where excellent players often cannot display their potential under the new conditions, cf. for example Stichweh, 2005: 7.

29 We expect especially information about the exact differentiation between transformation respectively system breakdown and 'normal' social change. Cf. Mayntz, 1996: 142, who suggests that societal upheavals are a special type of social discontinuities, that is rapidly progressing, extensive (radical) changes at the macro-level that involve the micro- and meso-level at the same time. Moreover, the reconstruction of the process opens up independent chances of insight that can be theoretically generalized. (cf. ibid: 144)

30 For critic and partial justification of equilibrium models cf. e.g. Esser, 1999: 356 et seq. and Smelser, 1968.

References

Best, Heinrich (Hg.) (2004). Challenge and Response. Das Forschungsprogramm des SFB 580 in den Jahren 2004 bis 2008 (*Mitteilungen des SFB 580*, H. 15, Juli 2004).

Best, Heinrich (2007). Der Challenge-Response-Ansatz als forschungsleitende Perspektive für die Transformationsforschung. In de Nève/Reiser/Schnapp 2007, 11–23.

Booth, David (Hg.) (1994). *Rethinking social development. Theory, research and practice.* Harlow: Longman Scientific & Technical.

Chen, X., Cen, G., Li, D., & He, Y. (2005). Social functioning and adjustment in Chinese children: The impact of historical time. In *Child Development*, 76, 182–195.

Cioffi-Revilla, Claudio (2005). A canonical theory of origins and development of social complexity. In *Journal of Mathematical Sociology*, 29(2). London [u.a.]: Taylor & Francis, 133–153.

Coleman, James (1990). *Foundations of social theory.* Cambridge: Harvard University Press.

Costa, Sérgio, Dominguez, Mauricio, Knöbl, Wolfgang, & da Silva, Josué P. (Hg.) (2006). *The plurality of modernity decentring sociology.* München: Rainer Hampp Verlag.

Eisenstadt, Shmuel N. (2000). Multiple modernities. In *Daedalus*, 129, 1–29.

Dittrich, Eckhard (Hg.) (2001). Wandel, Wende, Wiederkehr. *Transformation as epochal change in Central and Eastern Europe: Theoretical concepts and their empirical applicability.* Würzburg: Ergon-Verlag.

Esser, Hartmut (1991). Einleitung: Probleme der Modellierung sozialer Prozesse. In Esser, Troitzsch 1991: 13–25.

Esser, Hartmut (1999). *Soziologie.* Spezielle Grundlagen. Bd. 2: Die Konstruktion der Gesellschaft, Frankfurt a.M. [u.a.]: Campus.

Esser, Hartmut & Troitzsch, Klaus G. (Hg.) (1991). *Modellierung sozialer Prozesse.* Bonn: Informationszentrum Sozialwissenschaften.

Haverkamp, Hans & Smelser, Neil J. (Hg.) (1992). *Social change and modernity.* Berkeley: University of California Press.

Hopfmann, Arndt & Wolf, Michael (Hg.) (2001). *Transformationstheorie – Stand, Defizite, Perspektiven.* Münster, Hamburg, & London: Lit.

Inglehart, Ronald & Welzel, Christian (2005). *Modernization, cultural change, and democracy. The human development sequence.* Cambridge [u.a.]: Cambridge University Press.

Joas, Hans & Knöbl, Wolfgang (2004). *Sozialtheorie. Zwanzig einführende Vorlesungen.* Frankfurt a. M.: Suhrkamp.

Kaase, Max & Lepsius, Rainer (2001). Transformationsforschung. In Bertram/Kollmorgen 2001: 343–363.

Knöbl, Wolfgang (2001). *Spielräume der Modernisierung. Das Ende der Eindeutigkeit.* Weilerwist: Velbrück.

Kollmorgen, Raj (Hg.) (2005). *Transformation als Typ sozialen Wandels: postsozialistische Lektionen, historische und interkulturelle Vergleiche.* Münster: Lit.

Kollmorgen, Raj & Schrader, Heiko (Hg.) (2003). *Postsozialistische Transformationen: Gesellschaft, Wirtschaft, Kultur. Theoretische Perspektiven und empirische Befunde.* Würzburg: Ergon-Verlag.

Linz, Juan J. & Stepan, Alfred C. (1996). *Problems of democratic transition and consolidation: Southern Europe, South America, and post-communist Europe.* Baltimore: Johns Hopkins University Press.

Lutz, Burkart (2003). Verpasste Gelegenheiten und nachzuholende Lektionen. Einige (selbst-) kritische Überlegungen zur deutschen Transformationsforschung der 90er Jahre. In Brussig, Martin/Ettrich, Frank/Kollmorgen, Raj (Hg.) 2003: *Konflikt und Konsens: Transformationsprozesse in Ostdeutschland.* Opladen: Leske + Budrich: 287–305.

Mayntz, Renate (1996). Gesellschaftliche Umbrüche als Testfall soziologischer Theorie. In Clausen 1996: 141–153.

Merkel, Wolfgang (1999). *Systemtransformation. Eine Einführung in die Theorie und Empirie der Transformationsforschung.* Opladen: Leske + Budrich.

Nève, Dorothée de, Reiser, Marion, & Schnapp, Kai-Uwe (Hg.) (2007). *Herausforderung – Akteur – Reaktion. Diskontinuierlicher Wandel aus theoretischer und empirischer Perspektive.* Baden-Baden: Nomos.

Rosa, Hartmut (2004). Four levels of self-interpretation. A paradigm for social philosophy and political criticism. In *Philosophy and Social Criticism*, Vol. 30, No. 5–6 2004: 691–720.

Rosa, Hartmut (2006). The universal underneath the multiple: Social acceleration as a key to understanding modernity. In Costa, Dominguez, Knöbl, & da Silva 2006: 23–42.

Rosa, Hartmut & Schmidt, Steffen (2007). Which challenge, whose response? Ein Vier-Felder-Modell der *Challenge-Response-Analyse* sozialen Wandels. In de Nève & Reiser, & Schnapp 2007: 53–72.

Reiser, Marion & Schnapp, Kai-Uwe (2007a). Jenseits der Linearität – konzeptionelle Grundlagen für die Beschreibung diskontinuierlicher Entwicklungsprozesse. In de Nève, Reiser, & Schnapp 2007: 25–51.

Reiser, Marion & Schnapp, Kai-Uwe (2007b). Herausforderung – Akteur – Antwort. Eine fruchtbare Heuristik zur Analyse sozialen Wandels. In de Nève, Reiser, & Schnapp 2007: 221–232.

Schelkle, Waltraud, Krauth, Wolf-Hagen, Kohli, Martin, & Elwert, Georg (Hg.) (2000). *Paradigms of social change: Modernization, development, transformation, evolution.* Frankfurt a. M. [u.a.]: Campus.

Smelser, Neil J. (1968). Toward a general theory of social change. In ders., *Essays in Sociological Theory.* Englewood Cliffs, NJ: Prentice-Hall: 193–268.

Smelser, Neil J. (1992). External and internal factors in theories of social change. In Haferkamp & Smelser 1992: 369–394.

Stichweh, Rudolf (2005). Transfer in Sozialsystemen: Theoretische Überlegungen. In Paper on http://www.unilu.ch/deu/prof._dr._rudolf_stichwehpublikationen.

Taylor, Charles (1985). Interpretation and the Sciences of Man. In ders., *Philosophical Papers Bd. 2.* Cambridge: Cambridge University Press: 15–57.

Therborn, Göran (2000a). 'Modernization' discourses, their limitations, and their alternatives. In Schelkle et al. 2000: 49–72.

Therborn, Göran (2000b). At the birth of second century of sociology: times of reflexivity, spaces of identity, and modes of knowledge. In *British Journal of Social Theory*, 6(3): 293–305.

Zapf, Wolfgang (2000). *How to evaluate German unification?* Berlin: WZB.

2

LIFE MANAGEMENT IN DEVELOPMENTAL SETTINGS OF MODERNITY: CHALLENGES TO THE ADAPTIVE SELF

Jochen Brandtstädter

The developmental settings of modernity are shaped by accelerated cultural change, growing interconnectedness ('globalization') in areas of production and communication, and increasing pluralization of life forms. By extending ideals of maximal efficiency from the sphere of economic production to personal life policies, contemporary societies put increasing emphasis on the efficient use of temporal, physical, and psychological resources. These general trends call for increased self-regulatory and compensatory effort in many areas of life and personal development; notions of maximization, optimization, and compensation are emblematic of the cognitive-theoretical orientations and values that characterize modernity and its use of human and cultural resources. Ideals of self-perfection, which since antiquity have been prominent in philosophical thought on human development (see also Tetens, 1777), currently resurface in debates about successful life management, mostly however centering on physical fitness, social competence, or attractive appearance, rather than on self-cultivation in the traditional sense that integrates moral, intellectual, and esthetic virtues. Popular guides on techniques of self-regulation and maximizing personal efficacy are well-selling; a growing need for compensatory support, however, also indicates that efforts to increase personal efficacy in many areas of life are approaching a 'production possibility frontier' (Brandtstädter & Wentura, 1995).

In the wake of these changes, there has been a gradual blurring of normative timetables for organizing one's life course (e.g., Mayer & Diewald, 2007; Settersten, 1999); accordingly, notions of agency and intentional self-development have gained currency in discussions on positive development and successful life-managment (cf. Brandtstädter, 1998, 2001;

Brandtstädter & Lerner, 1999; Carstensen & Lang, 2007; Emmons, 2003; Greve, Rothermund, & Wentura, 2005; Heckhausen, 1999). Institutions and norms that traditionally have structured the individual's life course have lost much of their regulative force, which gives people greater freedom and choice in the selection of developmental options, but also leaves them with less orientation and support in processes of life-management; this is also reflected in a tendency to postpone transitions such as parenthood or marriage (cf. Arnett, 2004). Personal development over the life span has become a 'reflexive project' (Giddens, 1991) requiring planful competence and informed selection among alternative options for personal development over the life span. At the same time, changing role structures and work environments call for flexible adjustment of personal goals and life policies across the life span. These basic conditions pose conflicting adaptive challenges in various domains of life management. In the following, I shall discuss some of these quandaries in short compass.

1 Negotiating continuity and change: Adaptive quandaries

Planful competence contributes to success and well-being, and particularly so in times of uncertainty and change (cf. Clausen, 1991; Crockett & Silbereisen, 2000; Shanahan & Elder, 2002); personality dispositions generally seem to become more predictive of subjective life quality in contexts that impose less organizing structure on the life course (cf. Caspi & Moffitt, 1993; Mayer & Diewald, 2007). These same conditions, however, reduce the possibilities of anticipating one's course of development and the utility of acquired skills and knowledge for coping with new exigencies. Life management today seems to favor an open format of life-planning that from the outset reckons with the possibility that one's plans and projects may fail.

Difficulties of 'taking the long view'

Reduced possibilities of anticipating the future eventually also reduce the motivational potential of long-term goals. Temporally extended agency essentially involves a capacity to evaluate personal goals with regard to future risks and benefits; it also requires formation and maintenance of future-related commitments that are strong and stable enough to resist situational enticements and to warrant goal pursuit even in the absence of immediate tangible reinforcers (cf. Baumeister, Heatherton, & Tice, 1994). Concepts of self-control and will-power colloquially refer to this capacity; in the typical delay-of-gratification experiment, such competences are expressed in the willingness to sacrifice a small, immediate reward for a larger, but delayed one (e.g., Metcalfe & Mischel, 1999). If the future is uncertain, however, delayed rewards and long-term benefits tend to be discounted more strongly, so that going for the immediate advantage may become a rational strategy (Loewenstein & Prelec, 1993; see also Brandtstädter, Rothermund, Kranz, & Kühn, in press). Saving rates, for example, tend to decrease in times of uncertainty (cf. Browning & Crossley, 2001). Considering the processes of life management, the difficulty to construe representations of the self in future states thus promotes an orientation toward goals the value of which does not depend on expected future utilities. This may foster an increased orientation toward goals of intrinsic value, but may also go with a tendency of blunting out future risks and seeking 'shortcuts to happiness' (Seligman, 2002) that offer immediate hedonic gratification.

Identity and self-continuity

A related quandary concerns the maintenance of a diachronically stable and coherent identity. In its traditional sense, the notion of identity implies self-sameness over time; the development of personal identity is closely tied to the acquisition, and identification with, self-attributes that are stable over time and across situations (e.g., Greve, 2007). Accordingly, personal continuity is threatened when internal or external structures supporting it become unstable. The developmental environments today involve recurrent processes of de- and resocialization over the life course; increased demands of mobility and flexible adjustment to changing work environments likewise tend to undermine stable identifications and long-term attachments. Under such conditions, skillful impression management and a readiness to attune one's behavior to changing role expectations become strategies of personal success; the construct of 'self-monitoring' (Snyder, 1979) refers to these particular skills. In the extreme, however, a chameleon-like adjustment to situational demands and expectations may amount to estranging oneself from one's self, if not to a 'corrosion of character' (Sennett, 1998).

Choice and regret

Modern societies offer a broad assortment of alternative options for personal development over the life span. This fosters feelings of freedom and choice, but also has less positive side effects. The plurality of options renders selective decisions more stressful and demanding; when attractive developmental options are easily available for 'upward' comparisons, people also tend to be less satisfied with their current situation and more likely to experience 'counterfactual emotions' of anger, disappointment, or regret (Kahneman & Miller, 1986). As Schwartz (2004) has noted, the 'explosion of choice' is a pervasive trend in modern societies, which however does not generally predict increased well-being, but often seems to reduce satisfaction. When attractive options are beyond the person's reach but nonetheless retain their positive valence, feelings of dissatisfaction easily turn into depression. This points to the potential benefits of processes that help the individual to disengage from blocked goals and to downsize ambitions of maximization and optimal choice.

Erosion of shared meanings

It has often been noted that rapid cultural change also reduces and fragments the sphere of shared meanings that form the basis for communication, mutual understanding, and respect within and between generations. This obviously has problematic effects on social cohesion; it increases the 'biographical distance' between age groups (Brandtstädter, 1985) and promotes 'social atomism,' as Taylor (1991) has put it. Traditional sources of meaning such as religious commitments or family values have lost much of their orienting potential for navigating the life course; as Seligman (1990) has argued, this 'waning of the commons' partly accounts for epidemiological findings of an increasing incidence of depression among younger people. An increasingly competitive orientation toward individualistic and materialistic conceptions of the 'good life' (see also Baumeister & Vohs, 2002) involves a correspondingly higher risk of set-backs and disappointments. Under such conditions, cultivating and improving personal efficiency becomes an important developmental strength; on the other side, however, moderating personal ambitions and adjusting goals to the feasible range appears equally important for maintaining a positive outlook on self and personal development. While largely deriding attitudes of humility and modesty as obsolete, modern societies ironically set the stage for a revival of such traditional values.

Cultural change and obsolescence

People strive for security, continuity, and stable identity; these motivations are basic to human agency and life management. To the extent that they threaten these strivings, contemporary societies contribute to the notorious 'discontents in modernity' (cf. Berger, Berger, & Kellner, 1975; Marsh, Caputo, & Westphal, 1992). At this juncture, it may be worth noting that the adaptive challenges that characterize the developmental settings of modernity are comparable to those imposed by the processes of aging (cf. Brandtstädter & Rothermund, 2003). In both contexts, personal future becomes insecure, which renders long-range planning problematic; moreover, questions concerning the optimal use and allocation of resources become urgent. While 'successful aging' is largely defined today in terms of maintaining youthful vigor and efficiency as long as possible, acceleration of cultural change renders this task more and more difficult; by the same token, there is a growing demand for compensatory interventions by means of 'prothetics, athletics, cosmetics' (Sloterdijk, 2005). At the same time, however, the limits of compensatory efforts are increasingly felt. Metaphorically speaking, the acceleration of time in times of rapid cultural change also accelerates subjective aging: Feelings of obsolescence, of being unable to keep pace with the processes of change, are experienced more frequently and at increasingly earlier points in the life course; moreover, personal experience and expertise are devalued when acquired skills and problem solutions can no longer be transferred to the future. By eroding traditions and habitual patterns of life at an increasing pace, cultural change breeds feelings of 'homelessness,' in that respect again resembling experiences of aging; at the same time, it may also create a longing for congenial environments and for 'timeless sources of meaning' (cf. Brandtstädter et al., in press; Mittelstraß, 1992; van Selm & Dittmann-Kohli, 1998).

2 The stability-flexibility dilemma in life management

In nonstationary developmental contexts where ontogenetic age-graded changes fuse and interact with historical influences and nonnormative-accidental events, negotiating continuity and change requires tenacity in pursuing personal goals, as well as sufficient flexibility in adjusting them to contextual and developmental changes. Today more than in the past, positive development and successful life management crucially hinge on the integration of these partly opposed and antagonistic adaptive demands.

Already on the level of action regulation, a basic dilemma consists in reconciling the demands of stability and flexibility, or of tenacious goal pursuit and flexible goal adjustment: Focal goals have to be shielded against distractive influences, and concurrent action tendencies must be inhibited in order to maintain a chosen course of action and prevent preference reversals that might be regretted in hindsight (e.g., Fishbach, Friedman, & Kruglanski, 2003; Gollwitzer, Fujita, & Oettingen, 2004). On the other hand, action regulation needs to be flexible enough to adjust to changes in contextual conditions, to be sensitive to new promising options, and to avoid entrapment in barren projects and life-paths. This stability-flexibility dilemma (Bak & Brandtstädter, 1998; Grossberg, 1987) is aggravated under conditions of uncertainty and change. In situations where efforts to maintain goals and ambitions approach limits, this quandary often gives rise to a stressful conflict between maintaining and relinquishing prior commitments. Personality traits such as strong internal control beliefs and high persistence are known to contribute to personal achievement and satisfaction; it tends to be overlooked, however, that these dispositions may also render people more liable to miss the 'right' point for relinquishing barren projects and life paths (see also Brockner, 1992). There is, however, also the obverse risk of premature resignation, of unstable and vacillating commitment, and of leaving developmental resources unexploited.

A basic requirement of efficient life management, thus, apparently consists in finding a balance between tenacious goal pursuit and flexible goal adjustment, which enables the person to successfully pursue personal projects and overcome obstacles, but at the same time also to remain responsive to internal and external changes that affect the range of feasible goals and developmental options. Developmental research in the past has largely neglected these adaptive processes; or, as Brim (1988, p. 49) puts it: 'That process of arranging and managing our lives to keep the right balance between achievement and capacity is ... one of the most important, fascinating, and overlooked aspects of adult development.'

It should be noted at this juncture that every adaptive system, including the social and cultural macrosystem, is subject to the dilemmatic tension between securing continuity and being open to innovative change. How this dilemma is negotiated in a particular societal context depends not only on how given contextual conditions organize and structure the life course, but also on the ways in which they regulate and constrain individual agency – which however is not only 'agency within structure,' but also contributes to the evolution and change on the macrolevel. The degree to which individual agents are intentionally involved in these macrolevel processes generally differs between individuals. In processes of social change, for example, there typically are early innovators who are at the frontiers of change, and laggards who are less prone to give up habitual life patterns; the majority will presumably range between these extremes. Active engagement at the frontiers of innovation and change mostly involves dissatisfaction with the status quo and a readiness to tenaciously pursue goals in the face of obstacles; active opposition against such changes may likewise require tenacity and persistence. These same dispositions, however, may reduce the readiness to adjust, or make one's peace with, externally imposed social change. Such differences make a difference on personal and social levels of 'well-being'; they also appear related to the adaptive dynamics and dispositions which are addressed in the following.

3 Adjusting goals and ambitions to capacities and constraints, and vice versa: the dual-process model

As William James (1890) and other psychologically minded philosophers before him (e.g., Schopenhauer, 1851) have noted, satisfaction and life quality basically depend on the relation between success and pretensions; this formulation implies that both increasing success as well as downsizing ambitions can contribute to well-being. A similar insight also recurs in philosophical distinctions between 'offensive' and 'defensive' concepts of happiness (Tatarkiewicz, 1976), which however represent different schools of thought that are often considered as inherently opposed. Classical ideals of equanimity and ascetism seem of course antithetical to contemporary life policies. While emphasizing the personal and societal benefits of ambitious goal striving, modern societies have largely neglected a central implication of James's formula, viz., that goals can be both sources of meaning and satisfaction as well as potential sources of dissatisfaction and frustration. This central tenet of Stoic philosophy also recurs in some religious systems (e.g., Buddhism; see also Tugendhat, 2003). Action-theoretical perspectives on human development offer vantage points for integrating both perspectives, and for elucidating how the relation between goals, ambitions, and competences is negotiated over the life span.

In the course of their development, humans acquire the competences and interests to actively shape and control their development (cf. Brandtstädter, 1998; Lerner & Walls, 1999); to quote from Charlotte Bühler's (1933) seminal work, development in adulthood thus becomes a permanent task in and of itself. People strive to keep the balance of 'gains' and 'losses' over the life span within favorable margins; such efforts may be enhanced or constrained by contextual factors that change on ontogenetic and historical dimensions. They can be successful, however, only if goals and ambitions are commensurate with the person's developmental potentials, as well as with contextual constraints.

To elaborate these points theoretically, we have to recognize that the self-system engages a variety of mechanisms to defend and maintain stability and permanence over time. For example, people prefer or actively seek contexts that fit with personal values, competences, and self-beliefs; they try to maintain threatened self-attributions through increased compensatory effort or through rejecting and defensively interpreting self-discrepant evidence; eventually, they may also disengage from goals they cannot identify with (e.g., Caspi & Roberts, 1999; Greenwald, 1980; Greve, 2005). Self-discrepancies and divergences between desired and actual developmental paths can obviously be reduced in two different, but complementary ways: (a) Through intentional efforts to shape or modify one's behavior, development, and circumstances of life so that they accord with the goals and values that constitute the person's desired or 'ought' self; or (b) through adjusting goals, ambitions, and self-standards to available action resources and situational constraints. We have denoted these activities and processes as *assimilative* and *accommodative*, respectively

(Brandtstädter 1989; Brandtstädter & Renner, 1990). The concepts of assimilation and accommodation have been used in different theoretical contexts; in particular, they figure prominently in Piaget's model of cognitive development (e.g., see Flavell, 1963). In the present context, however, the concepts denote different modes of negotiating divergences between desired and factual conditions of personal development, and of neutralizing negative emotions that typically accompany such goal discrepancies. Whereas the assimilative mode supports tenacious persistence in goal pursuit and enduring effort in the face of obstacles, accommodative mechanisms prevent the wasting of resources in barren goals and enhance reorientation toward new, more promising goals. Thus, both modes serve specific adaptive functions in the evolutionary architecture of the cognitive-motivational system. Assimilative and accommodative processes are antagonistically related insofar as tendencies of goal engagement are opposed to the processes disengaging from it. In concrete episodes of coping which often involve adaptive demands on different levels, however, both processes may complement and support each other. In particular under constrained resources or when capacity limits are reached, we must often relinquish particular goals in order to successfully achieve others.

Depending on personal goals and beliefs, as well as on available knowledge and procedural means, assimilative activities come in many shapes. For example, we acquire knowledge and skills to prepare for future tasks; we strive to increase fitness and attractiveness through physical exercise, cosmetics, or dieting; we try to prevent age-related losses through compensatory activities such as increased training, 'brain jogging,' and the like; in navigating our lives, we follow normative expectations and self-ideals and form corresponding self-evaluative and self-corrective 'second order volitions' (Frankfurt, 1971; see also Bandura, 1989). Self-efficacy, self-cultivation, and self-preservation are the basic motivational vectors of assimilative acitivities, which can have a preventive, corrective, or optimizing focus. The values and beliefs that guide such activities are to various degrees informed by socially shared conceptions of the 'good life'; in particular, they are at the same time outcomes and antecedent conditions of personal development.

Assimilative efforts can of course fail or become ineffective; due to age-graded, historical, and accidental changes, intended goal states may become unattainable or so difficult to accomplish that the costs of problem-focused efforts outweigh expected benefits. At this point, accommodative processes are activated; a key feature of this adaptive mode is the flexible adjustment of personal goals and plans to situational constraints. This includes the downgrading of, and eventually disengagement from, blocked goals, as well as the rescaling of self-evaluative standards; accommodative processes also support a positive reappraisal of initially aversive circumstances, in particular when these seem not amenable to change. Although inhibiting further investment in barren projects, the accommodative process does not terminate assimilative activities altogether, but rather helps to direct action resources to new, more promising goals. In contrast to assimilative activities, however, accommodative processes cannot be considered as intentionally enacted; we cannot simply disengage from goals merely because we consider it as useful or benificial to our well-being. In other words, the eventual decision to relinquish a blocked goal is not the antecedent condition but rather the outcome of accommodative processes. As phenomena such as depression, rumination, or regret show, however, the shift from assimilative engagement to accommodation is not necessarily a smooth one. This draws attention to the preintentional or subpersonal mechanisms underlying both adaptive modes.

The dual-process model has evolved from research on goal orientations and control beliefs in adulthood and old age. Findings from questionnare studies as well as from interviews and experiments have contributed to further elaborate the model with regard to differential conditions and underlying cognitive mechanisms, and illustrate its implications for positive development and well-being over the life span (for overviews, see Brandtstädter, 2007; Brandtstädter & Rothermund, 2002).

Underlying cognitive mechanisms

Assimilative and accommodative processes engage cognitive sets that differ in important respects. In the assimilative mode, information processing is geared toward efficient goal pursuit; attractive valences of the goal as well as attainability beliefs become more salient, and there is a tendency of blunting out stimuli and action tendencies that would detract from the pursuit of the focal goal. When obstacles intervene, goal-related efforts are intensified; this reactant effect is often accompanied by an increase in goal valence (cf. Brandtstädter & Rothermund, 2002; Kuhl, 1987; Lavie & Fox, 2000).

As the system shifts toward the accommodative mode, the attentional field widens again, and the cognitive system becomes more responsive to stimuli and competing action tendencies that have been warded off in the assimilative phase; a heuristic-divergent, bottom-up mode of information processing replaces the convergent, problem-focused mode that characterizes goal-related efforts. As already intimated, the shift from assimilative to accommodative processes is not intentionally actuated; it critically depends on the erosion of attainability beliefs, which generally proceeds more slowly in people who harbor strong self-beliefs of control. Neurophysiological research suggests that the aforementioned changes in cognitive sets are mediated by dopaminergic neuromodulation (see also Ashby, Isen, & Turken, 1999).

Dispositional factors

Among the dispositional factors that influence the balance between assimilative and acommodative processes, self-beliefs of control are of prime importance; as long as the focal goal seems within the agent's span of control, accommodative processes are inhibited. People will also find it more difficult to relinquish goals or projects that are central to their life-design, and for which equivalent substitutes cannot easily be found. Accordingly, a self-structure that embraces alternative goals or life-projects supports accommodative flexibility and resiliency in the face of irreversible losses and constraints (cf. also Linville, 1987). This, however, also hints that individuals differ in the degree to which they prefer, or engage in, assimilative or accommodative modes of coping. The scales of Tenacious Goal Pursuit (TGP) and of Flexible Goal Adjustment (FGA) have been developed to assess such dispositional differences (Brandtstädter & Renner, 1990). On the dispositional level, assimilative persistence and accommodative flexibility as measured by these scales constitute largely independent adaptive competences; close to zero correlations have been found in most studies. Both scales, however, show substantial correlations with indicators of successful life management such as optimism, emotional stability, life satisfaction across all age levels (see also Becker, 2006). It appears, however, that tenacity and flexibility contribute to subjective life quality in different, and partly independent, ways: Whereas strength and frequency of positive emotions seem to depend more closely on assimilative dispositions, accommodative flexibility appears to contribute to well-being primarily through dampening negative emotions (see also Heyl, Wahl, & Mollenkopf, 2007). Most notably, assimilative persistence and accommodative flexibility show opposed regressions across adulthood on age; more specifically, the correlational pattern points to an increasing dominance of accommodative over assimilative modes of coping in later life. This finding has emerged in many replications (e.g., Brandtstädter, 1992; Heckhausen & Schulz, 1995); it points to the particular role of the accommodative process in coping with losses, impairments, and other undesired facticities of one's life.

Empirical findings and explanatory scope of the dual-process model

As noted above, assimilative as well as accommodative dispositions independently contribute to subjective life quality throughout adulthood. A broad array of findings, however, attests to the specific importance of accommodative modes for coping with irreversible losses and constraints, and for finding meaning and satisfaction even under adverse circumstances. In moderated regression analyses, accommodative flexibility (FGA) has been found to buffer the negative impact of bodily handicaps, impaired health, chronic pain, or loss in sensory functions on well-being and satisfaction (e.g., Boerner, 2004; Brandtstädter, Rothermund, & Schmitz, 1997; Brandtstädter & Wentura, 1994; Schmitz, Saile, & Nilges, 1996); flexible goal adjustment also appears to be an important source of resilience for parents with handicapped children (Seltzer, Greenberg, Floyd, & Hong, 2004). Congruent with the aforementioned analyses, experimental findings by Kühn (2008) hint that among individuals scoring high in accommodative flexibility, prior exposure to distressing or negatively valenced stimuli (pictures, melancholic music) enhances performance in tasks that involve divergent thinking and 'remote associations.' Furthermore, flexible individuals tend to accept advice and suggestions more easily; their greater reliance on open, data-driven or 'bottom-up' modes of information processing may even involve a heightened susceptibility to 'placebo' effects. In later life, people scoring high in accommodative flexibility also seem to be less affected by the prospect of life's finitude; for flexible individuals, a self-categorization as being 'old' also bears less negative connotations. Using techniques of semantic priming, we were able to show that accommodative dispositions enhance the finding of benefits in situations of loss and distress (Wentura, 1995; Wentura, Rothermund, & Brandtstädter, 1995). In partnership and family contexts, people scoring high in accommodative flexibility report higher satisfaction and stability (e.g., Brandtstädter & Felser, 2003); problems and conflicts in particular areas of life also affect their general well-being to a lesser degree. When looking back on their past development, flexible individuals also appear to be more proud and satisfied with past achievements, and more prone to accept the less fortunate facticities of their life (cf. Kalicki, 1996; Meulemann, Birkelbach, & Hellwig, 2001; Schmitz, 1998).

These findings highlight the particular readiness or capacity of flexible individuals to adjust ambitions to constraints, and to find positive meaning in adversity. The dual-process-model, however, proposes that processes of benefit finding are most strongly activated when efforts to actively solve the problem remain ineffective. This proposition is substantiated by the experimental finding that perceptual tendencies of blunting out negative stimuli or 'danger signals' increase when the negative effects are seen as beyond personal control (Brandtstädter, Voss, & Rothermund, 2004). This does not imply, however, that efficacy and control would be negatively influenced by accommodative processes. Self-beliefs of power and efficacy are primarily rooted in the experience or belief of having control over personally valuable areas of life; accordingly, downgrading the importance of unattainable goals can help to maintain a sense of control over personal development. As findings by Brandtstädter and Rothermund (1994) illustrate, losses of control in particular goal domains affect the individual's global sense of control to a lesser degree when the personal importance of the respective domain is reduced. Together with the observation of an age-related increase in accommodative flexibility, this also offers an explanation for the seemingly counterintuitive but robust finding that control-beliefs remain quite stable in the transition to old age (e.g., Fung, Abeles, & Carstensen, 1999; Krampen, 1987).

While partly converging with control-theoretical accounts of depression (e.g., Peterson, 1999), the two-process approach thus suggests that beyond a loss of control over personally valued areas of life, a second important risk factor in the etiology of depression and hopelessness consists in maintaining, or being unable to relinquish, barren goals and attachments. From the perspective of the dual-process model, feelings of hopelessness and depression indicate difficulties in shifting from assimilative to accommodative modes. At the same time, however, these mood states appear functional to enhance disengagement from barren commitments; for example, deconstrual of positive control biases and a more sober appraisal of personal control potentials, that are characteristic of depressive reactions (Alloy & Abramson, 1979), can contribute to inhibit further effort investment and thus facilitate accommodative processes.

In line with this argument, people scoring high in accommodative flexibility also seem to be less vulnerable to persistent feelings of disappointment and regret, which often indicate lasting attachment to unachieved goals or missed opportunities. Feelings or anticipations of regret can stabilize a chosen course of action against enticements and activate efforts to undo earlier mistakes, but lose much of this adaptive value when mistakes are irreversible, or when dysphoric rumination hinders reorientation toward new goals. Whereas assimilative tendencies and self-beliefs of control seem to promote anger and regretful rumination (see also Wrosch & Heckhausen, 2002), accommodative flexibility has been found to effectively dampen ruminative regret in situations where mistakes appear irreversible (Kranz, 2005). In experimental settings, regret over prior choices has likewise been found to be particularly virulent as long as the decisions can be revoked; conversely, acceptance of untoward consequences is enhanced when alternative options are no longer available (e.g., Lyubomirsky & Ross, 1999). This effect is easily explained in terms of accommodative processes; as theoretically predicted, it has been found to be more strongly expressed among individuals scoring high in the FGA measure. These findings also converge with the observation of enhanced 'spreading' or 'endowment' effects, i.e., flexible individuals are more prone to emphasize positive aspects and to blunt out negative aspects of chosen options or life circumstances, while the reverse pattern holds for rejected ones (Kühn, 2008). In a similar vein, Baumeister (1994) has argued that this cognitive disposition is most effective to prevent chronic dissatisfaction and a 'crystallization of discontent.'

4 Planning and action in development

From a developmental point of view, planful life management requires the capacity to contrast self-representations in the temporal modalities of past, present, and future, and to envision possible alternative courses of personal development. These particular cognitive and representational competences typically emerge during adolescence, or – in Piagetian terms – on the level of formal-operational thought, and they involve self-representations that change over the life span. Development-related planning is thus itself subject to developmental change; how people perceive, evaluate, and organize their life depends on the beliefs, values, knowledge resources, and technical means that are available to them in a given developmental phase or setting. The causal and social contexts within which we organize our lives, however, are partly intransparent and uncontrollable; we don't even have complete knowledge of our own wishes and beliefs, and cannot surely predict and control how they may change over time. As Bruner (1990) has noted, 'trouble' is a basic ingredient in life stories, which are always a mixture of intended and unintended, expected and unexpected, as well as of desired and undesired outcomes. For these reasons, optimal development and successful life management cannot simply be conceived in terms of planful competence and efficient goal pursuit; although success-driven societies place a premium on such criteria, a more comprehensive account of successful life management should also consider the processes and resources that help people to cope with, and eventually come to terms with, discrepancies between intended or desired and factual paths of life. In contemporary developmental contexts, the balanced interplay between goal pursuit and goal adjustment, disengagement and commitment, or tenacity and flexibility becomes a basic requirement of successful life management, and the 'art' of life essentially consists in achieving this balance.

The processes and capacities of life management that characterize human development are central resources of adaptation, but only to the extent that they themselves can adapt to a changing field of affordances and constraints. Persistence and flexibility in pursuing personal goals and plans are basic requirements of adaptive life management (cf. Brandtstädter, 2007; Sternberg & Spear-Swerling, 1998). These criteria point to the stability-flexibility dilemma mentioned above; effortful goal pursuit should not obstruct the view to new, perhaps more promising options.

As argued above, the functional states and mind-sets that prevail in the assimilative mode shield focal goal pursuit against distractions; in cases where obstacles intervene, action reserves are mobilized, and the negative aspects of possible failures are rendered more salient by anticipations of anger and regret. Temporally extended plans typically involve a sequence of intermediary decisions and steps; planning for an academic career, for example, may start with forming a preference for a particular subject area and applying for a particular university and course of study; in the further course, one eventually chooses a special subject for a thesis, a mentor, and so on. In this way, the agent's horizon of rational deliberation and decision becomes gradually narrow and focalized, and tendencies to reconsider preceding decisions remain inhibited – at least as long as no obstacles intervene that are strong enough to activate accommodative processes.

While stabilizing planful goal pursuit, this ensemble of processes reduces the openness and sensitivity of the system for new and promising options. The conflict between two adaptive tendencies may even amount to something like a dilemma of rationality, as far as the reasons or arguments that support persistence in a chosen life path or course of action suggest refraining from actions that, in the current situation, seem reasonable (see also Bratman, 1999). The tendency to emphasize, in the assimilative mode, positive goal valences and to underestimate costs and negative side effects typically results in overpredicting both the negative emotional consequences of failure and the satisfaction value of intended outcomes; this may lead to the biases of 'miswanting' (Gilbert & Wilson, 2000). Related to this is the risk of rigidly adhering to plans and projects even to the point where costs and difficulties exceed prior expectations, and to miss the 'right' moment for relinquishing barren projects. In personal life management – and in particular under conditions of instability and rapid change – such 'escalation of commitment' may have disastrous consequences; examples from other areas of management such as politics and business come easily to mind (cf. Arkes & Blumer, 1985; Staw, 1997).

As experimental research has amply documented, 'planning in tasks fraught with complexity and uncertainty might benefit from less of the discipline imposed by a top-down process' (Hayes-Roth & Hayes-Roth, 1979, p. 306). This holds particularly true for life planning in contemporary societies; here, an open, incremental format of planning seems more adequate that remains sensitive to a changing horizon of options, avoids premature closure, and allows for a flexible adjustment of aspirations to personal and contextual resources (see also Meyer & Rebok, 1985). Flexible life management, however, not only involves strategic adjustments of means and procedures, but eventually also a complete disengagement from previous goals or projects. The processes of commitment and disengagement contribute to well-being in particular when they match with the specific demands of role transitions in the life course (see Nurmi, 2004; Salmela-Aaro, Nurmi, Saisto, & Halmesmäki, 2001). At this juncture, it is useful to conceive of goals as knowledge structures (Kruglanski, 1996) that not only comprise means-end beliefs and procedural knowledge, but also relate a given goal to other, eventually higher-level goals and values. Meaning and valence of goals primarily depend on such 'upward' cognitive links, which tend to be inhibited, however, when the search for effective means remains futile. In other words, accommodative processes typically start at the procedural level; when procedural adjustments remain ineffective, doubts about the 'Why' of goal pursuit are activated, which eventually set the stage for downgrading or relinquishing higher-level goals. Such critical reflections involve a more holistic processing and may open new horizons of meaning; when reaching such levels, accommodative processes may approximate ideals of wisdom (cf. Baltes, Smith, & Staudinger, 1992). In early phases, however, when accommodative processes are not yet strong enough to fully inhibit assimilative tendencies, doubts about the meaning and value of actual strivings and related conflicts between 'hanging on' and 'letting go' may breed feelings of disorientation, uncertainty, and stress (cf. Pyszczynski & Greenberg, 1992).

These accommodative dynamics critically depend on procedural resources that facilitate effective replacements of ineffective means, as well as on meaning resources which could help substituting equivalent goal orientations for blocked or relinquished ones. The availability of such resources, however, varies between individuals and across contexts.

Being sensible to the typical biases and risks which are implied by the cognitive processes of commitment to, and disengaging from, personal goals and temporally extended projects may help to avoid some pitfalls of planning reason. In diverse contexts of planning and decision-making, such information could be of particular advantage for individuals with a strong but unbalanced disposition toward either assimilative tenacity or accommodative flexibility.

5 Developmental resources and assets: toward open models of positive development

From an action-theoretical point of view, positive development and successful life management can hardly be defined by a fixed set of criteria that would apply to all people at all times. A more promising approach consists in focusing on developmental strengths or assets that help people to thrive in various and changing developmental contexts.

Continuously adjusting goals to given action potentials and constraints, critically evaluating progress in chosen action paths, scrutinizing own motivations and capacities, selecting goals and implementation strategies that harmonize with other personal goals and enlarge the range of future options, economizing action reserves, not least to a readiness to accept the facticities of one's past life course, could be considered as general examples, which also correspond to general principles of prudence and practical wisdom (Korsgaard, 1997).

Such developmental strengths are supported by resources on various levels of a developmental system (cf. Lerner & Benson, 2003; Lerner, Theokas, & Jelicic, 2005). The resource concept refers to personal and contextual assets that are broadly instrumental to a diversity of goals (see also Benson, Scales, Hamilton, & Sesma, 2006; Hobfoll, 1989). This also includes 'metaresources' that contribute to build or maintain personal and contextual resources across the life span; personal dispositions such as creativity, planfulness, cooperativeness, honesty, kindness, gratitude, generosity, curiosity, diligence, self-regulatory skills may be considered as examples (see also Peterson & Seligman, 2003); the adaptive strengths of assimilative persistence and accommodative flexibility may be added to this list (see also Carver & Scheier, 2003). At this point, it should also be noted that common criteria of mental health or positive well-being such as 'environmental mastery' or 'purpose in life' (e.g., Ryff & Singer, 2003) refer not just to personal strengths, but should be conceived in terms of person-context relations: For example, in order to maintain environmental mastery in later life, adjusting home and work environments to individual capacities as well as, on the other side, mobilizing compensatory potentials and reserve capacities are complementary strategies; the chances of finding meaning and purpose in life similarly depend on both personal resources and contextual affordances. The processes of coadjusting goals and projects to situational affordances and constraints are obviously basic to such person-context coordinations, which in turn are crucial to well-being and successful life management across the life span.

On a more abstract level, which again spans personal and contextual factors, we can distinguish between action resources and resources of meaning; whereas the former contribute to successful goal pursuit and enhance the availability of equifinal means or alternative solutions to given problems, the latter fuel intrinsically motivated strivings, enhance benefit finding in adversity, prevent experiences of void and alienation, and support reorientation to new goals when habitualized modes of life are challenged. Both categories of resources thus support adaptive competence in situations of change and uncertainty; it appears, however, that whereas meaning resources can compensate for losses in action resources, the obverse does not hold. For example, age-comparative findings by Brandtstädter, Meiniger, and Gräser (2003) suggest that resources of meaning contribute most strongly to well-being when action resources are reduced; under narrowing life-time reserves, accommodative flexibility also appears to facilitate an orientation toward sources of meaning that transcend the horizon of personal life.

Well-being and subjective life quality over the life span crucially depend on the possibility to actualize personal competences and 'signature strengths' (Seligman, 2002), and to bring them to bear in meaningful activities and commitments over the life cycle. This principle can be traced back to Aristotle's writings; it gains particular weight in contemporary societies. Considering the growing diversity of developmental options, the 'Aristotelian principle' (Rawls, 1971) underscores the importance of person-environment coordinations over the life span, which – as proposed above – crucially hinges on the interplay of active-assimilative and accommodative processes. It also highlights the need, however, of institutionalizing services of developmental counseling in order to support the processes of life management and intentional self-development across the life span.

References

Alloy, L.B. & Abramson, L.Y. (1979). Judgement of contingency in depressed and nondepressed students: Sadder but wiser? *Journal of Experimental Psychology: General, 108*, 441–485.

Arkes, H.R. & Blumer, C. (1985). The psychology of sunk cost. *Organizational Behavior and Human Decision Processes, 35*, 124–140.

Arnett, J.J. (2004). *Emerging adulthood: The winding road from the late teens through the twenties.* New York: Oxford University Press.

Ashby, F.G., Isen, A.M., & Turken, A.U. (1999). A neuropsychological theory of positive affect and its influence on cognition. *Psychological Review, 106*, 529–550.

Bak, P.M. & Brandtstädter, J. (1998). Flexible Zielanpassung und hartnäckige Zielverfolgung als Bewältigungsressourcen: Hinweise auf ein Regulationsdilemma. *Zeitschrift für Psychologie, 206*, 235–249.

Baltes, P.B., Smith, J., & Staudinger, U.M. (1992). Wisdom and successful aging. In T. Sonderegger (Ed.), *Nebraska Symposium on Motivation* (Vol. 39, pp. 123–167). Lincoln, NE: University of Nebraska Press.

Bandura, A. (1989). Self-regulation of motivation and action through internal standards and goal systems. In L.A. Pervin (Ed.), *Goal concepts in personality and social psychology* (pp. 19–85). Hillsdale, NJ: Erlbaum.

Baumeister, R.F. (1994). The crystallization of discontent in the process of major life change. In T.F. Heatherton & J.L. Weinberger (Eds), *Can personality change?* (pp. 281–297). Washington, DC: American Psychological Association.

Baumeister, R.F., Heatherton, T.F., & Tice, D.M. (1994). *Losing control: How and why people fail at self-regulation.* San Diego, CA: Academic Press.

Baumeister, R.F. & Vohs, K.D. (2002). The pursuit of meaningfulness in life. In C.R. Snyder & S.J. Lopez (Eds), *Handbook of positive psychology* (pp. 608–618). New York, NY: Oxford University Press.

Becker, P. (2006). *Gesundheit durch Bedürfnisbefriedigung.* Göttingen: Hogrefe.

Benson, P.L., Scales, P.C., Hamilton, S.F., & Sesma, A., Jr. (2006). Positive youth development: Theory, research, and applications. In R.M. Lerner (Ed.), *Theoretical models of human development* (Handbook of child psychology, Vol. 1, 6th ed., pp. 894–941). New York: Wiley.

Berger, P.L., Berger, B., & Kellner, J. (1975). *Das Unbehagen in der Modernität.* Frankfurt/M.: Campus.

Boerner, K. (2004). Adaptation to disability among middle-aged and older adults: The role of assimilative and accommodative coping. *Journal of Gerontology: Psychological Sciences, 59B*, 35–P42.

Brandtstädter, J. (1985). Entwicklungsprobleme des Jugendalters als Probleme des Aufbaus von Handlungsorientierungen. In D. Liepmann & A. Stiksrud (Eds), *Entwicklungsaufgaben und Bewältigungsprobleme der Adoleszenz* (pp. 5–12). Göttingen: Hogrefe.
Brandtstädter, J. (1989). Personal self-regulation of development: Cross-sequential analyses of development-related control beliefs and emotions. *Developmental Psychology*, 25, 96–108.
Brandtstädter, J. (1992). Personal control over development: Some developmental implications of self-efficacy. In R. Schwarzer (Ed.), *Self-efficacy: Thought control of action* (pp. 127–145). New York: Hemisphere.
Brandtstädter, J. (1998). Action perspectives on human development. In R.M. Lerner (Ed.), *Theoretical models of human development* (Handbook of child psychology, Vol. 1, 5th ed., pp. 807–863). New York: Wiley.
Brandtstädter, J. (2001). *Entwicklung – Intentionalität – Handeln.* Stuttgart: Kohlhammer.
Brandtstädter, J. (2007). *Das flexible Selbst: Selbstentwicklung zwischen Zielbindung und Ablösung.* Heidelberg: Elsevier/Spektrum Akademischer Verlag.
Brandtstädter, J. & Felser, G. (2003). *Entwicklung in Partnerschaften: Risiken und Ressourcen.* Bern: Huber.
Brandtstädter, J. & Lerner, R.M. (Eds). (1999). *Action and self-development: Theory and research through the life span.* Thousand Oaks, CA: Sage.
Brandtstädter, J., Meiniger, C., & Gräser, H. (2003). Handlungs- und Sinnressourcen: Entwicklungsmuster und protektive Effekte. *Zeitschrift für Entwicklungspsychologie und Pädagogische Psychologie*, 35, 49–58.
Brandtstädter, J. & Renner, G. (1990). Tenacious goal pursuit and flexible goal adjustment: Explication and age-related analysis of assimilative and accommodative strategies of coping. *Psychology and Aging*, 5, 58–67.
Brandtstädter, J. & Rothermund, K. (1994). Self-percepts of control in middle and later adulthood: Buffering losses by rescaling goals. *Psychology and Aging*, 9, 265–273.
Brandtstädter, J. & Rothermund, K. (2002). The life-course dynamics of goal pursuit and goal adjustment: A two-process framework. *Developmental Review*, 22, 117–150.
Brandtstädter, J. & Rothermund, K. (2003). Intentionality and time in human development and aging: Compensation and goal adjustment in changing developmental contexts. In U.M. Staudinger & U. Lindenberger (Eds), *Understanding human development: Dialogues with lifespan psychology* (pp. 105–124). Boston: Kluwer Academic Publishers.
Brandtstädter, J., Rothermund, K., Kranz, K., & Kühn, W. (in press). Final decentrations: Personal goals, rationality perspectives, and the awareness of life's finitude. *European Psychologist*.
Brandtstädter, J., Rothermund, K., & Schmitz, U. (1997). Coping resources in later life. *European Review of Applied Psychology*, 47, 107–114.
Brandtstädter, J., Voss, A., & Rothermund, K. (2004). Perception of danger signals: The role of control. *Experimental Psychology*, 51, 24–32.
Brandtstädter, J. & Wentura, D. (1994). Veränderungen der Zeit- und Zukunftsperspektive im Übergang zum höheren Erwachsenenalter: entwicklungspsychologische und differentielle Aspekte. *Zeitschrift für Entwicklungspsychologie und Pädagogische Psychologie*, 26, 2–21.
Brandtstädter, J. & Wentura, D. (1995). Adjustment to shifting possibility frontiers in later life: Complementary adaptive modes. In R.A. Dixon & L. Bäckman (Eds),

Compensating for psychological deficits and declines: Managing losses and promoting gains (pp. 83–106). Mahwah, NJ: Erlbaum.

Bratman, M.E. (1999). Toxin, temptation, and the stability of intention. In M.E. Bratman, *Faces of intention: Selected essays on intention and agency* (pp. 58–90). Cambridge, UK: Cambridge University Press.

Brim, O.G., Jr. (1988). Losing and winning. *Psychology Today, 22,* 48–52.

Brockner, J. (1992). The escalation of commitment to a failing course of action: Toward theoretical progress. *Academy of Management Review, 17,* 39–61.

Browning, M. & Crossley, T.F. (2001). The life-cycle model of consumption and saving. *Journal of Economic Perspectives, 15,* 3–22.

Bruner, J.S. (1990). Culture and human development: A new look. *Human Development, 33,* 344–355.

Bühler, C. (1933). *Der menschliche Lebenslauf als psychologisches Problem.* Leipzig: Hirzel.

Carstensen, L.L. & Lang, F.R. (2007). Sozioemotionale Selektivität über die Lebensspanne: Grundlagen und empirische Befunde. In J. Brandtstädter & U. Lindenberger (Eds), *Entwicklungspsychologie der Lebensspanne. Ein Lehrbuch* (pp. 389–412). Stuttgart: Kohlhammer.

Carver, C.S. & Scheier, M.F. (2003). Three human strengths. In L.G. Aspinwall & U.M. Staudinger (Eds), *A psychology of human strengths: Fundamental questions and future directions for a positive psychology* (pp. 87–102). Washington, DC: American Psychological Association.

Caspi, A. & Moffitt, T.E. (1993). When do individual differences matter? A paradoxical theory of personality coherence. *Psychological Inquiry, 4,* 247–271.

Caspi, A. & Roberts, B.W. (1999). Personality continuity and change across the life course. In L.A. Pervin & O.P. John (Eds), *Handbook of personality: Theory and research* (2nd ed., pp. 300–326). New York: Guilford Press.

Clausen, J.S. (1991). Adolescent competence and the shaping of the life course. *American Journal of Sociology, 96,* 805–842.

Crockett, L.J. & Silbereisen, R.K. (Eds). (2000). *Negotiating adolescence in times of social change.* New York: Cambridge University Press.

Emmons, R.A. (2003). Personal goals, life meaning, and virtue: Wellsprings of a positive life. In C.L.M. Keyes & J. Haidt (Eds), *Flourishing: Positive psychology and the life well-lived* (pp. 105–128). Washington, DC: American Psychological Association.

Fishbach, A., Friedman, R.S., & Kruglanski, A.W. (2003). Leading us not unto temptation: Momentary allurements elicit overriding goal activation. *Journal of Personality and Social Psychology, 84,* 296–309.

Flavell, J.H. (1963). *The developmental psychology of Jean Piaget.* New York: van Nostrand.

Frankfurt, H.G. (1971). Freedom of the will and the concept of a person. *Journal of Philosophy, 68,* 5–20.

Fung, H.H., Abeles, R.P., & Carstensen, L.L. (1999). Psychological control in later life: Implications for life-span development. In J. Brandtstädter & R.M. Lerner (Eds), *Action and self-development: Theory and research through the life span* (pp. 234–372). Thousand Oaks, CA: Sage.

Giddens, A. (1991). *Modernity and self-identity: Self and society in the late modern age.* Cambridge, UK: Polity Press.

Gilbert, D.T. & Wilson, T.D. (2000). Miswanting: Some problems in the forecasting of future affective states. In J.P. Forgas (Ed.), *Feeling and thinking: The role of affect in social cognition* (pp. 178–197). Cambridge, UK: Cambridge University Press.

Gollwitzer, P.M., Fujita, K., & Oettingen, G. (2004). Planning and the implementation of goals. In R.F. Baumeister & K.D. Vohs (Eds), *Handbook of self-regulation: Research, theory, and applications* (pp. 211–228). New York: Guilford Press.

Greenwald, A.G. (1980). The totalitarian ego: Fabrication and revision of personal history. *American Psychologist, 35,* 603–618.

Greve, W. (2005). Maintaining personality: The active and adaptive self as core of individuality and personhood. In W. Greve, K. Rothermund, & D. Wentura (Eds), *The adaptive self: Personal continuity and intentional self-development* (pp. 49–70). Göttingen: Hogrefe & Huber.

Greve, W. (2007). Selbst und Identität im Lebenslauf. In J. Brandtstädter & U. Lindenberger (Eds), *Entwicklungspsychologie der Lebensspanne. Ein Lehrbuch* (pp. 305–336). Stuttgart: Kohlhammer.

Greve, W., Rothermund, K., & Wentura, D. (Eds). (2005). *The adaptive self: Personal continuity and intentional self-development.* Göttingen: Hogrefe & Huber.

Grossberg, S. (1987). Competitive learning: From interactive activation to adaptive resonance. *Cognitive Science, 11,* 23–63.

Hayes-Roth, B. & Hayes-Roth, F. (1979). A cognitive model of planning. *Cognitive Science, 3,* 275–310.

Heckhausen, J. (1999). *Developmental regulation in adulthood: Age-normative and sociostructural constraints as adaptive challenges.* New York: Cambridge University Press.

Heckhausen, J. & Schulz, R. (1995). A life-span theory of control. *Psychological Review, 102,* 284–304.

Heyl, V., Wahl, H.-W., & Mollenkopf, H. (2007). Affective well-being in old age: The role of tenacious goal pursuit and flexible goal adjustment. *European Psychologist, 12,* 119–129.

Hobfoll, S.E. (1989). Conservation of resources: A new attempt at conceptualizing stress. *American Psychologist, 44,* 513–524.

James, W. (1890). *The principles of psychology.* New York: Holt.

Kahneman, D. & Miller, D.T. (1986). Norm theory: Comparing reality to its alternatives. *Psychological Review, 93,* 136–153.

Kalicki, B. (1996). *Lebensverläufe und Selbstbilder: Die Normalbiographie als psychologisches Regulativ.* Opladen: Leske & Budrich.

Korsgaard, C.M. (1997). The normativity of instrumental reason. In G. Cullity & B. Gaut (Eds), *Ethics and practical reason* (pp. 215–254). Oxford: Clarendon Press.

Krampen, G. (1987). Entwicklung von Kontrollüberzeugungen: Thesen zu Forschungsstand und Perspektiven. *Zeitschrift für Entwicklungspsychologie und Pädagogische Psychologie, 19,* 195–227.

Kranz, D. (2005). *Was nicht mehr zu ändern ist. Eine bewältigungstheoretische Untersuchung zum Gefühl der Reue.* Berlin: Wissenschaftlicher Verlag Berlin.

Kruglanski, A.W. (1996). Goals as knowledge structures. In P.M. Gollwitzer & J.A. Bargh (Eds), *The psychology of action: Linking cognition and motivation to behavior* (pp. 599–618). New York: Guilford Press.

Kuhl, J. (1987). Action control: The maintenance of motivational states. In F. Halisch & J. Kuhl (Eds), *Motivation, intention and volition* (pp. 279–291). Berlin: Springer.

Kühn, W. (2008). *Entscheidungsabhängige Bewertungen als Funktion akkommodativer Flexibilität.* Unveröffentlichte Dissertation. Trier: Universität Trier.

Lavie, N. & Fox, E. (2000). The role of perceptual load in negative priming. *Journal of Experimental Psychology: Human Perception and Performance, 26,* 1038–1052.

Lerner, R.M. & Benson, P.L. (Eds). (2003). *Developmental assets and asset-building communities: Implications for research, policy, and practice.* New York, NY: Kluwer/Plenum.

Lerner, R.M., Theokas, C., & Jelicic, J. (2005). Youth as active agents in their own positive development: A developmental systems perspective. In W. Greve, K. Rothermund, & D. Wentura (Eds), *The adaptive self: Personal continuity and intentional self-development* (pp. 31–48). Göttingen: Hogrefe & Huber.

Lerner, R.M. & Walls, T. (1999). Revisiting 'individuals as producers of their development': From dynamic interactionism to developmental systems. In J. Brandtstädter & R.M. Lerner (Eds), *Action and self-development: Theory and research through the life span* (pp. 3–36). Thousand Oaks, CA: Sage.

Linville, P.W. (1987). Self-complexity as a cognitive buffer against stress-related illness and depression. *Journal of Personality and Social Psychology, 52,* 663–676.

Loewenstein, G.F. & Prelec, D. (1993). Preferences for sequences of outcomes. *Psychological Review, 100,* 91–108.

Lyubomirsky, S. & Ross, L. (1999). Changes in attractiveness of elected, rejected, and precluded alternatives: A comparison of happy and unhappy individuals. *Journal of Personality and Social Psychology, 76,* 988–1007.

Marsh, J.L., Caputo, J.D., & Westphal, M. (Eds). (1992). *Modernity and its discontents.* New York: Fordham University Press.

Mayer, K.U. & Diewald, M. (2007). Die Institutionalisierung von Lebensverläufen. In J. Brandtstädter & U. Lindenberger (Eds), *Entwicklungspsychologie der Lebensspanne. Ein Lehrbuch* (pp. 510–539). Stuttgart: Kohlhammer.

Metcalfe, J. & Mischel, W. (1999). A hot/cool-system analysis of delay of gratification: Dynamics of willpower. *Psychological Review, 106,* 3–19.

Meulemann, H., Birkelbach, K., & Hellwig, J.-O. (2001). Life satisfaction from late adolescence to mid-life. The impact of life success and success evaluation on the life satisfaction of former Gymnasium students between ages 30 and 43. *Journal of Happiness Studies, 2,* 445–465.

Meyer, J.S. & Rebok, G.W. (1985). Planning-in-action across the life span. In T.M. Shlechter & M.P. Toglia (Eds), *New directions in cognitive sciences* (pp. 47–68). Norwood, NJ: Ablex.

Mittelstraß, J. (1992). Zeitformen des Lebens: Philosophische Unterscheidungen. In P.B. Baltes & J. Mittelstraß (Eds), *Zukunft des Alterns und gesellschaftliche Entwicklung* (pp. 386–407). Berlin: de Gruyter.

Nurmi, J.E. (2004). Socialization and self-development: Channeling, selection, adjustment, and reflection. In R.M. Lerner & L. Steinberg (Eds), *Handbook of adolescent psychology* (2nd ed., pp. 85–124). New York: Wiley.

Peterson, C. (1999). Personal control and well-being. In D. Kahneman, E. Diener, & N. Schwarz (Eds), *Well-being: The foundations of hedonic psychology* (pp. 288–301). New York: Russell Sage Foundation.

Peterson, C. & Seligman, M.E.P. (2003). *The VIA classification of strengths and virtues.* Washington, DC: American Psychological Association Press.

Pyszczynski, T. & Greenberg, J. (1992). *Hanging on and letting go: Understanding the onset, progression, and remission of depression.* New York: Springer.

Rawls, J. (1971). *A theory of justice.* Cambridge, MA: Belknap Press of Harvard University Press.

Ryff, C.D. & Singer, B. (2003). Ironies of the human condition: Well-being and health on the way to mortality. In U.M. Staudinger & L.G. Aspinwall (Eds), *A psychology of human strengths: Fundamental questions and future directions for a positive psychology* (pp. 271–287). Washington, DC: American Psychological Association.

Salmela-Aro, K., Nurmi, J-E., Saisto, T., & Halmesmäki, E. (2001). Goal reconstruction and depressive symptoms during the transition to motherhood: Evidence from two cross-lagged longitudinal studies. *Journal of Personality and Social Psychology, 81*, 1144–1159.

Schmitz, U. (1998). *Entwicklungserleben älterer Menschen. Eine Interviewstudie zur Wahrnehmung und Bewältigung von Entwicklungsproblemen im höheren Alter.* Regensburg: Roderer.

Schmitz, U., Saile, H., & Nilges, P. (1996). Coping with chronic pain: Flexible goal adjustment as an interactive buffer against pain-related distress. *Pain, 67*, 41–51.

Schopenhauer, A. (1851). *Parerga und Paralipomena: kleine philosophische Schriften.* Berlin: A.W. Hayn.

Schwartz, B. (2004). *The paradox of choice: Why more is less.* New York: Harper Collins.

Seligman, M.E.P. (1990). Why is there so much depression today? The waxing of the individual and the waning of the commons. In R.E. Ingram (Ed.), *Contemporary psychological approaches to depression: Theory, research, and treatment* (pp. 1–9). New York: Plenum.

Seligman, M.E.P. (2002). *Authentic happiness: Using the new positive psychology to realize your potential for lasting fulfillment.* New York: Free Press.

Seltzer, M.M., Greenberg, J.S., Floyd, F.J., & Hong, J. (2004). Accommodative coping and well-being of midlife parents of children with mental health problems or developmental disabilities. *American Journal of Orthopsychiatry, 74*, 187–195.

Sennett, R. (1998). *The corrosion of character.* New York: Norton.

Settersten, R.A. (1999). *Lives in time and place: The problems and promises of developmental science.* Amityville, NY: Baywood.

Shanahan, M.J. & Elder, G.H., Jr. (2002). History, agency, and the life course. In L.J. Crockett (Ed.), *Motivation, agency, and the life course* (Nebraska Symposium on Motivation, Vol. 48, pp. 145–186). Lincoln, NE: University of Nebraska Press.

Sloterdijk, P. (2005). *Optimierung des Menschen?* [Video]. Tübingen: Zentrum für Datenverarbeitung (ZDV) der Universität Tübingen.

Snyder, M. (1979). Self-monitoring processes. In L. Berkowitz (Ed.), *Advances in experimental social psychology* (Vol. 12, pp. 85–128). New York: Academic Press.

Staw, B.M. (1997). The escalation of commitment: An update and appraisal. In Z. Shapira (Ed.), *Organizational decision making* (pp. 191–215). Cambridge: Cambridge University Press.

Sternberg, R.J. & Spear-Swerling, L. (1998). Personal navigation. In M. Ferrari & R.J. Sternberg (Eds), *Self-awareness: Its nature and development* (pp. 219–245). New York: Guilford Press.

Tatarkiewicz, W. (1976). *Analysis of happiness.* The Hague, Netherlands: Martinus Nijhoff.

Taylor, C. (1991). *The malaise of modernity.* Toronto: House of Anansi Press.

Tetens, J. (1777). *Philosophische Versuche über die menschliche Natur und ihre Entwicklung* (2 Bde.). Leipzig: M.G. Weidmanns Erben und Reich.

Tugendhat, E. (2003). *Egozentrizität und Mystik. Eine anthropologische Studie.* München: Beck.

van Selm, M. & Dittmann-Kohli, F. (1998). Meaninglessness in the second half of life: The development of a construct. *International Journal of Aging and Human Development, 47,* 81–104.

Wentura, D. (1995). *Verfügbarkeit entlastender Kognitionen. Zur Verarbeitung negativer Lebenssituationen.* Weinheim: Psychologie Verlags Union.

Wentura, D., Rothermund, K., & Brandtstädter, J. (1995). Experimentelle Analysen zur Verarbeitung belastender Informationen: differential- und alternspsychologissche Aspekte. *Zeitschrift für Experimentelle Psychologie, 42,* 152–175.

Wrosch, C. & Heckhausen, J. (2002). Perceived control of life regrets: Good for young and bad for old adults. *Psychology and Aging, 17,* 340–350.

3

CONCEPTUALIZING THE DYNAMICS OF LIVES AND HISTORICAL TIMES: LIFE COURSE PHENOMENA, INSTITUTIONAL DYNAMICS AND SOCIOHISTORICAL CHANGE

Ross Macmillan and *Arturo Baiocchi*

The concept of human agency sits a central theme in life course research. At the same time, its specific meaning and role in life course processes is fairly vague. Few would dispute the idea that individuals exercise agency. They think, they choose, and they act. And by virtue of these things, they are able to shape future events. In much life course research, particularly that aligned with social psychology, variation in the ways in which individuals think about their lives, be it aspirations, expectations, sense of self, planfulness, or any other aspect of cognition, is used to understand the different ways in which human lives unfold, different achievements, and different experiences.

A focus on agency, however, is always tempered by the recognition of social structure. Articulated best by Elder (1994), lives unfold in historical contexts that provide systems of opportunity and constraint that are resources and challenges for individual actors. Some people live in times of immense opportunity and expansion and their life choices and chances reflect some conditions. Others live in times of turmoil and strife that place limits on freedoms and undermine the capacity to achieve wanted goals. Be they economic downturns, times of war, times of disaster, the broader social landscape can greatly dampen human will. Most historical periods, of course, comprise a mix of opportunities and constraints and hence provide a highly complex and a variable context for human lives. When considered in concert, agency and social structure represent an ongoing relationship between the life course and social change. As sociohistorical conditions change over time, they create new contexts for the unfolding life course that in turn provide the terrain in which agency shapes life course progress.

This view of agency, structure, and social change that dominates traditional life course inquiry is immensely useful in that it provides a framework for both conceptualizing life course processes and structuring empirical research. At the same time, it presents a rather unidimensional perspective. Specifically, it suggests that structure is somewhat 'outside' of individual actors, their thoughts, and their actions and that agency involves social action as the navigation of structural circumstance. By extension, social change is something that actors encounter rather than create. Such a view contrasts with much work in sociological theory that seeks to articulate a more dialectical and dynamic relationship (Bourdieu, 1977; Coleman, 1990; Giddens, 1984; Sewell, 1992). Equally important, such a view ignores the role of individuals in producing social change. Here, individual expressions of agency, directly and indirectly, personally and collectively, reconfigure social landscapes and in the process create new social structures that serve to shape life course fortunes. To date, there have been few attempts to articulate or study this aspect of the agency-structure relationship in life course study. Such a perspective, however, is a necessary precursor to a fuller, more dynamic, dialectical theory of the life course.

This chapter seeks to articulate a general theory of the life course that captures the dialectic dualism of agency and structure during broad sociocultural change. It does so by juxtaposing the tradition to view agency as contingent upon social structure with life course scholarship that connects the dynamics of social roles over time to broader systems of structure and stratification. We then go on to introduce a set of mechanisms by which life course structures may themselves contribute to social change through a process of production and reproduction of social structures and mental schemas. Next, we draw upon an empirical case of profound social change, emerging cultural legitimacy of same-sex relationships, to examine how the dialectic dynamics of the life course provide the social space, and structural impetus that make change possible. Finally, we conclude with a discussion of implications for theory and research.

Lives in time and place: Agency as contingent

A traditional focus in life course theory is the idea that human experience occurs through the interaction of agency and sociohistorical conditions. Although empirical work is scarcer than we might like (cf. Shanahan et al., 1998), the core idea, best expressed by Elder (1994) is that:

> ... differences in birth year expose individuals to different historical worlds, with their constraints and options. Individual life courses may well reflect these different times. Historical effects on the life course take the form of a cohort effect in which social change

differentiates the life patterns of successive cohorts, such as older and younger women before World War II. History also takes the form of a period effect when the effect of change is relatively uniform across successive birth cohorts... As a rule, any personal implications would be contingent on what people bring to the change process as well as on the nature and severity of the change itself (pp. 5–6).

The insights offered by Elder and his many collaborators are significant and have spawned varied research. In one tradition, the life course itself is studied in the context of changing sociohistorical conditions. Elder's (1999 [1974]) own investigations of *Children of the Great Depression* stands as the classic work that examines the unfolding of lives in the context of significant historical change. In a different manner, Hogan (1978) systematically examines variation in the order of life course transitions (i.e., work, marriage, and parenthood) across cohorts in the first half of the twentieth century as a way of teasing out the dynamic relationship between changing macro-historical conditions and the basic patterning of the life course. More recently, Shanahan and colleagues (1998) demonstrate a second avenue of research in directly examining variation in agency in different historical contexts. Here, 'planfulness,' an operationalization of agency by John Clausen (1991), is only significant for educational attainment for those born in the second decade of the twentieth century, those who came of age after the Great Depression and experienced a period of increased opportunity and varied options. In contrast, those born earlier avoided the tight labor markets of the Great Depression by extending higher education, making planfulness an insignificant factor in shaping life course fortunes. In mapping out the dynamic relationship between demography and history, as well as the connections between psychological orientations, historical context, and life course fortunes, the central theme that life courses are embedded within and dependent upon historical contexts stands as one of the enduring features of life course theory in the social sciences.

The theoretical gains that are apparent in such a perspective nonetheless also highlight a key weakness. In the above model, social structure, as indexed by sociohistorical context, is something that sits outside of human agency and the life course. Here, life course dynamics and expressions of agency are contingent upon or contextualized by social conditions. While such a view is not in error, it is rather unidimensional. Actors exist and operate within structural contexts and the nature of action is a function of the specific opportunities and constraints of a given context. Missing from such a perspective is the ways in which actors produce and reproduce, apprehend and modify social and cultural conditions and hence are an engine of social change that creates new cultures and contexts that serve to shape and reshape future life course trajectories. Articulating such a perspective expands theoretical and empirical frontiers and fleshes out the complex relationships between the life course and social change.

Agency, social structure and the life course

It is not surprising that life course theory articulates a unidimensional view of structure and agency given that the agency-structure relationship remains the central problematic for social and sociological theory (Coleman, 1990; Sewell, 1992). At the same time, much contemporary social theory attempts to integrate structure and agency. Giddens (1984), for example, offers a theory of structuration whereby agency and structure represent a dualism where agents reproduce social structures that are simultaneously rules and resources for future action. Likewise, Bourdieu's (1977) emphasis on habitus articulates the dynamic relationship between 'mental structures' and the 'world of objects' as a general 'theory of practice.' The key feature of such perspectives is an emphasis on a dynamic, mutually constitutive relationship between structure and action that moves beyond static visions of structure as outside of and constraining of human action and experience.

Sewell (1992) offers a particularly useful version of social structure that lends itself well to conceptualization and analysis of the life course and life course processes (Macmillan & Eliason, nd). For Sewell, social structures involve a dual character of schema and resources. Schemas are 'generalizable procedures applied in the enactment/reproduction of social life' (Sewell, 1992, p. 8). They are virtual, existing in personal and collective memory and can be applied in a variety of contexts, even contexts that are outside their traditional or designated realm. Schemas are representations of things and models for doing things and serve to structure action in both productive and constraining ways. The complement to schemas is a conception of resources as anything, human and non-human, that can serve as a source of power in social interactions. The dual character of social structures is that they are 'composed simultaneously of schemas, which are virtual, and resources, which are actual' (Sewell, 1992, p. 13).

Moreover, resources depend on schemas to define the social meaning of actions and the utility of things, translating resources from their inert base state to a condition of virtual power. Likewise, schemas are sustained and reproduced over time only through the accumulation of resources, which provide the actual validation that their enactment engenders. That is, schemas lacking connection to resources will eventually disappear, just as resources without schemas to direct their use will have little meaning. Schemas and resources consequently constitute structures when they mutually imply and sustain each other over time.

Such a view of social structures has important applications for a life course perspective. At the outset, a life course perspective is inherently a role-based perspective (Alwin, 2008; Macmillan, 2004; Macmillan & Eliason, nd). The unfolding life course exists as movement into, through, and out of social roles. Roles are combined and linked in varied ways that essentially constitute the life course. Moreover, roles, role configurations, and pathways (through multiple roles) determine the actual experience of roles and what they mean for given individuals and collectives.

From this starting point, a role-based life course involves the interplay of schema and resources. In the former case, roles are inherently cultural in that schemas provide rules, examples, and templates for how one acts in a given role. Although such things are dynamic and sometimes contested, role-related action derives from the internalization of schema and schema dictate how one *is* a student, is a worker, is a husband/wife, is a parent, or lives independent of parents and family. Extending out, schemas also provide templates for how individuals can or should put different roles together. Here, schemas involve both normative and proscriptive elements and describe roles that are complementary and reinforcing, such as marriage and parenthood, those that are contradictory and perhaps stigmatized, such as schooling and parenthood, and those that are contested or variable (e.g., working and parenthood among women). Finally, life course schema include pathway schema which proscribe the timing and ordering of social roles in the life course. Role sequences here can have a 'taken-for-granted' logic such as finishing school, entering full-time work and then moving into family roles of marriage and parenthood. Yet, roles can also be 'off-time' such as teenage parenthood or early work and 'disorderly' when entry into some role(s) offsets or undermines other social roles (i.e., teenage parenthood may limit educational attainment, disrupt smooth movement into full-time work, and even limit prospects for later marriage). Schema thus differentially define and differentially validate the variable pathways that characterize movement through roles over the life course.

Complementing the schematic character of roles, role configurations, and pathways is their resource character. Although neither life course scholarship nor social psychology has explicitly articulated this, the essence of social roles is their resource capacity. Schooling is intrinsically related to the acquisition of human capital that is the fundamental resource for a wide variety of social action. Work is intrinsically about the acquisition of (financial) capital, as well as human capital. Likewise, marriage involves the pooling of resources and expenses and thus contributes to capital accumulation, in addition to its role in reinforcing and fostering social capital. Parenthood is perhaps the role with the most complicated capital potential given that parenthood typically requires capital expenditure with a gamble on capital remuneration in the distant future. At the same time, there is little doubt that parenthood fosters social capital at both individual and collective levels.

The resource potential of roles is also dependent upon the nature of role configurations and life course pathways. In the former respect, there are numerous research literatures that attest to the contingent nature of social roles and how their meaning and implication is dependent upon the presence of other roles. As one example, considerable research examines parenthood with and without marriage and points to the myriad resource implications, social and psychological, that accrue from either circumstance (see for example, Furstenberg, Brooks-Gunn, & Morgan 1987). Schooling in the context of paid employment, marriage with or without employment, as well as virtually any other combination of roles has also attracted research attention because of the varied impacts that such configurations represent (Mortimer, 2003). Although examining the impacts of these types of contingencies has dominated traditional inquiry, research has also explored the temporal aspects of such configurations, the consequences of life course timing. For example, whether schooling occurs before or after movement into full-time work, marriage, or parenthood has important implications for the acquisition of human capital (Cameron & Heckman, 1993). Likewise, parenthood before rather than after marriage also conditions the acquisition and significance of various capitals (McLanahan & Sandefur, 1996). Ultimately, the overall timing and order of roles in the life course and how these define distinct pathways over the life span is fundamental to identifying the resource potential of any given role.

The dual nature of life course structures stems from the mutually constitutive character of role schema and role resources over time. Roles, role configurations, and pathway schema define how roles are/can be enacted, how roles are/can be combined, and how roles are/can be timed and ordered. Moreover, roles, role configurations, and pathways are variably generative of material, human, social, and cultural capitals and those that are more so are likely to have greater validation, a more 'taken-for-granted' legitimacy, and greater prevalence within the population (Macmillan & Eliason, nd).

Life course social structures and sociocultural change

Given this backdrop, how might we conceive of social change? Although social structures of any sort, including life course ones, imply some sense of stability and reproduction, even the most cursory examination of history reveals their inherent fragility and often ephemeral character. As a result, questions of agency and social change are intimately connected to studies of social structure.

In general, Sewell (1992) offers a number of ways and mechanisms by which social structures shape and engender the potential for social change. These include the multiplicity of structures, the transposibility of schema, the unpredictability of resource accumulation, the polysemy of resources, and the intersection of structures. All are important in understanding social change as an endemic process, that is, aspects of change not contingent on external force and influence, but by virtue of a society's already embedded diversity. Change happens through the continual re-workings of schema and resources, and the structural consequences such recombination engenders. When considering the life course, these mechanisms illustrate processes by which social change is both possible as a consequence and catalyst for life course roles and pathways.

In any given society, there are a variety of distinct and interlocking structures and institutions that exist at multiple levels. This allows for structures and institutions to operate in different ways, but also produces a rich variability of ideas, schema and life course configurations. In the context of the life course, schema of school, work, and family vary depending upon the domain from which they exist. Few would argue that the meaning of schooling is exactly the same in inner-city schools struggling to graduate the majority of their students as it is in 'prep' schools, where the real question is what elite university students will attend. Likewise, the meaning and practice of work varies significantly across social classes and across time, as does the meaning of marriage and parenthood. Yet, while schema are variable within each of these domains, schema also vary and are subject to contestation across domains. One of the clearest examples of this is the contested view of family within work domains. In general, family is a valued cultural state, yet it is also viewed with some skepticism in work domains that denounce the 'greedy' character of family life to impede on one's ability to fully engage with the work role (Coser, 1974). Although less developed, education schema are also somewhat contested in contemporary work domains given the general disconnection between any standard curriculum and the requirements of paid labor and the consequent importance of on-the-job training. As a result, actors have knowledge of a wide variety of schemas and access to a range of role-related resources in their everyday practices and life course structures have multiple meanings and multiple resource potentials.

An important implication of this is that schema can be applied across a wide range of circumstances, including those that are not necessarily typical or predictable. Agency thus involves the extension of schema to new contexts where implication and result are uncertain.

Social change, via the mutual reinforcement of schema through resources, results from the successful application of schema in unfamiliar terrain.

With respect to the life course, the transposibility of schema is again possible within and across domains.

Within domain, a particularly salient example is the adaptability and claims for adaptability of family schema. Traditionally, family schema have been connected with blood kin and heterosexual relationships. Yet, the contemporary era has seen the application of 'family' to a wide variety of relationships including non-parental couples, single parenthood households, same-sex couples, as well as long-term cohabitations. Although examples abound, one of the most salient indicators of this change is the move to rename the premier American journal for family studies, the *Journal of Marriage and the Family* to the *Journal of Marriage and Family*. One can similarly think about how work and schooling schema have been adapted to a wide variety of practices (e.g., flex-work, contingent or contract employment, home schooling, on-line degrees). Moreover, transposibility of life course schema extends to both role configurations and pathways where schema combine within and across time and reconfigure in light of structural contingencies to ultimately produce new schema and scripts of action and organization, hence contributing to social change.

A third feature of social structures that contributes to social change is the unpredictability of resource accumulation. Given the transposibility of schema and the ever present possibility of extending them to new and untested contexts, the acquisition of resources is neither predictable nor ensured. In one regard, the enactment of schema in a given, perhaps common, situation may result in unanticipated failure. In another, schema extended to new contexts may meet with startling success. Given this unpredictability, schemas will be differentially validated by resources and subject to adaptation and revision. Similarly life course roles, role configurations, and pathways are likewise amenable to variable resource consequences given the multiple ways that become enacted. Sociologist Aaron Pallas, for example, argues that education in the contemporary US no longer occupies a particular life stage with individuals variably and flexibly connected to educational institutions through their 20s, 30s and even older. Importantly, this transforms the resource implications of education by reconfiguring the content of education, altering the social networks that accrue through schooling, and changing its capitalization potential (Cameron & Heckman, 1993; Pallas, 2006; Rosenbaum, 2001). Similarly, Carol Stack's (1974) study of African-American families shows how single parenthood may allow for, and foster broader acquisition of, social capital because of the meshing together of inter-generational ties. The resource potential of work is also quite variable, particularly given the transformations of the labor force, the increasingly polarity of compensation, and its contemporary ephemeral character. Moreover, the complex ties and interconnections between roles, both within and across time, complicate resource potentials. Social change emerges as the purposeful action of life courses and their constitutive roles have intended and unintended consequences.

Resources can also have multiple meaning given their embodiment by cultural schemas. As Sewell (1992, p. 19) notes, 'any array of resources is capable of being interpreted in varying ways and, therefore, of empowering different actors and teaching different schemas.' For life course social structures, the degree to which roles are perceived as and consequently are resources is highly variable. Consider, for example, education and marriage. There is a wealth of research that links educational attainment to 'better' marriage. Goldstein and Kenney (2001), for instance, show that greater education is associated with higher likelihood of marriage. Yet, this only holds for white women. In contrast, African-American women with higher levels of education actually have lower prospects for marriage. In the context of the polysemy, this can be interpreted as education having variable values in marriage markets; being a resource for white women, yet a liability for African-American women. As a more temporal example, social change within and beyond the family can emerge given changing values of given life course states. Here, some speculate that marriage has simply gotten less valuable given the predominance of more material resources, notably higher education and personal employment (Oppenheimer, 1997). Regardless, social change can manifest itself from the polysemy of life course roles, role configurations, and pathways.

Finally, and likely most importantly, is the fact that social structures intersect and overlap and do so for both the schema and resources. Schema and resources can be claimed and deployed by a wide variety of actors and actors, individual and corporate, operating at vastly different levels and connected to multiple social structures. This latter point is particularly significant in that it implies the role of large-scale structures that organize people on the basis of class, gender, race, ethnicity, age, nativity, community, country, and any other large-scale structure in conditioning role-based life course structures. In one respect, it can shape the prevalence, order and timing of life course roles. In the United States, race has been particularly important in structuring the transition to adulthood, shaping when people finish school, if and when they move into full-time work, if and when they get married, and if and when they have children. When jointly considered, racialized social structures become important determinants of life course pathways which have consequent implications for the role-resource nexus and the overall capitalization of the life course. It creates the conditions for the reproduction of inequalities, what many life course scholars call processes of 'cumulative disadvantage.' Yet, life course structures also create the conditions for social change by reconfiguring structures at both the macro- and life course levels and producing new schema and resource nexuses. Again using the example of race, the newly engendered life course patterns for African-Americans in the post-civil rights era ultimately created new opportunity structures and when such structures translate into high capitalization life course structures, produced a new middle class with high education, stronger labor force activity, more stable families, and intergenerational prospects that would not have been imaginable in earlier times (Wilson, 1987). Intersectionality of life course and extra-life course structures across multiple levels and across time is thus pivotal in creating both social reproduction and social change.

Life course and sociocultural change: An empirical example of schematic change

A view of life course as social structure suggests that structures of the life course can be a significant vehicle of social change. Few would dispute that the most profound changes in the life course over the past few decades have centered on the family and sexuality. In one respect, the family as a social institution has been in serious decline and this manifests itself in a radical restructuring of the role of family in the life course. This includes declines in age at first marriage and childbirth, increases in cohabitation, increases in marital dissolution, albeit with a significant prevalence of remarriage, and dramatic increases in out-of-wedlock childbearing. When considered together, the twentieth-century norm of children in households with two biological parents has withered markedly.

An equally profound transformation has occurred with respect to the cultural meaning of families, specifically with respect to sexuality and attitudes towards same-sex relationships. While the traditional family was strongly heteronormative, new visions of the family and social life increasingly feature same-sex unions. Both moderate and radical elements of the queer movement have thrived in an era of identity politics (Fraser & Honneth, 2003) gaining not only legitimacy for 'alternative lifestyle' but also growing constituents of allies and activists that have made significant headways in progressive government policies. Indeed, if the transformation of the traditional family has been a major demographic change in the contemporary life course, attitudes towards and beliefs surrounding same-sex unions represent a significant political and cultural change in the contemporary life course. Put in the context of a theory of social structure, such change reflects changing salience of schema around heterosexuality, homosexuality, relationships, and family. We use this change as an example of how changing structures of the life course connect to broader patterns of cultural change and hence can be seen as an engine for change rather than mere consequence. Our purpose here is not to fully model the dynamic relationships outlined above but instead to provide an empirical example of the missing side of the equation, the effects of the changing life course on large-scale cultural change.

Measuring legitimacy of same-sex relationships

To do so, we draw upon data from the General Social Survey (GSS), cross-sectional data representative of the adult, household population of the United States. The GSS has been conducted on an almost yearly basis since 1972, polling the American population's attitudes and values on a variety of topics. Using a multi-stage probability design for most cycles, the survey samples approximately 1,400 English-speaking adults each year, for its structured, face-to-face interviews. Over the 30 years of the GSS (1976–2006), a question was asked in a consistent manner that assesses a normative view on same-sex relationships. Specifically, the question asks: What about sexual relations between two adults of the same-sex – do you think it is always wrong, almost always wrong, wrong only sometimes, or not wrong at all? (GSS, 2006, question # 218). For our purposes, the key utility of the question is that more positive (or less negative) responses to this question represent a puncturing of the heteronormative culture that underpins both family life and consequent social organization across the life course. Implicitly, it is a measure of the *legitimacy of same-sex relationships* in American society and the data itself are intriguing. Even in 2006, the majority of Americans (61 per cent) responded that such sexual relations are 'always wrong,' or 'almost always wrong,' attesting to the continued hegemony of heteronormativity. Still, trends over time also show dramatic change. Whereas only 11–15 per cent of Americans viewed homosexuality as 'never wrong' between 1972 and 1979, this proportion of respondents grew almost three-fold (32 per cent) through 2006. In many respects, this is a quite remarkable example of cultural change.

Modeling the life course context of sociocultural change

To understand the role of life course dynamics in such cultural change, we use a two-pronged strategy. First, we make use of unique items concerning the number of gay acquaintances that we administered to a random subset of respondents ($\approx$1,252 depending upon missing data) in the 2006 GSS survey. Specifically, respondents were asked the number of gay acquaintances in general, in their family, at work (current or previous), in their neighborhood, or through volunteer activities and could report 'none,' 'one,' 'two to five,' 'six to ten,' or 'more than ten.' We use this measure to index *network diversity* that is associated with, productive of, and reinforced by, specific life course states/social roles. We also focus on a general item of one's political orientation ranging from 'extremely conservative' to 'extremely liberal' as also associated with, productive of, and reinforced by life course social roles. We view the latter as a measure of *cultural tolerance* which, in concert with expanded social networks, should increase the legitimacy of schemas of same-sex relationships. Empirically, we model the relationship between life course states and both network diversity and cultural tolerance, as well as the mediating effects of network diversity and cultural tolerance.

Our second strategy makes use of the longitudinal nature of the GSS data. As the legitimacy of same-sex relationships was asked in a consistent manner over a 30-year period, along with a standard set of sociodemographic questions regarding schooling, work, and family, we use a pooled multiyear sample as a vehicle to explore how the changing nature of the life course is intimated in such changing conceptions of relationships. We plot these graphically to show (a) the time trend for attitudes regarding homosexuality, (b) the trend in population prevalence of given life course roles, and (c) the time varying association derived from logistic regression analyses between the two. To us, this is one way of modeling the dynamic relationship between the individual life course contexts, changing life course patterns, and large-scale cultural change.

Indexing the life course

Following from Alwin (2008), we index life course dynamics in the context of specific social roles and then examine their relationship to the changing context of schema of same-sex relationships. First, we examine marriage. Marriage can be seen as an inherently conservative institution. For almost all of human history, schema of marriage has implied heterosexual relationships and claims to marriage and defense of marriage have been fundamental aspects of political debates over gay rights in the twenty-first century (Hull, 2006). The earlier incarnation of this was claims for equality of same-sex couples with respect to employment and benefits, essentially a claim for equality of resources for marital and same-sex relationships. More recently, the debates have turned more symbolic and have emphasized claims for and contestation of schema of family and marriage among same-sex and heterosexual couples. One side articulates the essential sameness of same-sex unions and hence their compatibility with traditional notions of marriage. The other side 'defends' marriage by emphasizing the importance of a heteronormative conception and the deviant nature of same-sex unions. From a role standpoint, marriage, by definition, implies greater embeddedness and psychological investment in heterosexual relations.

In many respects, marriage can be contrasted with both *divorce* and *never married* statuses. Unlike marriage, divorce and being single might be seen as more liberalizing life course states. From a role perspective, both states have a greater potential for more diverse networks and hence exposure to broader or more varied schema of social life. Moreover, given recent historical trends, divorce and remaining single, at least for longer periods of the life course, are increasingly normative and accepted life course stages that have a similarly 'taken-for-granted' status as conventional marriages. This is increasingly the case given the divorce revolution of the 1980s which made divorce a lifestyle choice, similar to same-sex unions.[1] Similarly, the diffusion of higher education across the population in recent decades has yielded both marriage delays and marriage declines with increasing time spent single in the life course (Goldstein & Kenney, 2001). From this perspective, the increased prevalence of divorce and singlehood, much like the decline of marriage, opens up space for cultural change and might increasingly do so over time.

Parenthood is a complementary family domain, but social change here is complicated. In one respect, total fertility rates have been declining worldwide and rates in most Western industrial nations are at or have dipped below replacement fertility (i.e., 2.1 children per female 15–45). At the same time, prevalence of parenthood has remained stable with people foregoing larger families rather than foregoing parenthood (Fischer & Hout, 2006). As a life course state, parenthood is largely heteronormative and may be increasingly so over time given its increased concentration in recent decades.

Another significant life course realm is schooling and education. As noted earlier, the latter decades of the twentieth century saw a dramatic change in education in terms of a marker of social attainment and a life course stage. Specifically, higher education, either through two, four, or professional/graduate degrees, became increasingly socially and statistically normative (Rosenbaum, 2001). From a life course perspective, higher education increasingly occupies the age-space traditionally reserved for movement into full-time (career-type) work, marriage, parenthood, and independence from parents. Given this, it is important to consider the nature of educational change from both an institutional standpoint and a demographic one. In the former case, the 1980s, 1990s, and 2000s were characterized by a tremendous diversification of higher education away from the traditional university/college model that was organized around a liberal arts/science curriculum and towards an integration of traditional curricula with technical and vocational degrees. In the latter case, there was tremendous demographic diversification with increased access to higher education for the lower classes, racial minorities, women, those with disabilities, first and second generation immigrants, etc. In light of this, we expected that college education would be, in general, a liberalizing life course state that would foster alternative and more diverse sexuality schema. We expect this, given the general 'liberal' character of education, the role that universities have played in counter-culture, and the broader social networks that exist in educational institutions. Education may also connote the independence of resource capitalization from heterosexuality, particularly for women, and hence indicate the viability of same-sex unions within the broader society. Still, social change regarding education also leads us to anticipate that its association with cultural beliefs regarding same-sex unions might weaken over time, given the institutional changes that have tightened the schema of work and education, that have eroded the generic resource potential of higher education, and have increasingly homogenized college and non-college populations.

The final life course domain we consider is the world of work. Much has been written about social change and the life course context of employment in recent years, and such work flags changes at both the life stage involving the transition into work (Booth, Crouter, & Shanahan, 1999) and the life stage involving the transition out of work (Han & Moen, 1999). Although we considered a range of employment conditions, including full-time and part-time work, the most significant and interesting associations observed corresponded to retirement and homemaker states. In the former case, an aging population means that the proportion of Americans who are retired is increasing. The GSS data bear this out with the prevalence of retirees increasing from 10 per cent in the late 1970s to over 15 per cent in the early 2000s. In the latter case, homemaker status has seen significant declines in prevalence. In the late 1970s, over a quarter of the US population were homemakers; 30 years later this rate had dropped to only 10 per cent. Both retirement and homemaker status might be seen as inherently conservative life course states in that they separate people from the more diverse networks of workplaces and hence a potentially 'horizon-broadening' environment. As a consequence, we expect both to be associated with more conservative schema of same-sex relations and to remain stable over time.

Life course statuses, network diversity and cultural tolerance, and legitimacy of same-sex relationships

The first phase of our empirical work seeks to tease out the theorized mechanisms that link life course statuses to attitudes towards same-sex relationships. We do so by estimating a series of regression models, OLS and logits that first examine the relationship between life course statuses and network diversity and cultural tolerance and then the mediating effects of the latter on perceived legitimacy of same-sex relationships. This is shown in Table 3.1. First, four of our five focal life course stages have significant associations with network diversity. Consistent with our expectations, those homemakers and those retired have less diverse networks

Table 3.1 Network diversity, cultural tolerance, and support of same-sex relationships by life course status, GSS 2006

	OLS		Logit	
	Network diversity	Cultural tolerance	Attitudes towards same-sex relationships	
	(1)	(2)	(3)	(4)
Retired	−1.019***	−0.194	−0.575**	−0.385
	(.258)	(.226)	(.247)	(.267)
Homemaker	−0.588*	−0.090	−0.029	0.089
	(.309)	(.270)	(.277)	(.296)
Divorced/Separated	0.962***	0.698***	0.638***	0.368
	(.253)	(.220)	(.220)	(.242)
Widowed	0.392	0.727***	0.297	0.030
	(.353)	(.307)	(.324)	(.350)
Never Married	0.979***	1.506***	0.800***	0.391
	(.234)	(.204)	(.193)	(.214)
College Graduate	0.899***	0.577***	0.698***	0.538***
	(.202)	(.175)	(.170)	(.185)
Network Diversity	–	–	–	0.168***
				(.026)
Cultural Tolerance	–	–	–	0.221***
				(.032)
Constant	1.859	6.964	−1.291	−3.302
	(.169)	(.147)	(.154)	(.304)

Note: *p < 0.05, **p < 0.01, ***p < 0.001.

(b = −1.019 and −.588, respectively). By extension, this means that those working in paid labor or in school have more diverse networks. At the same time, marriage is clearly a state that constrains network diversity, as those who are divorced/separated or never married have more diverse networks (b = .962 and .979, respectively). Also consistent with our expectations, college graduates have more diverse networks (b = .899).[2]

We next consider effects on cultural tolerance. Here, effects are more varied. There are no significant differences with respect to employment. In contrast, divorced/separated, widowed, and single respondents report significantly higher cultural tolerance (b = .698, .727, and 1.506, respectively). By implication, marriage is associated with greater conservatism and less cultural tolerance. Also consistent with expectations, college graduates report greater cultural tolerance (b = .577).

The third set of models employs logistic regression to examine the mediating effect of network diversity and cultural tolerance on attitudes towards same-sex relationships. In the first of these models, four of our five focal life course states have significant associations with attitudes towards same-sex relationships. Consistent with expectations, those who are retired are 44 per cent less likely than those working or in school to view same-sex relationships as legitimate ($e^{-.575} = 0.56$). Those who are divorced/separated or single are more likely to hold an opposite view. In comparison to respondents who are married, those divorced or separated are 89 per cent more likely ($e^{.638} = 1.89$) and those single are 123 per cent more ($e^{.800} = 2.23$) likely to see same-sex relationships as normative. Likewise, college graduates are also more likely to view same-sex relationships as legitimate ($e^{.698} = 2.01$). The only effect that is not consistent with our expectations is that for homemaker. While we expected that homemakers would view same-sex relationships as less legitimate, they are no different from those working or in school ($\beta = -.029$, ns).

On the specific issue of mediation through network diversity and cultural tolerance, our expectations are also supported. First, network diversity and cultural tolerance both have strong and similar effects on attitudes. In the former case, increases in network diversity are associated with 18 per cent increases in the likelihood of viewing same-sex relationships as normative ($e^{.168} = 1.182$). At the same time, increases in cultural tolerance are associated with 25 per cent increases in the likelihood of similar attitudes ($e^{.221} = 1.247$). Equally important, the logic of statistical mediation requires that the effects of life course state would be substantially reduced with the inclusion of network diversity and cultural tolerance, and this is seen. While the effect of retirement is reduced by a third to non-significance, the effects of marital status see even larger reductions (42 and 50 per cent for divorce/separated and single respectively) and are also non-significant. Even in the case of college education, which continues to have a statistically significant effect, the effect is still reduced by almost a quarter in the final model ($\beta = .538$, $p < 0.01$).

Although our models only use data from 2006, the models clearly show that life course states influence network diversity and cultural tolerance, as well as attitudes towards same-sex relationships, and that network diversity and cultural tolerance mediate the former's effect on the latter. While some of our expectations are not borne out, the overall pattern reveals, at least partially, the mechanism by which life course states are associated with cultural beliefs surrounding same-sex relationships.

Life course dynamics and sociocultural change

Having demonstrated the mechanisms by which life course states, and by implication life course dynamics, influence the legitimacy of same-sex relationships, we next consider the interlocked temporal dynamics of life course states and attitudes towards same-sex relations. We do so by estimating a multivariate logit model that examines the independent and

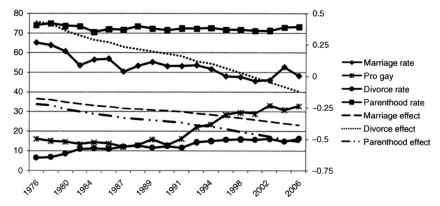

Figure 3.1 Marriage and parenthood and attitudes towards same-sex relationships, US GSS 1976–2006.

time-varying effects of our focal life course states on attitudes towards same-sex relationships.[3] Beginning with marital status (see Figure 3.1), there are several interesting features. First, there is a clear decline in prevalence over time. In the mid-1970s, over 65 per cent of the population (18–85 and older) was married. This declines quite steadily through the 80s and 90s such that just under 50 per cent are married in the early 2000s. This trend corresponds strongly with the increasing prevalence of positive attitudes towards homosexuality. From our perspective, changing structures of the life course, in an unintended manner, open up space for cultural change by diluting a particularly powerful schema-resource nexus. This interpretation is further fostered by the dynamic relationship between marriage and attitudes over time where marriage has a negative association that becomes increasingly strong in recent decades. Specifically, it begins with an effect that reduces the odds of feeling that same-sex relationships are 'not wrong at all' by 18 per cent ($e^{-.20} = .82$) but this declines to 33 per cent ($e^{-.40} = .67$) by 2006. As a life course state, marriage can be seen as increasingly conservative, but at the same time decreasingly prevalent in the population. In other words, as marital structures become less hegemonic they become more intense. Still, as they become less hegemonic, social space is opened up for alternative social schema.

In the case of divorce or separation, our expectations are only partially borne out (also see Figure 3.1). In one respect, the GSS data show that divorce is an increasingly common life course state. Between 1976 and 2006, its prevalence rose from just over 5 per cent to over 15 per cent, a threefold increase and this, to some degree, tracks the normalization of attitudes towards same-sex relationships. Bracketing the issue of spuriousness for the moment, one might conclude that the liberalizing of attitudes towards same-sex unions has occurred alongside the weakening of marriage as an institution. Equally interesting, and in contrast to our argument, divorce was most associated with positive attitudes towards same-sex unions in the late 1970s and has become increasingly heteronormative over time. Specifically, the odds of positive attitudes towards same-sex unions are almost 50 per cent greater ($e^{.40} = 1.49$) among the divorced in the late 1970s, but this declines to 18 per cent lower ($e^{-.20} = .82$) during the early 2000s. One explanation for this may be that, as divorce becomes more statistically normative, its population tends to resemble socially and culturally that of the married and hence cultural schema with respect to same-sex unions tend to take on a similar form.

When we examine parenthood (see Figure 3.1), our expectations have more support. In general, the prevalence of parenthood has remained stable; between 70 and 75 per cent of the US population has a child and this does not track with the significant declines in heteronormativity through the 1990s and early 2000s. At the same time, there is a significant negative association with attitudes towards same-sex relationships. For example, through the 1970s and early 1980s, parenthood is associated with an average decrease in the odds of feeling favorable to same-sex unions of about 18 per cent ($e^{-.20} = .82$). Moreover, the association increased in strength over time. While the effect on odds was an 18 per cent decrease for parents in the 1970s and early 1980s, it grew to a 30 per cent ($e^{-.35} = .70$) decrease by the mid-1990s and to a 40 per cent ($e^{-.50} = .60$) decrease by the 2006.

Turning to the effects of increased education, the GSS data bear out expectations (see Figure 3.2). The increasingly normative nature, at least in a statistical sense, of college completion is clearly seen with the proportion of Americans with college degrees increasing from 15 per cent in the late 1970s to 30 per cent during the first decade of the twenty-first century. Although we do not show it, almost all of this increase is seen among those in 20s, 30s, and 40s with comparatively low rates of college attainment for those in mid-life and older. When considered in relation to trends in

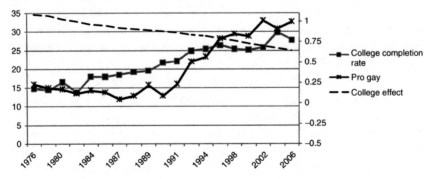

Figure 3.2   College completion and attitudes towards same-sex relationship, US GSS 1976–2006.

beliefs around same-sex unions, there is a clear, positive correlation and the association is somewhat larger than those seen for family life course states. Perhaps even more important, we see strong evidence that the college effect is both profoundly liberalizing and has declined significantly over time. For example, through the late 1970s, college education almost tripled the odds of being favorable to same-sex unions ($e^{1.0} = 2.73$) and the increase in odds remains above two throughout most of the time period. However, the effect does decline such that the increase in odds declines to 2.2 ($e^{.80} = 2.23$) by the early 1990s and to 1.9 ($e^{.60} = 1.87$) by 2006. As a central feature of life course attainments in the contemporary era, college completion clearly fosters space for schemas supportive of same-sex unions but has grown weaker in this capacity as the educational landscape has changed.

In contrast but consistent with expectations, retirement is associated with generally lower odds of feeling favorable to same-sex unions (see Figure 3.3). For example, from the mid-1970s to the mid-1990s, retirees have odds 22 per cent lower ($e^{-.25} = .78$) than others outside of the labor force. There are however some moderate declines in the effect: in the late 1970s, retirees had odds 18 per cent lower ($e^{-.20} = .82$), yet 31 per cent lower ($e^{-.37} = .69$) by the early 2000s. Still, the association, in general, is relatively flat, suggesting a small negative association that has remained relatively constant. Finally, when we examine homemakers, the trend in the prevalence of this life course state shows the rise of the dual earner couples and two income families. In the late 1970s, over a quarter of the US population were homemakers; 30 years later this rate had dropped to only 10 per cent. Given this, the association between trends in homemaker status and beliefs regarding same-sex unions was fairly strong. Much like retirement, we anticipate that homemaker status would be associated with greater influence of immediate kin and narrower social networks and hence would be

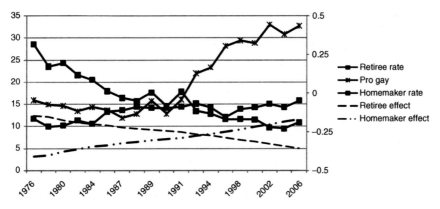

Figure 3.3 Retirement and attitudes towards same sex relationships, US GSS 1976–2006.

negatively associated with positive values towards same-sex unions. The GSS data bear this. Through the late 1970s and 1980s, homemakers have odds that are approximately 25 per cent lower ($e^{-.30} = .75$). Still, there is also some evidence of liberalization. In the late 1970s, homemakers had odds 33 per cent lower ($e^{-.40} = .67$); by the early 2000s, this difference had declined to only 20 per cent ($e^{-.20} = .80$). As homemaking has become less prevalent, its negative association with same-sex values has declined precipitously.

As a final issue, the model we estimated began with just a conditional effect of time on attitudes to index the extent of cultural change and then added the various life course states and their contingencies by time and age. In doing so, we account for just under a quarter of the effect of time. Put another way, a relatively simple accounting of the changing structure of the life course accounts for a quarter of the change in attitudes over time. Given the fact that our model was intentionally simplistic, we think it makes a particularly significant case for the role of life course social structures as a mechanism for broad based social and cultural change.

Concluding comments

At an abstract level, a life course perspective is intrinsically connected to issues of social change. Indeed, the seminal statements, including those associated with luminaries such as Bronfenbrenner, Elder, Furstenberg, Hogan, Mayer, Modell, and Shanahan, explicitly emphasize human development as contingent upon sociohistorical context. Such a perspective is important and has contributed to a making a life course perspective particularly powerful as social explanation. At the same time, it seems incomplete, given the well-recognized dynamic relationship between individual action and sociocultural change and persistent questions about the role of human agency in the reproduction and reconfiguration of social structures (Bourdieu, 1977; Giddens, 1984; Sewell, 1992). This chapter articulates a structural theory of the life course that explicitly elaborates the life course processes that can be mechanisms for social change. By design, our work is partial in that it focuses on the undeveloped aspect of a more dynamic and multidimensional conceptualization. In doing so, it helps flesh out previously unarticulated aspects of the life course as a vehicle for social change.

Over three decades ago, Norman Ryder (1965) offered the social sciences a provocative essay on 'cohort' as a vehicle of social change. Ryder's insight was profound. Each society is continually faced with its own reproduction and production given the cyclical nature of human lives. As older generations die off, they are replaced with new ones that encounter different environments, have different experiences, and formulate different goals and values. Such a process provides a constant mechanism for social change. The ideas we offer in this chapter extend Ryder's ideas by situating them in a life course context. Through the idea of life course social structures, cohorts matter because they have particular relations to life course states both in terms of if and when people move into school, work, and family and the degree to which these states introduce life course and extra-life course schema and resources. One aspect of this, an aspect we do not emphasize in this chapter, is the production and reproduction of life pathways that involve unique combinations of the timing and order of multiple role entries and exits. The other aspect of this, that is highlighted in this chapter, is the role that life course states, their timing, order and resultant pathways play in creating cultural spaces for the solidification of hegemonic values, for the diversification of values, or for the emergence of counter-cultural perspectives. As one moves from the individual to the population, life course social structures become an engine, in and of themselves, for both the reproduction of society and cultural and (extra-life course) structural innovation.

Central to our argument is the idea that different life course states provide different balances of cultural consolidation and innovation. They do so because they manipulate exposure to and the salience of social schema. At the same time, they provide exposure to and experience of schema-resource nexuses that shape how people envision core social action, fundamental social relations, and broad aspects of social organization. In our example, we characterized marriage, retirement, and homemaking as sexually conservative institutions, and higher education, singlehood, and divorce as more liberalizing institutions. For our purposes, we view them as conservative or liberal in the context of the diversity of social networks and the types of schema and discourses that they foster and reinforce. It is important to recognize that we did this for the specific example at hand, an examination of the changing sexual norms over the last quarter of the twentieth century. Other research will need to conceptualize the specific schema and resource nexuses of life course social roles and how these relate to unique examples of social and cultural change.

Another theoretical implication is the utility of thinking about life course states, roles, role configurations, and pathways, as having unique schematic character that extend beyond the specific schema that determine the how of roles, role configurations, and pathways. James Coleman's (1990) quasi-rational choice theory of action suggests that life course states may facilitate or inhibit purposeful action such as social movement activity directed at producing social change. Such a view is consistent with McAdam's (1987) note that participants in the freedom summer project, a classic example of high-stakes activism, were 'free' from the demands of family, marriage, and full-time work and hence more available to express their political values through action. Future work might further explore the complex mechanisms that link life course states, social activism, and socio-cultural change.

At the same time, Sewell (1987) has noted that Coleman's thesis is overly purposeful and leaves little room for unintended consequences. Indeed, social history is filled with examples of purposeful action that yielded unintended consequences and actions that only seem purposeful when social scientists, post hoc, identify the apparent 'rationality' of ideation and action. Given this, a complementary avenue of research would further consider more unintended consequences of life course dynamics and processes of social change. Such work would be a fundamental starting point for understanding mechanisms, selection and causation, by which life course states and pathways provide the contexts for large-scale structural and cultural change.

Extending such work, there is clearly a need for broader, more dynamic and multidimensional models of the life course. Here, life course theory might begin with the basic schema-resource framework and think about modeling contingent phenomena without explicit concern for causation. Doing so would remove the constraints of cause and effect that are so seductive yet so arbitrary in life course research and instead articulate a more descriptive model that would flesh out the range of factors, across levels and across time, that infuse a life course perspective (see Abbott, 1998 for similar argument). Although these theoretical issues still need to be worked out, the basic aspects of a life course perspective seem uniquely poised to address key issues in social theory (Emirbayer & Mische, 1998).

More worrisome is the methodological aspects of contemporary life course research. Although the perspective is quite distinct with its emphasis on contingency and temporality, typical research readily adopts the conventional methods of social and statistical analysis, methods that do not usually reflect the core conceptual features of a life course perspective. This may be problematic. Conventional tools usually suit conventional problems and ignore the subtleties of specific theoretical perspectives. Given the issues we outline in this chapter, there are two methodological issues that should be considered. First, research needs to be multi-level *and* multi-dimensional. Importantly, this is different from the adoption of 'multi-level' or 'hierarchical' models. Such models typically adjust for the independence of units, across space or time, by re-estimating standard errors rather than examining multi-level contingencies and the conditions under which they exist. As the essence of our argument is the intersection of social structures, as well as the within-time and across-time contingencies of life course social roles, future research needs to focus explicitly, variably and statistically, on n-way interactions and interaction models that examine embeddedness and contingency and their implications. Models of cluster analysis, latent class analysis, and newly emergent Bayesian approaches offer considerable promise for modeling life course phenomena.

Second, there seems to be a need for either better data or more creative use of data. A cursory scan indicates that many countries have decennial census data, annual (or semi-annual) public opinion data, one, if not many, national or regional longitudinal samples, and, in some cases, the latter data that characterize different historical periods. The challenge for life course researchers is to integrate social and cultural context, historical period, and longitudinal studies to provide a more multidimensional, multifaceted, and multi-level set of measures of life course pathways and sociohistorical context. As one example of this, the National Longitudinal Series (NLS) in the United States includes longitudinal panels beginning 1966, 1968, 1979, and 1997. Such data could fruitfully be combined, with appropriate statistical adjustments, with public opinion data from the General Social Survey series (1972 to 2006), and the census (1960, 1970, 1980, 1990, and 2000) to flesh out the fuller dimensionality of life course and extra-life course schema-resource nexuses and their relationship to social reproduction and social change. Data organizations such as the IPUMS program at the University of Minnesota have considerable expertise in harmonizing data across time and space and are invaluable resources for the building of such data infrastructure.

Regardless of the complexities that these issues imply for future research, this chapter offers a small but significant re-conceptualization of the relationship between life course and social change. Without abandoning the traditional foci of life courses unfolding in given sociohistorical contexts, a new and more powerful era of life course research requires attention to the role that life course social structures play in the production of social cultures and contexts and how these fit into a broader, more dynamic perspective of social structures of the life course in contemporary societies that examine the dynamic interplay of schema and resources of both a life course and extra-life course character. It is hoped that the example shown provides some glimpse into the role that the life course might play in the production of socio-cultural change and suggest avenues for future research. And in doing so, it is hoped that this will lead to both greater consideration and greater incorporation of dynamic context into models of the life course. An accurate accounting of the unfolding of human lives in different sociohistorical contexts requires nothing less.

Notes

1 While this may seem overstated, it is important to note that the central tenet of the divorce revolution was the move to 'no-fault' divorce which removed the necessity of the traditional grounds for divorce (i.e., abuse, cruelty, abandonment).

2 Although determining magnitude is complicated, such effects likely fall into the moderate range given that almost half of respondents report having no gay acquaintances at all and a very small number report more than ten.
3 We also control for age given the potential importance of cohort effects on such attitudes.

References

Abbott, Andrew (1998). The casual devolution. *Sociological Methods & Research*, 27, 148–181.

Alwin, D. (2008). Integrating varieties of life course concepts. Unpublished paper, Center on Population Health and Aging, Penn State University, University Park, PA 16801.

Booth, A., Crouter, A. & Shanahan, M. (1999). *Transitions to adulthood in a changing economy: No work, no family, no future?* New York: Greenwood.

Bourdieu, P. (1977). *Outline of a theory of practice*. Cambridge: Cambridge University Press.

Cameron, S. & Heckman, J. (1993). The non-equivalence of high school equivalents. *Journal of Labor Economics*, 11, 1–47.

Clausen, John (1991). Adolescent competence and the shaping of the life course. *American Journal of Sociology*, 96, 805–842.

Coleman, J. (1990). *Foundations of social theory*. Cambridge: Harvard University Press.

Coser, L. (1974). *Greedy institutions: Patterns of undivided commitment*. New York: The Free Press.

Elder, G. (1999) [1974]. *Children of the Great Depression*. Chicago: University of Chicago Press.

Elder, G. (1994). Time, human agency, and social change. *Social Psychology Quarterly*, 57, 4–15.

Emirbayer, M. & Mische, A. (1998). What is Agency? *American Journal of Sociology*, 103, 962–1023.

Fischer, C. & Hout, M. (2006). *Century of difference: How America changed in the last hundred years*. New York: Russell Sage.

Fraser, N. & Honneth, A. (2003). *Redistribution or recognition? A political-philosophical exchange*. Brooklyn: Verso.

Furstenberg, F., Brooks-Gunn, J. & Morgan, P. (1987). *Adolescent mothers in later life*. Chicago: University of Chicago Press.

Giddens, A. (1984). *The constitution of society: Outline of the theory of structuration*. Berkeley: University of California Press.

Goldstein, Joshua & Kenney, C. (2001). Marriage delayed or marriage foregone? *American Sociological Review*, 66, 506–519.

Han, S. & Moen, P. (1999). Clocking out: Temporal patterns of retirement. *American Journal of Sociology*, 105, 191–236.

Hogan, D. (1978). The variable order of events in the life course. *American Sociological Review*, 43, 573–586.

Hull, K. (2006). *Same-sex marriage: The cultural politics of love and law*. Cambridge: Cambridge University Press.

Macmillan, R. (Ed.) (2004). *The structure of the life course: Advances in life course research*, Vol. 9. London: Elsevier.

Macmillan, R. & Eliason, S. (nd). Social differentiation in the structure of the life course: Latent pathways in the transition to adulthood. Unpublished manuscript.

McAdam, D. (1987). *Freedom summer*. New York: Oxford University Press.

McLanahan, S. & Sandefur, G. (1996). *Growing up with a single parent: What hurts, what helps*. Cambridge: Harvard University Press.

Mortimer, J. (2003). *Working and growing up in America*. Cambridge: Harvard University Press.

Oppenheimer, V. (1997). Women's employment and the gain to marriage: The specialization and trading model. *Annual Review of Sociology*, 23, 431–453.

Pallas, Aaron (2003). A subjective approach to schooling and the transition to adulthood, pp. 173–198. In Ross Macmillan (Ed.)., *Constructing adulthood: Agency and subjectivity in adolescence and adulthood, advances in life course research*, Vol. 11. New York: Elsevier.

Rosenbaum, J. (2001). *Beyond college for all*. New York: Russell Sage.

Ryder, N. (1965). Cohort as a concept in the study of social change. *American Sociological Review*, 30, 843–861.

Sewell, William H. Jr. (1987). Theory of action, dialectic, and history: comment on Coleman. *American Journal of Sociology*, 93, 166–172.

Shanahan, M., Elder, G. & Miech, R. (1997). History and agency in men's lives: Pathways to achievement in cohort perspective. *Sociology of Education*, 70, 54–67.

Shanahan, M., Miech, R. & Elder, G. (1998). Changing pathways to attainment in men's lives: Historical patterns of school, work, and social class. *Social Forces*, 77, 231–256.

Stack, C. (1974). *All our kin: Strategies for survival in a black community*. New York: Harper & Row.

Wilson, W. (1987). *The truly disadvantaged*. Chicago: University of Chicago Press.

Part II

DETERMINANTS ON THE INDIVIDUAL LEVEL

4

GLOBALIZATION, INSTITUTIONAL FILTERS AND CHANGING LIFE COURSE. PATTERNS IN MODERN SOCIETIES: A SUMMARY OF THE RESULTS FROM THE GLOBALIFE-PROJECT

Dirk Hofäcker, Sandra Buchholz, and *Hans-Peter Blossfeld*

Over the last two decades, globalization has had a lasting impact on modern societies. However, it is notable that, up to now, research on globalization largely has been confined to the effects of the globalization process on national aggregates with the help of macro data. Although there is no denying that this type of research has made a major contribution to the understanding of globalization, it can be assumed that there has been an equally fundamental influence on the micro-level, particularly on the development of individual life courses in modern societies. A major research endeavor to analyse these micro-macro linkages systematically has been the GLOBALIFE research project, supported by a 1.7 million Euro grant from the Volkswagen Foundation in Germany, which was carried out at the Universities of Bielefeld and Bamberg from 1999 to 2006. Based on a cross-nationally comparative empirical analysis of the effects of the globalization process on the life-courses of women and men in 17 advanced OECD-type societies, this project not only empirically described the impacts of globalization on individual life courses as such but also demonstrated how far national institutional structures 'filter' the globalization process in specific ways, thus producing outcomes on the level of individual life courses that differ from country to country.

This chapter summarizes the key findings of this research. It starts by outlining theoretically the characteristics of the globalization process and its effects on individual life courses. Subsequently, we confront these theoretical considerations with the most important empirical findings of the GLOBALIFE project. In doing so, we will discuss not only the general changes in central transitions of the life course resulting from globalization but also the *country-specific form* that these changes take and how these changes can be traced back to the cross-nationally varying design of nation-specific 'filters' as embodied in welfare state and labor market institutions.

Features and effects of the globalization process

Basically, globalization is understood as a combination of processes that have led to growing worldwide interconnectedness (Alasuutari, 2000; Robertson, 1992). While this is certainly no fundamentally new phenomenon (Robertson, 1990; Sutcliffe and Glyn, 1999), nobody would deny that most industrial nations have seen an enormous increase in the intensity and scope of cross-border interactions over the last two decades – be they economic transactions or processes of informational, cultural, and political exchange (Alasuutari, 2000; Castells, 2004; Dreher, 2006; Held et al., 2000; Robertson, 1990; Sutcliffe and Glyn, 1999; Raab et al., 2008). Particularly through the rapid advances in information technologies in recent years, the fall of the Iron Curtain with the resulting abrupt opening of new markets, and the economic boom in Asian countries, there has been a marked intensification of cross-border exchange between modern states that has attained a new and previously unattained quality.

Nowadays, most social scientists assume that the globalization process is characterized by the simultaneous co-action of four macro-structural trends that have become increasingly dominant, particularly since the 1980s (see also Figure 4.1). These are:

1 The increasing internationalization of markets and the associated growth in competition between countries with very different wage and productivity levels as well as different social and environmental standards.
2 The intensification of competition between nation states and the resulting tendency for modern states to reduce business taxes and to engage in deregulation, privatization, and liberalization while strengthening the market as a coordination mechanism.
3 The rapid worldwide networking of persons, companies, and states through new information and communication technologies, and, as a result, the increasing global interdependence of actors along with the increasing acceleration of social and economic interaction processes.
4 The fast growth in the importance of globally networked markets and the accompanying increase in the interdependence and volatility of local markets that are ever more vulnerable to scarcely predictable social, political, and economic 'external shocks' and events throughout the world (such as wars, economic and financial crises, sub-prime mortgage turbulences, Oil price shocks, consumer fashions, technological innovations).

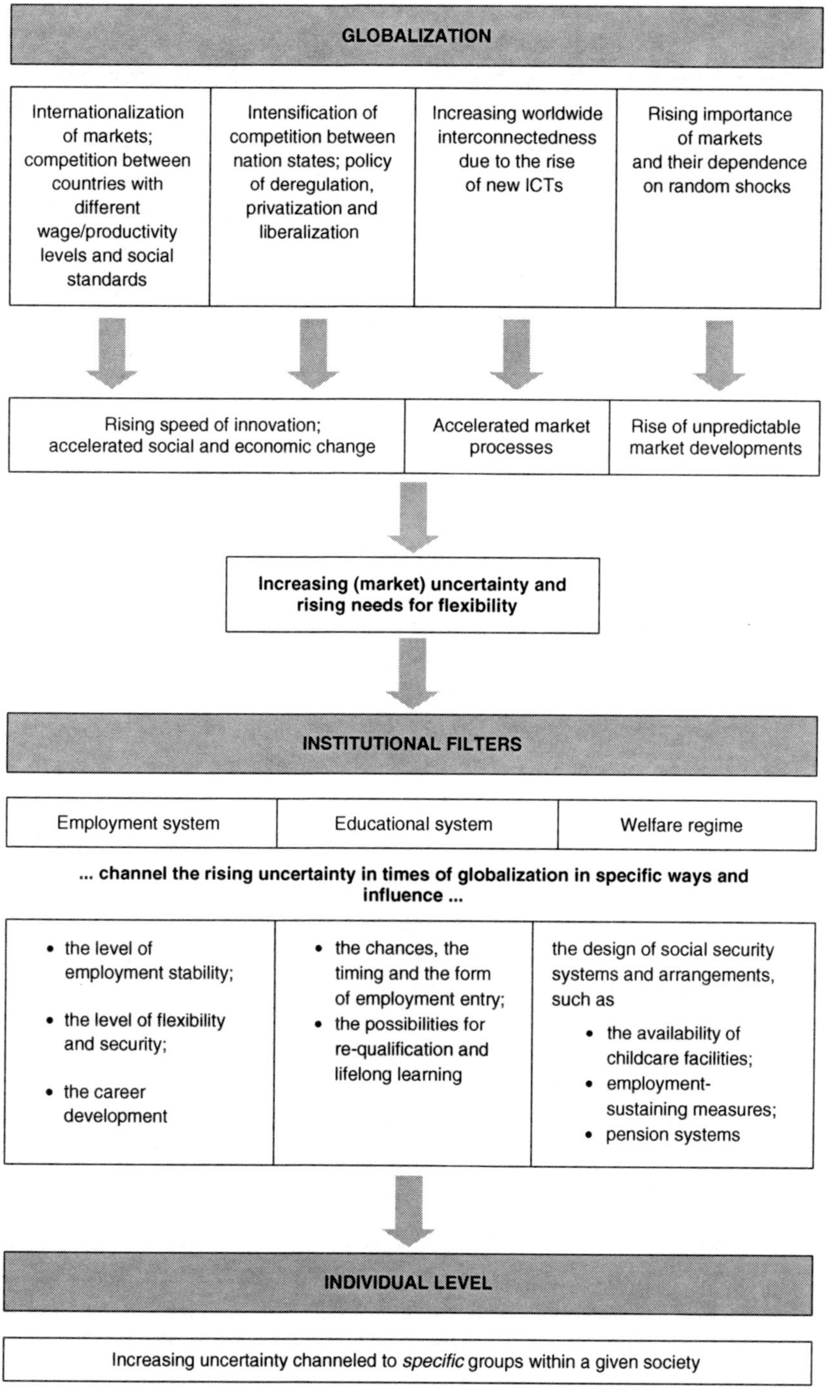

Figure 4.1 Globalization and rising uncertainties in modern societies.
Source: Own illustration following Mills and Blossfeld (2005).

As previous research within the scope of the European Research Network TransEurope[1] has demonstrated (see Raab et al., 2008), globalization processes have been clearly more advanced in the OECD countries than in the less developed regions of the world. Comparing the nation-specific degree of globalization across countries and time using a multidimensional index – the so-called 'GlobalIndex' (ibid.) – shows that in global comparison, modern countries have been exposed disproportionately to globalization influences in recent decades. For these countries, globalization, on the one hand, has certainly increased productivity and improved the general standard of living in broad population strata of modern societies. Nonetheless, it has been simultaneously accompanied by a growth in unexpected market trends in an increasingly changing global economy, by more rapid processes of social and economic change, by an ever stronger decline in the predictability of economic and social trends, and, as a result of this, by a general increase in uncertainty (see Figure 4.1). This rise in uncertainties has impacted significantly on various aspects of the private and employment lives of individuals in modern societies. However, nation-specific institutions such as different types of welfare state arrangements and labor market regulation have mediated these 'main effects' of globalization and have thereby led to cross-nationally varying outcomes of globalization, reflected in different patterns of life course development under globalization. In the following, we will outline these differentiated effects of globalization in more detail. Following the approach taken in the GLOBALIFE project, we will differentiate analytically between four central transitions in the life course and employment career of women and men:

1   The transition from youth to adulthood and the accompanying process of becoming established on the labor market during this period along with its effects on family formation and fertility (Blossfeld et al., 2005).
2   The transitions during the employment course of men in mid-career (Blossfeld, Mills and Bernardi, 2006).
3   The transitions during the employment course of mid-life women, paying particular attention to family formation and motherhood (Blossfeld and Hofmeister, 2006).
4   The changes in late careers and the transition to retirement (Blossfeld, Buchholz and Hofäcker, 2006).

The data underlying the following analyses originate from a total of 17 OECD-type countries. Analyses were based on most recent longitudinal data sets such as national surveys, retrospective panel studies and public administrative data bases, covering a time span from the 1970s until present.[2]

For structuring the following overview of institutional and cultural characteristics, we classify these 17 countries into five different welfare and labor market regimes[3]: *liberal* (Canada, Great Britain, and the United States), *conservative* (Germany, the Netherlands, and France), *social-democratic* (Norway, Denmark, and Sweden), *family-oriented* (Italy, Spain, Ireland, and Mexico), and *post-socialist* (Estonia, Hungary, the Czech Republic, and Poland).

Globalization and the role of institutional filters

It is not essentially increasing uncertainty as such that is important if we analyse the consequences of globalization. Increasing uncertainty does not impact all regions, states, organizations or individuals in the same way. There are institutional settings and social structures, historically grown and country-specific, that determine the degree to which people are affected by rising uncertainty (DiPrete et al., 1997). These institutions have a tendency to persist (Nelson, 1995; Esping-Andersen, 1993) and act as a sort of intervening variable between global macro forces and the responses at the micro level (Hurrell and Woods, 1995; Regini, 2000). Thus, we do not expect that increasing uncertainty leads to a rapid convergence of life courses in all modern societies (see for example Meyer, Ramirez and Soysal, 1992, Treiman, 1970; Treiman and Yip, 1989) but claim that there are path-dependent developments within countries (Nelson, 1995; Mayer, 2001). The institutions that most impact life courses are employment relations, educational systems, national welfare state regimes, and the family.

Countries differ significantly in their *employment relations systems*, for example with respect to types of work councils, collective bargaining systems, the strength of unions versus employer organizations, labor legislation, and administrative regulations. They produce distinct national variations of occupational structures and industries, patterns of labor-capital negotiations, strike frequencies and collective agreements on wages, job security, labor conditions, and work hours (Soskice, 1993; Streeck, 1992). How these systems diverge has been characterized as 'coordinated' and 'uncoordinated' market economies (Soskice, 1998), 'individualist' or 'collective' regimes (DiPrete et al., 1997), or 'open' and 'closed' employment relations (Sørensen, 1983). The open employment relationship is represented by countries such as the United States, Canada, Ireland, and Britain (after Margaret Thatcher), and is characterized as decentralized, dualistic and based on free market forces and competition. Employment relations are open in the sense that protective factors such as labor unions, legislation related to job security and stability are weak. Shielding of workers from market risk is at a minimum, market mechanisms are central and individuals' labor market resources or human capital such as education, labor force experience are crucial (DiPrete et al., 1997). These market-based types of systems tend to generate a high level of inequality between workers with different amounts of human capital.

Many European countries, on the other hand, such as Sweden, Norway, Germany, France, the Netherlands, Italy and Spain, are often classified as having labor markets with relatively closed employment relationships and centralized procedures for negotiating wages (Regini, 2000). Sweden and Germany are countries with particularly strong labor unions, while Southern European countries like Spain and Italy are taken as extreme cases of 'insider-outsider' labor markets. Within these systems, most of the already employed workers, the so-called 'insiders,' will be relatively shielded against the growing uncertainty and flexibility demands of the world market, while at the same time, globalization in these countries tends to create a new kind of underclass of the socially excluded with low levels of job security and low wages.

There are also great differences among nations in the way in which their *educational systems* (1) differentiate the maximum number of school years attended by all and tracking (stratification), (2) value certificates or ability-based learning (qualificational versus organizational), and (3) standardize the quality of education (standardization). In unstratified systems, exemplified by most Anglo-Saxon countries, a larger proportion of a cohort attains the maximum number of school years provided by the general educational system. Only after this broad universal education does stratification into different school tracks take place. Standardization in both the general educational system as well as in vocational training is low and unified occupational certificates are not widespread. As a consequence, most job-specific knowledge is transferred via on-the-job training at the specific workplace. Under globalization, these unstandardized and unstratified systems can be highly flexible and adaptable to new demands. At the same time, however, they provide little orientation for both employers and employees and often lead to high search costs on the labor market, reflected in often high levels of occupational mobility.

In contrast, in most conservative countries, educational opportunities are more differentiated as youth are streamed into specific educational tracks already at younger ages. Vocational training systems are highly differentiated and provide a large number of specific 'tracks' geared towards accurate qualification for specific occupational demands. Successful completion of these tracks is acknowledged by standardized certificates that serve as preconditions for access to specific types of jobs. These types of jobs 'direct' leavers of the educational system precisely accurate to specific types of jobs and have therefore been highly effective in providing for a smooth transition from education employment and to keep unemployment before labor market entry low. Under globalization, however, these systems carry the danger of creating strong and rigid occupational boundaries that may make it difficult for employees to adapt to new skill demands induced through technological changes. Furthermore, education often remains restricted to early parts of an individual's life course, thereby fostering a depreciation of individual skills. In order to avoid these effects, many Scandinavian countries have combined a standardized system of education and training with opportunities for lifelong learning and skill upgrading for workers of all ages.

Finally, the impact of increasing uncertainty in a globalizing world on individual life courses is strongly dependent on the nation-specific design of *welfare state policies*. Modern countries have created different welfare regimes implying diverse national ideologies about social solidarity (Flora and Alber, 1981) as well as gender and social equality (Esping-Andersen, 1999; Orloff, 1996). Previous research has differentiated five different types of welfare regimes: the liberal, the social-democratic, the conservative, the family-oriented and post-socialist.

To varying degrees, the United States, United Kingdom, and Canada are viewed as liberal welfare regimes characterized by passive labor market policies, moderate support for the underprivileged, and relatively small public sector employment. Together with the flexible design of both labor relations and educational systems, this welfare model has proved to be highly effective in generating generally high employment levels, though often at the expense of greater inequality and poverty.

Norway, Denmark, and Sweden are in contrast often considered as examples of the social-democratic welfare regime model. Active labor market and taxation policies in these countries are aimed at full employment (using Keynesian demand policies and mobility stimulating measures such as retraining, mobility grants, and temporary jobs), gender equality at the workplace as well as at home, and a 'fair' income distribution with a high degree of wage compression. The large participation of women in full-time employment in these countries rests on both the rapid expansion of job opportunities in the service and public sector, engendered in particular by the demands of social services and the highly progressive individual income tax that makes a second household income necessary for most families (Blossfeld and Drobniè, 2001).

Germany and the Netherlands are often cited as examples of conservative welfare regimes. Social policies in these countries are not so much designed to promote employment opportunities, job mobility, but rather to ensure that workers who leave employment because of job loss, disability, or early retirement are protected against serious declines in living standards. This type of welfare regime is therefore strongly transfer-oriented, with decommodifying effects for those who are economically inactive. It is also committed to the traditional division of labor in the family that makes wives economically dependent on their husbands, often referred to as the 'male-breadwinner model.' Correspondingly, welfare state provisions (e.g., day care) are far less developed than in the social democratic model and female economic activity rates are considerably lower and mostly restricted to part-time jobs (Blossfeld and Hakim, 1997).

Southern European countries like Italy and Spain, and to some extent Mexico and Ireland, also share common features. They have developed a welfare regime model that might be called 'family-oriented' (Jurado Guerrero, 1995). In terms of labor market policy, support for the less privileged, and the importance of public sector employment, this welfare regime is very similar to the liberal one. Unlike the latter, however, it is characterized by a strong ideological – and indeed practical – involvement of family and kinship networks in protecting its members against economic and social risks. Due to the meager or non-existent safety net (e.g., family support, unemployment benefits), the state shifts the responsibility for the support of the unemployed and other vulnerable 'outsider' groups to families. In this model the family culturally represents an important institution of reciprocal help and family members thus are expected to support each other.

Finally, the post-socialist welfare regime includes countries in the former socialist Eastern Europe, such as Estonia, Hungary, the Czech Republic, and Poland. Welfare state patterns in these countries tend to be not unique. Hungary is perhaps closer to the social democratic regime, characterized by both egalitarianism and de-familialization. While the dual-earner family model is favored by fiscal arrangements, there is only a highly conditional to limited degree of support for the unemployed (Róbert and Bukodi, 2005). In contrast, Estonia has taken a more liberal direction with limited next to non-existent unemployment and family benefits (Katus, Puur and Sakkeus, 2005). However, considering the rapid transformations after 1990, the trajectory of these welfare regimes is still in evolution.

Changing life courses in the globalization process

Table 4.1 synthesizes the results of the previous institutional overview. In the following, we will demonstrate, how these country-specific institutional backgrounds have influenced the way in which globalization has affected the family and employment lives of individuals in different modern societies. Following the logic of the life course, we will discuss the developments in four different pivotal transitions that guided the analyses within the framework of the GLOBALIFE project.

Table 4.1 Country-specific institutional packages

Country studies of GLOBALIFE project	USA, Great Britain, Canada	Sweden, Denmark, Norway, (the Netherlands)	Germany, France, (the Netherlands)	Italy, Spain, Ireland, Mexico	Hungary, Estonia, Poland, Czech Republic
Employment relationships/ production regime	Weakly regulated	Moderately regulated	Strongly regulated	Strongly regulated	Transition to market economy
Welfare regime	Liberal	Social-democratic	Conservative	Family-oriented	Post-socialist
	Residual public security system	Public security system plus active employment policies	Transfer-oriented; basic public support for not employed population	High public support for (former) insiders	Under transformation
Occupational and educational systems	On-the-job-training; incentives for re-qualification	Vocational qualification in schools; strong orientation on re-qualification	Dual system; little incentives for re-qualification	On-the-job-training; little incentives for re-qualification	Under transformation

Source: Own illustration.

Note: The Netherlands cannot be classified definitely. With regard to employment policy they show similarities to the social-democratic welfare regimes; with regard to other welfare state arrangements – e.g. pension policies – they show similarities to conservative regimes.

Youth and young adults: The losers of globalization

The first research phase of the GLOBALIFE project took a cross-national comparative perspective to compare how adolescents and young adults manage to enter the labor market under the conditions of globalization, and how changed labor market entry and early patterns in young persons' lives impact on familial decisions such as marrying or having a baby. Results show that young individuals face a strong increase in uncertainties when entering the labor market (Blossfeld et al., 2005; Golsch, 2005). These uncertainties manifest particularly in the form of a major increase in precarious, atypical forms of employment (e.g., short-term jobs, part-time jobs, precarious forms of self-employment, and, compared with older cohorts, lower income) which tend to make young people the 'losers' of the globalization process. At first glance, this seems to be contra-intuitive given that the young generation is far more educated than the older and many of these young people have spent a longer part of their life abroad. However, they are affected particularly strongly, because they frequently lack job experience and strong ties to business networks, particularly in internal labor markets. Often they are unable to fall back on established contacts, and do not possess the negotiating powers to demand stable and continuous employment. Thus, it is comparatively easy for employers and unions to adjust young people's work contracts and make them more flexible and less advantageous at their expense.

The concrete effects of the globalization process on the labor market positions of young adults vary according to the specific welfare-state and labor market regime. The regulated, rigid insider-outsider markets of Southern Europe (but, in part, also Germany) reveal increasing phases of unemployment and/or above all short-term work contracts (Bernardi and Nazio, 2005; Kurz, Steinhage and Golsch, 2005; Simó Noguera, Castro Martin and Soro Bonmati, 2005). Particularly in Southern Europe, forms of precarious self-employment can be found, while in the Netherlands, there is a massive increase in part-time jobs for young women and men (Liefbroer, 2005). In these countries, strong employment protection has, on the one hand, shielded the 'core workforce' (mostly men in their mid-careers), but has, on the other hand, promoted a 'flexibilisation at the margins' (Buchholz, 2008). In contrast, in the open employment systems of the liberal countries (United States, Great Britain), the effects of the globalization process are rather manifesting across generations particularly in increasing income losses for young persons (Berkowitz King, 2005; Francesconi and Golsch, 2005).

The increasing experience of employment uncertainties in young adulthood has consequences for familial decision processes. Growing economic and temporal uncertainties lead young people more and more to postpone or even to forgo family formation (Blossfeld et al., 2005). On the societal level, this leads to a dilemma, because not only improved conditions for labor market flexibility in the sense of greater competitiveness but also rising birthrates are viewed as desirable. Young adults have developed four behavioral and adaptive strategies as a reaction to growing uncertainties in the life course (Mills, Blossfeld and Klijzing, 2005): (1) They increasingly postpone decisions requiring a long-term commitment; the youth phase becomes more and more of a 'moratorium,' and transitions to gainful employment often take a chaotic course. (2) They switch increasingly to alternative roles instead of employment (e.g., they spend longer in the education system instead of letting themselves be defined as 'unemployed'). (3) They are increasingly forming more flexible forms of partnership (e.g., consensual unions) that permit an adaptation to rising uncertainty without having to make long-term commitments (Nazio and Blossfeld, 2003; Nazio 2008). (4) Particularly in the family-oriented welfare states of Central and Southern Europe, they have developed gender-specific strategies to deal with uncertainty: Men are increasingly less able to guarantee any long-term income security as the 'breadwinner' for a household, often leading to delay in family formation. In contrast, many unqualified women who 'have nothing to lose' react to the growing uncertainties on the labor market by turning to the security of the family and the traditional roles of mother and housewife (as a strategy to reduce uncertainty). Vice versa, the tendency for highly qualified women to have children in increasingly uncertain labor markets depends on whether they can protect their careers by making family and career compatible. When childcare facilities are underdeveloped, as is particularly the case in Southern Europe, many qualified women decide in favor of their careers rather than for children (Bernardi and Nazio, 2005; Simó Noguera, Castro Martin and Soro Bonmati, 2005). Hence, a paradoxical outcome of the globalization process is that precisely in traditional family-oriented societies, the birth rate is declining markedly because of the growing experience of employment uncertainties for young men and the incompatibility of family and career for qualified women. Founding a family calls for at least a minimum of economic and social certainty regarding the future that, under the global conditions of increasing labor market uncertainty, can often be achieved only after a long transition period following the exit from the education system. Therefore, economically and socially speaking, young people who forgo having children are making a rational response to structural trends. A similar restrained fertility behavior can also be found in the transformation countries of Eastern Europe in which uncertainties have grown enormously since the collapse of socialism and support through public family policy institutions simultaneously have declined (Katus, Puur and Sakkeus, 2005; Róbert and Bukodi; 2005). In contrast, in Scandinavian countries in which the state provides comparatively generous universal services for young adults and families, along with childcare facilities while engaging in an active employment policy, the birthrate is comparatively high, though still below the net reproduction rate (Bygren, Duvander and Hultin, 2005; Nilsen, 2005).

It is important to point out in this context that it is not the *absolute* level of uncertainty that is decisive for the structuring of decisions on family formation, but the subjectively perceived *relative* level of uncertainty in the specific country's labor force (Blossfeld et al., 2005). In each country, young adults compare themselves in daily life with 'significant others' (such as friends, relatives, acquaintances) when judging their individual labor market situation. In the United States, for example, the absolute level of uncertainty for the young generation is higher as a whole than in many European countries. People lose their jobs more frequently, but the unemployed can rely on soon finding another job, that is, becoming an 'insider' again, because of the low mobility barriers on the labor market. This is why labor market uncertainty, career mobility, and flexibility possess a different social significance in the United States. On the other hand, in the insider-outsider markets of Europe, 'being an outsider' often means an identity-threatening, long-term exclusion from work in a climate in which flexible work arrangements are often viewed as only a stop-gap solution on the way toward a permanent job. 'Flexibilized' young adults in these labor markets therefore experience their fate as being far more negative than their peers in the United States.

Men in mid-career: The winners of globalization?

The second phase of the GLOBALIFE project focused on the employment trajectories of mid-career men. Results showed that younger men are indeed confronted with a somewhat greater labor market uncertainty than those from older birth cohorts (Blossfeld, Mills and Bernardi, 2006). However, globalization in no way leads to an increasing erosion of traditional male employment relationships or to the spread of 'patchwork careers' and 'job hopping' as frequently assumed by 'individualization theorists' (cf. Beck, 1992). Quite the opposite: The employment careers of well-qualified male employees who are established on the market are still comparatively stable and broadly protected from any flexibilization by employers. An explanation for this paradoxical result may be that, although the globalization process forces companies to respond more flexibly and therefore to try to reduce their own market risks and pass these on to their employees by imposing more short-term-oriented employment relationships, a completely flexibilized workforce is neither desirable nor efficient for a company. In times of greater (international) competition, a secure and long-term cooperation with qualified and experienced staff is still important for employers in order to ensure the flow of information in the company, productivity, and also innovations. The comprehensive introduction of flexible employment relationships would threaten the reliable and permanent cooperation between management and qualified staff, and additionally carries the threat that a company will be faced with high recruitment costs and qualification losses when hiring new employees (Breen, 1997; Mills, Blossfeld and Bernardi, 2006). Hence, employers have no interest in withdrawing from long-term commitments to *all* the employees on their staff, but try not to threaten the *trust relationship* to those in qualified positions. These ambivalent company goals in the globalization process, namely, flexibility on the one side but stability and continuity on the other, lead to an increasing *segmentation* of labor into core groups and peripheral groups (Blossfeld, Mills and Bernardi, 2006), with the demarcation cutoff between those belonging to the 'insiders' and those belonging to the 'outsiders' is being raised increasingly higher. Essentially, this is disadvantaging the lowly qualified and people who are less established on the labor market such as those completing education, young adults, and women.

Even if qualified mid-career men can generally be described as the winners of the globalization process, there are still major differences across and within the various regimes studied in the GLOBALIFE project (Mills and Blossfeld, 2006). In all the countries of the GLOBALIFE project, it was possible to identify a significant group of low-qualified males who are increasingly long-term unemployed and who fail to re-enter the labor market – in particular in those countries with rigid insider/outsider labor markets. There is a further group of mid-career men, mostly unskilled or with low occupational status, who 'oscillate' between unemployment and jobs. The relative size of these 'male globalization losers' varies from country to country; nonetheless, it is comparatively large particularly in the less regulated labor markets of the United States and some former socialist countries. In contrast, the *majority* of mid-career men in countries with conservative, family-oriented, and social democratic structures enjoy a high degree of stability in their employment careers, because they are comprehensively protected by strong employment protection (Blossfeld, Mills and Bernardi, 2006).

Women in mid-life: Marginalization in the globalization process

The effects of the globalization process on the middle phase of women's life courses differ markedly from those on men in mid-career. Whereas mid-career male employment lives have remained comparatively stable in the globalization process, women reveal a trend toward *marginalization* on the labor market (Blossfeld and Hofmeister, 2006). As the GLOBALIFE study has shown, although in a series of countries, women have become increasingly integrated into modern labor markets as a result of the globalization process, this integration has often been rather precarious.

Due to quantitative and qualitative improvements in their access to education, young women show not only a greater interest in their own careers but also have improved their preconditions for successful labor market participation compared with women in earlier generations. Moreover, the increasing instability of families, along with the declining security in the employment careers of husbands in more recent generations in some countries, have contributed to greater female participation on the labor market. As a result of these changes, women's incomes have become increasingly important for the material security of women and their families. This increasing work *supply* of women on the one side has been matched by a growth in the *demand* for female labor on the other side in the expanding (private and public) service sector (Blossfeld and Hakim, 1997).

At the same time, it still is almost exclusively women who continue to perform the unpaid familial and care duties in all modern societies. During the family phase, married couples tend to invest far more in the continuing working career of the husband rather than that of the wife (Blossfeld and Drobniè, 2001). This practice not only limits women's earning capacities but can also impair their continuity of employment and career chances in the long term, particularly when wives give up their jobs completely in favor of those of their husbands, or adapt them to those of their husbands in terms of time or space. As a result, women are disproportionately overrepresented in the flexible forms of work emerging within the globalization process (Blossfeld and Hofmeister, 2006), such as precarious, insecure, and low-paid jobs; part-time jobs or jobs with variable work shifts; jobs with little autonomy, control, or responsibility; and jobs with only slight possibilities of promotion and high risks of downward career mobility or unemployment (Hofmeister and Blossfeld, 2006). Hence, globalization contributes to a marginalization of women as 'outsiders' of the labor market.

Despite this general tendency, the GLOBALIFE project once again reveals different patterns of development in the various regimes: In conservative and, to a lesser extent, Southern European countries, the creation of new, flexible job options in the globalization process has contributed to a better *integration* of women into national labor markets previously characterized by the dominance of a stable 'standard male employment relationship', even though often on a precarious basis (Buchholz and Grunow, 2006; Kalmijn and Luijkx, 2006; Pisati and Schizzerotto, 2006; Simó Noguera, 2006). An increasing integration of women can also be observed in the liberal states that offer little state support for families and pursue a flexible 'laissez-faire' labor market policy. As a consequence of this residual institutional design, it is above all low-qualified women who enter the labor market to support their families financially, and this is frequently in low-income jobs (Hofmeister, 2006). The social-democratic and also former socialist countries, in which active labor market and generous family policies have supported high female employment rates for decades, have largely managed to stabilize their exceptionally high proportion of employed women while retaining job security in the globalization process (Korpi and Stern, 2006) though the proportion of working women in Denmark has dropped moderately since the recent introduction of vacation regulations (Grunow, 2006; Grunow and Leth-Sørensen, 2006). In the former socialist countries, in contrast, integration into the world economy, accompanied by rising economic turmoil and a decline in public policies to support women's employment, has led to stagnating or even negative developments in female employment rates (Bukodi and Róbert, 2006; Hamplová, 2006; Helemäe and Saar, 2006; Plomien, 2006).

Late-career employees: Increasingly confronted with accelerating structural change in the globalization process

Finally, the fourth and final phase of research in the GLOBALIFE project showed that the work careers of older employees have also undergone a remarkable transformation in the globalization process (Buchholz, Hofäcker and Blossfeld, 2006). Companies facing global market competition have a growing need to adapt flexibly to changing economic conditions. However, in light of these new flexibility demands through globalization, older employees reveal several *competitive disadvantages* compared with their younger competitors (Buchholz, Hofäcker and Blossfeld, 2006): They mostly possess only obsolescent technological knowledge and vocational qualifications that make it harder for them to adapt to accelerating technological changes under globalization. As a consequence, the decisive advantage that older employees used to have, namely, their work *experience* compared with young labor market entrants, is rapidly losing importance. The costs of re-qualifying older employees through further training programs and on-the-job training measures are often too high for employers because of the poor returns to investments due to the few years of employment left. Young employees, in contrast, possess more modern qualifications, their training is often to the latest occupational and technological standards, and the costs of further training can be recouped over a longer period of time. In a number of countries, older employees also earn higher 'seniority wages' and employment protection through the logic of internal labor markets. This often makes them far more expensive than their younger competitors, without these competitive advantages being linked with higher productivity. In contrast, young employees have been exposed to a destabilization and flexibilization in their employment careers within the globalization process (Blossfeld et al., 2005). Their work contracts are correspondingly less regulated and they often earn less. Companies thus perceive older employees as being less flexible, inadequately qualified, and cost-intensive. It is therefore in the interest of not only companies, but also policymakers concerned with the attractiveness of their national business location, to find solutions for this discrepancy between increasing demands for flexibility under globalization and the limited flexibilization potential of older employees (Blossfeld, Buchholz and Hofäcker, 2006). One major option for resolving this contradiction has been to offer attractive financial incentives for early employment exit. Indeed, comparative labor market data reveal a trend toward an increasingly early retirement of older employees in almost all Western industrial societies since the 1970s (cf. OECD, 2006).

Detailed analyses in the GLOBALIFE project have shown, however, that the *magnitude* of this trend varies markedly between different institutional regimes (cf. Hofäcker and Pollnerová, 2006; Hofäcker, Buchholz and Blossfeld, 2006). To cope with the problematic labor market situation of older employees in the globalization process, modern societies appear to pursue various strategies that can be classified according to three different ideal types (cf. Buchholz, Hofäcker and Blossfeld, 2006).

Particularly Central and Southern European states pursue a strategy of one-sidedly promoting the *employment exit* of older employees in order to cope with the global competitive pressure and the structural changes in the economy (Blossfeld, Buchholz and Hofäcker, 2006). The discrepancy between growing demands for flexibility in the globalization process and the flexibilization potential of older employees is particularly large in these countries. Due to a highly standardized education system, which largely restricts vocational training to the early life course and which offers few possibilities of in-service or further training, older employees often have major qualification disadvantages compared with their younger labor market competitors. At the same time, extensive protection from dismissal and a well-established system of seniority wages limit the possibilities of making their work contracts more flexible. As a way out of this dilemma, the Central and Southern European states have extended existing early retirement options and furthermore created new early retirement pathways, in part by additional interim welfare state provisions to bridge the gap to full retirement (Beckstette, Lucchini and Schizzerotto, 2006; Buchholz, 2006, 2007; Henkens and Kalmijn, 2006).

In contrast, other societies have broadly rejected such early retirement measures, and have made it possible for older employees to adapt flexibly to the challenges of structural and technological change. Empirically, two strategies for the *employment maintenance* of older employees can be distinguished (Blossfeld, Buchholz and Hofäcker, 2006): Liberal states (Great Britain, United States) broadly follow a model of maintaining older employees through *market mechanisms*. The policy for adjusting older workers to new flexibility demands is to place broad trust in a flexible labor market and an only weakly standardized education and training system. Low mobility barriers on the labor market and a decentralized organization for acquiring relevant qualifications 'on-the-job' enable older employees to adapt flexibly to changing demands through labor market and job mobility. At the same time, low state pensions and a strong emphasis on private schemes based on capital investments or company pensions limit the possibilities of an early exit from employment. Older employees in the liberal states have correspondingly long employment careers and often retire comparatively late. Due to the residual policy approach and the trust in market mechanisms, however, the liberal system tends to strengthen social inequalities on the labor market, sometimes even beyond retirement age: Employees with meager financial resources often have to carry on working after retirement age, or they return to the labor market because they are unable to survive on their pensions alone (cf. Warner and Hofmeister, 2006).

In contrast, social-democratic states (Sweden, Norway, and Denmark) actively engage in supporting the ability of older employees to adapt to the flexibility demands due to globalization (i.e., by maintaining older employees through *state mechanisms*). An active labor market policy as well as state promotion of life-long learning and further vocational qualification help to keep them employable so that their employment careers are more continuous and stable. At the same time, pension systems with lower incentives for early retirement favor a long work career. Despite the recent introduction of some isolated early retirement options in response to growing unemployment rates, the labor market participation of older employees in these countries remains markedly higher than the international average (cf. Aakvik, Dahl and Vaage, 2006; Hofäcker and Leth-Sørensen, 2006; Sjögren Lindquist, 2006).

Summary

This chapter summarized the results of the GLOBALIFE project carried out from 1999 to 2006 at the Universities of Bielefeld and Bamberg and funded by the Volkswagen Foundation. The goal of the project was to perform an empirically based cross-national comparative analysis of the effects of globalization on labor market flexibilization in different countries that each have their own specific institutional contexts.

As the results of the GLOBALIFE project show, the globalization process has impacted very differently on these different phases of the life course. Qualified men in mid-career are broadly protected from the effects of globalization and their careers continue to be very stable in modern societies. Globalization thus has in no way led to the increase in the erosion of traditional standard male employment relationships or a massive spread of flexibilized 'patchwork careers', frequently postulated by individualization theorists. In contrast, young adults, women in mid-life, and people approaching retirement have had to accept a clear change in their life courses as a result of the globalization process, although the ways in which the life courses of these groups have changed vary greatly. In all, it can be seen that it is particularly young adults who can be described as the losers of the globalization process as their labor market situation has deteriorated profoundly in recent years and they see themselves confronted with fundamental uncertainties in working life.

Another central finding has been that the globalization process has *not* led to the same outcome in the various modern societies. Though life courses in modern societies have changed profoundly as a result of the globalization process in almost any country under study, the form and extent of these changes vary strongly and are shaped decisively by the given *configuration* of country-specific labor market structures, welfare states, and education systems. Hence, the results of the GLOBALIFE project explicitly contradict the frequent assumption in globalization research of a decline in the significance of national state regulations in the course of the globalization process leading to the *same* outcomes in different countries (Beck, 2000; Meyer, Ramirez and Soysal, 1992; Ohmae, 1990; Treiman and Yip, 1989). It is far more the case that the globalization process in different national contexts runs up against various firmly anchored institutional structures such as welfare state institutions, specific ways of regulating labor markets, or local norms and values. These national institutions filter the increasing uncertainty due to globalization in a *specific* way, thus leading to special forms of labor market flexibilization that, in turn, have shaped and changed the life courses and structures of social inequality in modern societies in very different ways. Globalization thus must be conceived right from the start as a contingent and pluralistic process in which the historically developed country-specific institutional and social structures have to be assigned a strong tendency to persist. The previous analyses for differential life phases have demonstrated vividly that these institutional systems and social structures of modern societies are interwoven arrangements with a high degree of internal complementarities which can only be grasped adequately in their *totality* as country-specific institutional *packages*.

Notes

1. The Research Network TransEurope, funded by the European Science Foundation (ESF) and comprising a total of seven different European countries, aims to advance further both the empirical measurement of globalization as well as the analysis of its consequences for individual life course patterns. For further information the reader is referred to the project's website: www.transeurope-project.org.
2. Data sets were chosen based on the proven expertise of national project collaborators. These selected experts in their field of research provided nation-specific country studies for any phase of the project and selected appropriate data sets for empirical analyses, given the overall design and specific research questions of the GLOBALIFE project. Given the need for longitudinal data to adequately capture the highly dynamic phenomenon of globalization and its life course consequences, on the one hand, and the present lack of a satisfying cross-national longitudinal data set covering the last two to three decades, on the other, this design appears to be most appropriate.
3. This was based on Esping-Andersen's (1990) regime classification, which is well established in comparative social research and distinguishes between liberal, social-democratic, and conservative welfare regimes. It was supplemented with the family-oriented regime covering not only the South-European countries, which Ferrera (1996) views as a distinct type of regime, but also Mexico and Ireland. What these family-oriented countries studied in the GLOBALIFE project have in common is that they aim to secure individual welfare by placing more trust in familial solidarity and networks than in universal state services. The post-socialist regime is a further extension to Esping-Andersen's classic welfare state typology. Although this regime is relatively heterogeneous, all these countries share the abrupt transition from a comparatively isolated, planned socialist economy to an open market economy exposed to the forces of globalization.

References

Aakvik, A., Dahl, S.-A. & Vaage, K. (2006). Late careers and career exits in Norway. In H.-P. Blossfeld, S. Buchholz, & D. Hofäcker (Eds), *Globalization, uncertainty and late careers in society*. London & New York: Routledge, pp. 235–254.

Alasuutari, P. (2000). Globalization and the nation-state: An appraisal of the discussion. *Acta Sociologica, 43*, 259–269.

Beck, U. (1992). *Risk Society*. London: Sage.

Beck, U. (2000). What is globalization? In D. Held, & A. McGrew (Eds), *The global transformations reader. An introduction to the globalization debate*. Cambridge: Polity Press, pp. 99–103.

Beckstette, W., Lucchini, M., & Schizzerotto, A. (2006). Men's late careers and career exits in Italy. In H.-P. Blossfeld, S. Buchholz, & D. Hofäcker (Eds), *Globalization, uncertainty and late careers in society*. London & New York: Routledge, pp. 101–118.

Berkowitz King, R. (2005). The case of American women. Globalization and the transition to adulthood in an individualistic regime. In H.-P. Blossfeld, E. Klijzing,

M. Mills, & K. Kurz (Eds), *Globalization, uncertainty and youth in society*. London & New York: Routledge, pp. 305–325.

Bernardi, F. & Nazio, T. (2005). Globalization and the transition to adulthood in Italy. In H.-P. Blossfeld, E. Klijzing, M. Mills, & K. Kurz (Eds), *Globalization, uncertainty and youth in society*. London & New York: Routledge, pp. 349–374.

Blossfeld, H.-P., Buchholz, S., & Hofäcker, D. (2006). *Globalization, uncertainty and late careers in society*. London & New York: Routledge.

Blossfeld, H.-P. & Drobnič, S. (2001). *Careers of couples in contemporary societies. From male breadwinner to dual-earner families*. Oxford: Oxford University Press.

Blossfeld, H.-P. & Hakim, C. (1997). *Between equalization and marginalization. Women working part-time in Europe and the United States of America*. New York and Oxford: Oxford University Press.

Blossfeld, H.-P. & Hofmeister, H. (2006). *Globalization, uncertainty and women's careers in international comparison*. Cheltenham, UK & Northampton, MA/USA: Edward Elgar.

Blossfeld, H.-P., Mills, M. Klijzing, E., & Kurz, K. (2005). *Globalization, uncertainty and youth in society*. London & New York: Routledge.

Blossfeld, H.-P., Mills, M., & Bernardi, F. (2006). *Globalization, uncertainty and men's careers in international comparison*. Cheltenham, UK & Northampton, MA/USA: Edward Elgar.

Breen, R. (1997). Risk, recommodification and stratification, *Sociology*, *31*(3): 473–49.

Breen, R. (2005). Explaining cross-national variation in youth unemployment. *European Sociological Review*, *21*, 125–134.

Buchholz, S. (2006). Men's late careers and career exits in West Germany. In H.-P. Blossfeld, S. Buchholz, and D. Hofäcker (Eds), *Globalization, uncertainty and late careers in society*. London & New York: Routledge, pp. 55–77.

Buchholz, S. (2007). *Beschäftigungsflexibilisierung in der Bundesrepublik Deutschland: Eine Flexibilisierung an den Rändern. Eine Analyse von Erwerbseinstiegs- und Erwerbsausstiegsprozessen in Ost und West*. Dissertation Bamberg: Otto-Friedrich-University.

Buchholz, S. (2008). *Die Flexibilisierung des Erwerbsverlaufs. Eine Analyse von Einstiegs- und Ausstiegsprozessen in Ost- und Westdeutschland*. Wiesbaden: VS Verlag für Sozialwissenschaften.

Buchholz, S. & Grunow, D. (2006). Women's employment in West Germany. In H.-P. Blossfeld, & H. Hofmeister (Eds), *Globalization, uncertainty and women's careers. An international comparison*. Cheltenham, UK & Northampton, MA/USA: Edward Elgar, pp. 61–83.

Buchholz, S., Hofäcker, D. & Blossfeld, H.-P. (2006). Globalization, accelerating economic change and late careers. A theoretical framework. In H.-P. Blossfeld, S. Buchholz, & D. Hofäcker (Eds), *Globalization, uncertainty and late careers in society*. London & New York: Routledge, pp. 1–23.

Bukodi, E. & Róbert, P. (2006). Women's career mobility in Hungary. In H.-P. Blossfeld, and H. Hofmeister (Eds), *Globalization, uncertainty and women's careers. An international comparison*. Cheltenham, UK & Northampton, MA/USA: Edward Elgar, pp. 171–198.

Bygren, M., Duvander, A.-Z., & Hultin, M. (2005). Elements of uncertainty in life courses. Transitions to adulthood in Sweden. In H.-P. Blossfeld, E. Klijzing, M. Mills, and K. Kurz (Eds), *Globalization, uncertainty and youth in society*. London & New York: Routledge, pp. 135–158.

Castells, M. (2004). *Der Aufstieg der Netzwerkgesellschaft. Das Informationszeitalter.* Opladen: Leske + Budrich.

Dreher, A. (2006). *KOF Index of Globalization.* Zürich: Konjunkturforschungsstelle ETH Zürich.

DiPrete, T., de Graaf, P.M., Luijkx, R., Tåhlin, M. & Blossfeld, H.-P. (1997). Collectivist versus individualist mobility regimes? Structural change and job mobility in four countries. *American Journal of Sociology,* 103, 2, 318–358.

Esping-Andersen, G. (1990). *The three worlds of welfare capitalism.* Cambridge: Polity Press.

Esping-Andersen, G. (1993). Post-industrial class structures: An analytical framework. In G. Esping-Andersen (Ed.), *Changing classes.* London: Sage, 7–31.

Esping-Andersen, G. (1999). *Social foundations of postindustrial economies.* Oxford: Oxford University Press.

Ferrera, M. (1996). The 'Southern model' of welfare in social Europe. *Journal of European Social Policy,* 6, 17–37.

Flora, P. & Alber, J. (1981). Modernization, democratization and the development of welfare states in Western Europe. In P. Flora and A.J., Heidenheimer (Eds), *The development of welfare states in Europe and America.* New Brunswick and New Jersey: Transaction Books, pp. 37–80.

Francesconi, M. & Golsch, K. (2005). The process of globalization and transitions to adulthood in Britain. In H.-P. Blossfeld, E. Klijzing, M. Mills & K. Kurz (Eds), *Globalization, uncertainty and youth in society.* London & New York: Routledge, pp. 249–276.

Golsch, K. (2005) *The impact of labour market insecurity on the work and family life of men and women. A comparison of Germany, Great Britain and Spain.* Europäische Hochschulschriften, Reihe 22: Soziologie, Frankfurt am Main: Lang.

Grunow, D. (2006). *Convergence, persistence and diversity in male and female careers – does context matter in an era of globalization. A comparison of gendered employment mobility patterns in West Germany and Denmark.* Opladen: Barbara Budrich Publishers.

Grunow, D. & Leth-Sørensen, S. (2006). Danish women's unemployment, job mobility and non-employment, 1980s and 1990s: Marked by globalization? In H.-P. Blossfeld & H. Hofmeister (Eds), *Globalization, uncertainty and women's careers. An international comparison.* Cheltenham, UK & Northampton, MA/USA: Edward Elgar, pp. 142–167.

Hamplová, D. (2006). Women and the labor market in the Czech Republic: Transition from a socialist to a social-democratic regime? In H.-P. Blossfeld & H. Hofmeister (Eds), *Globalization, uncertainty and women's careers. An international comparison.* Cheltenham, UK & Northampton, MA/USA: Edward Elgar, pp. 224–246.

Held, D., McGrew, A., Goldblatt, D. & Perraton, J. (2000). Rethinking globalization. In D. Held & A. McGrew (Eds), *The global transformation reader. An introduction to the globalization debate.* Cambridge: Polity Press, pp. 99–104.

Helemäe, J. & Saar, E. (2006). Women's employment in Estonia. In H.-P. Blossfeld & H. Hofmeister (Eds), *Globalization, uncertainty and women's careers. An international comparison.* Cheltenham, UK & Northampton, MA/USA: Edward Elgar, pp. 199–223.

Henkens, K. & Kalmijn, M. (2006). Labor market exits of older men in the Netherlands. An analysis of survey data 1979–99. In H.-P. Blossfeld, S. Buchholz & D. Hofäcker (Eds), *Globalization, uncertainty and late careers in society.* London & New York: Routledge, pp. 79–99.

Hofäcker, D., Buchholz, S. & Blossfeld, H.-P. (2006). Late careers in a globalizing world. A comparison of changes in twelve modern societies. In H.-P. Blossfeld, S. Buchholz, & D. Hofäcker (Eds), *Globalization, uncertainty and late careers in society*. London & New York: Routledge, pp. 353–371.

Hofäcker, D. & Pollnerová, S. (2006). Late careers and career exits. An international comparison of trends and institutional background patterns. In H.-P. Blossfeld, S. Buchholz & D. Hofäcker (Eds), *Globalization, uncertainty and late careers in society*. London & New York: Routledge, pp. 25–53.

Hofäcker, D. & Leth-Sørensen, S. (2006). Late careers and career exits of older Danish workers. In H.-P. Blossfeld, S. Buchholz & D. Hofäcker (Eds), *Globalization, uncertainty and late careers in society*. London & New York: Routledge, pp. 255–278.

Hofmeister, H. (2006). Women's employment transitions and mobility in the United States: 1968 to 1991. In H.-P. Blossfeld & H. Hofmeister (Eds), *Globalization, uncertainty and women's careers. An international comparison*. Cheltenham, UK & Northampton, MA/USA: Edward Elgar, pp. 302–326.

Hofmeister, H. & Blossfeld, H.-P. (2006). Women's careers in an era of uncertainty: Conclusions from a 13-country international comparison. In H.-P. Blossfeld & H. Hofmeister (Eds), *Globalization, uncertainty and women's careers. An international comparison*. Cheltenham, UK & Northampton, MA/USA: Edward Elgar, pp. 433–450.

Hurrell, A. & Woods, N. (1995). Globalization and inequality, millennium. *Journal of International Studies*, 24, 3, 447–470.

Jurado Guerrero, T. (1995). Legitimation durch Sozialpolitik? Die spanische Beschäftigungskrise und die Theorie des Wohlfahrtstaates, *KZfSS*, 47, 727–752.

Kalmijn, M. & Luijkx, R. (2006). Changes in women's employment and occupational mobility in the Netherlands: 1995 to 2000. In H.-P. Blossfeld & H. Hofmeister (Eds), *Globalization, uncertainty and women's careers. An international comparison*. Cheltenham, UK & Northampton, MA/USA: Edward Elgar, pp. 84–112

Katus, K., Puur, A. & Sakkeus, L. (2005). Transition to adulthood in Estonia. Evidence from FFS. In H.-P. Blossfeld, E. Klijzing, M. Mills & K. Kurz (Eds), *Globalization, uncertainty and youth in society*. London & New York: Routledge, pp. 215–247.

Korpi, T. & Stern, C. (2006). Globalization, deindustrialization and the labor market experiences of Swedish women, 1950 to 2000. In H.-P. Blossfeld & H. Hofmeister (Eds), *Globalization, uncertainty and women's careers. An international comparison*. Cheltenham, UK & Northampton, MA/USA: Edward Elgar, pp. 115–141.

Kurz, K., Steinhage, N., & Golsch, K. (2005). Case study Germany: Global competition, uncertainty and the transition to adulthood. In H.-P. Blossfeld, E. Klijzing, M. Mills & K. Kurz (Eds), *Globalization, uncertainty and youth in society*. London & New York: Routledge, pp. 51–82.

Liefbroer, A.C. (2005). Transition from youth to adulthood in the Netherlands. In H.-P. Blossfeld, E. Klijzing, M. Mills & K. Kurz (Eds), *Globalization, uncertainty and youth in society*. London & New York: Routledge, pp. 83–103.

Mayer, K.-U. (2001). The paradox of global social change and national path dependencies: Life course patterns in advanced societies. In A. Woodward & M. Kohli (Eds), *Inclusions and exclusions in European societies*. New York: Routledge, pp. 89–110.

Meyer, J.W., Ramirez, F.O. & Soysal, Y.N. (1992). World expansion of mass education, 1970–1980. *Sociology of Education*, 65, 128–149.

Mills, M., & Blossfeld, H.-P. (2005). Globalization, uncertainty and the early e: course: A theoretical framework. In H.-P. Blossfeld, E. Klijzing, M. Mills & K. Kurz (Eds), *Globalization uncertainty and youth in society*. London/New York: Routledge Advances in Sociology Series, pp. 1–24.

Mills, M. & Blossfeld, H.-P. (2006). Globalization, patchwork careers and the individualization of inequality? A 12-country comparison of men's mid-career job mobility. In H.-P. Blossfeld, M. Mills & F. Bernardi (Eds), *Globalization, uncertainty and men's careers. An international comparison*. Cheltenham, UK & Northampton, MA/USA: Edward Elgar, pp. 467–492.

Mills, M., Blossfeld, H.-P. & Klijzing, E. (2005). Becoming an adult in uncertain times: A 14-country comparison of the losers of globalization. In H.-P. Blossfeld, E. Klijzing, M. Mills & K. Kurz (Eds), *Globalization, uncertainty and youth in society*. London/New York: Routledge Advances in Sociology Series, pp. 393–411.

Mills, M., Blossfeld, H.-P., and Bernardi, F. (2006). Globalization, uncertainty and men's employment careers. A theoretical framework. In H.-P. Blossfeld, M. Mills & F. Bernardi (Eds), *Globalization, uncertainty and men's careers. An international comparison*. Cheltenham, UK & Northampton, MA/USA: Edward Elgar, pp. 3–37.

Nazio, T. (2008). *Cohabitation, family and society*, New York (NY) and Abingdon (UK): Routledge.

Nazio, T. & Blossfeld, H.-P. (2003). The diffusion of cohabitation among young women in West Germany, East Germany, and Italy. *European Journal of Population*, 19, 47–82.

Nelson, R.R. (1995). Recent evolutionary theorizing about economic change. *Journal of Economic Literature*, 33, 48–90.

Nilsen, O.A. (2005). Transition to adulthood in Norway. In H.-P. Blossfeld, E. Klijzing, M. Mills & K. Kurz (Eds), *Globalization, uncertainty and youth in society*. London & New York: Routledge, pp. 159–176.

OECD (2006). *Ageing and employment policies: Live longer – work longer*. Paris: OECD.

Orloff, A. (1996). Gender and the welfare state, *Annual Review of Sociology*, 22: 51–78.

Ohmae, K. (1990). *The borderless world*. New York: Harper Business.

Pisati, M. & Schizzerotto, A. (2006). Mid-career women in contemporary Italy: Economic and institutional changes. In H.-P. Blossfeld and H. Hofmeister (Eds), *Globalization, uncertainty and women's careers. An international comparison*. Cheltenham, UK & Northampton, MA/USA: Edward Elgar, pp. 352–375.

Plomien, A. (2006). Women and the labor market in Poland: from socialism to capitalism. In H.-P. Blossfeld & H. Hofmeister (Eds), *Globalization, uncertainty and women's careers. An international comparison*. Cheltenham, UK & Northampton, MA/USA: Edward Elgar, pp. 247–271.

Raab, M., Ruland, M., Schönberger, B., Blossfeld, H.-P., Hofäcker, D., Buchholz, S. & Schmelzer, P. (2008). GlobalIndex – A sociological approach to globalization measurement. *International Sociology*, 23(4), 599–634.

Regini, M. (2000). Between deregulation and social pacts: The responses of European economies to globalization'. *Politics and Society*, 28(1), 5–33.

Róbert, P. & Bukodi, E. (2005). The effects of the globalization process in the transition to adulthood in Hungary. In H.-P. Blossfeld, E. Klijzing, M. Mills & K. Kurz (Eds), *Globalization, uncertainty and youth in society*. London & New York: Routledge, pp. 177–214.

Robertson, R. (1990). Mapping the global condition: Globalization as the central concept. *Theory, Culture & Society, 7*, 15–30.

Robertson, R. (1992). Globality, Global culture, and images of world order. In H. Haferkamp & N.J. Smelser (Eds), *Social change and modernity*. Berkeley: University of California Press, pp. 396–412.

Simó Noguera, C. (2006). Hard choices: Can Spanish women reconcile job and family? In H.-P. Blossfeld & H. Hofmeister (Eds), *Globalization, uncertainty and women's careers. An international comparison*. Cheltenham, UK & Northampton, MA/USA: Edward Elgar, pp. 376–401.

Simó Noguera, C., Castro Martin, T. & Soro Bonmati, A. (2005). The Spanish case. The effects of the globalization process on the transition to adulthood. In H.-P. Blossfeld, E. Klijzing, M. Mills & K. Kurz (Eds), *Globalization, uncertainty and youth in society*. London & New York: Routledge, pp. 375–402.

Sjögren Lindquist, G. (2006). Late careers and career exits in Sweden. In H.-P. Blossfeld, S. Buchholz & D. Hofäcker (Eds), *Globalization, uncertainty and late careers in society*. London & New York: Routledge, pp. 211–233.

Sørensen, A.B. (1983). The structure of allocation to open and closed positions in social structure. *Zeitschrift für Soziologie, 12*, 203–224.

Soskice, D. (1993). The institutional infrastructure for international competitiveness: a comparative analysis of the UK and Germany. In A.B. Atkinson & R. Brunetta (Eds), *The economics of the new Europe*. London: Macmillan, pp. 45–66.

Soskice, D. (1998). Divergent production regimes: Coordinated and uncoordinated market economies in the 1980s and 1990s. In H. Kitschelt, P. Lange, G. Marks & J. Stephens (Eds), *Continuity and change in contemporary capitalism*. Cambridge: Cambridge University Press, pp. 101–134.

Streeck, W. (1992). *Social institutions and economic performance. Studies in industrial relations in advanced capitalist economies*. London: Sage.

Sutcliffe, B. & Glyn, A. (1999). Still underwhelmed: Indicators of globalization and their misinterpretation. *Review of Radical Political Economics, 31*, 111–132.

Treiman, D.J. (1970). Industrialization and social stratification. In E.O. Laumann (Ed.), *Social stratification: research and theory for the 1970s*. Indianapolis: Bobbs Merrill, pp. 207–234.

Treiman, D.J. & Yip, K.-B. (1989). Educational and occupational attainment in 21 countries. In M.L. Kohn (Ed.), *Cross-national research in sociology*. Newbury Park (CA): Sage, pp. 373–394.

Warner, D. & Hofmeister, H. (2006). Late career transitions among men and women in the United States. In H.-P. Blossfeld, S. Buchholz & D. Hofäcker (Eds), *Globalization, uncertainty and late careers in society*. London & New York: Routledge, pp. 141–181.

5

DEMANDS OF SOCIAL CHANGE AND PSYCHOSOCIAL ADJUSTMENT: RESULTS FROM THE JENA STUDY

Rainer K. Silbereisen, Martin Pinquart, and *Martin J. Tomasik*

Psychological research on German unification and its psychosocial consequences was rather naive in the beginning in a methodological sense. Given the rapid change that seemed to affect one part of the country in collective, and left the other, Western part virtually unaffected, studies borrowed the cohort comparison model from sociology and compared same-aged samples from East and West at different time periods during the 1990s (e.g., Silbereisen, Reitzle, & Juang, 2002). With the overlay of the rapid structural changes by the gradual changes due to the world-wide challenges of globalization, however, it soon became clear that changes may take various directions. In psychological research on the consequences of the societal changes the notion then had flourished that many changes on the structural level qualify as stressors on the individual level, and thus can be analysed with relevant models on stress and coping. Only after some time, however, the huge variation in the degree to which individuals are actually exposed to changes became clear. Globalization targets individuals in a cascaded fashion, with various 'filters' between society and individuals (Hofäcker, Buchholz, & Blossfeld, Chapter 4 this volume). Change in international cooperation, for instance, will affect local labor markets, and the increased risk of lay-offs or loss of qualification do apply to novices in the labor market more than to those higher in seniority because of politically guaranteed, institutional protection. Moreover, the more gradual the changes on the societal level are, the more time individuals have to adapt. Consequently interindividual differences in resources and skills, generally speaking, become important.

Our own study on individuals' dealing with the stressors induced by social change had a model in life-course sociology and developmental psychology, namely Elder's landmark studies on the Great Depression (Elder, 1974), and studies led by Conger on the farm crisis in Iowa during the 1980s (Conger & Elder, 1994). In essence the authors and their colleagues assumed and confirmed that the consequences for well-being of negative economic changes on the societal level are due to how people deal with the everyday manifestations at their doorstep, so to speak. According to the model, the reduction of income due to a radical economic recession is perceived as a growing and threatening gap between what one was used to and what one can afford. This results in attempts to compensate for the mismatch by various helpful and often also inadequate means, such as cutbacks on even necessary expenditures for securing a family's functioning. The after-effects of these more or less successful adaptations for the parents' mood and the marital quality of the couple induce problem behaviours in the offspring – unless there are enough human and social resources that provide protection (Conger et al., 1992).

Coping with societal challenges

We (Pinquart & Silbereisen, 2004) used this approach as a starting point to develop our own model of how individuals cope with social change, thereby utilizing ideas from various other research fields that address more specifically the kind of responses possible. As opposed to previous research (e.g., Elder, 1974; Conger & Elder, 1994), however, we were interested in a broad portfolio of current social changes. Consequently we needed a more generic approach to how people deal with the many challenges on the societal level that could be equally applied to various issues that require readjustment.

The starting point of any individual response is the everyday manifestations of the societal challenges. What are the characteristics of the transformation period since about the late 1990s in Germany (for details and references of the following figures see Silbereisen et al., 2006)? Various changes are rooted in globalization and, related to that, an enormous spread of information technologies. On the individual level these trends primarily concern the world of work. Information technologies became ubiquitous, indicated by a radical increase of computers and internet connections in private households to meanwhile 63.0 per cent and 47.1 per cent in 2004, almost two times and six times greater, respectively, compared to 1998. Consequently, the need for renewing one's qualification and accepting work below one's original training and expertise increased. At the same time the unemployment rate increased from 4.9 per cent in 1991 to 9.1 per cent in 2005, and this average camouflaged the fact that the rates in the East were twice as high as those in the West. Parallel to this the number of employees working part-time increased from 5.8 million in 1991 to 7.2 million in 2004, and the transition from school to training and work became more precarious. Globalization and the opening of European boarders also resulted in the fact that meanwhile about one-fifth of the German population have a personal history of migration, which increased the need to deal with cultural variation in everyday life. Particularly in the Eastern part of the country such changes increased feelings of insecurity, and the intergenerational nexus concerning experiences with work and planning for career was interrupted.

The second major characteristic is individualization and increased plurality of the life course. The standard biographical sequence of the past, from education and training to permanent employment, followed by family formation, no longer applies in general. In the domain of work, people are forced to change their job more often. For instance, the number of employees who changed their job within one year was raised by about 30 per cent between 1992 and 2002. In the domain of family, the figures of informal cohabitations increased and those of marriages decreased. In the cohort of those born between 1968 and 1982, 38 per cent lived single in 2000, up from 21 per cent of those born between 1944 and 1957. The divorce rates almost doubled over the last 15 years such that one-third of marriages are estimated to end in divorce, and related to that the share of single parents also increased. In a nutshell, the family has increasingly been deinstitutionalized so that people had fewer successful role models, and important decisions have to be settled without a partner.

In sum, the challenges on the societal level require, in their everyday manifestation, dealing with insecurities one was not accustomed to, and learning new skills in order to negotiate the developmental tasks of adulthood in work, family, and public life. How people deal with such challenges on the individual level was formulated in our model of coping with social change (Pinquart & Silbereisen, 2004). Its basic structure is shown in Figure 5.1.

The model builds on research in the stress and coping tradition, but it is more specific in at least three aspects. First, we see all the processes and outcomes embedded and influenced by the various developmental contexts Bronfenbrenner (1979) distinguished. They carry the changes from the societal level over to the individual. Changes of the social and political order in its most abstract sense concern the macro-system with its characteristic belief systems. However, they are manifested in institutions that address more specific issues with more specific measures, such as the organization of education, training, and work. These contexts have a more or less direct influence on the family, the most central micro-context for psychosocial adjustment and development of a person, and structural changes on the

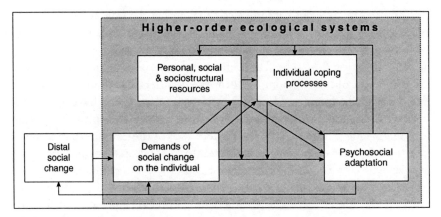

Figure 5.1 Model of coping with social change (adopted from Pinquart & Silbereisen, 2004).

higher levels will be experienced here as an imposed change of aims and behaviours to pursue them. Against the scenario of a cascade of changes on the contexts and their dynamics, our model presumes that how individuals cope with the demands and to what end is a function of the interplay of opportunities and constraints evolving from the contexts on the various levels. Although we will become more specific on this issue when presenting our results on the moderating effects of the local context at the end of this chapter, it is important to mention upfront that the social, economic and cultural contexts can be considered moderators of the impact of demands on the outcomes, thus influencing the relationships between the different constructs in the model.

Second, the demands as such are characteristic of the model. In principle they represent the new claims or opportunities for negotiating one's life tasks given the changes on the societal level and their manifestations in contexts. Depending on circumstances, individuals may appraise them as threats or challenges, and may believe that they have the resources and action potentials necessary to respond or not (Pinquart & Silbereisen, 2004; Lazarus & Folkman, 1984). We primarily referred to threats rooted in growing insecurities concerning the resolving of typical biographical tasks in adulthood, and we assess them in the mode of retrospective temporal comparisons over a period of time deemed significant.

Third, we assumed that the outcomes of being confronted with social change are manifold. In principle all aspects of successful development during adulthood are compatible with the model, such as developing competencies and forming an identity based on achievements in the major domains of life, enjoying psychological well-being, and also becoming a citizen contributing to the common good (Silbereisen et al., 2006). Of particular interest was civic engagement because some believe that this behaviour may be an answer to the growing number of people who are no longer needed in ordinary jobs (see Erlinghagen, 2000).

The specific features of our model concerning the interplay between demands and psychosocial outcomes are the coping processes on the one hand, and the resources on the other. As shown by the pattern of arrows in Figure 5.1, in both cases we assumed three principle ways of influence, namely, a direct effect on the outcomes, a buffering effect on the demands, and a mediating effect by which demands and outcomes are connected via coping and resources, respectively. The direct effect of demands refers to influences that are not buffered by the coping strategies or resources particularly addressed. A moderating effect reduces the salience of the demands focused and thus protects the individual from the negative outcome. Mediation means that particular modes of coping are provoked by the demands, and once utilized allow a more or less adequate dealing with the demands.

We presume the same pattern of effects to apply to the personal and social resources. Personal resources entail various forms of financial and human capital, from education to particular competences and capabilities, like problem-solving skills, self-efficacy, and optimism. People who were particularly stressed after German unification due to their closeness to the forgone political system in East Germany fared better if they had shown higher self-efficacy in the past, before the political changes took place (Pinquart, Juang, & Silbereisen, 2004). Similarly, a study in Russia also revealed associations between higher self-efficacy and lower perceived affectedness by social change (Shteyn, Schumm, Vodopianova, Hobfoll, & Lilly, 2003).

The model further presumes that the psychosocial outcomes themselves have consequences on all other components. Thus, success or failure in dealing with demands may strengthen or weaken the resources and may influence the ways of coping that people choose in the future. Furthermore, the demands themselves and the societal challenges that gave rise to them may be changed in the long run as well. Concerning the latter, there is a group of potential psychosocial outcomes such as civic engagement or political participation that might be especially relevant for feedback effects on the societal challenges themselves.

Work and family demands

Obviously what we call the demands of social change on the individual level are the core of the link between macro and micro according to the model. Against the backdrop of official statistical indicators of globalization and individualization, and informed by a series of informal interviews and structured pre-tests, we developed a set of measures with the aim of catching representative everyday manifestations of the societal challenges described (Silbereisen et al., 2006). Early on a decision was made to assess these stressors in the particular mode of subjective temporal comparisons, thereby comparing the person's current circumstances with the state of affairs a few years ago. Thus, the focus of interest was on the perceived self-referred change over this period of time, in particular issues reminiscent of the broader societal changes in Germany. These assessments represent the demands that provide the base for individuals' dealings with the challenges on the structural level.

Assessment of demands

Given the fact that a multi-theme survey as planned did not allow lengthy assessments, we had to limit ourselves to six issues per domain (work, family, public life) that were formulated in a closed format. Thus, the mode of assessment was to provide the participants with a statement addressing change over the last five years, and then to ask them for their endorsement, expressed on a scale from 1 (does not apply at all) to 7 (fully applies). An example is 'When considering the past five years, it has become more difficult to plan my career path.' The presumed pace of the change was not assessed as such, but was built into the statement. The 'quantifier' used was based on the information from the literature and population statistics that led to the choice of the topic, and also was found in several pretests as adequately representing the severity of the topic. The idea was to address issues and find formulations that would apply to a considerable portion of the population in the age range between 16 and 43 years, irrespective of age and gender.

More specifically, concerning the domain of work we formulated two statements describing difficulties and insecurities in career planning (the one mentioned is an example), two concerning potential job loss, and one each with regard to changes in work arrangements, that is, full-time versus part-time work, and working below one's actual qualification. As the situation for those out of work differs somewhat in the issues addressed compared to those who are employed, the formulation for the statements was slightly different dependent on the status. The domain of family was covered in a similar way by six statements. Two concerned the stability of intimate relationships – 'When considering the past five years, it is now more likely that my partner could leave me' is an example. Moreover, two statements were used to tap into the difficulties of finding direction and independence in one's life. One refers to ambivalence about having a child, and one addresses the possibility that one may stay or become financially dependent on one's parents. The domain of public life also addressed six statements that referred to issues such as trust in social institutions and cultural diversity. As our

Table 5.1 Means and standard deviations of the endorsement of demands

Demands: When considering the past five years	M	(SD)
… it has become more difficult to plan my career path.	4.15	(2.15)
… today I have to be prepared more for the possibility of reluctantly only working part-time instead of full-time.	4.43	(2.24)
… the risk of losing my job has increased.	4.84	(2.12)
… my career plans were more often hindered by unforeseen events and circumstances.	4.39	(2.02)
… it is now more likely that I will be forced to accept a job requiring lower qualifications than those I have.	4.59	(2.12)
… there are currently fewer job opportunities for me.	5.15	(2.02)
… I now have to take more things into account when it comes to decisions concerning the relationship with my partner or family.	4.72	(2.06)
… it is more difficult to decide, given my present life circumstances, whether I want to have a(nother) child or not.	4.47	(2.32)
… the knowledge and experiences of my parents now provide less sense of direction in my life.	3.84	(1.91)
… it is more likely that I now have to reckon with being or once again becoming financially long-term dependent on my parents.	2.57	(1.93)
… my personal contacts are now less reliable.	3.24	(1.87)
… it is now more likely that my partner could leave me.	3.26	(2.11)

Note: $N = 2{,}154$.

first analyses showed that this domain was hardly associated with measures of subjective well-being, it is left out in the following. Table 5.1 lists the wording of all demand statements together with their mean endorsement in our sample.

As can be seen from the topics, the demands concern structural claims affecting individuals' chances to fulfill the age-typical developmental tasks in work and family, or more specifically, obstacles against being able to live up to the expectations held for a productive worker and caring partner. The fact that the statements were formulated against the backdrop of the objective figures concerning societal processes is not to say that there is a one-to-one relationship. Whether we indeed find a difference between East and West in the temporal comparisons and of which size is an empirical question. In order to provide or actually endorse such a direct change estimate, people obviously need a memory of the past state of affairs. But due to the salience of such experiences and because we avoided asking for evaluative judgments, the biographical memory should suffice (Rutter,

Maughan, Pickles, & Simonoff, 1998). But beyond that the demands as assessed in this study obviously entail a personal element of biographical construction and self-reference (Foster & Caplan, 1994), and we believe that this is of interest in itself.

The data were gathered as part of the Jena Study on Social Change and Human Development (Silbereisen et al., 2006), a study embedded in the interdisciplinary research consortium SFB 580 funded by the German Science Foundation. Respondents were drawn from four federal States of Germany. Within each region, one state stood for a relatively prospering economy (East: Thuringia, West: Baden-Württemberg), and one for a relatively precarious economy (East: Mecklenburg-Western Pomerania, West: Schleswig-Holstein), as indicated by a selection of major economic and social indicators of productivity and employment. Within each state, smaller regional districts (*Landkreise* and *kreisfreie Städte*) were chosen and within each district sampling points were selected at random from the ADM register which is representative for the German household population aged 14 and older (von der Heyde & Loeffler, 1993). Trained personnel of a professional survey institute conducted face-to-face interviews, based on a random route procedure (77 per cent response rate). The sample used for the current analyses (excluding participants still in education) comprised 2,154 German adolescents and adults aged 16 to 42 years. The share of males (44 per cent) and females was almost alike, and due to the sampling design the share of the federal states was about one-fourth of the entire sample.

Differences between regions and status in work and family

In the following and actually for all analyses thus far, we used a measure of cumulated demand load, assessed as a sum of all endorsements per domain that entailed the extreme ratings of 6 or 7. Thus, participants' scores were the number of strongly endorsed statements. We found this kind of assessment particularly fitting to the general notion of dealing with stress. A few mild stressors can be coped with rather easily, whereas when it comes to a pressing load the potentials and resources for adjustment are overtaxed and result in the kind of negative effects for psychosocial adjustment we have in mind (e.g., Sameroff, 2000). The average load scores for the domain of work were 2.4 highly endorsed demands, and for the domain of family 1.5.

We expected that the demand load reported in the East is higher than that in the West. The post-transformation period meant that the consequences of unification-related challenges, such as the much higher unemployment rates in the East, were aggravated by the challenges from globalization, resulting in lasting structural changes in the various sectors of employment, and this should be revealed in a higher demand load. Following the notion of the micro-contexts of work and family as 'filters' or protective shields (Hofäcker et al., Chapter 4 this volume), we further expected differences as a function of the status in these two domains. More specifically, we expected those who are not in work to experience a higher demand load, due to their lower legal protection and acquired privileges, and those not married also to experience a higher demand load, due to the lack of support and buffer against strains from work.

The data were analysed (see Tomasik & Silbereisen, 2009) using a linear regression model, with the cumulated demand load as the dependent variable, and conducted separately for the domains of work and family. In line with how the demand statements were conceived, we indeed found virtually no differences as a function of age and gender in the first step of the analyses, and what little there vanished once the other predictors were included. Table 5.2 shows the results of the second step of the analyses; target variables are the load of demands in the domains of work and family, respectively.

As can be seen, the political regions differed as expected in both domains. Those living in the East experienced on average about three-quarters of a demand in work, and about one-half of a demand in family more than those in the West. Concerning the employment status, compared to those in work both being unemployed or otherwise outside the labor market corresponded to a higher demand load as expected. Being unemployed corresponded to

Table 5.2 General linear model for the prediction of demand load in work and family (Step 2)

Variable	Work B (SE_B)	Family B (SE_B)
(Intercept)	1.85 (.30)***	1.44 (.22)***
Age	.00 (.01)	−.01 (.01)
Gender[1]	.02 (.09)	.04 (.07)
Region[2]	.72 (.09)***	.53 (.07)***
Employment status[3]		
unemployed	2.02 (.13)***	.34 (.10)***
outside labor market	.72 (.11)***	.22 (.08)**
Partnership status[4]		
Cohabitating	.14 (.13)	.09 (.09)
Single	.10 (.13)	−.05 (.09)
Divorced/separated/widowed	.49 (.15)***	.34 (.11)**
Education[5]	−.48 (.11)***	−.05 (.08)

Note: Unstandardized regression coefficients (B) together with the respective standard errors (SE_B) are presented; Work: $R^2 = .163$; $AIC = 9163$ Family: $R^2 = .052$ $AIC = 7795$; [1]Reference category: male; [2]Reference category: Western Germany; [3]Reference category: employed; [4]Reference category: married; [5]Reference category: no formal degree or basic schooling only. **$p < .01$; ***$p < .001$

two more highly endorsed demands in the domain of work, being otherwise outside the labor force to two-thirds of a demand. The difference between these two categories is that although both refer to groups of people who are not currently employed, the first group was actively searching for a job in the last four weeks and was willing to accept an offer in the next two weeks, whereas the latter group did not qualify in this regard. This distinction reflects the definition of unemployment as used by the International Labor Office (ILO). The effects of occupational status concerning the family domain were small (one-third of a demand and lower) compared to those on work. Concerning the partnership status, also as expected, being divorced, separated or widowed corresponded to about one-half (work) and one-third (family) higher cumulated demand load.

Beyond the hypotheses and results on the direct effects, we also expected that the filtering function of employment and relationship status would be moderated by the political region. Concerning the domain of work, one has to bear in mind that the pace and depth of structural change and challenges in the East since German unification was much faster and profound than what people in the West experienced. Living in the East meant coping with demands against a backdrop of much smaller cumulated financial assets that provide a major resource in dealing with post-transformation strains (Huster, 1997). Thus, we expected an aggravation of the negative effects of being out of employment in the East. Concerning the domain of family, in contrast, we expected an aggravation of the demand load in the West. Divorce and separation have been more normative in the East, and also the consequences were less severe (Böttcher, 2006), in part related to the higher labor force participation of women before unification. Although this has changed, the less traditional family values should have survived the times since then.

In order to test these hypotheses two-way interactions were added to the analyses reported thus far. In the work domain, both interactions with the region were significant. In line with expectations, those from the East outside the labor market reported about one-half more cumulated demands compared to the West, but this did not apply to the unemployed proper. Concerning partnership status, as expected those from the West divorced or separated reported almost one higher demand load. In the family domain, however, neither the role of employment status nor the role of relationship status was aggravated by the region.

In essence it was particularly the work-related demands of insecurities concerning career planning, potential job loss, and deficiencies of the job that clearly distinguished the ecological niches comprised of region, employment status, partnership status, education and their interplay. Compared to that, the insecurities regarding relationship stability, difficulties in finding directions in life, and ambivalence concerning having a child and remaining independent from one's parents were less pronounced, and possible consequences of work status and marital status were similar for people living in the West and in the East.

Biographical backdrop of demands

According to our model, the demands assessed represent the antecedents to the processes that result in the outcomes for psychosocial adaptation (Pinquart & Silbereisen, 2004; Silbereisen et al., 2006). They are, however, also related to biographical trajectories that may make individuals vulnerable to experiencing demands. Given this crucial role it is important to get some further insight into the life circumstances of people who were confronted with these demands. We want to do this by briefly presenting two different approaches. The first will show associations of recent demands with perceived career trajectories, the second illuminates precocious autonomy in adolescence as risk factor for the experience of demands.

The first insight into the subjective reality of the demands is whether they correspond to views people have of their own situation concerning work and family. We have data on perceived career histories, indicated by participants' endorsement of a set of icons that shows a range of prototypic trajectories one may have experienced since the first job (such as continuous or stepwise upward, continuous or stepwise downward, stability, and zigzag patterns; for details see Reitzle & Körner, 2008).

Given the multitude of societal changes addressed one could have imagined that traditional criteria of economic success and promotion in status would not correspond to the particular career history individuals identify. As Reitzle and Körner (2008) reported, the opposite was true and this was in line with other research showing that traditional criteria of career success, such as income and occupational status, remain important (Kuijpers, Schyns, & Scheerens, 2006). Those in employment endorsed stable or upwardly directed career histories more if they enjoyed higher or increasing incomes, were not struck by financial problems, had a higher occupational status, worked on open-ended contracts, and felt satisfied with the conditions and nature of their work. In contrast, those indicating unsteady or downward career histories via the icon chosen showed the opposite pattern.

Our actual interest, of course, refers to the role of the demands. Differences in the demand load turned out to be the best single characteristic describing a dimension from overall decline to stability and increase in the career history. The only exception was the unemployed in the East where work-related demands played no role, and instead personal resources, such as self-efficacy with regard to issues of social change, described the dimension distinguishing between the icons. This particularity of the unemployed in the

East is probably related to the fewer job opportunities and more wide-spread demands they have to face.

The demands people experience certainly are not only a reflection of regional opportunities and the status concerning employment and family as discussed thus far. Rather, they are probably also a function of people's psychosocial development in the past that makes them vulnerable to demands. Our second attempt refers to this, further illuminating what the demands possibly imply. In research published elsewhere, we (Haase, Tomasik & Silbereisen, 2009) showed that the cumulated demands were more pronounced among young adults who shared pre-existing personal vulnerabilities. We analysed samples of late adolescents (16 to 21 years) and young adults (25 to 30 years) who had experienced behavioural autonomy prematurely compared to the prevalent cultural standards, evidenced by that fact that they could come and go without parental consent at the age of 16 years or earlier (less than 20 per cent of the samples). Adolescents with premature curfew autonomy differed from their age mates in the earlier timing of some developmental transitions, such as the age at first sexual experiences, and they also revealed indications of less than optimal adjustment, such as lower planfulness and higher deviancy. But there were no differences concerning the educational level aspired for in late adolescence. The picture was different among the young adults where we found differences in the educational levels attained. More interesting were those with premature curfew autonomy who reported higher cumulated demands of social change in all three domains of life. Note that there was no difference in the employment and family status. Thus, at first glance, premature individuals appeared similarly adjusted compared to their normative peers with regard to work, family, and public life. However, they were more burdened by demands of social change within these domains.

As discussed by Haase et al. (2009), probably the premature freedoms and their consequences had distracted them from really pursuing their aspirations and investing in school and education. And consequently they lacked the crucial capitals that are known to help overcome challenges of social change that otherwise would hurt (Pinquart et al., 2004; Shteyn et al., 2003).

Dealing with the demands

In order to assess how people deal with all these demands, we chose the life-span theory of control as formulated by Heckhausen and Schulz (1995). The authors differentiate between adaptive reactions that are targeted at the external world, such as the circumstances resulting in higher difficulties in career planning, called primary control, and adaptive reactions that are directed towards the self, such as attempts to assemble one's motivational energy in finding a solution, called secondary control. Both strategies come in two variants of functionality. Either individuals are selecting among various options for action, or they have to compensate for foreclosed options or insufficient personal resources. The four different modes of adaptive reactions are described with reference to the demands of social change in question.

Selective primary control concerns investments of personal resources (ability, time, affect) in order to resolve a demand or remove difficulties in achieving a satisfying solution. Thus, people challenged by difficulties in their career could actively search for opportunities to increase their qualification, and towards that end accept long days filled with even more duties. All such activities require motivation and will power in order not to give in during the course of dealing with the new claims and the effort it takes, and this is addressed as selective secondary control. In this mode individuals may empower themselves by envisioning the positive consequences of their action, be it a better job or a more satisfying relationship, they may increase the personal salience of overcoming the claims, and also actively avoid any interferences and distractions by other issues. If the demands cannot be coped with in a satisfying fashion, compensatory primary control comes in, meaning that people expand their potentials for resolving the demands by seeking social support in their network.

All three strategies mentioned thus far concern goal engagement (Heckhausen, 2005; Tomasik & Pinquart, 2008), that is, resolving the demands in work and family remained in the focus and the circumstances of the negative changes perceived were pursued. But obviously positive adaptation is not possible for all issues, and consequently the fourth mode addresses failure and how individuals can protect themselves from the negative after-effects. This compensatory secondary control also comes in many ways, and we (Tomasik & Pinquart, 2008) particularly referred to two options. One is to preserve the motivational potentials for future action, rather than to deplete them in fruitless efforts prone to fail. The other is to reduce the costs of disengagement by devaluing the personal significance of the demand. Such activities sound like having a defensive undertone, but if opportunities are really lacking, this way of action is probably better than sticking to a mission that cannot be achieved.

Given the fact that the demand load in the East was higher than that reported in the West, Tomasik and Pinquart (2008) expected that the control strategies would also reveal similar differences between the regions. This was the case for selective primary control and compensatory primary control. Participants from the East in particular endorsed reactions which implied the utilization of social support more than those from the West, but in terms of actively pursuing the demands there was also a difference in the expected direction. Thus, against some public prejudice, but consistent with our theoretical concept, those more under pressure of demands seemingly resorted to proactive attempts at resolving the situation. Note that this effect was independent from other conditions, such as employment status and education that also played a role as expected. More specifically, and again for the domain of work and family alike, those in employment endorsed both forms of selective control more than those out of work, and concerning the distancing from a failed resolution of demands, unemployed participants and those low in education were more in agreement to downgrade the salience for their life. The effects just described remained basically the same when controlled for overlap by multivariate analyses.

After having discussed the demands and how people deal with them, we now turn to the issue of psychosocial outcomes addressed in the model. Within the scope of this chapter, we only can focus on two outcomes we deem particularly relevant. The one is civic engagement, the other one subjective well-being.

Demands and civic engagement

Given the recent challenges particularly concerning the labor market, some scholars believe that an alternative to traditional gainful employment may be other forms of activities, such as working in social projects to the advantage of the community with a modest financial compensation (see Erlinghagen, 2000). Against this backdrop, we (Silbereisen, Tomasik, & Grümer, 2008) wanted to test whether the experience of the demands related to social change would relate to higher civic engagement. Although one could assume that the perception of the pressures we deal with alerts to the structural causes and thereby provokes teaming up with others for a change, the opposite expectation is actually more plausible. Being confronted with claims in salient developmental tasks requires focusing on these issues, and this should mean that people retreat from activities that are not directly related to this aim. Beyond the negative relationship between the demands and civic engagement, we also predicted that goal engagement modes of dealing with the demands are irrelevant. Attempts at overcoming the particular demands in this way are probably incompatible with engagement for other purposes. Disengagement concerning the demands in work and family, however, may be related to getting involved in alternative social activities, the reason being that this could represent a sphere of life to turn to if one sees no hope concerning the jeopardized career issues or the overwhelming claims concerning partnerships.

The multinomial logistic regression model used in analysing the data included sociodemographic variables, demands, control strategies, personal and social resources that are also well-known to support civic engagement, and a list of life goals. As dependent variables, we defined four distinct groups of civic engagement. Civic engagement in the strict sense corresponded to people who had volunteered to improve the fate of others over the last year, and had achieved this while being actively involved in an association, church, or initiative (13 per cent of the sample). Beyond those who reported neither (57 per cent), there was the case of being involved in an organization only (24 per cent), and volunteering only (6 per cent). In the following we concentrate on the volunteering plus organization.

The most noteworthy result was that only the work demands played a role at all. Although the association was negative as expected, the effect size was very small. Much more relevant were the personal and social resources, whereas the control strategies were not significant. Finally, those who revealed interest in politics, endorsed as important life goals of achieving social status and enjoying a large social network, and discounted high income and an exciting life as unimportant, revealed a higher likelihood of belonging to the organized volunteers rather than to the inactive group. Once all variables were utilized in the hierarchical multinomial regression, the negative effect of the work-related demands was no longer significant, although the size of the coefficient had not changed much.

In contrast to the above, the disengagement mode was relevant among those who had joined an organization without an emphasis on volunteering. Thus, being involved with other activities outside one's core responsibilities for work and family may indeed serve as a substitute for issues too difficult to resolve in these fields. Whatever the type of civic engagement people chose, it was interesting to see that goals related to self-improvement did not play a role. Thus it seems that these activities are pursued as an expansion of personal strengths, not as compensation for opportunities one has missed. In this regard it is noteworthy that parenthood belonged to the strongest predictors of volunteering plus organization.

In the remainder we report evidence that a higher load of work-related demands corresponds to lower well-being, but that in line with our model this relationship seemed further influenced by how people dealt with the situation, and whether they lived in a context that was more or less affected by negative consequences of social change in Germany.

Demands and well-being: Contextual moderation

The demands imply growing uncertainties, and their negative effects on well-being broadly speaking are to be expected (Greco & Roger, 2003). If we are able to show a connection between well-being and stressors we have conceived for social change, this represents a corroboration of the general approach. Given our general interest in the two political regions with their differences in opportunities and constraints, the contextual dimension of the model can also be addressed.

Well-being is one aspect in a broader concept of the subjective quality of life, and we (Grümer & Pinquart, 2008) were interested in whether the experience of high demand loads would be reflected in a lower well-being, as indicated by the experience of positive affects over the last month, and the satisfaction with work, family, leisure, and finances. The results showed lower well-being with higher loads in work-related demands. Furthermore, we also found better well-being among those with higher social support and more personal resources, a variable comprised of optimism, self-efficacy related to social change, and curiosity. Interestingly enough, the family-related demands did not play a role, and the expected moderation of the demands by the resources was only relevant for work-related demand loads and social resources. Thus, the overall negative association between work demands and well-being was obviously in part due to those who had few social supports. Put differently, when faced with growing problems and insecurities in the domain of work, it helps if one can rely on others who offer encouragement, and also get engaged in practical help. This is in line with other research (Cohen, Hettler, & Park, 1997) and the results taken together underscore that the demands, particularly in the work domain, address stressors that require a response.

Moderating effects of contexts

The analyses and results reported thus far do not address the most crucial facet of our model. We presumed that the relationship between demands, coping, and outcomes would be conditioned by the contexts and their dynamic. The Jena Study allowed getting closer to the immediately surrounding ecology by the features of the design that allowed comparing individuals due to the 77 regional districts covered by the sample.

We (Pinquart, Silbereisen, & Körner, 2008) assessed the regional units in terms of their economic situation and their family friendliness. Concerning the economics, the indicators chosen were drawn from public statistics, such as the average salary level and the gross domestic product per employee, a proxy for the standard of living in the region, the unemployment rate, and the welfare rate. For the family friendliness indicators were used addressing the compatibility between family and work and the welfare condition of young people.

The first results showed some differences between the regional units in the levels of the demand load, the control strategies, and well-being. Well-being was indexed by the frequency of ten positive effects during the last month. Lower levels on the gross domestic product per employee and the income level as the economic indicator at the regional level corresponded to higher demand loads in work and family, and higher levels of engaging control strategies at the individual level. But the level of well-being was not different between the administrative regions, a somewhat surprising result that can be understood by the moderating effects reported below. Given the fact that the work-related demands were confined to those in employment, it is probable that the demands were rooted in economic circumstances that corresponded to relatively lower wages and lower productivity. The other aspect of the regional economy, covering unemployment and social welfare, however, was related to the family demands, probably indicating insecurities originating in the compatibility between work and family. The family friendliness index, however, revealed only few differences in the levels of the individual variables mentioned.

In hindsight the context indicators chosen were highly complex, and this implied difficulties in interpreting their moderating role on the relationships between demands, coping, and well-being. Consequently, in a more refined analysis we (Pinquart, Silbereisen, & Körner, 2009) concentrated on the role of unemployment/welfare in the region and the demands related to work among employed people between 16 and 42 years of age, utilizing a complex hierarchical modeling approach.

The individual level associations between the variables were according to the conceptual model as expected (Pinquart & Silbereisen, 2004; Silbereisen et al., 2006). Higher demand loads corresponded to lower well-being, as did higher goal engagement and lower goal disengagement. Thus, participants had experienced a positive effect on fewer occasions over the recent month if things became worse concerning work and career over a period of the last five years. Actually we had also expected buffering effects of goal engagement such that the negative effects of the demands on well-being would be lowered. That this was not the case may be due to the general difficulty of finding interaction effects in unselected samples because the relevant cases are rare (Cohen, Cohen, West, & Aiken, 2003).

The core of the analyses concerned the conditioning of these associations by the regional variation in economic prosperity. The psychological rationale behind this assumption is that people are aware of the situation indexed by the regional rates of unemployment and welfare even if they are not affected themselves. They are aware, first, because of the public discourse over the facts as such and their likely causes related to social change. And they are aware of the situation, second, because they observe manifestations, such as neighbors who are unemployed because of changes in the local labor market that discounts their qualification, or who receive welfare because they cannot cope with the increased competitiveness.

Living in economically disadvantaged vicinities implies that there are many people around who are affected by the same work-related demands such as unemployment or career uncertainty. Against all naive expectations, the personal experience of demands under these circumstances may become less relevant for psychological well-being compared to more prosperous ones. Individuals may laterally compare themselves to the reference group of others in a similar situation, and consequently discount the demands as relatively normative (e.g., Schieman, Pearlin, & Meersman, 2006). Beyond that and perhaps more importantly, the demand load may be attributed to the structural constraints rather than personal misdeeds, thereby limiting its effect on well-being. In line with such a view, Clark (2003) found that unemployed men showed better mental health if the unemployment rate was higher in the region. Similar results were recently reported by Eggers, Gaddy, and Graham (2006).

Our results show that the negative relationship between demands and well-being found on the individual level becomes less negative, or more positive so to speak, for people living in regions characterized by higher levels of unemployment and welfare payments. This effect is indicated by a positive cross-level interaction coefficient. Its meaning can be exemplified by comparing particular regions at the opposite ends of the economy continuum. In a region in a well-off state in the West, traditionally characterized by many privately owned small businesses and a high share of home owners, the relationship is negative and significant, whereas in an economically challenged area in a federal state in the East, characterized by deindustrialization and high levels of unemployment, it was not significantly different from zero.

Concerning the association between goal engagement and well-being, the idea was that to live in economically better-off administrative units would offer more opportunities in general, and in particular positive role models of how to master job-related difficulties would be more visible. The results confirmed the prediction. The positive relationship found for the individual was stronger in more affluent regions. Against our expectations the relationship between disengagement and well-being, however, did not vary by the region. This could mean that even bad circumstances in the region as assessed do not convey the visible evidence that giving in to the new claims is a viable option.

According to our model, how people deal with the demands has the potential to buffer the effects on well-being. Although we did not find such an overall effect on the individual level, the situation with regard to the level of regional units is probably different. The variation in the economic prosperity is large by design, and this should entail better opportunities for gaining from adequate adaptive activities. Consequently we expected that the buffering effect of goal engagement would be found when living in economically more prosperous regions. Concerning disengagement strategies, we presumed that in economically weak regions giving in and looking for alternatives would buffer the effects of the demands on well-being. Whereas goal engagement revealed no buffering effect, the interaction concerning disengagement was significant as expected. Higher levels of endorsed demands were no longer associated with impaired subjective well-being if individuals used high levels of distancing from these demands and at the same time lived in regions with high levels of unemployment and poverty.

Limitations and outlook

For this chapter we chose affective and cognitive aspects of well-being not only as convenient indicators of psychological adjustment, but also as a potent trigger to future success in the spheres of work and family. This is particularly relevant in times of social change when people have to make long-ranging decisions concerning their future life trajectories in order to succeed. Other variables were addressed only in passing, such as the resources. It would be particularly interesting to see whether the known role of self-efficacy and social support (e.g., Pinquart et al., 2004) on the individual level would be augmented or diminished by variation across the regional units. The indicators of prosperity we chose may also be a proxy for differences in the accessibility of support beyond people's immediate circle, or differences in the collective efficacy of the residents.

The individual level data were exclusively self-reports throughout the Jena Study. For instance, we had no independent evidence for the changes in work demands as reported by others, such as people familiar with their economic plight, or objective data on the economic situation in their firm or profession. Nonetheless, the differences in reported demands were reflected in the objective measures of regional conditions.

As the demands are the focal variable in our approach, some additional thoughts are in order. We assessed them as retrospective temporal comparisons that address negatively connotated claims from insecurities concerning the fulfillment of age-typical expectations in the domains of work and family. As assessed they are obviously not equivalent to computed change scores from a baseline, and consequently, with the current data, we cannot distinguish between increasing insecurity from a comfortable level, versus a change that is devastating given the already negative state of affairs at the outset. But in conjunction with our demand load index, we believe that the accumulation of strong endorsements of negatively connotated changes taps into the severity of the experiences. Individuals in general attempt to maintain or improve their self-image (Keyes, 2006), and consequently perceive negative self-referential changes as a threat. This means that the endorsement of the temporal comparisons given to the participants may tend to underestimate the actual changes experienced. As this would not work in favor of our hypotheses, such a conservative bias could be tolerated.

The results refer to samples of adults between their twenties and forties, gathered around 2005 in the East and West of Germany in a particular historical situation, and this historical context is probably unique for Germany. Nevertheless, in other transformation societies of the former Eastern Bloc many people may be confronted with similar demands. The aim of our beginning collaboration with Polish researchers is to compare the demands and their role between the two countries. Generally, we expect corresponding psychological ramifications of demands in the two countries (see Kohn, 1987). The role of particular ecological niches as studied here may be different though. For instance, the strong family supports typical of the Polish context may reduce the cross-over effects between work and family that we found.

Another comparative dimension we want to utilize is that of life-span. The current research addressed a period of the life-span not characterized by many normative changes as is common for childhood and adolescence. Rather, change in psychosocial adaptations originates from differences in dealing with life tasks, such as those involved in work and family. Differences as a function of chronological age were not expected and were, indeed, on average, not found. In older age-groups this may be different, and thus a study is planned for people in the age-range of 55 to 75 years. The content of the demands may differ, their changeability and also the contextual affordances, but otherwise we would expect similar processes to take place.

The results on the interplay between contexts and individuals coping with demands of social change probably have consequences for intervention. Strengthening a habit to attempt coping in the mode of goal engagement only makes sense if the context becomes enriched in opportunities at the same time. Somewhat ironically, but following our results, those who have been facing high demands in an affluent environment would probably be worse off in psychological well-being than others. They would see the opportunities for others but could not get solace from comparing themselves with others who suffer more, and also would have difficulties in attributing the situation to external circumstances. Only improving adaptive behaviours would certainly not be enough, and consequently a program in the making for school leavers of vocational tracks should address broader issues of exploration of opportunities, pursuing goals, and implementing the results.

Beyond all limitations and questions still to be resolved, our research confirmed that studying the challenges of current social change by utilizing a modified stress and coping paradigm provides new insights in how adults deal with the demands in work and family. Our main aim was to demonstrate the interplay between forces in the contexts and processes of dealing with the demands on the individuals. In the long run this research will not only provide pivots for how to increase people's chances to cope with demands and maintain psychosocial adjustment, but also induce further research on how people could use their strengths in forming collective action for the improvement of the societal challenges themselves. To be confronted with undeserving insecurities in one's life, however, is not enough to become engaged as our results on the negligible role of the demands for civic engagement showed.

References

Bötcher, K. (2006). Marital union and dissolution in East and West Germany: The impact of women's labor force participation on martial stability. *Kölner Zeitschrift für Soziologie und Sozialpsychologie, 58*, 592–616.

Bronfenbrenner, U. (1979). *The ecology of human development*. Cambridge: Harvard University Press.

Clark, E. (2003). Unemployment as a social norm: Psychological evidence from panel data. *Journal of Labor Economics, 21*, 323–351.

Cohen, J., Cohen, P., West, S.G., & Aiken, L. (2003). *Applied multiple regression/correlation analysis for the behavior sciences* (3rd Ed.). Mahwah, NJ: Erlbaum.

Cohen, L.H., Hettler, T.R., & Park, C.L. (Eds) (1997). *Social support, personality, and life stress adjustment*. New York: Plenum Press.

Conger, R.D., Conger, K.J., Elder, G.H., Lorenz, F.O., Simons, R.L., & Whitbeck, L.B. (1992). A family process model of economic hardship and adjustment of early adolescent boys. *Child Development, 63*, 526–541.

Conger, R.D. & Elder, G.H. (1994). *Families in troubled times: Adapting to change in rural America*. New York: de Gruyter.

Eggers, A., Gaddy, C., & Graham, C. (2006). Well-being and unemployment in Russia in the 1990s: Can society's suffering be individuals' solace? *The Journal of Socio-Economics, 35*, 209–242.

Elder, G.H. (1974). *Children of the Great Depression: Social change in life experiences*. Chicago: University of Chicago Press.

Erlinghagen, M. (2000). Arbeitslosigkeit und ehrenamtliche Tätigkeit im Zeitverlauf. Eine Längsschnittanalyse der westdeutschen Stichprobe des Sozio-oekonomischen Panels (SOEP) für die Jahre 1992 und 1996 [Unemployment and volunteering over time. A longitudinal study on the West German sample of the socio-economic panel]. *Kölner Zeitschrift für Soziologie und Sozialpsychologie, 52*, 291–310.

Foster, D.A. & Caplan, R.D. (1994). Cognitive influences on perceived change in social support, motivation, and symptoms of depression. *Applied Cognitive Psychology, 8*, 123–139.

Greco, V. & Roger, D. (2003). Uncertainty, stress, and health. *Personality and Individual Differences, 34*, 1057–1068.

Grümer, S. & Pinquart, M. (2008). Zusammenhänge zwischen Anforderungen des sozialen Wandels, psychosozialen Ressourcen, Einstellungen zum sozialen Wandel und subjektivem Befinden [Relationships between demands of social change, psychosocial resources, attitudes towards social change and subjective well-being]. In R.K. Silbereisen & M. Pinquart (Eds), *Individuum und sozialer Wandel* (pp. 211–255). Weinheim: Juventa.

Haase, C.M., Tomasik, M.J., & Silbereisen, R.K. (2008). Correlates of premature behavioral autonomy in late adolescence and young adulthood. *European Psychologist, 13*, 255–266.

Heckhausen, J. (2005). Competence and motivation in adulthood and old age: Making the most of changing capacities and resources. In C.S. Dweck & A. Elliott (Eds), *Handbook of competence and motivation* (pp. 240–256). New York: Guilford.

Heckhausen, J. & Schulz, R. (1995). A life-span theory of control. *Psychological Review, 102*, 284–304.

Huster, E.-U. (Ed.). (1997). *Reichtum in Deutschland – Die Gewinner in der sozialen Polarisierung* [Wealth in Germany – The winners of social polarization]. Frankfurt a. M.: Campus.

Keyes, C.L.M. (2006). Subjective change and its consequences for emotional well-being. *Motivation and Emotion, 24*, 67–84.

Kohn, M.L. (1987). Cross-national research as an analytic strategy: American Sociological Association 1987 Presidential Address. *American Sociological Review, 52*, 713–731.

Kuijpers, M.A., Schyns, B., & Scheerens, J. (2006). Career competencies for career success. *Career Development Quarterly, 55*, 168–178.

Lazarus, R.L. & Folkman, S. (1984). *Stress, appraisal, and coping*. New York: Springer.

Pinquart, M. & Silbereisen, R.K. (2004). Human development in times of social change: Theoretical considerations and research needs. *International Journal of Behavioral Development, 28*, 289–298.

Pinquart, M., Juang, L., & Silbereisen, R.K. (2004). Changes of psychological distress in East German adolescents facing German unification: The role of commitment to the old system and of self-efficacy beliefs. *Youth and Society, 36*, 77–101.

Pinquart, M., Silbereisen, R.K., & Körner, A. (2008). Das Zusammenspiel von Merkmalen der Region mit individuell erlebten wandelbezogenen Anforderungen und deren Bewältigung [The interaction between characteristics of the region with individually experienced demands of social change and their coping]. In R.K. Silbereisen & M. Pinquart (Eds), *Individuum und sozialer Wandel* (S. 256–290). Weinheim: Juventa.

Pinquart, M., Silbereisen, R.K., & Körner, A. (2009). Perceived work-related demands associated with social change, control strategies, and psychological well-being: Do associations between perceived social change, coping, and psychological well-being vary by regional economic conditions? Evidence from Germany. *European Psychologist, 14*, 207–219.

Reitzle, M. & Körner, A. (2008). Aufstieg, Abstieg, Berg und Tal – psychologische und demografische Korrelate von Erwerbsverläufen [Ups and downs, peaks and valleys – Psychological and demographical correlates of career patterns]. In R.K. Silbereisen & M. Pinquart (Eds), *Individuum und sozialer Wandel* (pp. 149–176). Weinheim: Juventa.

Rutter, M.L., Maughan, B., Pickles, A., & Simonoff, E. (1998). Retrospective recall recalled. In R.B. Cairns, L.R. Bergman, & J. Kagan (Eds), *Methods and models for studying the individual* (pp. 219–243). Thousand Oaks, CA: Sage Publications.

Sameroff, A.J. (2000). Developmental systems and psychopathology. *Development and Psychopathology, 12*, 297–312.

Schieman, S., Pearlin, L.I., & Meersman, S.C. (2006). Neighborhood disadvantage and anger among older adults: Social comparisons as effect modifiers. *Journal of Health and Social Behavior, 47*, 156–172.

Shteyn, M., Schumm, J.A., Vodopianova, N., Hobfoll, S.E., & Lilly, R. (2003). The impact of the Russian transition on psychosocial resources and psychological distress. *Journal of Community Psychology, 31*, 113–127.

Silbereisen, R.K., Reitzle, M., & Juang, L. (2002). Time and change: Psychosocial transitions in German young adults 1991 and 1996. In L. Pulkkinen & A. Caspi (Eds), *Paths to successful development: Personality in the life course* (pp. 227–254). New York: Cambridge University Press.

Silbereisen, R.K., Pinquart, M., Reitzle, M., Tomasik, M.J., Fabel, K., & Grümer, S. (2006). *Psychosocial resources and coping with social change. Mitteilungen des SFB 580, 19,* 1–132.

Silbereisen, R.K., Tomasik, M.J., & Grümer, S. (2008). Soziodemografische und psychologische Korrelate des bürgerschaftlichen Engagements Anfang 2000 in Deutschland [Sociodemographic and psychological correlates of civic engagement at the beginning of the new millennium in Germany]. In R.K. Silbereisen & M. Pinquart (Eds), *Individuum und sozialer Wandel* (pp. 197–227). Weinheim: Juventa.

Tomasik, M.J. & Pinquart, M. (2008). Adaptiver Umgang mit Anforderungen sozialen Wandels [Adaptive coping with demands of social change]. In R.K. Silbereisen & M. Pinquart (Eds), *Individuum und sozialer Wandel* (pp. 99–125). Weinheim: Juventa.

Tomasik, M.J. & Silbereisen, R.K. (2009). Demands of social change as a function of the political context, institutional filters, and psychosocial resources. *Social Indicators Research, 94,* 13–28.

von der Heyde, C. & Loeffler, U. (1993). Die ADM Stichprobe [The ADM sample]. *Planung und Analyse, 20,* 49–53.

6

GLOBALIZATION, SOCIAL INEQUALITY, AND INDIVIDUAL AGENCY IN HUMAN DEVELOPMENT: SOCIAL CHANGE FOR BETTER OR WORSE?

Jutta Heckhausen

There is much attention in life-course sociology and life-span psychology to processes of deregulation and individualization believed to become dominant in the wake of economic globalization. Some researchers focus on the risks in terms of social exclusion, marginalization, and downward social mobility that these processes of deregulation and destabilization of the social structure bring along (Bynner & Parsons, 2002; Furstenberg, Kennedy, McLoyd, Rumbaut, & Settersten, 2004). In contrast to this critical view of social change associated with globalization, many life-span developmental psychologists and life-course sociologists emphasize the potential that modernity (Beck, 1986) and the effects of globalization on society bring about for self-direction and individualization in development across the life course (Heinz, 2002b; Shanahan, Mortimer, & Krüger, 2002; Wrosch & Freund, 2001), constructing an individualized career (Hall, 2004), and even envisage new arenas and developmental phases for self-fulfillment (Arnett, 2000). However, other life-course sociologists and life-span psychologists have warned to not throw the baby out with the bathwater and declare the end of social structure and institutions when they continue to shape life courses and trajectories of development (Brueckner & Mayer, 2005; Heckhausen, 1999).

This chapter brings together our motivational psychology approach to individual agency in life-span development (Heckhausen & Heckhausen, 2008; Heckhausen & Schulz, 1995, 1999; Heckhausen, Wrosch, & Schulz, in press; Schulz & Heckhausen, 1996) and a life-course sociological approach to globalization and its impact on individual life courses (Blossfeld et al., 2007; Buchholz et al., 2009). The life-span theory of control provides a motivational and action-theoretical framework to conceptualize how biological and societal conditions and their changes across the life-span interface with the development-related agency of the individual. Regarding the societal conditions, the life-course sociological approach of Blossfeld and colleagues identifies the pertinent changes associated with globalization, and how these vary in different countries. When integrating the two approaches, we arrive at hypotheses about which individual differences in developmental regulation should be more adaptive in which society. Finally, we discuss some recent empirical findings from our research program about motivation in life-span development in light of these new conceptual ideas about individual agency under conditions of social change. It is important to keep in mind that these empirical studies were originally not planned with the goal to investigate individual control striving in settings of social change, and therefore the findings are merely suggestive and may serve as guideposts for future research.

How societal structure and institutions set up the action field for developmental agency of the individual

The life-span theory of control addresses the role of human agency in life-span development (Heckhausen, 1999; Heckhausen & Schulz, 1995; Heckhausen et al., in press; Schulz & Heckhausen, 1996). Human development and behavior across the life span is only weakly determined by biological processes and changes. Within the phylogeny of mammals, a biological strata characterized by open behavioral programs (Mayr, 1974), humans have evolved as a species with unprecedented variability and flexibility in the regulation of behavior and ontogeny. There is an immense degree of freedom for human developmental change, particularly during adulthood. The great variability and flexibility of human behavior and development is an advantage in terms of enhanced adaptive potential. However, the organism needs to organize his/her resource investment by making choices and focusing resources accordingly. Thus, life-span development inherently raises the question of how to decide on which domain or goal to select (Baltes & Baltes, 1990; Carstensen, Isaacowitz, & Charles, 1999; Freund & Baltes, 2002; Marsiske, Lang, Baltes, & Baltes, 1995), and how to remain focused on a domain or goal that has been chosen (Heckhausen, 1999; Heckhausen & Schulz, 1999).

Many decisions individuals make about career and family goals and life-course paths are strongly influenced by the societal structure and age-graded institutions such as schools, career and promotion patterns, and retirement. These social institutions provide 'adaptive challenges' (Heckhausen, 1999) by channeling the individual's goal investments into constrained developmental pathways (Heckhausen & Schulz, 1993, 1999) and offering age-graded and sequential timetables for the individual's attempts to co-produce his or her own development. Under conditions of globalization, these developmental pathways become (at least partially) deregulated and thus may lose some of their constraining but also some of their supporting and guiding capacity.

Developmental regulation as goal engagement and disengagement

Individual agency plays a crucial part in human development across the life span (Baltes, Lindenberger, & Staudinger, 1998; Brandtstädter, 2006; Heckhausen, 1999; Lerner & Busch-Rossnagel, 1981). In a given society there is much consensus about normative developmental tasks for each age segment of the life course (Havighurst, 1952). Individuals base their own mental representations about desired outcomes of life-course transitions and developmental processes on these normative conceptions. Typically, these desired outcomes or developmental tasks are adopted by the individual as goals to strive for and can thus organize the active attempts of individuals to influence their own development. Many developmental researchers therefore focus on goal-related concepts when investigating individual contributions to life-span development and life-course events and transitions (Brandtstädter, Wentura, & Rothermund, 1999). Development-related goal concepts are adapted for the life-course context by addressing developmental processes of life-course transitions, and aim at intermediate levels of aggregation (e.g., enroll in college, find a girl friend, become less dependent on my parents) and intermediate future time extension (i.e., five to ten years). (Heckhausen, 1999)

The way in which individuals can actively influence their own development and life-course is by choosing and pursuing developmental goals. Just encountering opportunities for entering college in a given developmental ecology (e.g., a high school graduate in a middle-class American family) is in itself not sufficient to put the individual on the trajectory for a college education. The individual has to make an active choice for the respective developmental goal of attaining a B.A., volitionally commit to it, and persist in goal pursuit until the goal is attained. This goal engagement requires the activation of certain control strategies of *primary control* (i.e., invest time and effort into goal pursuit) and typically also selective *secondary control* to maintain the focus and commitment on the goal in spite of challenges and distractions (Heckhausen, 1999; Heckhausen et al., in press; Wrosch & Heckhausen, 1999). When thinking in terms of the example of striving for a career promotion, the person who has set this goal for herself will invest more time and effort into work (i.e., selective primary control), imagine the positive consequences and pride that would come with achieving the promotion (i.e., selective secondary control), and seek advice from more advanced colleagues on effective strategies to foster career success (i.e., compensatory primary control).

As the individual moves along the age axis, the capacity for primary control in most domains of life will change and force the individual to respond to this loss of control by disengaging from the goal (Heckhausen & Schulz, 1993; Heckhausen et al., in press; Wrosch, Scheier, Carver, & Schulz, 2003). In contrast to the motivational mind set of goal engagement, *goal disengagement* requires *compensatory secondary control*. Compensatory secondary control encompasses deactivating the obsolete goal, and using self-protective strategies, such as self-protective causal attribution (avoiding self blame), the focusing on successes in other domains, and downward social comparisons.

Changing opportunities and constraints across the life course

Individuals have to adjust, cope with, and take advantage of the changing opportunities and constraints to what they can accomplish at different points in life. Biological maturation and aging, and societal institutions (e.g., education, labor market, retirement) set up a roughly inverted U-shape curve of control capacity across the life span, with a steep increase during childhood and adolescence, a peak in young adulthood, and a decline in advancing age. This more general life-course encompassing trajectory of first increasing and then decreasing opportunities is overlaid with more domain-specific trajectories of improving and declining opportunities for achieving specific developmental goals. Societal institutions such as the educational system, vocational careers, and welfare systems elaborately structure the life span in terms of critical transitions (e.g., school entry, promotions, retirement) and sequential constraints (e.g., educational qualifications as prerequisites for certain careers). These time-organized opportunity structures present significant regulatory challenges to the individual to take advantage of the opportunities in a time/age-sensitive way. Moreover, the individual needs to come to terms with diminished chances to attain important life goals, once the opportunities vanish. In summary, any effective theory of life span development needs to address the way in which life-course variations of opportunities and constraints are met with individuals' attempts to master their own development.

Societal canalizations of human life-course development

In a given society, mechanisms of life-course canalization perpetuate social inequality both across generations and within individual life courses. For example, across generations access to higher education can be facilitated or hindered by parents' own educational background and experience. Within individual life-courses, people can use a major life-course transition (e.g., after graduating from high school) as a spring board to launch an upwardly mobile trajectory into a higher social strata (e.g., by entering college and going on to medical school training). Changing one's social position in society between normative life-course transitions is less common, particularly in societies with less flexible career patterns, and might well involve an extraordinary event that either derails the individual in his path (e.g., by a severe illness, large inheritance) or disrupts societal canalization processes (e.g., by extensive societal transformation, such as associated with German reunification). These mechanisms of societal canalization of individual life courses vary across historical time and across different countries in terms of how rigid, stable, and impermeable they are, leaving more or less potential control to the individual agent. Societal canalization mechanisms within a system of social inequality have an ambivalent nature. On the one hand, they constrain an individual's upward mobility, and on the other hand they serve as adaptive scaffolds for an individual's developmental goal setting and goal engagement, and protect from an otherwise ubiquitous risk for downward social mobility.

Globalization-related social change and how it affects life courses in different countries

One of the major questions, if not the key question for evaluating social change in its effects on individual life courses, is whether or not and in what way it affects social inequality in a given society. Major social change typically affects the way in which social inequality in a given society is transferred from one generation to the next and/or how it is maintained across an individual's life course. Societies across historical time and across different continents, or across developed versus developing countries, vary greatly in the extent they allow individuals to break loose from their social origins and across their life-course climb socially into classes of higher social status and greater access to resources than their parents belonged to. The flip-side of this potential for upward social mobility is, of course, the risk of downward social mobility. Modern societies offer greater overall social mobility, which entails both the chance for social ascent and the risk of social descent. The following paragraphs provide a brief summary of the findings of GLOBALIFE, a research program on globalization processes and their impact on life courses (Blossfeld et al., 2007; Buchholz et al., 2009) and also a discussion of some implications from a life-span developmental and motivational psychology perspective. The focus here is to view the dimensions of social change identified by GLOBALIFE as parameters of the action field for the individual agent who is trying to optimize his or her life course in the context of the respective society's system of social inequality.

Blossfeld and colleagues (Blossfeld et al., 2007; Buchholz et al., 2009) have identified the major consequences of the globalization process in terms of challenges for individual agents in managing their life courses. Specifically, these are decreasing transparency, decreasing predictability of long-term consequences of individual decisions, increasing erosion of social security, and increasing asymmetry in power relations between employers and employees.

In their multi-country research program GLOBALIFE on the consequences of globalization processes, Blossfeld and his colleagues identified different consequences for young adults just entering the workforce and women and older adults leaving the workforce. The hardest hit by increasing lack of transparency and greater uncertainty about one's life-course trajectory, were younger adults (Blossfeld, Klijzing, Mills, & Kurz, 2005). They had to put up with lower income, part-time or short-term jobs, often without or with fewer benefits (health insurance, social security, retirement benefits). Some authors who study the mental health consequences of such patterns of employment refer to it as 'underemployment' (Dooley, 2003), and show that it is associated with plummeting self-esteem and depression (Dooley, Prause, & Ham-Rowbottom, 2000), and even with lower birth weight in babies born to mothers experiencing a switch to such inferior forms of employment during their pregnancy (Dooley & Prause, 2005). Another group that was disproportionately affected were women at midlife (Blossfeld & Hofmeister, 2006), particularly those that had interrupted their careers to raise their children. On the other hand, men at midlife, and particularly those with high vocational or professional qualifications, seem to be protected from unemployment and hardship in most countries (Blossfeld, Mills, & Bernardi, 2006). Finally, older adults were also disadvantaged by the consequences of globalization processes in terms of more rapidly outdated qualifications and skills.

However, these consequences for the different groups of the population are not universal, but critically depend on the rigidness versus flexibility of the labor market and its career tracks, and on the kinds of welfare provisions the respective national states offer, and also on the role of the traditional family to support members that get pushed out of traditional forms of employment (Blossfeld et al., 2007; Buchholz et al., 2009). These state and family-based support systems provide a filter or buffer for the impact of universal globalization processes on the individual (Hofäcker, Buchholz, & Blossfeld, Chapter 4 this volume).

Table 6.1 shows the five categories of countries identified by the GLOBALIFE research program and indicates how these countries differ in important ways for individual life-course agency. Individuals try to exert

Table 6.1 GLOBALIFE categories of welfare states (Blossfeld et al., 2007) and their characteristics as societal contexts for individual agency directed at social mobility across one's life course

	Liberal	Social-democratic	Conservative	Family-oriented	Post-socialist
	USA, GB, Canada	Sweden, Denmark, Norway	Germany, France	Italy, Spain, Ireland, Mexico	Hungary, Estland, Poland, Czech Rep.
Flexibility, permeability	High	High	Low	Low	???
Individual responsibility	High	Medium	Low	Low	???
Opportunity for upward mobility	High	High	Low	Low	???
Resources from community	Low	High	For insiders	For insiders	???

their own control over where they stand and where they end up over time in the respective society's system of social inequality. Countries in the different GLOBALIFE categories differ in important parameters that determine the effectiveness of individual agency directed at social mobility. First of all, there is the issue of flexibility in vocational careers, a dimension Hamilton referred to as 'permeability' (Hamilton, 1994) which sets the stage for individual action. Low flexibility or permeability seriously constrains the individual's range of effective action in moving from a lower social trajectory to a higher one. The conservative and family-oriented welfare states provide relatively little flexibility and thus less potential for social mobility than the liberal and the social-democratic welfare states. Next is the degree to which an individual is expected to assume responsibility for their life-course trajectory. Individual responsibility is high in the liberal welfare states, moderate in the social-democratic welfare state, and low in the conservative and family-oriented welfare states. Flexibility and individual responsibility are pre-conditions for the effectiveness of individual agency, but as we discussed in the previous section, individual agency is incapacitated when there are no or few opportunities for upward mobility in the sense of educational and training institutions and supportive contexts for upward mobility (e.g., step and ladder-type educational institutions). Such upward-mobility opportunities are relatively plentiful in liberal and social-democratic welfare states, but underdeveloped or absent in conservative and family-oriented welfare states. Finally, societal systems differ with regard to the degree of resources the social community (e.g., state, family) provides for individuals who try to move up in society. Here liberal and social-democratic welfare states differ. Liberal welfare states such as the U.S. provide relatively few resources, whereas social-democratic welfare states provide relatively rich support. Conservative and family-oriented welfare states show their preference for supporting insiders (those that hold qualified jobs) while outsiders can expect little support.

Given the findings from GLOBALIFE, it seems that globalization processes do not level the playing field by conveying greater opportunity for upward mobility to individuals. Instead, disadvantaged groups with low personal and social capital, such as youth, older adults and women, are more vulnerable to become marginalized and relegated to precarious forms of employment. This is particularly true for countries with conservative or family-oriented welfare states, such as Germany, France, Italy, Spain, Ireland, and Mexico, because they are founded on a labor market with relatively inflexible and non-permeable vocational career paths, which leave little room for individual agency and provide sparse opportunities for upward mobility. Conditions for individual agents to fight off the risks and optimize the chances for upward mobility are better in countries that offer more flexibility in career paths, such as those with liberal and social-democratic welfare states. The next section will address the question how young adults as a group that is vulnerable to globalization losses, try to attain optimal outcomes under the conditions of contrasting societal conditions in the U.S. with its liberal welfare state on the one hand and Germany with its conservative welfare state on the other hand.

Individual agency of youth in the transition to adulthood: A contrast between liberal and conservative welfare states

In this final section, we will take a look at the individual agency during the transition after graduating from secondary education (high school or equivalent) in work or college. First, the increasing role of education under conditions of globalization is considered. Second, I outline a set of research questions addressing individual agency during the transition to adulthood in societies varying along the four dimensions (see rows in Table 6.1) of permeability of educational and career tracks, individual responsibility, community resources supporting individual agency, and opportunities for upward mobility. Moreover, as a first empirical example, the characteristics of goal choice and goal engagement of youth in two different educational and career systems, California, USA and Berlin, Germany, are considered. It is important to note that neither of these longitudinal studies was planned with a systematic comparison of the societal canalization in mind. The findings, however, were indicative of country-specific characteristics in the societal organization of the school to work and college transition as the critical cause of differences in the choice and effectiveness of individual agents' strategies. These differential effects in turn are suggestive of how globalization-related social change may affect the choices individual agents make in their developmental regulation and how effective these choices may turn out to be.

As a general consequence of the decreased predictability, greater permeability of career paths, and uncertainty of long-term careers that comes with globalization processes across different countries with their varying welfare systems, the role of general education as a form of personal capital has become ever more important (Blossfeld, Klijzing, Mills, & Kurz, 2005; Bynner, 2005; Bynner & Parsons, 2002; Mills & Blossfeld, 2003). Reading, writing, mathematics, computer literacy and knowledge of information technology are essential intellectual skills required in a wide variety of careers and industries. In addition, advanced degrees reflect higher level intellectual abilities, problem-solving and self-regulatory skills, and an expertise that can serve as a blueprint for developing expertise in other domains. As it turns out, many youth respond to the increased uncertainty and their reduced prospects to enter a vocational career with long-term employment and promotion prospects, by spending a longer time in educational institutions and thus delaying both the entry into the labor market and the beginning of a family. Far from this being a reflection of identity search in emerging adults (Arnett, 2000), most such strategies are rational if desperate responses to the increase in uncertainty, long-term predictability, and decreasing value of highly specialized and non-transferable knowledge and training (Bynner, 2005).

When we look at the different categories of welfare states, the role of personal resources in terms of aptitude, education, and motivational self-regulatory skills, can be expected to be greatest in liberal welfare states, where not only the flexibility and opportunities for upward mobility is high, but also individual responsibility is high with low support from the community (Schoon, 2007, August). In such societal settings, individuals with high ambitions (and the motivational propensity for high investments (selective primary control) and strong commitment (selective secondary control) to overcome the status of their family of origin in the system of social inequality have better chances to fulfill their ultimate goals, particularly when opportunities for upward mobility are institutionalized in the educational or career system.

In contrast, the conservative and family-oriented welfare states offer far less degrees of freedom for individual agency. In these countries, individuals have to focus on fitting in and aligning themselves with the 'insiders' who hold stable employment and serve as gate-keepers (Blossfeld, Klijzing, Mills, & Kurz, 2005; Buchholz et al., 2009). These societal settings would provide good developmental ecologies for those who are content to strive for goals that are closely calibrated to what they already achieved (e.g., previous school grades), and attuned to getting support from others (compensatory primary control). Career agency orientations that focus on a role in a given company are likely to be more successful in such societal settings than agency orientations that are directed at autonomy, self-growth and self-employment. Heinz has identified among young adult workers in Germany types of 'biographical agency,' for example 'company identification' and 'wage worker habitus,' that would represent an orientation towards fitting in with an insider system. This may be contrasted to other types identified in Heinz' research that express an orientation towards individual autonomy and breaking free from insider systems (e.g. 'personality growth or autonomy,' 'self-employment habitus') (Heinz, 2002a, 2008). These types of orientations in individual life-course agency are both a result of self-socialization within a given societal system, and may have the potential to contribute towards social change.

Another intriguing area of research is the relationship between educational and career systems. In more conservative systems, educational qualifications and career prospects are very closely related, and offer little flexibility once a certain path (e.g., vocational versus academic track) is taken. In such a system, ambitious educational goals and motivational investments work hand in hand with career aspirations. The more flexible liberal systems do not necessarily require certain educational qualifications for many careers. Instead, individuals can learn on the job and work their way up. This might well mean that among young high-school graduates aspirations and motivational investment in educational and career goals compete with each other, so that, for example, a high commitment to ambitious career goals takes away motivational resources from educational pursuits.

Finally, individual agents and globalization processes are involved in transactional influences, such that individuals adapt to the increase in uncertainty and non-contingency of vocational tracks and societal institutions become transformed in the process. An example may be young Germans who complete their apprenticeships and instead of waiting for an employment within the same vocation, which due to globalization-based de-regulation of vocational career tracks has become extremely rare, venture out to neighboring or even further removed careers. In a sample of about 1,000 apprentices (Heinz, 2002b), Heinz found that within the first year after completing the apprenticeship about one-sixth of the freshly graduated journey-men worked in other occupations, and eight years after graduation about half of the 1,000 journey-men had worked in occupations they were never specifically trained for. In the long run, the combination of de-regulated vocational careers and individual choices will render apprenticeships less dominant and may even erode them as institutions of vocational training.

Empirical example: School to work and to college transition in Germany and the United States

The increasing relevance of education as personal capital for channeling the individual's life-course potential under conditions of globalization, moves the question of how access to post-secondary and vocational education is regulated, to center stage. The question arises whether the same individual characteristics of ambitiousness of goal setting and intensity and persistence in goal engagement lead to superior outcomes in terms of educational attainment and career entry across societies differing in critical features of their welfare states. Our life-span developmental and motivational approach proposes that those individuals fare better who have motivational preferences which match their countries' characteristics of the labor market and welfare state.

Under conditions of relatively stable and non-permeable education and employment tracks as in Germany, youth should closely calibrate their goals for vocational training and careers and pursue their goals with intense primary control, striving to achieve better outcomes. In contrast, high-school graduates in the U.S. with its more permeable educational and career system, should profit more from very ambitious goals which lead them to find their way from lower to higher education and employment, sequentially utilizing educational and employment opportunities along an upward social trajectory. Two empirical examples of contrasting social institutionalization of a life-course transition are briefly discussed here: (1) The transition from high school (middle-tier track) to vocational training and work in Germany, and (2) the transition from high school to college in California, USA Note that these studies were not jointly planned, but do speak to the possible differential effect of non-permeably segregated versus step-by-step accessible (i.e., California Master Plan of Higher Education) transition outcomes.

The transition from the German middle-tier high school 'Realschule' (after completing grade 10) to vocational training in the dual system (i.e., two days of school combined with three days of vocational training in company-based apprenticeships) is highly institutionalized and follows narrow channeling according to a youth's previous school performance and behavior in a personnel interview or test (Heckhausen & Tomasik, 2002). Vocational training positions are in short supply, and therefore over-ambitious goals for apprenticeships with high social prestige (e.g., for banking and insurance careers) bear the risk of not obtaining any training position. As a consequence, closely adjusted vocational aspirations should be most adaptive when trying to secure one of the coveted vocational training positions in company-based apprenticeships. Moreover, the scarcity of positions makes it mandatory that goal engagement is high.

We studied 768 students from two East and two West-Berlin middle-tier schools (Realschule), one school each for lower-class and middle-class neighborhoods, and followed three cohorts throughout the 10th (final) grade of school and two years after graduation. The study was funded by the German Research Foundation. We found a substantial relationship between vocational aspirations measured as social prestige score for the vocation a youth expressed an interest in, and school achievement measured as school grades in core subjects (mathematics, German, history) (Heckhausen & Tomasik, 2002). The indices were standardized within school to allow for an optimized local validity. Students overall kept their school grades in mind when expressing preferences for vocations ($r = .37$). Students with lower aspirations were more likely to obtain an apprenticeship. In further analyses utilizing the bi-monthly data collections during grade 10, we investigated trajectories most likely to result in apprenticeships with relatively high vocational prestige given a youth's level of school achievement. Such trajectories were conceptualized to start slightly above one's own achievement level and then adjust downward until an apprenticeship is obtained (Tomasik, Hardy, Haase, & Heckhausen, 2009). It is noteworthy that youth who exhibited this adaptive trajectory of vocational aspirations were also the ones who reported the strongest control strivings for goal engagement (selective primary control and selective secondary control) and the lowest levels of goal disengagement (compensatory secondary control). High goal engagement with searching for an apprenticeship was also found to be decisive for girls in their success with attaining an apprenticeship, and predictive of positive changes in affective well-being for both girls and boys (Haase, Heckhausen, & Köller, 2008).

In the United States, we studied the transition after high school (12th grade) into post-secondary education and work (only the educational trajectory will be discussed here). The educational system in the U.S. differs fundamentally from the German system in that it is integrated until high-school graduation, whereas the German system is three-tiered starting at 4th grade (in some states 6th grade). This is not so say that the U.S. school system is egalitarian. Far from it, high schools in neighborhoods of varying social-economic status differ greatly in their quality of instruction and the number of graduates that go on to enroll in four-year colleges. However, the educational system does not constrain upward mobility by formalized institutional barriers as it does in the German educational system. To the contrary and particularly in California, the college system provides educational institutions for everyone which are regulated by the California Master Plan for Higher Education, an educational masterplan in such a way as to allow a step-by-step upward mobility from high-school graduate to community college student to then transfer either to the California State system or the University of California system (California Code, 1960). Such a societal context enables highly ambitious students to make their way upward step by step from humble beginnings to high-flying educational qualifications.

In our longitudinal study of high-school graduates in the Los Angeles Unified School District, we surveyed 1,183 high school seniors and then followed up one, two, three and four years after graduation (Chang, Chen, Greenberger, Dooley, & Heckhausen, 2006; Chang, Greenberger, Chen, Heckhausen, & Farruggia, in press; Heckhausen, et al., 2007). Vocational and particularly educational aspirations were high, with a large majority anticipating to complete a Bachelors degree, even if their own senior-year grades were too low to enter a four-year college right after high school (Heckhausen, et al., 2007). Such high aspirations would lead to unrealistic choices and failure in a system that is more segregated and less permeable. However, in California the youth with the most ambitious educational expectations ended up being most successful in enrolling in and completing four-year college degrees (Heckhausen, et al., 2007). Moreover, strong goal engagement with highly activated selective primary and secondary control strategies also predicted better subjective well-being and mental health after high-school graduation.

In sum, the societal differences between Germany and the United States in facilitating individual agency in the school to work and college transition reflect three important dimensions: flexibility or permeability of educational tracks, individual responsibility, and opportunity or institutional scaffolding of upward mobility. The three dimensions facilitate upward mobility in the context of the postsecondary educational system in California, USA. In the German educational and vocational training system, youngsters are channeled into segregated paths. However, with the demise of traditional vocational career paths from apprenticeship to employment, individuals manage to break out of traditional employment patterns and may play a role in the transformation of vocational training systems in this conservative welfare state.

These examples illustrate how certain characteristics of the social and institutional structure in a given society can foster different patterns of social mobility across major life course transitions, and how this differentially may affect subgroups of the population with more or less access to educational, social support, and individual agency resources. Accordingly, social change into and out of such life-course conditionings will affect the effectiveness of individual agency in human development. Thus, social change associated with economic globalization is rendering the playing field less even for individual agents with unequal access to personal and social resources.

References

Arnett, J.J. (2000). Emerging adulthood: A theory of development from the late teens through the twenties. *American Psychologist, 55,* 469–480.

Baltes, P.B. & Baltes, M.M. (1990). Psychological perspectives on successful aging: The model of selective optimization with compensation. In P.B. Baltes & M.M. Baltes (Eds), *Successful aging: Perspectives from the behavioral sciences* (pp. 1–34). New York: Cambridge University Press.

Baltes, P.B., Lindenberger, U., & Staudinger, U.M. (1998). Life-span theory in developmental psychology. *Handbook of Child Psychology, 5,* 1029–1143.

Beck, U. (1986). *Risikogesellschaft. Auf dem weg in eine andere moderne* [Risk society. On the way into another modernity]. Frankfurt, Germany: Suhrkamp Verlag.

Blossfeld, H.-P. & Hofmeister, H. (2006). *Globalization, uncertainty and women's careers in international comparison.* Cheltenham, U.K.: Edward Elgar.

Blossfeld, H.-P., Mills, M., & Bernardi, F. (2006). *Globalization, uncertainty and men's careers in international comparison.* Cheltenham, U.K.: Edward Elgar.

Blossfeld, H.-P., Klijzing, E., Mills, M., & Kurz, K. (Eds). (2005). *Globalization, uncertainty and youth in society.* London, U.K.: Routledge.

Blossfeld, H.-P., Buchholz, S., Hofäcker, D., Hofmeister, H., Kurz, K., & Mills, M. (2007). Globalisierung und die veränderung sozialer ungleichheiten in modernen gesellschaften. *Kölner Zeitschrift für Soziologie und Sozialpsychologie, 59,* 667–691.

Brandtstädter, J. (2006). Action perspectives on human development. In R.M. Lerner & W. Damon (Eds), *Handbook of child psychology* (6th Ed.) (Vol. 1, *Theoretical models of human development,* pp. 516–568). Hoboken, NJ: John Wiley & Sons.

Brandtstädter, J., Wentura, D., & Rothermund, K. (1999). Intentional self-development through adulthood and later life: Tenacious pursuit and flexible adjustment of goals. In J. Brandtstädter & R.M. Lerner (Eds), *Action and self development: Theory and research through the life span* (pp. 373–400). Thousand Oaks, CA: Sage.

Brueckner, H. & Mayer, K.U. (2005). De-standardization of the life course: What it might mean? And if it means anything, whether it actually took place? *Advances in Life Course Research, 9,* 27–53.

Buchholz, S., Hofäcker, D., Mills, M., Blossfeld, H.-P., Kurz, K., & Hofmeister, H. (2009). Life courses in the globalization process: The development of social inequalities in modern societies. *European Sociological Review, 25.*

Bynner, J. (2005). Rethinking the youth phase of the life course: The case for emerging adulthood? *Journal of Youth Studies, 8,* 367–384.

Bynner, J. & Parsons, S. (2002). Social exclusion and the transition from school to work: The case of young people not in education, employment or training (neet). *Journal of Vocational Behavior, 60,* 289–309.

California Code (1960). The California master plan for higher education (Vol. 66010.1–66010.8): California Education Code.

Carstensen, L.L., Isaacowitz, D.M., & Charles, S.T. (1999). Taking time seriously: A theory of socioemotional selectivity. *American Psychologist, 54,* 165–181.

Chang, E.S., Chen, C., Greenberger, E., Dooley, D., & Heckhausen, J. (2006). What do they want in life? The life goals of a multi-ethnic, multi-generational sample of high school seniors. *Journal of Youth and Adolescence, 35,* 321–332.

Chang, E.S., Greenberger, E., Chen, C., Heckhausen, J., & Farruggia, S.P. (in press). Non-parental adults as social resources in the transition to adulthood. *Journal of Research on Adolescence*.

Dooley, D. (2003). Unemployment, underemployment, and mental health: Conceptualizing employment status as a continuum. *American Journal of Community Psychology, 32*, 9–20.

Dooley, D. & Prause, J. (2005). Birth weight and mothers' adverse employment change. *Journal of Health and Social Behavior, 46*, 141–155.

Dooley, D., Prause, J., & Ham-Rowbottom, K.A. (2000). Underemployment and depression: Longitudinal relationships. *Journal of Health and Social Behavior, 41*, 421–436.

Freund, A.M. & Baltes, P.B. (2002). Life-management strategies of selection, optimization and compensation: Measurement by self-report and construct validity. *Journal of Personality and Social Psychology, 82*, 642–662.

Haase, C.M., Heckhausen, J., & Köller, O. (2008). Goal engagement during the school-to-work-transition: Beneficial for all, particularly for girls. *Journal of Research on Adolescence, 18*, 671–698.

Hall, D.T. (2004). The protean career: A quarter-century journey. *Journal of Vocational Behavior, 65*, 1–13.

Hamilton, S.F. (1994). Employment prospects as motivation for school achievement: Links and gaps between school and work in seven countries. In R.K. Silbereisen & E. Todt (Eds), *Adolescence in context: The interplay of family, school, peers, and work in adjustment* (pp. 267–303). Cambridge, UK: Cambridge University Press.

Havighurst, R.J. (1952). *Developmental tasks and education*. New York: McKay Company.

Heckhausen, J. (1999). *Developmental regulation in adulthood: Age-normative and sociostructural constraints as adaptive challenges*. Cambridge, U.K.: Cambridge University Press.

Heckhausen, J. & Heckhausen, H. (Eds). (2008). *Motivation and action*. New York: Cambridge University Press.

Heckhausen, J. & Schulz, R. (1993). Optimization by selection and compensation: Balancing primary and secondary control in life span development. *International Journal of Behavioral Development, 16*, 287–303.

Heckhausen, J. & Schulz, R. (1995). A life-span theory of control. *Psychological Review, 102*, 284–304.

Heckhausen, J. & Schulz, R. (1999). Biological and societal canalizations and individuals' developmental goals. In J. Brandtstädter & R. Lerner (Eds), *Action and self-development: Theory and research through the life-span* (pp. 67–103). Thousand Oaks, CA: Sage Publications.

Heckhausen, J. & Tomasik, M.J. (2002). Get an apprenticeship before school is out: How German adolescents adjust vocational aspirations when getting close to a developmental deadline. *Journal of Vocational Behavior, 60*, 199–219.

Heckhausen, J., Chang, E.S., & Lessard, J. (2007, August). Developmental regulation in German and American adolescents during the transition from school to work. Paper presented at the 13th European Conference on Developmental Psychology, Jena, Germany.

Heckhausen, J., Wrosch, C., & Schulz, R. (in press). A motivational theory of lifespan development. *Psychological Review*.

Heinz, W.R. (2002a). Self-socialization and post-traditional society. In R.A. Settersten & T.J. Owens (Eds), *Advances in life-course research: New frontiers in socialization*. New York: Elsevier.

Heinz, W.R. (2002b). Transition continuities and the biographical shaping of early work careers. *Journal of Vocational Behavior, 60*, 220–240.

Heinz, W.R. (2008). The many faces of emerging adulthood: Social pathways from youth to adulthood. Unpublished manuscript, Bremen, Germany.

Lerner, R.M. & Busch-Rossnagel, N.A. (Eds). (1981). *Individuals as producers of their development: A life-span perspective*. New York: Academic Press.

Marsiske, M., Lang, F.R., Baltes, P.B., & Baltes, M.M. (1995). Selective optimization with compensation: Life-span perspectives on successful human development. In R.A. Dixon & L. Bäckman (Eds), *Compensating for psychological deficits and declines: Managing losses and promoting gains* (pp. 35–79). Hillsdale, NJ: Erlbaum Associates.

Mayr, E. (1974). Behavior programs and evolutionary strategies. *American Scientist, 62*, 650–659.

Mills, M. & Blossfeld, H.-P. (2003). Globalization, uncertainty and changes in the early life course. *International Journal of Behavioral Development, 2*, 188–218.

Schoon, I. (2007, August). School engagement and transitions into adult roles. Paper presented at the European Conference for Developmental Psychology. Retrieved.

Schulz, R., & Heckhausen, J. (1996). A life-span model of successful aging. *American Psychologist, 51*, 702–714.

Shanahan, M.J., Mortimer, J.T., & Krüger, H. (2002). Adolescence and adult work in the twenty-first century. *Journal of Research in Adolescence, 12*, 99–120.

Tomasik, M.J., Hardy, S., Haase, C.M., & Heckhausen, J. (2009). Adaptive adjustment of vocational aspirations among German youths during the transition from school to work. *Journal of Vocational Behavior. 74*, 38–46.

Wrosch, C. & Freund, A.M. (2001). Self-regulation of normative and non-normative developmental challenges. *Human Development, 44*, 264–283.

Wrosch, C. & Heckhausen, J. (1999). Control processes before and after passing a developmental deadline: Activation and deactivation of intimate relationship goals. *Journal of Personality and Social Psychology, 77*, 415–427.

Wrosch, C., Scheier, M.F., Carver, C.S., & Schulz, R. (2003). The importance of goal disengagement in adaptive self-regulation: When giving up is beneficial. In *Self and Identity, 2*, 1–20.

Part III

TRANSITIONS AND TRANSFORMATIONS IN INTERNATIONAL PERSPECTIVE

7

INSTITUTIONAL RESPONSES TO SOCIAL CHANGE IN COMPARATIVE PERSPECTIVE: GERMANY AND POLAND

Reinhold Sackmann

During the last two decades we could observe an experiment in intended and planned social change during which most post-communist countries tried to restructure their fundamental institutions following a given model of modernity. Many former European communist countries implemented a transformation or transition of their societies at the beginning of the 1990s by introducing market economies and democratic political structures. 'Big decisions' had to be made at the primary stage of transformation to define basic features of the institutional order. Despite the wish to follow given Western models, the ambiguity of the varieties of these orders produced a high degree of uncertainty about these decisions. As the building of new societal constitutions *ab ovo* is a rare event in social reality, these meta-decisions received a lot of attention from social scientists of different disciplines. We are now in a second stage of transformation which is dominated by the everyday procedures of transformation. Although not as spectacular as in the days of revolution, shock therapy and controversies on constitutions, it is equally important. The second stage is driven by questions concerning the unintended consequences of transformation either in the form of economic or political crises. As the quality of modern institutional orders is based upon their capacity to cope with unintended change, the medium-term range success of transformations can be compared by their coping capacity with regard to unintended consequences of fundamental change. At least in theory, market economies and democratic political decision making are highly efficient institutional systems which are able to come to terms with the unexpected, to adapt to unforeseen situations and to structure sensible responses to surprising challenges.

How do the institutions of transformation societies respond to the unintended consequences of transformation? The answer to this empirical question could help us to understand the logic of institutional coping strategies in societies confronted with major social change. It can also give us an idea of the prerequisites of a successful transformation. The aim of this chapter is to give an answer to this question by analysing comparative data in two very different transformation societies, Poland and (East) Germany. Both countries re-introduced modern institutions of market economy and democracy in 1989 and 1990 after 40 years of communist rule. However, Poland did this in a mainly autonomous way following the preferences of their elites (in a globalizing world and with regard to the neighboring European Union), whereas the East German transformation was the only one in the form of an incorporation into an existing society (West Germany). It was also different in its institutional set-up with the import of West German elites in top economic, political, judicial, scientific, administrative and media organizations. The two countries also differed in the economic resources available to cushion the transformation of infrastructure, people and organizations, with (West) Germany financially subsidizing the transformation of East Germany to a considerable degree with no significant equivalent in Poland. What are the effects of these differences in autonomy and resources for responses to unintended consequences of transformation?

The area of unintended consequences of transformation is wide. To get a good field for comparison, areas with linear developments and long-term consequences in the future are quite useful as they allow the modeling of the similarity and dissimilarity of processes of problem recognition, strategic decision formation, responses and their effects in a systematic way. Demographic change is a good example, because it is a linear development which will continue in the foreseeable future. Demographic change in transformation countries consists of a considerable drop in the birth rate, a rise in longevity, migration and a change in the timing of births. It constitutes a major unintended consequence of transformations, which we find in nearly all European transformation countries. For example, in 2005 the total fertility rates in the transformation countries Estonia (1.5), Germany (1.3), Latvia (1.3), Lithuania (1.3), Poland (1.2), Slovakia (1.2), Slovenia (1.3), Czech Republic (1.3), Hungary (1.3), Bulgaria (1.3) and Romania (1.3) are all very similar and all well below the reproduction rate. Demographic change during the last two decades confronts these countries with the challenge of how to react to the new situation of demographically aging populations. As there are stable trends in birth rates and other demographic indices, challenges in this policy field can be foreseen with considerable precision for a medium-term time range of decades. For example, fewer children usually mean fewer pupils, fewer students and fewer young workers. Most policies directed at altering demographic change itself were not successful as there are profound shifts of life course regimes which are behind the drop of birth rate in post-communist countries. Therefore, the center of interest for this case study of response strategies to unintended consequences lies in the adaptive measures taken. Furthermore, response to demographic change is the empirical material on which this chapter is based. How do local authorities respond to demographic change in their personnel policy? There is a whole range of options for them, they can ignore demographic developments, they can transpose agendas, they can close down schools, they can raise the level of schooling, or they can change working contracts, to name just a few response strategies available to local authorities. The responses of local government to demographic change and their consequences are important as they have considerable impact on the future agency of municipalities with regard to indebtedness, public service and human capital development. As local government is seen as a school for democracy, it also has some influence on the mid-term success of democratization in transformation societies.

The chapter will first outline an institutionalist theory of challenge and response. Most literature on transformation is either macrosocial, concentrating only on models of the functioning of institutional orders, or microsocial focusing only on the effects of transformation upon individuals or groups. The approach of the chapter is a combined one in the form of an institutionalist challenge response model. As the focus of the chapter is on grounded theory, different approaches are combined into a heuristic instrument, rather than simply deducting a general model from one theory. In the second part, a short outline of the methods used for collecting and analysing data is given and some hypotheses are developed. The main part concentrates on how municipalities responded to demographic change. It has been shown that the perception of the importance of demographic change of the local authorities systematically differ in the two countries. Whereas response in general administration is quite similar, in organizational fields that are very sensitive to demographic change we find considerable innovations which differ in direction and instruments used in Poland and (East) Germany. In a discussion of the results explanations for the different response strategies are discussed and the medium-term consequences are evaluated.

1 Challenge and response as theoretical model

The historian Arnold Toynbee (1947, 1957) proposed a down-to-earth theory of history as a chain of challenges and responses as opposed to evolutionary and deterministic theories of history. Within this heuristic approach, the unintended consequences as challenges for development and responses in form of coping are the cornerstones of a theory of social change. This approach will be explained in more detail, first by differentiating the three major components of an institutionalist challenge response model, and then by presenting some hypotheses for comparing the transformation societies of Poland and (East) Germany.

Challenge response models are best seen as combining models which concentrate on the challenge aspect of a situation with the reflexivity of agency and the institutionalist structuration of responses (cf. Fig. 7.2). A good starting point is a model of the challenge. Challenge response models depict a challenge as a change in the objective situation of the actor, group of actors or societies, which cannot be overcome with routine behavior and/or available resources. In contrast to simplistic behavioristic models, the challenge is not seen as stimulus for only one possible reaction to the new situation. Instead, as Elder & Caspi (1988, 1990) suggested, a challenge in general is a loss of resources that can be answered by either a new mobilization of resources or by an adjustment of aspirations to the new level of resources. Both processes include reframing and coping activities. The situation remains problematic if a new equilibrium of aspirations and resources is not achieved. In this model, lowering aspirations, like the fox does in his description of sour grapes in the fable of Aesop, is a possible adequate response besides regaining resources (Elster, 1983).

However, it is useful to add some components to a challenge response model which account more precisely for the agency of the responding actor. As empirical work of the theorist of morphogenesis, Margaret Archer (2003, 2007) has shown, different forms of actors' reflexivity create divergent causal effects. Reflexivity is the ability to consider oneself in relation to his/her (social) context and vice versa, mainly by internal conversation. Actors thus mediate structural and cultural constraints and enablements, turning objective situations into subjective actions, e.g. by activating projects. Archer differentiates between communicative reflexivity, autonomous reflexivity, meta-reflexivity and fractured forms of reflexivity. Communicative reflexive practice consists mainly of talking things through with other people, which often results in a reproduction of structure. Autonomous reflexivity in contrast stresses self-reliance in decision making. Meta-reflexivity is characterized by orientation on ideals that foster incongruence with contexts. Autonomous reflexivity and meta-reflexivity in general activate a change in structure. Fractured reflexivity intensifies, with its internal conversation the disorientation rather than leads to purposeful courses of action.[1]

A further dimension of a challenge response model is that most responses to challenges are not fully shaped by a conscious or reflexive reaction to a new situation (especially if the actor is a corporate actor), but by response sets developed by institutions to meet ever new changes

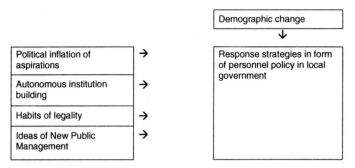

Figure 7.1 Explanatory model of response strategies in municipal personnel policy.

in environment. An objective for most institutions is to react efficiently to new challenges. Institutionalist approaches to be included in a general challenge response model focus on different aspects of institutions. Neo-institutionalism (Meyer, 2000; DiMaggio & Powell, 1983) conceptualizes organizations and individuals as guided by habits. In this Anglo-Saxon tradition of institutionalist theories, institutional actions mainly follow routines to which sometimes new accounts and new stories are added that proclaim a change of action, despite most basic proceedings still following given routines. This approach is skeptical with regard to the potential of institutional innovation in response strategies. In contrast, in the more continental European tradition of theories on institutions, an institutionalization of principles of action following guiding ideas is conceptualized (Lepsius, 1990). According to this approach some principles find a way into judiciary structures after a competition of ideas and interests. These principles then orientate action, apply sanctions to actions and therefore preselect and privilege certain types of action against others.

After these more general remarks on features of a challenge and response model the concept will be applied to a specific analysis of transformation processes and their challenge and response chains (cf. Fig. 7.1). As already mentioned, the transformation of a society consists of two different stages. In a first phase, 'big decisions' are reached to implement a new set of institutions. In the second stage, in which most transformation societies are now, the efficiency of these institutions can be evaluated by their potential to adapt to non-intended consequences of the transformation. An objective evaluation of the efficiency of institutions is difficult as it would presuppose unanimity on the criteria of success. In this chapter the focus is more on a comparison of the kinds of responses to foreseeable challenges, like demographic change to get information on the practice of adaptability of transformation societies.

It is presupposed that the dynamic of aspirations, an important aspect of the coping theory of Elder & Caspi (1990), differs between transformation societies. In all political systems cycles of political inflation and deflation are known, i.e., either collective aspirations are raised far beyond the possible realization or the level of distrust between groups within a society is increased (Parsons, 1963). But there are also differences in this process between societies. The observation of transformation societies already showed in the early 1990s that the dynamics of aspirations differ between autonomous transformation societies and incorporation transformations (Offe, 1996). In both types of transformation the change from a socialist to a market economy went hand-in-hand with a destruction of (productive and human) capital. In incorporation transformation countries like (East) Germany, a high transfer of resources was able to compensate this loss of capital, and the level of prosperity was even increased at the early stages of transformation. However, as most people thought that conditions of living should equalize in East and West Germany, the level of aspiration was even higher. In contrast to this development, in autonomous transformation countries the level of prosperity dropped significantly at the beginning of the transformation, but political elites could lower aspirations by appealing for a collective effort to tighten belts to achieve later successes. It is presupposed that the different dynamics of aspiration in transformation societies lead to different degrees of indebtedness as over-optimistic aspirations tend to lead to a higher level of debt which, according to this theory, would be more likely in East Germany. So, within the response dimension of strategy our thesis would be that the Polish response strategy should be more flexible with regard to adaptation of aspirations than their East German counterpart.

A second type of difference between the kinds of responses of transformation societies could be a result of differences in their reflexivity and agency. One can refer here to classic political sociology (Tocqueville, 2002) showing that even remote poor societies, like the US at the beginning of the nineteenth century, might have developmental advantages if they are allowed to set their own political path. In contrast, incorporation transformation societies mainly had to adapt to the given institution order of the incorporating society. It is supposed therefore that we should find less development of new institutions in East Germany and more forms of fractured or communicative reflexivity. In contrast to this, and despite strong influences from outside, especially international organizations and the European Union, Poland was able to develop its own transformation path autonomously. We postulate that we will find more autonomous reflexivity here and more signs of collective self-efficacy in mid-term development. With regard to the response dimension of deliberation our thesis would be that Polish public reflexivity should be more autonomous, thus allowing more structural innovation in the development of a path than their East German comparison group.

A third type of difference is the differences in labor law and the resulting flexibility this provides. We do not suppose great differences in the flexibility of labor markets as both countries draw on traditions of strong labor inflexibility under communist regimes and a loss of organized labor power in the process of transformation. However, we presuppose differences with respect to the habitual prerequisites of labor laws. In communist regimes the law itself had, both in the proceedings of administration as well as in the regulation of labor contracts, less importance than arbitrary political rulings. As the continuity of elites in all spheres of public life is higher in autonomous transformation countries, it is reckoned that habitual disrespect towards legal structures is higher. The binding power of legal regulations is lower in Poland and other transformation countries of this type. The hiatus between formal and informal elements of labor market structures is higher. Despite similar impulses towards a habitual peculiarity of legal structures we suppose a higher degree of legal practice in East Germany as both elite discontinuity and imported elites foster a break with (communist) tradition. So, with regard to the response dimension of (institutionalized) practice our thesis is that institutional habits of disrespect towards legal proceedings will continue communist practice in Poland to a higher degree than their East German counterparts.

A fourth type of difference between the responses of the public administrations of Poland and (East) Germany to demographic change could be a result of differences in the institutionalization of new ideas. Since the 1980s, international organizations, especially the OECD, have fostered a new ideology with respect to public administration: 'new public management'. Its reception in continental Europe, especially Germany, was very low because existing interests had a strong motive to resist it, pushing Germany towards a stronger development of internal forms of flexibility than exists in other countries. One might suppose that the hegemonic power of the concept of New Public Management is more easily achieved in acceding countries of the European Union, like Poland. Also, with regard to the response dimension of practice, our thesis is that new guiding ideas, reorienting (institutionalized) practice, are more influential in Poland so that a change of bureaucratic practice there would be greater than in East Germany.

In combination our hypotheses are that the response to demographic change in the transformation countries Poland and East Germany will systematically differ in the following ways: (a) aspirations will stay higher in East Germany, resulting in a higher rate of indebtedness; (b) as a result of a more autonomous path of political development there will be more new institutions in Poland than in East Germany; (c) the degree of informality will be higher in Poland, legal procedures being less habitualized, and (d) New Public Management ideas will be more important in Poland than in East Germany.

	Connection between challenge and response	Response	Dimension of response
	→	Coping (Elder/Caspi) - rise of resources - adaptation of aspiration	Strategy
Challenge	⇅	Reflexivity (Archer) - communicative - autonomous - meta-reflexive - fractured	Deliberation
	←	Structuration - habit - institutionalization	Practice

Figure 7.2   Challenge and response.

2 Design of study and methods

To test these hypotheses, data collection took place in 2006.[2] A sample of 14 local government units was drawn in the following two steps: (a) Firstly, two comparable federal units (federal state, voivodship) in East Germany and Poland were selected: one in each country is next to the capital of the country (Brandenburg, Mazowieckie) and one in each country is in a region of heavy economic restructuring (Saxony-Anhalt, Śląskie); (b) Secondly, units within these federal regions were chosen according to their affectedness by demographic change: two growing municipalities (Bautenbach-Feldow, Sentig-Sendow; Bracewo, Mielcz),[3] two stagnant communes (Pötzberg, Talstedt; Starów, Sierowice), two shrinking localities (Bolfin, Stechwitz; Buciszewo, Kołowina) and a big city (Linten, Goromierz). As many developments in East Germany are only understandable in comparison with West German procedures, a similar sample of communes was picked in West Germany. In the federal state of Rhineland Palatinate a major city (Kaulshafen), two growing (Wabental, Merzenfels), two stagnant (Streelenau, Bingenzell) and two shrinking municipalities (Dahrenberg, Giebelsdorf) were singled out. In each of the 21 handpicked communes at least two expert interviews were made with the mayor and with the person responsible for personnel in the area of public employment most hit by demographic change. In both countries a third interview was chosen in the area of education as a personnel-sensitive area for demography in municipalities. As local jurisdiction for educational affairs differs, the field of kindergarten was opted for in Germany, the field of schools was selected

	Poland	East Germany	West Germany	Total
Intermediaries	15	8	10	33
Local government (mayor, head of personnel, head of education/ social affairs)	24	18	20	62
Schools	14			14
	53	26	30	109

Figure 7.3   Number of expert interviews in 2006.

in Poland. Additionally, 33 interviews were conducted by experts employed by intermediate agencies like trade unions or representatives of organizations of municipalities in Germany and Poland.

All interviews were transcribed and coded with Max-QDA. Additionally, for all the communes that were studied, quantitative data on demography, revenues, expenditures, staff, local employment situation, economic strength, debts and participation in elections were obtained.

3 Response to demographic change in Poland and (East) Germany

For an analysis of the differences of response strategies to demographic change in Poland and East Germany it is useful to get a picture of the situation before we go into an explanation of the details and their potential causes. A common feature in all three areas of observation (Poland, (East) Germany and (West) Germany) is that they are affected by strong demographic change. Whereas in 1985 the levels of the total fertility rates differed considerably (Poland 2.3; East Germany 1.7; West Germany 1.3), they approached each other after the transformation (1995: Poland 1.5, East Germany 0.8, West Germany 1.3; 2005: Poland 1.2, East Germany 1.3, West Germany 1.4). Despite the similarities in these demographic developments – only diverging in the timing and momentum at the beginning of the nineties – we find strong divergence in the subjective experience of demographic change (Bartl, 2007). Whereas all Polish leaders in municipalities see demographic change as either irrelevant (five municipalities) or a challenge to be met (two communes), it is seen far more dramatically in East Germany, where it is interpreted as loss in four communes and as challenge in all municipalities studied.[4] How can these wide differences in the interpretation of the problem be explained?

3.1 Aspirations

One explanation could be that demography is higher on the political agenda in Germany than in Poland, which leads to differences in the interpretation of problems. Indeed we find a change in the German discourse on the problems of municipalities beginning in the second half of the 1990s from being attributed to economic restructuring, to being blamed on demographic change. This was endorsed by East German local authorities whereas West Germany's shrinking municipalities still preferred an economic interpretation of these processes (Glock, 2006). The Polish municipalities interpret the situation more like their West German counterparts than the East German discourse (Wróblewksi, 2008). Another argument for less accentuation on demography as the cause of the problem in Poland rests on the fact that demographic development happened later there. The drop in total fertility rates in Poland happened later than in East Germany and it is not as radical as it was there in the early 1990s when the lowest fertility rates in the world were reached in East Germany. However, despite the later lowering of the birth rate in Poland, which could lead to a postponement of demographic agenda setting, it surprises in so far as the overall amount of a drop of birth rate during the last decades is stronger in Poland than in Germany as the starting level was much higher.

To understand why Polish municipalities blamed demography less in accounting for their problems, it is useful to reconstruct why demography is a relevant subject for local authorities instead of only talking about general public affairs. Demography is an important point on local agendas as most revenues are distributed according to demographic criteria. Both in Poland and in Germany most revenues at the local level are not achieved by taxes exclusively for the local government but by getting a share of the tax volume of higher units of the state (central level, federal level). The main criteria for getting a share of these distributed taxes for local authorities are the number of their inhabitants. A fall in the demographic number of inhabitants therefore has to be registered by the local authorities since it has direct consequences for their budget. With this respect to differences in institutional awareness there are two components that can explain differences in the interpretation of demography in Poland and East Germany: One rests on differences in the registration of demographic processes. A loss in inhabitants caused by migration (which is important both in Poland with growing migration to European countries and East Germany with considerable migration to West Germany) is fragmentarily registered in Poland whereas more efficient data collection is practiced in East Germany (Gołata & Jonda, 2008). And, even more importantly, the financial situation in East Germany is far tighter than that of Poland, as Figures 7.4 and 7.5 show.

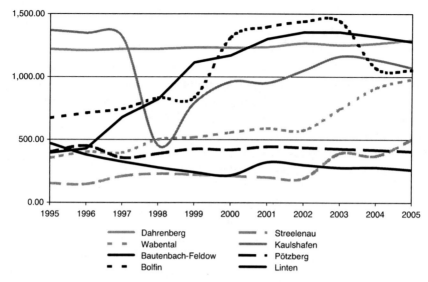

Figure 7.4 Debt per capita of German municipalities 1995–2005 (in € per capita).
Source: Rademacher (2007): 34; according to Statistical Offices.

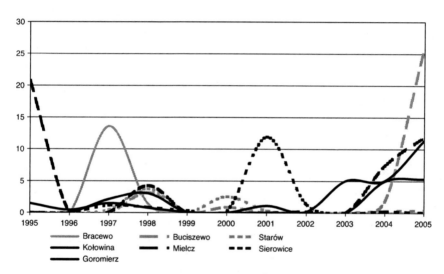

Figure 7.5 Debt per capita of Polish municipalities 1995–2005 (in €-equivalents per capita).
Source: Rademacher (2007): 35; according to GUS, NBP and ECB.

Polish municipalities had almost no debts during the whole period under consideration between 1995 and 2005, whereas most municipalities in both West and East Germany had a level of indebtedness of 500 to 1,500 Euro per capita. Shrinking localities like Dahrenberg in West Germany, Bolfin and Linten in East Germany, had the highest rates of indebtedness among the communes that were compared. Similar effects of the connection between indebtedness and shrinkage cannot be observed in Polish municipalities, as the shrinking units Kołowina and Buciszewo do not differ with regard to their level of debt. As in both Poland and Germany public law allows debts as a possible instrument for financing municipal budgets, and German law even controls the financial behavior of municipalities to a greater degree than higher levels of the state, like federal state and central state, one can conclude that a different degree of indebtedness is not an effect of different constraints for behavior, but seems to be the result of different preferences. Polish communes chose a prudent, careful financial policy, always readjusting aspirations to resources, whereas East German municipalities opted for an (over) optimistic financial policy with investments in oversized infrastructures. The unintended consequence of transformation, a loss of population for many municipalities, hit East German local governments by surprise. They had to register its financial effects that accentuated their debt problems as they had made themselves vulnerable by an overoptimistic financial policy.

One can conclude that the original hypothesis on differences in response strategies to unforeseen challenges between the transformation countries is supported by differences in their adjustability of their aspirations. The far higher rate of indebtedness in East German municipalities is an indicator for people holding on to higher aspirations in the early period of transformation in East Germany. This difference made them more vulnerable to the financial effects of demographic change than their Polish counterparts. Differences between the two countries regarding the awareness of the challenge of demographic change therefore rest on a different development of aspirations, resulting problems and mechanisms of institutionalized awareness registering effects of responses for resource development.

3.2 Autonomy

A second dimension of the comparison of response strategies to demographic change refers to the autonomy in agency and institution building. It was postulated rather generally that the nature of an incorporation transformation like in East Germany might hinder autonomy in institution building to a higher degree than the more self-driven path of the autonomous transformation in Poland. But is this really the case? Institutional economists would argue that more important than the self-directedness of the decisions of a voted elite is whether or not we find a whole range of competing units independently looking for the best solutions. Autonomy and agency in this institutionalist interpretation is not only an attribute of reflective input, but also a result of the relational structure of the units. We will see that both components of the concept of autonomy have an important influence on the divergence of responses to demographic change in the personnel policy of local authorities in the two countries.

To understand why the logic of response in Poland is different, it is useful to compare the institutional development of schools in Poland and Germany, even though these are not part of local government in Germany. Transformation of schools in East Germany encompassed among others three components. With regard to general governance the centralized state system in education was shifted towards a federal system as is common in West Germany. Instead of one central actor we now have five decisive actors in educational questions in East Germany. With respect to school structure, the communist comprehensive school system was changed to a system of early separation of pupils at about age 10, as is common in West Germany. This 'reform' is quite interesting as it is both against international trends and against post-war East German traditions. Its main logic is the adaptation to the West German school system and the traditions of its elites. East German institution building deviated to this structure only insofar as some federal states did not form three separate stratified school forms in their secondary school system, which is the usual structure in West Germany (Hauptschule, Realschule, Gymnasium), but only two separate stratified schools that combined the two lower ones (under different headings 'Sekundarschule,' 'Regelschule,' 'Oberschule,' 'Regionalschule') beside the 'Gymnasium.' This 'innovation' happened in most cases in the early days of transformation and it was not – different to standard controversies in Germany – structured by party politics because both conservative and social democratic governments took this route. With reference to the length of schooling, only some federal states in East Germany changed from the 12 years needed for earning the high school degree of 'Abitur', which was usual in the GDR, to the 13 years which was common in West Germany. Since the turn of the millennium, in both East and West German federal states there has been a move towards shortening the duration of schooling to 12 years.

One can conclude that with the exception of some variance in school differentiation, the main direction of school innovation in East Germany was the adaptation of West German forms. The number of decisive actors did not grow considerably. School reforms are neither direct nor indirect parts of responses to demographic change.

This situation is in sharp contrast to school innovations in Poland, which increased the autonomy of actors considerably and form a major part of indirect forms of response to demographic change. First of all the governance form of education was decentralized. Responsibility for most schools shifted in 1995 from central government to local authorities enumerating the number of independent key actors. In 1999 the position of the school director was strengthened so that he can now decide central aspects of the personnel policy of his school. With reference to school structure,

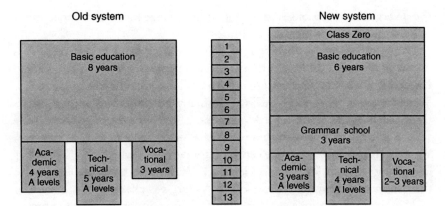

Figure 7.6 Change of Polish school structure in 1999 (Kopycka, 2008).

the communist comprehensive schools were prolonged and split along age markers in 1999. They were not transformed into a stratified system (cf. Figure 7.6). Classes 7 to 9 were formed in new schools called grammar schools (which are, the name notwithstanding, non-selective comprehensive schools). The number of independent schools was raised by 16 per cent between 1998 and 2002 by this reform, despite falling numbers of pupils.

With respect to school duration the education reform in 1999 prolonged the minimum duration of schooling for two extra years, one by starting at age six instead of seven, and one by prolonging it to a higher age as well. As the number of hours taught within one school year was raised as well, one can say that the amount of schooling per pupil was increased considerably by the reform. The effect of the school innovations which intentionally aimed at improving the quality of the school system, following bad results by Poland in international evaluations already in 1995, was that falling numbers of pupils as a consequence of demographic change did not lead to a falling number of teachers. As Figure 7.7 shows, quite the opposite happened: The quality reform of Polish schools at the end of the 1990s compensated the drop in pupils.

It is difficult to evaluate the financial and quality effects of this Polish response to demographic change yet. Financially, a main criterion for the central state to give tax revenues to local authorities follows the number of pupils in the municipalities. The amount of central state subsidies given to schools in municipalities did not keep up with expenses at this level and the gap that the locality has had to fill has been growing since 1995. However, as we have already seen, in most cases this does not mean that local authorities have to go into debt. With respect to output quality of education, the achievement of Polish pupils in PISA tests grew considerably between 2000 and 2003, which is an indicator that more input after the reform may have raised the quality of Polish schools.

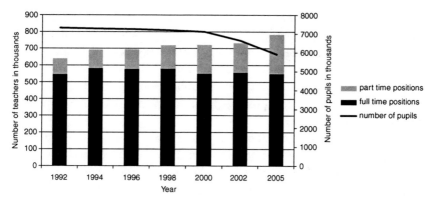

Figure 7.7   Teacher employment and number of pupils in Poland 1992–2005 (Kopycka, 2008).

It was postulated that the response strategy in the Polish transformation process would be better characterized by autonomous development of institutions than in the case of an incorporation transformation. Present data supports this hypothesis. Although there was a similar tendency towards elaborating the communist comprehensive school system in the transformation in East Germany, the main thrust of reform there was in efforts to adapt to the West German system. Federalization only slightly increased the number of independent actors. See-saw changes in the duration of schooling helped to undermine a feeling of collective efficacy in East Germany rather than foster it. School innovations did not have an impact on response strategies to demographic change. In contrast, autonomy of institutions was raised considerably by decentralization of state and school responsibility in Poland. Additionally, a side effect of reforms targeting school quality was that a drop of pupils due to demographic change did not lead to a drop of teachers, since the amount of schooling per pupil compensated for the fall of numbers. Response paths of educational reform in Poland – despite not being targeted to counter the effects of demographic change – are characterized by more innovations fostering autonomy of the system and augmenting the number of independent decisive actors. A response strategy of a rise of quality compensating for a fall in quantity was possible in this context.

3.3   Institutional response sets

A further important point of comparison between the response strategies of transformation societies refers to the personnel policy of organizations in the public sector. Demographic change implies fewer pupils, which, in economic terms, means less demand. In the public sector less 'demand' is not expressed in market demand, but in tax transfers according to the number of persons (pupils) served by an institution, which is also coupled to a drop in population and lower resources for the organization. Organizations are confronted with the problem of adapting their personnel to the new situation. As personnel flexibility in the public sector is regulated to a higher degree than in the private sector, response to this new situation is not easy for the organizations.

In the public sector reaction to demographic change, a big difference exists between general administration and those public sector areas which are very sensitive to demography, like schools and kindergarten. Despite the coupling of a remuneration of taxes to inhabitants, the effect of demography to general administration is not felt. As there is no budget squeeze in Poland, the main problem is not seen in adapting to demography but continually replacing old (regime) administrators by young (innovative) administrators.[5]

Staff in the municipal administration reflects a continuity of personnel since the time of the People's Republic: The same employees on the same position – mainly women. Like it was common in the old days they see applicants as uninvited guests. [...] In sum I can state that despite having in Starow an aging population, we prefer as administrators only young people for recruitment because they can be shaped (Starow, M: 34–35).

Constraints are felt more in Germany when we look at public administration demography in the form of budget. In municipalities there (including East German communes), a standard procedure to adjust to falling numbers of inhabitants (and lower taxes) in public administration in this situation is to stop recruitment and use intergenerational exchange as a way to reduce the number of staff. As budgetary problems are quite common in East (and West) German municipalities, this strategy is widespread.

We now look at the demography sensitive areas. In Polish schools, due to the huge drop of pupils, response strategies are more complex (Kopycka, 2007). The headmaster, in general a former teacher of the school he manages, either uses early retirement, redundancies, fixed term contracts, part-time employment, reduction of weekly working hours, multiple tasking, overtime, combining posts and changes between schools for the adaptation of staff to changing number of pupils. As a result of the decisions of different headmasters, which are diverse, one can discern an ideal-type of a pattern of adaptation strategy which is common in Polish schools at the beginning of the millennium. Figures 7.8 and 7.9 show its general features.

Figure 7.8 shows an internal labor market in a situation with no demographic downturn. Characteristic for it are numerous entrants who move on to secure positions. 'The major drawback of such systems lies in their relatively low responsiveness on changes in demand for workforce'

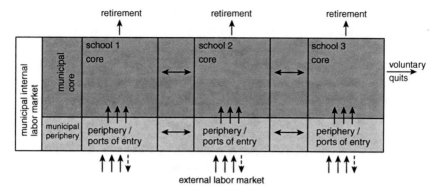

Figure 7.8   Ideal type of an internal labor market (Kopycka, 2007: 128).

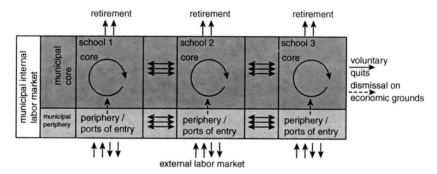

Figure 7.9   Ideal type of contemporary Polish school labor market (Kopycka, 2007, 129).

(Kopycka, 2007: 128). Figure 7.9 shows the present shape of the Polish school labor market. In comparison there is a lot more exchange between external and internal labor market, which is mainly a result of the widespread use of fixed-term contracts for (mostly) young teachers. A transfer from these positions to permanent positions in the meantime is quite rare, thereby increasing insecurity. There is more movement within and between schools. There are two factors bringing about these transfers. Headmasters have successfully encouraged teachers to widen their teaching portfolio from one to two subjects. Secondly, it is quite common within one municipality that schools cooperate in exchanging teachers or in jointly employing teachers. Redundancies (although possible with compensation payments) are quite rare as headmasters try to avoid this measure. Expert interviews show that headmasters have a priority in finding a way of reducing the teaching staff which, in some form, secures the income of teachers. 'Social costs are taken into consideration first, whereas the financial side of the implemented policies, although also very important, comes second' (Kopycka, 2007: 124).

One can conclude that combinations of internal and external flexibility are the major response in personnel policy in areas sensitive to demographic change in Poland.

To get an impression of organizational practices of personnel policy in East Germany in organizations most hit by demographic change one has to look at kindergartens because they are, unlike German schools, within the responsibility of the municipality. The main tools used are a moratorium on recruitment, redundancies, fixed-term contracts and contracted working time reductions. Especially in the late middle of 1990s, mass redundancies of kindergarten educators were a quite common reaction to demographic change. This is quite unusual as redundancies are taboo in the German public sector and complicated in legal terms (although there were some special regulations for East Germany). Both employers and employees disliked this instrument and tried to cushion it with voluntary arrangements and payments. The use of fixed-term contracts – similar to Poland – became more important.

We work a lot with fixed term contracts. That is especially important in the education ... in the educator area, because there we always have to adapt the work capacity according to the number of children. (Bautenbach-Feldow, M: 12).

A further major tool of personnel policy, which had a significant impact on the response strategy of East German municipalities, is time reduction contracts, often in a collective form. All educators, sometimes all the employees of a municipality, work less for less money during the term of a contract between employer and union.

We have reduced hours in the area daycare facilities for children. We did not lay off personnel, but we talked with everybody, in a number of staff meetings, and that it is necessary out of financial reasons because of a change of the children enhancement act and similar things that the hours are reduced. And there are only two options: Either we lay off personnel or we try to distribute it on shoulders, somewhat reconcilable. [...] And as I said, that was the discussion theme that we said: From 38, first to 31 and than we reduced in a second wave to 24 hours. (Bolfin, M: 16).

A decision was made by a collective agreement to adapt to the new situation by quite drastically reducing working hours (and wages.) The mayor of the East German municipality of Bolfin puts this down to showing solidarity. Collective agreements of this kind are quite common in East German municipalities.

All response strategies of personnel policy with regard to demographic change have their specific risks and potentials in the form of unintended consequences. We just want to discuss the most frequent: (a) A moratorium on recruitment – quite common in Germany – practiced for some years, leads to a rapidly aging workforce that might lose innovative force and functional flexibility; (b) Lay-offs and redundancies – seen mostly in East German municipalities – are a shock for organizations and promote mistrust. However, in mid-term perspective lay-offs have the potential that a rise in births (demand) directly results in new recruitment, as can already be experienced in some East German municipalities; (c) Fixed-term contracts – a major form in both Poland and Germany – introduce an element of dual labor markets into public sector employment as insecurity (and sometimes lower wages) are concentrated on the (on average young) entrants whereas stable professional work is shielded for the (older) insiders. After around about one to two decades, systems of dual labor markets come to a situation where the balance of permanent term contracts and fixed contracts may shift to the latter, having the potential to turn an internal labor market to an external flexible labor market. French youth unrest in 2005 can be interpreted as a conflict between these two forms of labor market regulation; (d) Collective working hours reduction – quite common in East Germany – is a response strategy that shifts problems from the presence to the future: it achieves quick financial savings which makes it attractive to the municipality, but as the working hours buffer is sometimes enormous, recruitment takes a lot longer after demand turns around. Therefore, the effects of an aging workforce are a common result of this strategy combined with an occasional drop in motivation as all employees, regardless of their individual efforts, have to renounce wages. Therefore, there is a risk of a Speenham land act equilibrium of a static low-wage, low-effort equilibrium (cf. Polanyi, 1944).

With regard to response strategies of organizations in the form of personnel policies differences between East Germany and Poland are not as large as was the case for aspiration dynamics and autonomy in institution building. Both countries have a similar pattern of internal labor market systems turning cautiously into labor market systems that allow for more external flexibility to react to 'demand shifts' like a drop of births. Manipulations of intergenerational exchange of workforce are the routine act of adaptation in both public sectors. In both countries lay offs are rarely used. Differences are mainly existent with regard to new combinations of external and internal flexibility. In Poland a dual labor market is constituted by fixed-term contracts for newcomers in addition to more internal mobility within organizations and more mobility between organizations in a municipality. Segmentation along cohort and age groups is on the rise and differences between entrants and insiders are augmented. However, collective agreements on working hours and wage reduction are a common feature in East Germany. Despite lowering the wages of insiders it is a strategy that cuts off links to potential outsiders trying to enter organizational employment to an even greater extent. 'Communities of survivors' are reinforced by this strategy. With respect to response sets in institutional personnel policy we do not find differences according to our hypotheses on more informal legal framing and more New Public Management thinking in Poland. There are similarities in organizational habits, which only differ in a slightly more dynamic approach in Poland and a slightly more wary approach in East Germany.

4 Summary

The aim of this chapter was to compare two transformation societies in their second phase of transformation occupied mainly by responding to unintended consequences of transformation. The coping capacity of Poland and East Germany was compared in one exemplary field of unintended consequences, namely demographic change causing shifts in resources and demand for the public sector. The challenge of falling birth rates and an aging population was quite similar in both Poland and East Germany with some differences in the volume and speed of the process. A fall of birth rates was quicker and sharper in East Germany at first, but the overall momentum in Poland was even stronger since the starting level in the 1980s was higher. Differences with regard to responses to this challenge are far more accentuated. Both flexibly adapt to the new situation, in so far as both societies are varieties of modern adaptive societies that can come to terms with the unexpected using principles of democratic market societies. But they also differ in kind and degree of their response strategy, as Figure 7.10 illustrates.

	Autonomous transformation (Poland)	Incorporated transformation (East Germany)
Coping (aspiration and resources) and its institutional effect	Slow rise of aspirations, slow rise of resources → Low level of municipal debt	Quick rise of aspirations, quick resource transfer → High level of municipal debt
Reflexivity and its institutional effect	Autonomous → Multi-actor structure. Collective self-efficacy path	Communicative, fractured → Adaptation. Few actors. Contradictory path
Structuration of personnel policy and its side-effects on identity	Slow shift of practice → Dual labor market. Young vs. old	Slow shift of practice → Communities of survivors

Figure 7.10 Response strategies to demographic change in the municipal public sector in autonomous and incorporated transformation societies.

Differences between the response strategies of autonomous and incorporated transformation countries mainly show up in the areas where the theoretical model would expect them: within the dynamic of aspiration and the reflexivity of collective actors. One fundamental difference lies in a direct effect of an incorporated transformation. Newly included populations think they are included on equal terms, i.e., their aspirations rise quickly. Despite considerable resource transfer from the incorporating society the inelasticity of aspirations results in debts of municipalities. The future room for maneuvering is restricted by this constellation. In contrast to this, autonomous transformation societies can move on a path of a slower rise of aspirations that accompanies the drop and slow rise of resources, usually accompanying transformations. As aspirations follow resources, debt in municipality then is avoided, giving room for future flexibility of action.

A second systematic difference of response strategies is a result of the reflexivity of the institutional actors. Incorporated transformation first develops forms of 'communicative reflexivity' (Archer, 2003) in trying to adapt to the society it is now part of. Neither in content of institution building nor in the figuration of an agency 'market' is there a drive towards reflected autonomy. 'Fractured reflexivity' (Archer, 2003) is also not uncommon as self-will is expressed either by hidden obstinacy or by moving on a contradictory path see-sawing between continuation of past tradition and adaptation. In contrast, in autonomous transformation countries one finds, as is to be expected, more forms of autonomous reflexivity. Characteristically, it takes longer to find solutions for the reform of the content of institutions, as new compromises between past and future have to be found. The strong basis of an autonomous structure is that it is institutionalized in an agency market of decentralized decision making, e.g., a local school governance structure. A collective self-efficacy path can be pioneered.

Response strategies in the dimension of structuration of practice differ less significantly between the two societies. Public sector personnel policy in both Poland and East Germany has shifted from an inflexible employment system to a more flexible public labor market, still with a strong leaning toward internal labor markets and its tendency to separate from the outside. However in detail there are minor differences. The Polish public sector labor market accentuates more dual labor markets with a strong rift between flexible, insecure young professionals and protected older professionals. This latent contentious division might have the potential for disruptive cleavages. The East German public sector cultivates defensive communities of survivors, also common in private companies after many organizations were terminated at the beginning of the 1990s.

Summing up, it seems that Tocqueville has still been right up to now: a higher degree of autonomy (however within the reach of the nearby European Union) might lead to more successful coping strategies in transformation societies than development by subordination to more resourceful countries. Both the dynamics of aspiration and the mode of reflexivity hinder sustainable innovative response strategies in incorporated transformation societies. It has to be seen whether this difference in response strategy between the two formations is only a phase of transformation or whether it is the beginning of diverging self-propagating paths.

Notes

1 At the time of our empirical work only some conceptual and qualitative work of Archer was available, which we used. In the meantime, there also exists a quantitative measurement instrument of reflexivity, the internal conversation indicator (ICONI) (Archer, 2007).
2 We thank the Collaborative Research Center 580, financed by the Deutsche Forschungsgemeinschaft, to enable our project. Principal investigators were Walter Bartl, Dr Bernadette Jonda, Katarzyna Kopycka, Dominika Pawleta and Christian Rademacher, besides the author.
3 Due to need for the privacy protection, the names of the interviewed experts and the names of the communes were kept anonymous.
4 Subjective experience of demographic change in West Germany lies in between these two extremes: demography is seen as irrelevant in three municipalities, and as a challenge in four localities.
5 In contrast to German municipalities we find in Poland also 'a party spoils system' similar to the US where top positions in administration are replaced after election of the mayor. As it is not related to demographic change, we do not comment on it.

References

Archer, Margaret S. (2003). *Structure, agency and the internal conversation*. Cambridge: Cambridge University Press.
Archer, Margaret S. (2007). *Making our way through the world*. Cambridge: Cambridge University Press.
Bartl, Walter (2007). Demographischer Wandel und Personalflexibilität von Kommunen in Ostdeutschland, Polen und Westdeutschland. In R. Sackmann, W. Bartl, K. Kopycka & C. Rademacher (Eds), Strategien zur Bewältigung des demographischen Wandels im öffentlichen Sektor. Sonderforschungsbereich 580 Mitteilungen 24. Jena, Sonderforschungsbereich 580, pp. 50–97.
DiMaggio, Paul, Powell, Walter (1983). The iron cage revisited: Institutional isomorphism and collective rationality. *American Sociological Review*, 48: 147–160.
Elder, Glen H., Caspi, Avshalom (1988). Human development and social change: An emerging perspective on the life course. In N. Bolger, A. Caspi, G. Downey & M. Moorehouse (Eds), *Persons in context. Developmental processes*. Cambridge: Cambridge University Press, pp. 77–113.

Elder, Glen H., Caspi, Avshalom (1990). Persönliche Entwicklung und sozialer Wandel. In Karl Ulrich, Mayer (Ed.), *Lebensverläufe und sozialer Wandel*. Opladen: Westdeutscher Verlag, pp. 22–57.
Elster, Jon (1983). *Sour grapes. Studies in the subversion of rationality*. Cambridge: Cambridge University Press.
Glock, Birgit (2006). Stadtpolitik in schrumpfenden Städten. Wiesbaden: VS Verlag.
Gołata, Elżbieta, Jonda, Bernadette (2008). Demographische Entwicklungen in Polen und Deutschland im Vergleich. In R. Sackmann, B. Jonda & M. Reinhold (Eds), *Demographie als Herausforderung für den öffentlichen Sektor*. Wiesbaden: VS Verlag, pp. 25–46.
Kopycka, Katarzyna (2007). Employment strategies in Polish public schools under changing demographic conditions. In R. Sackmann, W. Bartl, K. Kopycka & C. Rademacher (Eds), *Strategien zur Bewältigung des demographischen Wandels im öffentlichen Sektor*. Sonderforschungsbereich 580 Mitteilungen 24. Jena, Sonderforschungsbereich 580, pp. 98–141.
Kopycka, Katarzyna (2008). Reform des polnischen Bildungssystems – eine expansive Strategie des Staates gegenüber dem demographischen Wandel? In Nikolaus, Werz (Ed.), *Demografischer Wandel – Politische und gesellschaftliche Implikationen*. Baden-Baden: Nomos, pp. 111–124.
Lepsius, M. Rainer (1990). *Interessen, Ideen und Institutionen*. Opladen: Westdeutscher Verlag.
Meyer, John W. (2000). The 'actors' of modern society: The cultural constitution of social agency. *Sociological Theory*, 18, 100–120.
Offe, Claus (1996). *Varieties of transition: The East German and East European experience*. Cambridge: MIT Press.
Parsons, Talcott (1963). On the concept of political power. In *Proceedings of the American Philosophical Society, 107* (3), 232–262.
Polanyi, Karl (1944). *The great transformation*. New York: Rhinehart.
Rademacher, Christian (2007). Die kommunale Bewältigung demografischer Herausforderungen: Deskriptive Ergebnisse im deutsch-polnischen Vergleich. In R. Sackmann, W. Bartl, K. Kopycka & C. Rademacher (Eds), *Strategien zur Bewältigung des demographischen Wandels im öffentlichen Sektor*. Sonderforschungsbereich 580 Mitteilungen 24. Jena, Sonderforschungsbereich 580, pp. 11–46.
Tocqueville, Alexis de (2002). *Democracy in America*. Chicago: University of Chicago Press.
Toynbee, Arnold J. (1947). *A study of history*. Abridgement of Vols. I–VI by D.C. Somervell. Oxford: Oxford University Press.
Toynbee, Arnold J. (1957). *A study of history*. Abridgement of Vols. VII–X by D.C. Somervell. Oxford: Oxford University Press.
Wróblewski, Piotr (2008). Arbeitsmarkt und Kommunen in Oberschlesien: Chorzów – eine Stadt im Wandel. In R. Sackmann, B. Jonda, M. Reinhold, (Eds), *Demographie als Herausforderung für den öffentlichen Sektor*. Wiesbaden: VS Verlag, pp. 269–282.

8

CLASS, STRATIFICATION, AND PERSONALITY UNDER CONDITIONS OF APPARENT SOCIAL STABILITY AND OF RADICAL SOCIAL CHANGE: A MULTI-NATION COMPARISON

Melvin L. Kohn

This chapter attempts a rather sweeping overview of more than half a century of cross-national research that my collaborators and I have done on the relationship of social structure and personality. We have carried out rigorously comparative studies of the United States, Japan, Poland when it was socialist, Poland and Ukraine in their transition to nascent capitalism, and – currently – China, during 'privatization.' These studies have enabled us to compare capitalist and socialist, Western and non-Western, societies during times of relative social stability. They also have enabled us to assess whether the relationships of social structure and personality continue to obtain during periods of radical social change – by which I mean fundamental change in the social, economic, and political structure of the society, not just a period of dramatic events, nor necessarily rapid change.

All of these studies have been devoted to developing and testing an interpretation of the linkages of social structure, proximate conditions of life, and personality that had initially been developed in US studies, particularly a large-scale survey of employed US men (Kohn, 1969; Kohn & Schooler, 1983); extended to employed men in Poland when that country was socialist (Kohn & Slomczynski, 1990) – to see whether the findings and interpretation of the U.S. study applied as well to a socialist society; further extended to employed Japanese men (A. Naoi & Schooler, 1985; Schooler & A. Naoi, 1988; Kohn, A. Naoi et al., 1990) – to see whether the findings and interpretation were generalizable to that non-Western capitalist society; then to the wives of these men in all three countries (J. Miller et al., 1979; M. Naoi & Schooler, 1990; Kohn & Slomczynski, 1990, Chap. 7); and subsequently to the study of both men and women, whether or not employed, in Poland and Ukraine during the early stages of their transition from socialism to nascent capitalism (Kohn et al., 1997, 2000, 2002, 2004; Kohn, 2006, Chaps. 4–7) – to see whether the interpretation was valid even under conditions of radical social change. An ongoing study of China not only affords a unique opportunity to further assess the generality of the findings and interpretation of the relationships between social structure and personality during a much different type of transformation, but also to study whether and, if so, how large-scale social processes, particularly the extent and success of privatization, affect those relationships.

The main theme of these studies is that positions in the class structure and in the social stratification hierarchy are closely linked to such fundamental dimensions of personality as intellectual flexibility, self-directedness of orientation, and a sense of well-being or distress. Moreover, the *explanation* of the relationships between social-structural position and personality is much the same in all the times and places studied: Positions in the class structure and in the social-stratification hierarchy are highly correlated with job conditions that facilitate or limit the opportunity to be self-directed in one's work – notably the substantive complexity of one's work, how closely it is supervised, and how routinized it is. These job conditions, in turn, affect (and are affected by) intellectual flexibility, self-directedness of orientation, and (except for Poland when it was socialist) a sense of well-being or distress.

Conceptualization and indexing of social structure and of personality

Social structure

Our studies focus on two major dimensions of social structure – or, as I prefer to think of them – two complementary conceptualizations of the socio-economic structure of industrialized (and partially industrialized) society: social stratification and social class.

We have conceptualized *social stratification* as a single dimension of inequality, embodying power, privilege, and prestige, as indexed in industrial societies by occupational status, educational attainment, and income. In the earliest studies, we used the Hollingshead Index, which combined a rather *ad hoc* but very serviceable measure of occupational status with a measure of educational attainment. In later studies, as better validated methods of appraising occupational status were developed, we combined the Treiman International Index of Occupational Prestige (based on

Treiman, 1977 and subsequent revisions of the index) with one or more indices of occupational status developed for the particular country, as our index of occupational status. We thereby attempted to capture the reality of occupational status being highly consistent across countries, cultures, and economic systems with whatever variations there might be from country to country. We used confirmatory factor analysis to combine occupational status, educational attainment, and various measures of income.

Our conceptualization of *social class* is a modification of Erik Wright's (1976, 1978) elaboration of Marx's conceptualization to fit the complex realities of the late twentieth century. Our basic premise is that social class is *not* a single continuum of social inequality, but a nominal classification, the intersection of three separate dimensions of power and privilege: ownership and control of the means of production, control over the labor power of others, and (for non-owners who have little or no supervisory authority over others) the classic Marxist distinction between non-manual and manual workers. We have modified the implementation of this conceptual scheme to fit the different realities of capitalist and socialist economies, culture, and periods of stability and change.

Personality

Although our initial choice of dimensions of personality to index and to analyse in these inquiries was made in a search for aspects of personality likely to affect or be affected by social-stratificational position and job conditions linked to stratification for men employed in civilian occupations in the United States, our efforts in later studies have been directed to achieving cross-national and cross-gender comparability in meaning and measurement – to ensure that the concepts are meaningful in all the cultural contexts and social systems we study, and that, insofar as possible, our indices are cross-nationally equivalent.

As our studies developed, we came to focus more and more on three fundamental dimensions of personality that had proved to be related to social-structural position and to job conditions in the studies of the United States, Poland when it was socialist, and Japan: intellectual flexibility, self-directedness of orientation *versus* conformity to external authority, and a sense of well-being or of distress, the latter two being underlying ('second-order') dimensions of orientation to self and others, based on confirmatory factor analyses of several first-order dimensions. Self-directedness of orientation is reflected primarily in not having authoritarian-conservative beliefs and in being receptive to change, and secondarily in having personally responsible standards of morality, being trustful of others, and (in some models) not being fatalistic – all of which are in accord with our theoretical premises. Distress is reflected primarily in being self-deprecatory and anxious, secondarily in lacking self-confidence and being distrustful of others – which certainly appears to be face-valid. The second-order confirmatory factor-analytic models fit the data well for all the countries we studied, and are similar for all these countries, and for men and for women in each country.

Social structure and personality during times of apparent social stability

The basic formulation of our studies – that position in the larger social structure affects (and is affected by) personality through the linkages of social-structural position to more proximate conditions of life and thereby to personality – had been developed and rigorously tested in studies of the United States, including testing and decisively confirming the Weberian hypothesis of reciprocity of effects of job conditions and personality (Kohn & Schooler, 1983, Chaps. 5–7). But the crucial tests of the generalizability of the formulation to countries and conditions other than the United States and other than under conditions of social stability awaited cross-national research.

The first fully comparable cross-national study, proposed and sponsored by Wlodzimierz Wesolowski and carried out by Kazimierz Slomczynski and me, was a comprehensive assessment of whether the interpretation derived from the U.S. research applied to a socialist society, as Poland then was (Kohn & Slomczynski, 1990). A second comprehensive cross-national study, sponsored by Ken'ichi Tominaga and carried out by Atsushi Naoi & Carmi Schooler (Naoi & Schooler, 1985; Schooler & Naoi, 1988), asked whether the interpretation derived from U.S. research applied to a non-Western society, Japan.

For the comparative analysis of the United States, Japan, and socialist Poland, we adapted the same basic conceptualizations of class and stratification to the historical, cultural, economic, and political circumstances of each country. We hypothesized that men who are more advantageously located in the class and stratification structures of their society would be more likely to value self-direction for their children, to be intellectually flexible, and to be self-directed in their orientations to self and society than are men who are less advantageously located in the social structure of that society. This expectation was strikingly confirmed for both class and stratification in all three countries (Kohn, A. Naoi, et al., 1990).

We also hypothesized that in all three countries the job conditions that facilitate or impede the exercise of occupational self-direction would play a crucial role in explaining the psychological effects of both class and stratification. This is a very strong hypothesis. We defined social class in terms of ownership and control over the means of production and control over the labor power of others; but we hypothesized that the reason why social class affects personality is because class position is determinative of how much control one has over the conditions of one's own work. There is nothing in the classic definition of social class, nor in the criteria we employed to index social class, that speaks directly to the issue of control over the conditions of one's own occupational life. Yet, we hypothesized that what is psychologically important about having an advantaged class position is not the power over others that it affords, but the opportunity it provides to be self-directed in one's own occupational life. Similarly for social stratification: our fundamental hypothesis was that position in the social-stratification hierarchy affects personality, not primarily because of the status it affords, nor even the socio-economic rewards that it confers, but because of the opportunity it provides to be self-directed in one's work.

This hypothesis, too, was strikingly confirmed. The effects of class and stratification on intellectual flexibility, valuation of self-direction, and self-directedness of orientation (and its principal component dimensions – authoritarian-conservatism vs. open-mindedness, personally responsible standards of morality, and receptiveness to change) – proved to be largely a function of the varying opportunities for occupational self-direction enjoyed by men at various locations in the class structure and at varying levels of the stratification hierarchy. Occupational self-direction thus plays a major part in explaining the effect of class and stratification on all these facets of personality. Moreover, the effects of occupational self-direction on intellectual flexibility, valuation of self-direction, and self-directedness of orientation are cross-nationally consistent.

There is one apparent anomaly in the findings, a cross-national difference in the relationships of social class and of social stratification with feelings of well-being or distress (and its principal component dimensions: anxiety and self-deprecation). In the United States, managers had a strong sense of well-being and manual workers were distressed; in socialist Poland, just the opposite; and in Japan managers had a strong sense of well-being, but it was the non-manual workers, not the manual workers, who were most distressed (Kohn, Naoi et al., 1990). Correspondingly, in the United States there was a *negative* relationship between social stratification and distress, in Japan there was virtually no relationship between the two, and in socialist Poland the relationship was *positive*. The Polish-U.S. differences appear to be largely a function of differences in the conditions experienced by Polish managers, especially those who were not members of the Communist Party, and U.S. managers, and between Polish and U.S. manual workers (see Kohn & Slomczynski, 1990, pp. 215–24).

The employed segments of the populations of Poland and Ukraine during times of radical social change

With the demise of the Soviet Union, Krystyna Janicka, Valeriy Khmelko, Bogdan Mach, Vladimir Paniotto, & Wojciech Zaborowski joined Slomczynski and me in a comparative study of whether the relationships between social structure and personality were altered under the conditions of radical social change attendant on the transformation of Poland and Ukraine from socialism to nascent capitalism. These studies were based on surveys of representative samples of the entire adult populations of the urban areas of these countries – women as well as men, whether or not employed.

Insofar as the earlier findings for employed Polish men under socialism were similar to those that had been found for U.S. and Japanese men under capitalism – notably, in the relationships of class and stratification to intellectual flexibility and to self-directedness of orientation and its component dimensions of personality – nothing had changed (Kohn et al., 1997; Kohn, 2006, Chap. 4). Moreover, the magnitudes of the relationships of social class with both intellectual flexibility and self-directedness of orientation were nearly as large for Polish men during the transition to nascent capitalism as they had been under socialism, and a bit larger for Polish women. Similarly, the correlations of *social stratification* with intellectual flexibility and self-directedness of orientation were as large for Polish men and women during the transition as they had been for Polish men under socialism. Moreover, occupational self-direction continued to largely explain the relationships of class and stratification with intellectual flexibility and with self-directedness of orientation. In all these respects, the explanation of the relationships between social structure and personality remained much the same during the Polish transition as during apparently stable socialist times.

Insofar as the earlier findings for Polish men under socialism had *differed* from those for U.S. and Japanese men, however – in particular, in the relationship between social structure and a sense of *distress* or of well-being (and their principal component dimensions: anxiety and self-deprecation) – there had been very great change indeed. Now the pattern for Polish men was much the same as for U.S. men, with managers and experts now having the strongest sense of well-being, and manual workers now being the most distressed of all social classes. Similarly, there had been a reversal in the relationship of social stratification with distress: whereas higher social-stratification position was earlier associated with a greater sense of distress, now it was associated with a greater sense of well-being. These relationships are much the same for Polish women as for Polish men, and stronger in magnitude.

Moreover, whereas occupational self-direction played little or no role in explaining the relationships of social structure and distress for Polish men under socialism, it was now of decisive importance. By contrast, conditions of uncertainty – which had been conducive to distress in both the United States and socialist Poland – declined in importance to virtual irrelevance. Here, too, the findings are much the same for Polish women as for Polish men.

The findings for employed *Ukrainian* men and women in 1992–1993 are in all respects similar in *pattern* to those for employed Polish men and women, but the *magnitudes* of relationship are consistently smaller for the Ukrainians (see Kohn et al., 1997 or Kohn, 2006, Chaps. 4 and 6). Still, the findings for Ukraine differ from those for Poland not in kind but only in degree.

In short, any expectation that the process of radical social change might undermine the relationships of social structure and personality earlier found in countries enjoying apparently stable social conditions was not borne out. Instead, radical social change seemed to affect the relationships of social structure and personality for employed men and women primarily in that social structures in the process of transformation came to exhibit the patterns characteristic of the type of society they were in the process of becoming. By late 1992, Poland already exhibited the capitalist pattern. As of late 1992 and early 1993, Ukraine seemed to be following a similar trajectory, albeit at a slower pace.

In my presidential address to the American Sociological Association (Kohn, 1987, pp. 716–21), I had subscribed to the view of several cross-national scholars that our goal, when we find cross-national differences, should be to develop higher-level interpretations that encompass both the cross-national similarities and the cross-national differences. But I lamented that I had not yet achieved that goal with respect to my interpretation of the inter-relationship of social-structural position, proximate conditions of life, and feelings of well-being or distress. Perhaps that statement was overly cautious, for I had provided pertinent evidence that the conditions of work and life for both manual workers and managers were quite different in the United States and socialist Poland, and that this probably accounted for the difference in the relationships of class and stratification with distress in the two countries. But, I must not have thought that the evidence for this conclusion was definitive. That evidence became much stronger with the reversal of the relationships of class and stratification with distress when the proximate conditions of life associated with being a manager or a manual worker changed dramatically in Poland (and Ukraine) with the advent of nascent capitalism.

I would now put it that the key to understanding the relationships of social structure to personality lies in the proximate conditions associated with social-structural position, which affect and are affected by personality (no change in the formulation thus far), but that the proximate conditions associated with class position or stratificational level are not necessarily invariant for all countries or all times. It makes a huge difference in one's conditions of life to be a manager (particularly a non-Party manager) under socialism and under capitalism; similarly for being a manual worker.

The non-employed segments of the Polish and Ukrainian populations during times of radical social change

The transformation of the economic and social structures of Poland and Ukraine presented both the need and the opportunity to expand the study of social structure and personality from the class positions and social-stratification levels of the employed to include as well the social-structural positions of the non-employed. Major categories of non-employment, although not entirely new to these transitional societies, were greatly expanded and substantially altered in social composition. This was particularly true for the *un*employed (those who had lost their jobs and were actively seeking paid employment) and for housewives, especially in Poland at that time. Equally far-reaching had been changes in the conditions of life of both new (or newly expanding) and existing segments of the population, in particular the economic adversity experienced by the unemployed, many housewives, and the pensioners.

In our analyses of the non-employed, we extended the conceptualization of *complexity*, to encompass not only the complexity of *work*, whether in paid employment or in such other realms as housework, but also the complexity of people's activities in *non-work* realms. Our hypothesis was that engaging in complex activities in any realm of life that is psychologically salient, regardless of whether the activities are thought of as work, profoundly affects and is affected by personality. We even hypothesized that complexity of activities is of such pervasive importance that the magnitudes of relationship between the complexity of activities and personality would be nearly as great for non-employed segments of the population as for the employed, and that these relationships do not merely reflect the propensity of more highly educated people to engage in more complex activities, nor do they represent a carryover from the complexity of people's past jobs to their present personalities. All these hypotheses were confirmed (Kohn et al., 2000; Kohn, 2006, Chap. 5).

Further analyses of the non-employed were addressed to learning whether there are significant differences in personality between the non-employed and the employed, and among the different segments of the non-employed (the unemployed, housewives, and pensioners); and whether such differences can be explained (in part) by the complexity of people's activities and other proximate conditions of their lives. These analyses showed that unemployed men and women, housewives, and pensioners do differ in personality, not only from employed people of their own gender in their respective countries, but also from other segments of the non-employed. Although some of these differences in personality may be ascribed to the social compositions of the several segments of the populations, the analyses show that the relationships between structural location and personality are also, in substantial part, a function of the conditions of life experienced by people in the various segments of the population.

At least two such conditions are relevant to personality. The first is economic adversity, which helps to explain the relationship of social-structural position with feelings of well-being or distress, particularly the cross-nationally consistent distress of the unemployed (notably including formerly employed housewives who would have greatly preferred to be employed). Second are conditions that enhance or diminish the complexity of activities. The transformation not only exposed some segments of the non-employed to conditions of economic duress, but also resulted in the unemployed and pensioners engaging in less complex activities than those characteristic of work in paid employment. Complexity of activities (or the lack thereof) is pertinent for explaining the relationship of structural location with all three fundamental dimensions of personality that we studied, intellectual flexibility most of all (Kohn et al., 2002; Kohn, 2006, Chap. 6).

Thus, the interpretive model that explains the relationships of class and stratification to personality for the employed applies also to the non-employed: social-structural position affects personality, at least in substantial part, through the proximate conditions of people's lives attendant on their location in the social structure. I would now add that these proximate conditions differed for Poland and Ukraine, consonant with Poland being further along in its transformation.

The psychological dynamics of radical social change: A longitudinal analysis of employed and unemployed Ukrainian men and women

With the realization that Ukraine had been at an early stage of a very radical transformation at the time of their cross-sectional survey in 1992–93, Valeriy Khmelko and Vladimir Paniotto grasped the unique opportunity to secure the follow-up data that would make possible longitudinal analyses of the ongoing processes of radical social change. In the spring and summer of 1996 they re-interviewed all those men and women in the original sample who had been in the labor force at the time of the initial interview.

We know from Khmelko's (2002) analysis of macrosocial change in the first decade of Ukrainian independence that by 1996 (and even later), although Ukraine had left its former socialist economy far behind, it had not moved decisively to a capitalist social and economic structure. The longitudinal Ukrainian analysis, then, is *not* a study of Ukraine *before* and *after* its transformation from socialism to capitalism, nor of Ukraine *during* and *after* the transformation, but of Ukraine during the early stages of an ongoing transformation whose eventual outcome was still uncertain.

Our analyses of these precious data yielded two principal findings. One is that during a period of three to three and a half years of ongoing radical social change, there was extreme *instability* in urban men's and women's self-directedness of orientation and sense of well-being or distress, and substantial instability even in what past studies, our own included, had found to be the most stable facet of personality: intellectual flexibility. So unexpected was this finding that we devoted several months to verifying that it was not an artifact of some defect in method (see Kohn et al., 2004 or Kohn, 2006, Chap. 7). The other principal finding is that, despite radical social change and instability of personality, the relationships of social class and social stratification with personality remained similar in pattern after three to three-and-a-half tumultuous years.

Much of the longitudinal analysis was devoted to reconciling what, on its face, would seem to be an incompatibility in these findings. If personality is so unstable, how could the relationships of social structure and personality be consistent over time?

Our initial hypothesis was that the extraordinary instability of personality might be linked to social mobility – that people who moved from more advantaged to less advantaged structural locations might have suffered increased distress, a decline in self-directedness of orientation, perhaps even a decline in intellectual flexibility; and that (those few) people who moved from less advantaged to more advantaged structural locations might have enjoyed an increased sense of well-being, greater self-directedness of orientation, and increased intellectual flexibility. At the extreme – the extreme being movement into and out of the ranks of the employed – there was evidence in support of this hypothesis, in that such mobility was substantially and significantly related to change in self-directedness of orientation and distress, albeit not to any significant change in intellectual flexibility. Still, the great majority of urban adults were employed both in 1992–93 and in 1996, and for them there was little evidence of any substantial linkage between social mobility and change in personality.

What, then, does explain the consistently significant relationships of social class and social stratification with self-directedness of orientation and intellectual flexibility during a period of three to three and a half years of radical social change and despite great instability of personality? Our emerging hypothesis was that the same proximate conditions of life that link position in the larger social structure with personality in times of greater social stability continued to play a bridging role throughout this period of Ukraine's transformation. The underlying premise of this hypothesis, of course, is that massive social change, as experienced during this extended period of time in Ukraine, did not affect the linkages of structural location to people's immediately impinging conditions of life. In support of this premise, we found that class and stratification were as highly correlated with the substantive complexity of work during this period of radical social change in Ukraine as they have been shown to be in other societies during times of apparent social stability. And the substantive complexity of work was linked to self-directedness of orientation and to intellectual flexibility, just as in other countries in more stable times, although not quite as strongly.

Moreover, as hypothesized, the crucial proximate conditions of life were themselves highly stable. Our empirical analyses focused on one key condition, the substantive complexity of work. Its stability, even during these years of radical social change, proved to be very high – both for men and for women.

The ultimate test was to replicate for Ukrainian men and women the prototypic causal model of job conditions and personality that Carmi Schooler and I had developed to assess the reciprocal effects of the substantive complexity of work and intellectual flexibility for U.S. men (Kohn & Schooler, 1978, 1983, Chap. 5). If our rationale is valid, then the substantive complexity of work should affect the intellectual flexibility of Ukrainian men and women during this period of radical social change much as it had affected the intellectual flexibility of U.S. men during an extended period of social stability. Indeed, it did, for both employed men and employed women (Kohn, 2006, Figure 7.1). What was not expected, but perhaps should have been expected, was that the effect of intellectual flexibility on the substantive complexity of work, which in the U.S. model had been strong, in the Ukrainian models was small and statistically non-significant. How could it be otherwise? If personality is unstable, how can it substantially affect the individual's ability either to modify his or her job conditions or to affect processes of promotion, retention, and job selection?

The major lesson from the longitudinal analyses of Ukraine is one of stability despite change: stability in the relationships of social structure and personality despite ongoing massive change in the social and economic structure of the country, and despite massive instability of personality of the adult populace.

The ongoing study of social structure and personality during the transformation of urban China

My collaborators, Weidong Wang & Lulu Li, and I have extended the comparisons to the radically different type of transformation now taking place in China. Instead of the transformation of the economic system following the collapse of the political system, as in Eastern Europe and the former Soviet Union, in China the 'privatization' of the economic system is taking place under the aegis of the Communist Party, thus far with little or no evidence of the political system changing substantially.

The Chinese transformation is not only very different from those of Eastern Europe and the former Soviet Union, but it is proceeding unevenly in this huge and heterogenous society, providing a splendid opportunity to see whether and, if so, how, the relationships of social structure and personality may vary in different social and economic contexts. The contexts that might matter most would be the extent and success, thus far, of privatization. To pursue this objective, we systematically selected our samples from cities ranging from the highest to the lowest quartile of Chinese cities, ranked on a scale of privatization and wealth, adding one city (Tianjin) from the highest quartile but much larger than most cities in that quartile (see the rationale and methods of selection in Kohn et al., 2007).

Measurement of social class and social stratification in transitional China

Since our primary basis for comparison of transitional China is transitional Poland and Ukraine, we have made precisely the same categorization of social classes for China as we did for Poland and Ukraine in transition, with seven class categories: employers, self-employed, managers, supervisors, experts, non-manual workers, and manual workers.

Our index of social stratification also parallels those we used in studies of transitional Poland and Ukraine (and of other countries), including measuring occupational status by combining the standard international classification with a classification specific to the particular country, one recently developed for China (Li, 2005).

Conceptualization and measurement of personality

For our study of China, we began with the indices developed for the comparative analyses of Poland and Ukraine during the early stages of their transformations, and undertook intensive inquiry into the appropriateness of using these indices for China (see Liu, 2006; Kohn et al., 2007, pp. 414–26).

The confirmatory factor-analytic measurement models we developed for all these dimensions of personality provide the evidence for four principal conclusions: One is that the models fit the data very well. The second is that the models, and in particular the relationships of concepts to indicators, are very similar for China to those for all the other countries we have studied. The third is that the models are essentially invariant for the five cities we studied in China. The fourth is that the models are essentially the same for men and for women. From this evidence, we concluded that we have a firm basis in cross-national comparability of meaning and measurement of all the dimensions of personality we have studied and thus for assessments of the relationships between social structure and personality in transitional China and all the times and countries to which we compare transitional China (Kohn et al., 2007, pp. 414–26). The evidence is strong that the concepts apply to China much as they do to Poland and Ukraine in transition (and also to the United States, Japan, and Poland when it was socialist). We are not imposing Western psychological concepts on Chinese culture.

Class, stratification, and personality for China compared to transitional Poland and Ukraine

The relationships of social class and of social stratification with intellectual flexibility, self-directedness of orientation, and feelings of well-being or distress are the same in pattern for Chinese men and women as they are for Polish and Ukrainian men and women. Thus, more advantaged social classes – managers, experts, and (male but not female) employers are more self-directed in their orientations and more intellectually flexible than the average for employed people of their gender; less advantaged social classes – manual workers and the self-employed – are less self-directed and less intellectually flexible than the average for employed people of their gender.

Of critical importance for the comparison of social structure and personality under different socio-political conditions, Chinese managers, like Polish and Ukrainian managers during the transition of those countries from socialism to nascent capitalism, but unlike Polish managers during socialism, are among the least distressed of the social classes. Chinese manual workers (like Polish and Ukrainian manual workers during the transformation of those countries, but unlike Polish and Ukrainian manual workers during socialist days) are among the most distressed of all social classes.

The findings for social stratification are entirely consonant with those for social class, with positive correlations for social stratification always matching high scores for the more advantaged social classes. The signs of the correlations between social-stratification position and the three principal dimensions of personality are also entirely consonant with those for Polish and Ukrainian men and women. The correlations with intellectual flexibility, while uniformly positive, are not quite as large for Chinese men and women as for Poles of the same gender, are uniformly positive and of roughly similar magnitude to those for Poland vis-a-vis self-directness of orientation, and are uniformly negative, and stronger in magnitude than those for Poland vis-a-vis distress. The correlations of social stratification with all three dimensions of personality are of the same sign but stronger in magnitude for Chinese men and women than for Ukrainians of the same gender.

Are the correlations of social-stratification position with personality substantially related to the cities' degree of privatization and wealth? The short answer is *no* – not substantially, certainly not linearly. Nor do these correlations differ much for men and women, or for the megacity and the city of lesser size but roughly similar degree of privatization and wealth. The relationships of social structure and personality would appear to be quite the same for all of urban China. Moreover, these relationships for China in transition to a 'privatized' economy are altogether consonant with those for Poland and Ukraine in transition from socialism to nascent capitalism, particularly with those for Poland, at a later stage of transformation.

The job conditions conducive to and restrictive of occupational self-direction

We have not yet come to the heart of the findings of all previous studies: namely, that the relationships of class and stratification with personality are largely explained by the linkages of social structure to the job conditions that are conducive to or restrictive of the opportunity to be self-directed in one's work – the substantive complexity of work, closeness of supervision, and routinization. Is this, too, true of China? To a modest degree, it is: these job conditions *do* contribute to the relationships of social structure with all the aspects of personality that we have studied. But they do not do so to as great a degree as they do for Poland (and, for some comparisons, also for Ukraine). Specifically, the substantive complexity of work is not nearly as important in explaining the relationships of social structure with intellectual flexibility and with self-directedness of orientation for Chinese men and women as for Polish men and women and, in some comparisons, for Ukrainian men and women; routinization is essentially irrelevant for explaining *any* of the relationships of class and stratification with these dimensions of personality for China; but closeness of supervision does have considerable explanatory power, especially for explaining the relationships of social structure with a sense of well-being or distress. On average, although these three job conditions taken altogether account for half to two-thirds, or even more, of the magnitudes of relationship of class and stratification with intellectual flexibility, self-directedness of orientation, and distress (and their constituent dimensions) for Poland, they account for decidedly smaller proportions of these relationships for China (with the corresponding figures for Ukraine not being either consistently higher or lower than those for China).

Thus, the relationships of class and stratification with personality may be of similar magnitude for Poland and China, but the explanation of these relationships is less complete for China. This immediately raises the twin questions: why do these job conditions provide a less complete explanation of the relationships of class and stratification with personality for China than for Poland and, for at least some dimensions of personality, for Ukraine? And what other conditions of life (or other variables) contribute to the relationships of class and stratification being nearly as strong for China as for Poland? We are again faced with the necessity of enlarging the interpretation to account for both the cross-national similarities and the cross-national differences.

I do not believe that the answer to the first of these questions lies in any difference in the measurement models we developed for the three job conditions for China from those we developed for Poland and Ukraine, although I must admit that I have not yet fully checked out the possibility that small differences in the relationships of concepts to indicators might contribute to the differences in findings. What I can be certain of is that the cross-national differences in the explanatory power of the three job conditions do not reflect any differences in how strongly these job conditions are related to either social class or social stratification: all three job conditions are as strongly related to class and stratification for China as for Poland and Ukraine. The substantive complexity of work, in particular, is very strongly related (approximately 0.80) to both class and stratification for both Chinese men and women, and in all five cities that we have sampled.

It logically follows that the correlations of one or more of these job conditions with some or all of the dimensions of personality must be smaller for China than for Poland and perhaps also for Ukraine. We have confirmed this inference by systematic cross-national comparisons of the magnitudes of the correlations of each of the three job conditions with all ten dimensions of personality that we have measured. From this array of comparisons, we learn that the correlations of the substantive complexity of work with the several dimensions of personality are generally weaker in magnitude (particularly vis-à-vis intellectual flexibility, but not vis-à-vis distress) for Chinese men and women than for Polish men and women, but not generally weaker than those for Ukrainian men and women. For closeness of supervision, some correlations with personality are *stronger* for Chinese men and women than for Polish men and women (especially vis-à-vis distress and its component dimensions), others are weaker (particularly vis-à-vis intellectual flexibility); and almost all correlations are stronger for China than for Ukraine. For routinization, the correlations with personality are almost invariably weaker for Chinese than for Poles and Ukrainians.

We learn more by examining the same array of correlations from the perspective of the relative importance of the three job conditions for personality in each of the three countries. For Chinese men and women, closeness of supervision ranks a clear first in terms of the magnitude of its correlations with personality. This is true not only vis-à-vis distress and its component dimensions, but also vis-à-vis self-directedness of orientation and its component dimensions, albeit not for intellectual flexibility. The substantive complexity of work is only modestly related to most dimensions of personality for Chinese men and women, the major exception being intellectual flexibility, for which the correlations are 0.36 for men and 0.38 for women. Last in terms of the magnitudes of correlations is routinization. For Chinese men, routinization has even modest correlations only with self-directedness of orientation (-0.18) and two of its component dimensions, authoritarian conservatism and receptiveness to change ($+0.17$ and -0.21); but even these correlations are much lower than those for Poland and Ukraine. And routinization is essentially irrelevant to *all* the dimensions of personality that we have studied for Chinese women. For Poland, by contrast, the substantive complexity of work is the dominant job condition of the three, more strongly related to many aspects of personality than is closeness of supervision, with routinization not far behind the other two. For Ukraine, the *relative* potency of the three job conditions is different from both China and Poland: routinization is, overall, the most potent of the three job conditions (particularly vis-à-vis self-directedness of orientation), with the other two essentially tied.

What is most distinctive about the relationships of these three job conditions with personality for China, as compared to Poland and Ukraine, is the relative strength of the relationships to personality of closeness of supervision and the extreme weakness of the relationships to personality of routinization. The substantive complexity of work is certainly not as closely related to personality for China as for Poland, but is at least as closely related to personality for China as for Ukraine. Major questions for further analysis are to explain why closeness of supervision is as closely linked to personality as it appears to be for Chinese men and women; why the substantive complexity of work is not nearly as closely linked to personality for Chinese men and women as for Polish men and women; and why routinization of work is not nearly as closely linked to personality for Chinese men and women as for Ukrainian men and women.

Whatever the explanation of these cross-national differences in the relationships of the three job conditions to personality may be, there must be other proximate conditions of life that also contribute to the relationships between position in the larger social structure and personality being nearly as strong for transitional China as for Poland, and stronger than for Ukraine. These 'other proximate conditions' may well be job conditions other than those on which our analyses have thus far focused. Two sets of job conditions come immediately to mind, one because it may be especially important at a time of radical social change, the other because it has in the recent past been, and may still continue to be, uniquely important in China.

The first set of conditions pertains to people's direct experiences of change and uncertainty. In the studies of Poland and Ukraine in transition, these had little explanatory effect on the relationships between social structure and personality – not because the experience of change and uncertainty was irrelevant to personality, but because such experience was so widespread throughout the social structure that it didn't much affect the relationships of social structure and personality. In the belief that these experiences might be more differentially distributed in the uneven process of privatization of this vast and heterogeneous country, we asked about our respondents' experiences of change and uncertainty in the China survey. The second set of conditions that might contribute to a fuller explanation of the relationships between social structure and personality for transitional China are some distinctively Chinese aspects of the organization of work. A prominent example is the so-called 'work unit,' which has in the past provided many of the basic components of social welfare and may even now link position in the social structure to personality for some segments of the population. We have included questions that we hope will be adequate for assessing the relevance of such aspects of work organization for linking people's positions in the larger social structure to personality in some or all of the selected cities. It will be particularly interesting to see if 'work unit' is as relevant for those cities that are advanced in privatization and wealth as for those that are not.

Conclusions

The most general conclusion I can draw from our studies is that we have found overwhelming similarities in the interrelationships of class and stratification with job conditions and personality in all the countries we have studied, Western and non-Western, socialist and capitalist, during times of apparent social stability and of radical social change. We have also found one poignant difference between socialist Poland and the capitalist countries, which disappeared as Poland and Ukraine became capitalist and is nowhere to be found in transitional China.

In our current comparisons of social structure and personality in transitional China to those same relationships in transitional Poland and Ukraine, the findings are actually remarkably consonant: in China, as in Poland and Ukraine during their very different transformations, a more advantaged position in the class structure, and a higher position in the social-stratification hierarchy, are associated with a more self-directed orientation, greater intellectual flexibility, and a greater sense of well-being, in contrast to a sense of distress. This is true both for employed Chinese men and for employed Chinese women, and it appears to be equally true regardless of the degree to which the city in which they live has been privatized, regardless of its wealth and, our one pertinent comparison suggests, regardless of its size. In our findings for China, as in the findings for transitional Poland and Ukraine, there is no hint of the one major respect in which Poland under socialism differed from the capitalist United States and Japan, that is, in the stronger sense of well-being of the manual workers than of other social classes in socialist Poland, and the stronger sense of distress among the managers, particularly those who were not members of the Communist Party. In transitional China, as in transitional Poland and Ukraine and in the capitalist United States, it is the manual workers who are most distressed and the more advantaged social classes (and the higher social-stratificational strata) who have a greater sense of well-being.

Where transitional China differs from transitional Poland and Ukraine, and from the capitalist United States and Japan, is that the job conditions that facilitate or restrict the exercise of occupational self-direction do not explain the relationships of class and stratification with personality to nearly as great a degree as they do for Poland and, for some aspects of personality, Ukraine as well. We do not as yet fully understand why this is so, or what other conditions of life contribute to the explanation of those relationships. These are intriguing questions, which we intend to pursue as thoroughly as our data and our imaginations permit.

References

Khmelko, Valeriy (2002). Macrosocial change in Ukraine: The years of independence. *Sisyphus: Sociological Studies*, XVI, 125–136.

Kohn, Melvin L. (1969). *Class and conformity: A study in values*. Homewood, IL: Dorsey Press. (2nd ed. University of Chicago Press, 1977).

—— (1987). Cross-national research as an analytic strategy: American Sociological Association, 1987 Presidential Address. *American Sociological Review*, 52, 713–731.

—— (2006). *Change and stability: A cross-national analysis of social structure and personality*. Boulder, CO: Paradigm Publishers.

Kohn, Melvin L., Khmelko, Valeriy., Paniotto, Vladimir., & Hung, Ho-fung. (2004). Social structure and personality during the process of radical social change: A study of Ukraine in transition. *Comparative Sociology*, 3: 3–4, 1–46.

Kohn, Melvin L., Li, Lulu., Wang, Weidong., & Yue, Yin. (2007). Social structure and personality during the transformation of urban China: A preliminary report of an ongoing research project. *Comparative Sociology*, 6, 389–429.

Kohn, Melvin L., Naoi, Atsushi., Schoenbach, Carrie., Schooler, Carmi., & Slomczynski, Kazimierz M. (1990). Position in the class structure and psychological functioning in the United States, Japan, and Poland. *American Journal of Sociology*, 95, 964–1008.

Kohn, Melvin L., & Schooler, Carmi. (1978). The reciprocal effects of the substantive complexity of work and intellectual flexibility: A longitudinal assessment. *American Journal of Sociology*, 84 (July), 24–52.

—— With the collaboration of Joanne Miller, Miller, Karen A., Schoenbach, Carrie., & Schoenberg, Ronald. (1983). *Work and personality: An inquiry into the impact of social stratification*. Norwood, NJ: Ablex.

Kohn, Melvin L., & Slomczynski, Kazimierz M. (2006). With the collaboration of Carrie Schoenbach (1990). *Social structure and self-direction: A comparative analysis of the United States and Poland*. Oxford: Basil Blackwell. (2nd ed.), IFiS Publishers [Institute of Philosophy and Sociology, Polish Academy of Sciences], 2006.)

Kohn, Melvin L., Slomczynski, Kazimierz M., Janicka, Krystyna., Khmelko, Valeri., Mach, Bogdan W., Paniotto, Vladimir., Zaborowski, Wojciech., Gutierrez, Roberto., & Heyman, Cory. (1997). Social structure and personality under conditions of radical social change: a comparative analysis of Poland and Ukraine. *American Sociological Review*, 62, 614–638.

Kohn, Melvin L., Zaborowski, Wojciech., Janicka, Krystyna., Mach, Bogdan W., Khmelko, Valeriy., Slomczynski, Kazimierz., Heyman, Cory., & Podobnik, Bruce. (2000). Complexity of activities and personality under conditions of radical social change: A comparative analysis of Poland and Ukraine. *Social Psychology Quarterly*, 63, 187–208.

Kohn, Melvin L., Zaborowski, Wojciech., Janicka, Krystyna., Khmelko, Valeriy., Mach, Bogdan W., Paniotto, Vladimir., Slomczynski, Kazimierz M., Heyman, Cory., & Podobnik, Bruce. (2002). Structural location and personality during the transformation of Poland and Ukraine, *Social Psychology Quarterly*, 65, 364–385.

Li, Chunling (2005). Prestige stratification in contemporary China: Occupational prestige measures and socio-economic index, *Sociological Research*, 2, 74–102. [In Chinese].

Liu, Bei (2006). Social structure and personality in transitional urban China. Unpublished PhD dissertation, Johns Hopkins University.

Miller, Joanne, Schooler, Carmi, Kohn, Melvin L. & Miller, Karen A. (1979). Women and work: The psychological effects of occupational conditions, *American Journal of Sociology*, 85 (July), 66–94.

Naoi, Atsushi & Schooler, Carmi (1985). Occupational conditions and psychological functioning in Japan, *American Journal of Sociology*, 90, 729–752.

Naoi, Michiko & Schooler, Carmi (1990). Psychological consequences of occupational conditions among Japanese wives, *Social Psychology Quarterly*, 53, 100–116.

Schooler, Carmi & Naoi, Atsushi (1988). The psychological effects of traditional and of economically peripheral job settings in Japan. *American Journal of Sociology*, 94, 335–355.

Donald J. Treiman (1977). *Occupational prestige in comparative perspective*. New York: Academic Press.

Wright, Erik Olin (1976). Class boundaries in advanced capitalist societies. *New Left Review*, 98, 3–41.

—— (1978). *Class, crisis and the state*. London: New Left Books.

9

CHILDREN'S SOCIOEMOTIONAL FUNCTIONING AND ADJUSTMENT IN THE CHANGING CHINESE SOCIETY

Xinyin Chen and Huichang Chen

Developmental theorists have long argued that human lives carry the imprint of their social worlds, which are themselves subject to continuous historical change (Bronfenbrenner & Morris, 2006; Elder, 1974; Silbereisen, 2000). This argument has been supported by the results of cross-cultural studies in many traditionally rural societies during urbanization and modernization (e.g., Graves & Graves, 1983; Madsen & Lancy, 1981), where individuals experienced social, economic, and cultural transformation (Nadler, Romek, & Shapira-Friedman, 1979). The impact of macro-level societal changes on human development is demonstrated systematically in the research program conducted by Elder (1974) on the implications of the Great Depression in the 1930s in the United States for family organization, parenting and child behavior. Recent studies in Eastern European nations (Flanagan, 2000; Little, Brendgen, Wanner, & Krappmann, 1999; Silbereisen, 2000) also indicate the significant effects of dramatic social and political changes after the fall of the Berlin Wall on children and adolescents' relationships, behaviors, and life adjustment.

Social and cultural changes may affect children's socioemotional functioning and adjustment through shaping socialization goals, beliefs, and practices. Kagitcibasi and Ataca (2005), for example, found that the developmental goals of Turkish parents changed over the past three decades as a function of the transformation of the society. The urbanization and socioeconomic development were associated with decreased material dependence within the family and increased approval of the child's autonomy. Turkish parents in 2003, particularly in high SES urban families, valued autonomy more than those in 1975. Moreover, the parents in 2003 were more likely than the parents in 1975 to appreciate affective parent–child interactions. Consistently, Greenfield and her colleagues (e.g., Greenfield, Maynard, & Childs, 2000) found that in adapting to changes toward a commercial lifestyle, Mayan mothers increasingly encouraged their children to be independent in learning. Keller and her colleagues (Eickhorst, Lamm, Borke, & Keller, 2008; Keller & Lamm, 2005) also observed that, with the demands for individualization over the past 20 years in Germany, a more independent cultural model has been emphasized in many European middle-class families.

Chinese society has been changing rapidly and extensively since the early 1980s, particularly in the past 15 years. The full-scale reform during this period towards a market economy has led to increased variations in family income, decline in the government control of social welfare, massive movement of the population, and rapid rise in unemployment rate and competition (e.g., Zhang, 2000). Along with the social and economic changes, individualistic values and ideologies such as liberty and individual freedom have been introduced into China from Western countries and gradually accepted by many Chinese people, especially in the younger generation (Zhang, Wang, & Fuligni, 2006).

In this chapter, we focus on the implications of the societal change in China for children's socioemotional functioning and development. We first provide some background information about the socioemotional characteristics of Chinese children, particularly in comparison with those of their Western counterparts. Next, we review the literature concerning traditional Chinese socialization patterns, such as parenting goals, beliefs, and attitudes, and recent changes in socialization patterns. In the following section, we discuss the impact of the social and economic changes on Chinese children's socioemotional functioning, particularly shyness-inhibition, a characteristic that is highly susceptible to contextual influence. Then, we discuss the regional differences in social and economic development within China and how they are reflected in children's socioemotional functioning. Our chapter concludes with a discussion of future directions in the study of child development in the changing Chinese society.

Cultural background, economic reform, and social conditions for child development in China

As a country with one of the most sophisticated ancient civilizations, China has more than 4,000 years of recorded history. A major feature of Chinese history is that people in the country experienced repeated internal and external conflicts and wars and various waves of uprising and revolution. Highly concerned about social instability and turmoil, Confucianism, the predominant guideline for social activities in Chinese cultural system, asserts that, to maintain a harmonious society, it is important to establish a set of moral standards and social rules to regulate individual behaviors and guide interpersonal interactions (Luo, 1996). In the Confucian framework, the expression of individual needs or striving for autonomous behaviors is considered socially unacceptable. Behaviors that threaten group harmony are strictly prohibited. Individual behavioral constraint and obedience to the authority are required not only in social and political activities in the society but also in daily life social interactions. For example, the doctrine of *Xiao* (filial piety) stipulates that, in the family, children must pledge obedience and reverence to parents. In turn, parents are responsible for 'governing' (i.e., teaching, disciplining) their children. Another important indigenous belief system in Chinese culture is Taoism. Relative to Confucianism, Taoism advocates more passive attitudes and behaviors in social situations to pursue internal harmony. To reach internal harmony, Taoism believes that it is crucial for individuals to remain flexible and even take 'no action' in dealing with external challenges and adversities (Wang, 2006). Consistent with the traditional ideologies, the contemporary Chinese collectivistic orientation highly emphasizes the stability of the society. To achieve this goal, the collectivistic principles indicate that the interests of the individual must be subordinated to those of the group. Selfishness, including seeking individual benefits at the expense of group interests and indifference to group interests, is regarded as a cardinal evil (King & Bond, 1985).

China has been an agricultural society for thousands of years. Due to relatively limited resources, most people have lived under poor conditions during most periods of its history. The living standard in China did not improve substantially until the early 1980s. Since then, China has carried out massive reforms towards a market economy. The initial phase of the reforms was the 'internal vitalization' in rural areas and the 'open-door' movement in some Southern regions. Full-scale reforms were expanded to cities and other parts of the country in the early 1990s. In the past 15 years, the centrally planned command economy with the dominance of state-owned enterprises has rapidly been transformed into a market economy, which led to dramatic growth of domestic and foreign private enterprises and joint ventures. The economy in China is currently the fourth largest in the world and growing at the rate of approximately 10 per cent a year.

According to the National Bureau of Statistics of China (Bulletin, 2006), in comparison to the annual per capita income of 100 and 50 Yuan for urban and rural areas, respectively, in 1949, the annual per capita income was 10,493 Yuan (approx. US$1,312) for urban residents and 3,255 Yuan (approx. US$406) for rural residents in 2005. The total poverty-stricken population was 250 million in 1978, but dropped to 43 million in 1998.

Along with the economic transformation, the structure and organization of Chinese families have changed in the past decades. A traditional Chinese family is usually a large family, consisting of three or four generations. Due to the cultural emphasis on interdependence among family members, most families have very close social and financial connections across generations. The father has the most responsibility to maintain and enhance the reputation of the family and to help children achieve to the highest level (Ho, 1987). Over the past 20 years, the number of large families has decreased, and the number of small nuclear families has increased. The average family size was 4.79, 3.58, and 3.13 persons in 1985, 1999, and 2005, respectively (3.27 and 2.97 in rural and urban regions in 2005; Data, 2006). The divorce rate is generally low, but is growing (below 5 per cent in 1980, 11.4 per cent in 1995, and 13 per cent in 1997; Ni, 2000), especially in major cities (25 per cent in 1997; Ni, 2000).

Since the late 1970s, China has implemented the one-child-per-family policy. This policy has been highly successful in population control in urban areas. As a result, over 95 per cent of children in the urban areas are the only child (Chen and He, 2004). A 'four-two-one' structure (four grandparents, two parents, and one child) is the norm in urban families. Although the one child policy has not been so successful in rural areas, it is the case that most families do not have as many children today as traditional families used to have in the past.

The sociocultural and family conditions are likely to exert pervasive influence on socialization and socioemotional development in Chinese children. Moreover, the social and economic transformation in the past decades in China may affect children's experiences and developmental patterns. In the following sections, we review and discuss parental socialization beliefs and practices and children's socioemotional functioning in the changing Chinese context.

Childrearing beliefs and practices in the changing context

Developmental and cross-cultural researchers have paid a great deal of attention to the role of social and cultural context in shaping parental childrearing beliefs and practices (e.g., Super & Harkness, 1986; Whiting & Edwards, 1988). A number of studies have revealed that childrearing styles and behaviors of Chinese parents may be different from those of Western parents (e.g., Chen et al., 1998). However, traditional Chinese childrearing beliefs and practices are changing due to the requirements of different social and behavioral qualities for adaptation to the new environment.

Traditional Chinese childrearing beliefs and practices

The primary socialization goal in traditional Chinese society is to help children develop attitudes and behaviors that are conducive to collective well-being, such as interdependence within the family, orientation to the larger group, and obedience to the authority (Tamis-LeMonda et al., 2008). Accordingly, the main task of parents and other socialization agents is to train children to control individualistic behaviors and to display cooperative and obedient behaviors. To help children learn collectivistic norms and group-oriented behaviors, maintaining adults' authority is believed to be essential in childrearing (Luo, 1996). Thus, it has been argued that the Chinese culture endorses the use of high-power, directive, and restrictive childrearing strategies (e.g., Chao, 1994; Ho, 1986).

Findings from several research programs appeared to support the arguments about traditional childrearing attitudes and practices in Chinese parents. Compared with Western parents, Chinese parents were more controlling and power assertive, and less responsive and affectionate to their children (e.g., Chao, 1994; Chen et al., 1998; Dornbusch, Ritter, Leiderman, Roberts, & Fraleigh, 1987; Kelley, 1992; Wu, 1981). For example, Chinese parents were less likely to use inductive reasoning and were more authoritarian in parenting than Western parents. Chinese parents were also less likely to encourage their children to be independent and exploratory. Finally, Chinese parents were less sensitive and more punishment-oriented in parent–child interactions than North American parents (Chen et al., 1998; Wu, 1981).

Changes in parental childrearing attitudes and practices in China

The traditional Chinese childrearing attitudes and practices are clearly incompatible with the requirements of the market-oriented society that emphasizes individual initiative and competitiveness. In the new environment, it is important for children to learn assertive, self-reliant, and autonomous skills. In recent years, researchers and professionals in China have encouraged parents and educators to expand their childrearing and educational goals to include helping children develop social and behavioral qualities that are required for adaptation in the market-oriented society such as expression of personal opinions, self-direction, and self-confidence (Yu, 2002). In a study concerning socialization goal-oriented behaviors, Liu et al. (2005) found that, although Chinese mothers had higher scores on encouragement of relatedness and lower scores on autonomy support than Canadian mothers, mothers in both samples had significantly higher scores on encouragement of autonomy than on encouragement of relatedness. Chinese parents may have realized that, to function adequately and achieve success in the competitive environment, children need to attain competencies to behave in an independent and assertive manner.

In a recent study, our research team examined similarities and differences in parental childrearing attitudes between parents of elementary school children (grades 3 to 6) in two cohorts (1998 and 2002) in Shanghai, China. The 1998 cohort included 466 mothers and 442 fathers, and the 2002 cohort included 243 mothers and 236 fathers. Parents were requested to complete a parenting measure tapping four major dimensions: parental warmth (e.g., 'My child and I have warm, good times together,' 'I comfort my child when he/she is upset or afraid,' 'I like to play with my child'), power assertion (e.g., 'I do not allow my child to question my decisions,' 'I believe physical punishment to be the best way of discipline,' 'I believe that scolding and criticism make my child improve'), encouragement of autonomy and independence (e.g., 'I let my child make many decisions for him/herself,' 'When my child gets into trouble, I expect him/her to handle the problem mostly by him/herself,' 'I encourage my child to be independent of me'), and encouragement of achievement (e.g., 'I encourage my child always to do his/her best,' 'I encourage my child to do better than others'). We expected that, with the emphasis on individual independence and the acceptance of Western 'child-centered' approach in recent years, parents would endorse more warm and sensitive parenting practices and encourage more autonomous and exploratory behaviors in the child. At the same time, parents might choose less forceful and power assertive parenting styles in childrearing.

The results, as presented in Table 9.1, were consistent with our expectations. Both mothers and fathers in the 2002 cohorts had higher

Table 9.1 Means and standard deviations of the parenting variables in the 1998 and 2002 cohorts

Variables	1998 cohort		2002 cohort		F value
	M	SD	M	SD	
Maternal parenting					
Warmth	3.89	.70	4.19	.79	27.60***
Power assertion	2.89	.74	2.72	.84	8.58**
Encouragement of autonomy	4.07	.68	4.21	.68	8.72**
Encouragement of achievement	4.37	.70	4.48	.78	3.31
Paternal parenting					
Warmth	3.80	.72	4.09	.85	20.92***
Power assertion	2.86	.73	2.56	.78	25.52***
Encouragement of autonomy	4.13	.55	4.19	.70	1.90
Encouragement of achievement	4.41	.53	4.41	.71	.00

Note: N = 466 and 243 for mothers and 442 and 236 for fathers in the 1998 and 2002 cohorts, respectively.
**$p < .01$ ***$p < .001$

scores on parental warmth and lower scores on power assertion than those in the 1998 cohort. Mothers in the 2002 cohort also had higher scores on autonomy support than mothers in the 1998 cohort. Fathers did not differ on this variable although the pattern was in the expected direction. Finally, no differences were found between the cohorts on encouragement of academic achievement; parents at both times highly valued academic performance.

These results suggest that parents in China increasingly appreciate the importance of children's socioemotional well-being and the role of affective communication in parent–child interaction in promoting children's socioemotional competence. Moreover, parents, particularly mothers, in China are now less likely to endorse the use of power assertive parenting and more likely to encourage autonomy and independence. Consistent with the new socialization goals, parents may create opportunities for their children to explore in the challenging environment and to learn initiative-taking skills in social situations.

Children's socioemotional functioning and adjustment in the changing context

Among the various aspects of socioemotional functioning, developmental researchers have been interested in children's sociability-cooperation, aggression-disruption and shyness-inhibition (e.g., Masten et al., 1995; Rubin, Chen, McDougall, Bowker, & McKinnon, 1995). Cross-cultural research has indicated that Chinese children differ from their Western counterparts in these major aspects. The change toward a market-oriented society is likely to have an impact on the display and significance of socioemotional functioning in Chinese children (Chen, Wang, & DeSouza, 2006; Yu, 2002). This has been demonstrated in a series of studies that Chen and his colleagues have conducted concerning shyness-inhibition in childhood and adolescence (e.g., Chen, Rubin, & Sun, 1992; Chen, Cen, Li, & He, 2005).

Shyness-inhibition and its functional meaning in Chinese children

Shyness-inhibition, derived from internal anxiety and lack of self-confidence, is often manifested in wary, vigilant and sensitive behavior in challenging social situations (Asendorpf, 1990). It has been found that shyness-inhibition plays an important role in social and psychological adjustment in childhood and adolescence (see Rubin, Burgess, & Coplan, 2002). Children who display shy and wary behaviors are often viewed as socially incompetent and immature in Western cultures (e.g., Rubin et al., 2002). Accordingly, shy-inhibited children, especially during the school years, are likely to experience low peer acceptance and poor social adjustment (e.g., Coplan, Prakash, O'Neil, & Armer, 2004). When they are aware of their social difficulties through negative social feedback, these children tend to develop negative self-perceptions and emotions such as feelings of loneliness and depression (e.g., Rubin, Bukowski, & Parker, 2006). Therefore, it has been argued that shyness represents a major aspect of internalizing problems (Rubin et al., 2002).

The adjustment difficulties that shy-inhibited children experience may be related to the emphasis on assertiveness and self-expression in Western societies (e.g., Oyserman, Coon, & Kemmelmeier, 2002). Due to the cultural values, shy, wary, and restrained behavior tends to be negatively evaluated and responded to by peers and adults (e.g., Chen, DeSouza, Wang, & Chen, 2006; Coplan et al., 2004), which, in turn, constitutes an environment that facilitates the development of social, school and psychological problems in shy-inhibited children.

Chinese children tend to display more shy-inhibited behavior than North American children in challenging social situations (Chen et al., 1998; Chen & Tse, in press). Chen et al. (1998) found, for example, that relative to Canadian toddlers, Chinese toddlers stayed closer to their mothers and were less likely to explore in free play sessions. Moreover, Chinese toddlers displayed more anxious and vigilant behaviors when interacting with a stranger, as indicated by their higher scores on the latency to approach the stranger and to touch the toys when they were invited to do so.

Inconsistent with the Western literature (e.g., Rubin et al., 2002), shy-inhibited behavior is considered an indication of accomplishment and mastery in traditional Chinese culture and is associated with virtuous qualities such as modesty, cautiousness, and self-control; shy-inhibited children are often perceived as well-behaved and understanding. Accordingly, we have found that shyness-inhibition is associated with social experiences in China that are different from those in North America (Chen, Wang, & DeSouza, 2006). Compared with others, shy-inhibited children who made passive and low-power social initiations received fewer positive responses and more rejection from peers in Canada. However, shy-inhibited children who displayed the same behavior were more likely than others to receive positive responses and support in China. Consistently, unlike their Western counterparts, shy-inhibited children in China are accepted by peers and perform well socially and academically in childhood and adolescence (e.g., Chen, Rubin, & Sun, 1992; Chen, Rubin, Li, & Li, 1999). Further, shy Chinese children perceive themselves positively and do not feel lonely or depressed (e.g., Chen et al., 2004a). These results suggest that the functional meaning or significance of shyness-inhibition may be moderated by social and cultural contexts (e.g., Bornstein, 1995; Chen & French, 2008).

The implications of societal change for the adjustment of shy-inhibited children in China

The massive economic reform has led to considerable changes in various areas in China. For example, many Chinese schools have changed their education goals, policies, and practices to help children develop assertive and independent skills (e.g., Liu, 2003; Yu, 2002). A variety of strategies (e.g., encouraging students to engage in public debate and to propose and implement their own plans about extra-curricular activities) has been used to facilitate the development of these skills (Liu, 2003). The emphasis on individuality, social initiative, and self-expression in school education and other social activities are likely to make shy-inhibited behavior less adaptive. Shy-inhibited behavior that impedes self-expression and active social communication may be increasingly unsuitable with the requirements of society (Chen, Wang, & DeSouza, 2006; Hart et al., 2000). Consequently, shyness may become an undesirable characteristic in social and psychological adjustment, and shy children may be at a disadvantage in obtaining social approval and status.

In a cohort-design study, Chen et al. (2005) examined the relations between shyness and adjustment at different times of social transition in urban China. Data on shyness and adjustment were collected in three cohorts (1990, 1998 and 2002) of elementary school children in Shanghai. Whereas children in the 1990 cohort experienced relatively limited influence of the comprehensive reform and children in the 2002 cohort were socialized in an increased self-oriented cultural context, the 1998 cohort represented an intermediate phase in which children might have mixed socialization experiences. In the study, children's shyness was assessed using a peer assessment measure of social functioning. Social, school, and psychological adjustment was assessed through multiple methods, including sociometric nominations, teacher ratings, and self-reports.

Multi-group invariance tests revealed that overall there were significant cross-cohort differences in the relations between shyness and all adjustment variables. Further analyses indicated that, in general, shyness was positively associated with peer acceptance, leadership and academic achievement in the 1990 cohort. However, shyness was negatively associated with peer acceptance and school adjustment and positively associated with peer rejection and depression in the 2002 cohort. The patterns of the relations between shyness and peer relationships and adjustment variables were non-significant or mixed in the 1998 cohort (Chen et al., 2005). The results suggest that shyness was an adaptive social characteristic that was associated with indexes of positive adjustment in the early 1990s. By the early part of the twenty-first century as the country became more deeply immersed in a market economy, however, shyness was associated with social and psychological problems; shy-inhibited children were perceived as problematic and incompetent by teachers and rejected by peers, displayed various school problems, and reported high levels of depression.

An interesting finding of Chen et al.'s (2005) study was that shyness was positively associated with both peer acceptance and peer rejection in the 1998 cohort. The analysis of the sociometric classification (Coie, Dodge, & Coppotelli, 1982) revealed that shy children in this cohort were controversial; they were liked and disliked by peers at the same time. These results indicate mixed attitudes of peers toward shy-inhibited children, which may reflect the conflict between the new values of initiative and traditional Chinese values of self-control in a transitional period. Another interesting finding was that social evaluations and relationships such as peer rejection and teacher-rated competence were more sensitive than other aspects of adjustment such as academic achievement and depression to the change in social and cultural norms. The influence of contextual forces on children's school performance and psychopathological feelings may occur through complicated and prolonged interpersonal and intrapersonal processes. Thus, social and historical changes may impact different aspects of socioemotional functioning and adjustment gradually and cumulatively (Silbereisen, 2000). The finding also supports the argument that social attitudes and relationships serve as a major mediator of contextual influence on individual development (Chen & French, 2008; Chen, French, & Schneider, 2006).

Urban-rural differences in social functioning and adjustment in Chinese children

There are substantial regional, particularly urban-rural, differences in social and economic development within China. The massive social and economic reform, such as the opening of stock markets in China, has been largely limited to urban centers and cities. Families in rural China have lived mostly agricultural lives, and rural children do not have as much exposure as urban children to the influence of the market economy (Cui, 2003). The regional differences in China are likely to be reflected in socialization and socioemotional development.

Socialization values, childrearing attitudes, and socioemotional functioning in rural children

In many rural areas, traditional Chinese values such as social responsibility and self-control are still highly emphasized in interpersonal interactions (Fuligni & Zhang, 2004; Sun, 2006; Shen, 2006). Parents in rural families tend to maintain socialization goals and use childrearing practices that are consistent with the traditional beliefs and values such as filial piety, respect for elders, and self-sacrifice for the family (e.g., China Youth & Children Research Center, 2007; Shen, 2006). It has been reported that rural parents are less likely to display warmth toward children, are less engaged in play activities, and use more physical punishment as a response to children's misbehavior (Li, Cui, & Wu, 2005). Similar results were found in one of our recent studies concerning parenting attitudes and practices in China. In this study, we collected self-report data from groups of children in rural elementary schools in He Nan province and in urban elementary schools in Beijing. It was found that rural parents had significantly higher scores than urban parents on parental control and power assertion in childrearing, $M = 3.57$ and 3.06, $SD = 1.01$ and 1.02, for rural and urban mothers, respectively, $F(1,503) = 31.61$, $p < .001$, and $M = 3.55$ and 2.76, $SD = 1.10$ and 1.12 for rural and urban fathers, respectively, $F(1,503) = 61.57$, $p < .001$.

Consistent with the urban–rural differences in the emphasis on traditional values and practices in socialization, urban and rural children have been found to differ in their social experience and adjustment (e.g., Sun, 2006). Based on teacher evaluations and self-reports, for example, relative to urban children, rural children are more group-oriented and display greater social responsibility, and are less likely to pursue individual interests (Guo, Yao, & Yang, 2005). We also found in a study conducted in 2006 with a sample of rural children that, similar to the results in the early 1990s in urban China, shyness was associated with indexes of social, school, and psychological adjustment such as leadership and teacher-rated competence. Thus, shy rural children are still not regarded as problematic, and, like their urban counterparts in the early 1990s, continue to obtain approval and social support from peers and adults and achieve success in social and academic areas. It is important to note that many rural regions of China are currently undergoing rapid changes. Urban and Western values increasingly influence parental socialization beliefs and practices and children's socioemotional development in rural areas. It will be interesting to investigate how rural children adapt to the changing environment.

Socioemotional functioning and adjustment of rural-to-urban migrant children

China's policies and development strategies have created huge gaps between rural and urban populations in many aspects of life, including health care conditions, education opportunities, and income levels (Yang & Zhou, 1999). Rural population is generally at a disadvantage in these aspects. Since the early 1990s, the Chinese government has relaxed the enforcement of migration restriction and allowed cities to absorb surplus rural labor. As a result, a large number of rural people, mostly young adults, have moved to cities to seek opportunities. It is estimated that 120–150 million peasants have moved from the countryside to cities in the past two decades in China (e.g., Pan, 2002). With relatively limited education, most of rural-to-urban migrants become unskilled workers in the city in such sectors as manual labor (e.g., manufacturing, cleaning streets, transporting goods), construction, and commerce (e.g., street peddlers, small vendors).

Many rural migrant workers have brought their families, including children, to the cities. In 2005, approximately 20 million school age rural children lived in cities with their parents (Nielsen, Nyland, Nyland, Smyth, & Zhang, 2006). Rural migrant families often stay in the city for years while maintaining links to their villages of origin (e.g., Wang, 2004). Under the *hukou* system of household registration, migrant children do not have an urban registration and thus do not have the same privileges as urban children. Many rural children are unable to enter public city schools because of various obstacles such as extra fees they have to pay. In major cities such as Beijing and Shanghai, the municipal government and the migrant community have set up migrant children schools.

For many migrant children, adapting to the new urban environment is a significant challenge that may result in stress and distress. Chen, Wang, and Wang, (2009) compared rural migrant and urban elementary school children in Beijing and found that migrant children displayed more problems in school adjustment and felt more depressed than urban children. Similar results have been reported in other studies (e.g., Guo, Yao & Yang, 2005; Shen, 2006). The higher levels of depression of rural migrant children might be related to the difficulties they faced in the new environment such as being deprived of many privileges that urban children enjoyed (e.g., access to normal public schools). Migrant children may also experience prejudice and discrimination in the city during their interactions with urban residents (e.g., Sun, 2006; Zhan, Sun, & Dong, 2005). The adverse life conditions and the exposure to negative social feedback about personal and group status may facilitate the emergence of negative self-schemata (Cole, 1991) and the development of social and psychological problems.

Nevertheless, it has been argued that adverse conditions do not necessarily have a negative impact on social and school adjustment (Sam, Vedder, Libkind, Neto, & Virta, 2008), especially for children who are resilient and have social support systems. Moreover, given that migrant children live in the city and are exposed to urban culture, they are inevitably influenced by the urban culture after moving to the city. This may be the case even for migrant children who attend rural migrant schools because many of these schools attempt to follow the requirements of the Municipal Educational Bureau in curriculum, instruction, and other aspects of school organization that are similar to those in city schools. According to the constructivist perspective (e.g., Conzen, Gerber, Morawska, Pozzetta, & Vecoli, 1992; Garcia Coll et al., 1996), diverse family and social experiences can serve as resources for children to learn different values and skills that are beneficial for the development of social competence. When migrant children increasingly learn new values and behavioral styles, with time, they are likely to engage in the 'process of construction' that incorporates rural and urban values and develop strategies to function flexibly and effectively in different settings. Researchers should investigate in the future how rural migrant children integrate various social expectations and values and use them in adjustment.

Conclusions and future directions

China is undergoing a massive economic transformation toward a market-oriented system, which produces extensive changes in the social lives of Chinese people. As a result, new behavioral qualities and skills are required to achieve success, whereas the characteristics that used to be beneficial for adjustment may become maladaptive. To help children develop social competence and adaptive behaviors in the new context, parents and other socialization agents need to modify their socialization goals and practices.

During the social and economic transformation, Western individualistic ideologies and values such as assertiveness and autonomy have been introduced into the country and have been exerting influence on the views and behaviors of children and adults in China. However, Western values are unlikely to be adopted completely in their original forms, but instead, may be integrated with the Chinese cultural traditions. It will be interesting to investigate how children and adolescents in China develop in the culturally integrated and sophisticated settings.

In this chapter, we focus on parental socialization beliefs and attitudes and children's socioemotional functioning, particularly shyness-inhibition, in the changing Chinese society. There are other important areas of socioemotional development such as aggression and psychopathological symptoms that are likely to change as a consequence of the social, economic, and cultural transformation. Moreover, urban lifestyles, increased affluence, and new cultural values that are promoted by modernization may affect the functions of social relationships. It has been suggested, for example, that social relationships serve a more utilitarian function in societies or communities, where relying on others for basic needs is essential (Guthrie, 2006). The increased value on personal independence and social initiative may undermine the utilitarian function of relationships and enhance their role in providing emotional support and fulfilling individual psychological needs. Indeed, Tamis-LeMonda et al. (2008) have noticed that the traditional utilitarian and instrumental type of relationship, *Guan*

Xi, is losing significance in China as the society moves to a market economy and stronger legal infrastructure. Unfortunately, little research has been conducted on children's social relationships in China. Thus, it will be interesting to investigate how the societal change affects the nature and function of social relationships in Chinese children and adolescents.

The studies conducted by our team and others have indicated the implications of social and cultural changes for socioemotional development in Chinese children. An important task for researchers is to explore the processes in which the macro-level contextual change plays a role in determining children's socioemotional functioning and its significance. The processes likely involve factors at multiple levels, from institutional to personal, including social policies, school education guidelines and activities, family and peer group socialization practices, and individual life goals (e.g., Silbereisen, Reitzle, & Juang, 2002). The institutional or community-level processes may be particularly important because they may serve as mediators and moderators of the links between the societal change and individual development. Therefore, it will be necessary to examine children's social behaviors, relationships, and adjustment from a broader perspective. Moreover, a multi-level (individuals nested within the group or school in multiple communities), multi-disciplinary (sociological, anthropological, psychological), and multi-method (quantitative, ethnographic, historical) approach may be needed to achieve an in-depth understanding of the processes.

Chen and French (2008) argue that socioemotional functioning in changing societies should be understood in terms of its associations with culturally directed social evaluations and responses in interactions and its developmental antecedents, concomitants, and outcomes. Moreover, the impact of social and cultural context and its change on individual behaviors and relationships is a dynamic process, in which children play an increasingly active role during development. The transaction among personal, social, situational, and developmental factors in children's adaptation to the changing environment needs to be examined thoroughly in the future.

References

Asendorpf, J. (1990). Beyond social withdrawal: Shyness, unsociability, and peer avoidance. *Human Development, 33*, 250–259.

Bornstein, M.H. (1995). Form and function: Implications for studies of culture and human development. *Culture and Psychology, 1*, 123–138.

Bronfenbrenner, U. & Morris, P.A. (2006). The bioecological model of human development. In W. Damon (Series Ed.) & R.M. Lerner (Vol. Ed.), *Handbook of child psychology: Vol. 1. Theoretical models of human development* (pp. 793–828). New York: Wiley.

Bulletin of China's Economic and Social Development in 2005 (2006, February 28). Xin Hua She, Beijing.

Chao, R.K. (1994). Beyond parental control and authoritarian parenting style: Understanding Chinese parenting through the cultural notion of training. *Child Development, 65,* 1111–1119.

Chen, X., Cen, G., Li, D. & He, Y. (2005). Social functioning and adjustment in Chinese children: The imprint of historical time. *Child Development, 76,* 182–195.

Chen, X., DeSouza, A., Chen, H. & Wang, L. (2006). Reticent behavior and experiences in peer interactions in Canadian and Chinese children. *Developmental Psychology, 42,* 656–665.

Chen, X. & French, D. (2008). Children's social competence in cultural context. *Annual Review of Psychology, 59,* 591–616.

Chen, X., French, D., & Schneider, B. (2006). Culture and peer relationships. In X. Chen, D. French, & B. Schneider (Eds), *Peer relationships in cultural context* (pp. 3–20). New York: Cambridge University Press.

Chen, X., Hastings, P., Rubin, K.H., Chen, H., Cen, G., & Stewart, S.L. (1998). Childrearing attitudes and behavioral inhibition in Chinese and Canadian toddlers: A cross-cultural study. *Developmental Psychology, 34,* 677–686.

Chen, X. & He, H. (2004). The family in mainland China: Structure, organization, and significance for child development. In J.L. Roopnarine and U.P. Gielen (Eds), *Families in global perspective* (pp. 51–62). Boston: Allyn and Bacon.

Chen, X., He, Y., De Oliveira, A.M, Lo Coco, A., Zappulla, C., Kaspar, V et al., (2004) Loneliness and social adaptation in Brazilian, Canadian, Chinese and Italian Children, *Journal of Child Psychology and Psychiatry, 45,* 1373–1384.

Chen, X., Rubin, K.H., Li, B., & Li. Z. (1999). Adolescent outcomes of social functioning in Chinese children. *International Journal of Behavioural Development, 23,* 199–223.

Chen, X., Rubin, K.H., & Sun, Y. (1992). Social reputation and peer relationships in Chinese and Canadian children: A cross-cultural study. *Child Development, 63,* 1336–1343.

Chen, X. & Tse, H.C. (2008). Social functioning and adjustment in Canadian-born children with Chinese and European backgrounds. *Developmental Psychology, 44,* 1184–1189.

Chen, X., Wang, L., & DeSouza, A. (2006). Temperament and socio-emotional functioning in Chinese and North American children. In X. Chen, D. French, and B. Schneider (Eds), *Peer relationships in cultural context* (pp. 123–147). New York: Cambridge University Press.

Chen, X., Wang, L., & Wang, Z. (2009). *Shyness-sensitivity and social, school, and psychological adjustment in rural migrant and urban children in China.* Child Development, 80, 1499–1513.

China Youth & Children Research Center (2007). A study of adaption of children of migrant workers to the urban life. *Reports of the China Youth & Children Research Center,* November 16. http://www.cycs.org/Article.asp?Category=1&Column=130&ID=5809

Cole, D.A. (1991). Preliminary support for a competency-based model of depression in children. *Journal of Abnormal Psychology, 100,* 181–190.

Conzen, K.N., Gerber, D.A., Morawska, E., Pozzetta, G.E., & Vecoli, R.J. (1992). The invention of ethnicity: A perspective from the U.S.A. *Journal of American Ethnic History, 11,* 3–41.

Cui, C. (2003). Adapting to the city and adjusting rural-urban relations: A study of migrant children's school and live circumstances in Beijing. In B. Li (Ed.), *The peasant worker: An analysis of social and economic status of Chinese rural-to-urban migrants*. Beijing: Social Sciences and Documentation Publishing House.

Coie, J.D., Dodge, K.A., & Coppotelli, H. (1982). Dimensions of types of social status: A cross-age perspective. *Developmental Psychology, 18*, 557–560.

Coplan, R.J., Prakash, K., O'Neil, K., & Armer, M. (2004). Do you 'want' to play? Distinguishing between conflicted-shyness and social disinterest in early childhood. *Developmental Psychology, 40*, 244–258.

Dornbusch, S., Ritter, P., Leiderman, R., Roberts, D., & Fraleigh, M. (1987). The relation of parenting style to adolescent school performance. *Child Development, 58*, 1244–1257.

Eickhorst, A., Lamm, B., Borke, J., & Keller, H. (2008). Fatherhood in different decades: Interactions between German fathers and their infants in 1977 and 2001. *European Journal of Developmental Psychology, 5*, 92–107.

Elder, G.H. Jr. (1974). *Children of the Great Depression*. Chicago, IL: University of Chicago Press.

Flanagan, C.A. (2000). Social change and the 'social contract' in adolescent development. In L.J. Crockett & R.K. Silbereisen (Eds), *Negotiating adolescence in times of social change* (pp. 191–98). New York: Cambridge University Press.

Fuligni, A.J. & Zhang, W.X. (2004). Attitudes toward family obligation among adolescents in contemporary urban and rural China. *Child Development, 74*, 180–192.

Garcia Coll, C., Crnic, K., Lamberty, G., Wasik, B.H., Jenkins, R., Garcia, H.V., & McAdoo, H.P. (1996). An integrative model for the study of development competencies in minority children. *Child Development, 67*, 1891–1914.

Graves, N.B. & Graves, T.D. (1983). The cultural context of prosocial development: An ecological model. In D.L. Bridgeman (Ed.), *The nature of prosocial development* (pp. 795–824). San Diego, CA: Academic Press.

Greenfield, P.M., Maynard, A.E., & Childs, C.P. (2000). History, culture, learning and development. *Cross-Cultural Research, 34*, 351–374.

Guthrie, D. (2006). *China and globalization: The social economic and political transformation of Chinese society*, New York: Routledge.

Guo, L., Yao, Y., & Yang, B. (2005). Adaptation of migrant children to the city: A case study at a migrant children school in Beijing. *Youth Study, 3*, 22–31.

Hart, C.H., Yang, C., Nelson, L.J., Robinson, C.C., Olson, J.A., Nelson, D.A., Porter, C.L., Jin, S., Olson, S.F., & Wu, P. (2000). Peer acceptance in early childhood and subtypes of socially withdrawn behaviour in China, Russia and the United States. *International Journal of Behavioral Development, 24*, 73–81.

Ho, D.Y.F. (1986). Chinese pattern of socialization: A critical review. In M.H. Bond (Ed.), *The psychology of the Chinese people* (pp. 1–37). New York: Oxford University Press.

Ho, D.Y.F. (1987). Fatherhood in Chinese culture. In M.E. Lamb (Ed.), *The father's role: Cross-cultural perspectives* (pp. 227–245). Hillsdale, NJ: Erlbaum.

Kagitcibasi, C. & Ataca, B. (2005). Value of children and family change: A three-decade portrait from Turkey. *Applied Psychology: An International Review, 54*, 317–337.

Keller, H. & Lamm, B. (2005). Parenting as the expression of sociohistorical time: The case of German individualisation. *International Journal of Behavioral Development, 29*, 238–246.

Kelley, M.L. (1992). Cultural differences in child rearing: A comparison of immigrant Chinese and Caucasian American mothers. *Journal of Cross-Cultural Psychology, 23*, 444–455.

King, A.Y.C. & Bond, M.H. (1985). The Confucian paradigm of man: A sociological view. In W.S. Tseng & D.Y.H. Wu (Eds). *Chinese culture and mental health* (pp. 29–45). Harcourt Brace Jovanovich: Academic Press.

Li, J., Cui, C., & Wu, D. (2005). Influences on adolescents' personality between urban and rural parents' childrearing attitudes. *Chinese Journal of Behavioral Medical Science, 14*, 664.

Little, T.D., Brendgen, M., Wanner, B., & Krappmann, L. (1999). Children's reciprocal perceptions of friendship quality in the sociocultural contexts of East and West Berlin. *International Journal of Behavioral Development, 23*, 63–89.

Liu, S. (2003). Facilitating students' development of autonomy in school education reform. *Modern Education Science, 166*, 27–30.

Liu, M., Chen, X., Rubin, K.H., Zheng, S., Cui, L., Li, D., Chen, H., & Wang, L. (2005). Autonomy- vs. connectedness-oriented parenting behaviors in Chinese and Canadian mothers. *International Journal of Behavioral Development, 29*, 489–495.

Luo, G. (1996). *Chinese traditional social and moral ideas and rules*. Beijing, China: The University of Chinese People Press.

Madsen, M.C. & Lancy, D.F. (1981). Cooperative and competitive behavior: Experiments related to ethnic identity and urbanization in Papua New Guinea. *Journal of Cross-Cultural Psychology, 12*, 389–408.

Masten, A., Coatsworth, J.D., Neemann, J., Gest, S.D., Tellegen, A., & Garmezy, N. (1995). The structure and coherence of competence from childhood through adolescence. *Child Development, 66*, 1635–1659.

Nadler, A., Romek, E., & Shapira-Friedman, A. (1979). Giving in the kibbutz: Prosocial behavior of city and kibbutz children as affected by social responsibility and social pressure. *Journal of Cross-Cultural Psychology, 10*, 57–72.

Ni, S. (2000). How should we revise the Marriage Law? *The People's Daily (Oversea Edition)*, November, 3, p. 5.

Nielsen, I., Nyland, B., Nyland, C., Smyth, R., & Zhang, M. (2006). Determinants of school attendance among migrant children: Survey evidence from China's Jiangsu province. *Pacific Economic Review, 11*, 461–476.

Oyserman, D., Coon, H.M., & Kemmelmeier, M. (2002). Rethinking individualism and collectivism: Evaluation of theoretical assumptions and meta-analyses. *Psychological Bulletin, 128*, 3–72.

Pan, P. (2002). Poisoned back into poverty: As China embraces capitalism, hazards to workers rise. *Washington Post*, August 4, A01.

Rubin, K.H., Bukowski, W., & Parker, J.G. (2006). Peer interactions, relationships, and groups. In N. Eisenberg (Ed.), *Handbook of child psychology: Vol. 3. Social, emotional, and personality development* (pp. 571–645). New York: Wiley.

Rubin, K.H., Burgess, K.B., & Coplan, R.J. (2002). Social withdrawal and shyness. In P.K. Smith & C.H. Hart (Eds), *Blackwell handbook of childhood social development* (pp. 330–352), Malden, MA: Blackwell Publishers.

Rubin, K.H., Chen, X., McDougall, P., Bowker, A., & McKinnon, J. (1995). The Waterloo Longitudinal Project: Predicting internalizing and externalizing problems in adolescence. *Development and Psychopathology, 7*, 751–764.

Sam, D.L., Vedder, P., Liebkind, K., Neto, F., & Virta, E. (2008). Immigration, acculturation and the paradox of adaptation in Europe. *European Journal of Developmental Psychology, 5*, 138–158.

Shen, R. (2006). Problems and solutions for child education for migrant rural worker families. *Journal of China Agricultural University (Social Science Edition), 64*, 96–100.

Silbereisen, R.K. (2000). German unification and adolescents' developmental timetables: Continuities and discontinuities. In L.A. Crockett & R.K. Silbereisen (Eds), *Negotiating adolescence in times of social change.* Cambridge: Cambridge University Press.

Silbereisen, R.K., Reitzle, M., & Juang, L. (2002). Time and change: Psychosocial transitions in German young adults 1991 and 1996. In L. Pulkkinen & A. Caspi (Eds), *Paths to successful development: Personality in the life course* (pp. 227–256). New York: Cambridge University Press.

Sun, H. (2006). About the social adaptation of children of migrant workers in the city. *Reports of the China Youth & Children Research Center*, December, 2. http://www.cycrc.org/cnarticle_detail.asp?id=1421

Super, C.M. & Harkness, S. (1986). The developmental niche: A conceptualization at the interface of child and culture. *International Journal of Behavioral Development, 9*, 545–569.

Tamis-LeMonda, C.S., Way, N., Hughes, D., Yoshikawa, H., Kalman, R.K., & Niwa, E. (2008). Parents' goals for children: The dynamic co-existence of collectivism and individualism in cultures and individuals. *Social Development, 17*, 183–209.

Wang, B. (2006). *The philosophy of Zhuangzi.* Beijng, China: Peking University Press.

Wang, D. (2004). A survey of educational problems among children of migrant workers. *Chinese Population Science, 4*, 58–64.

Whiting, B.B. & Edwards, C.P. (1988). *Children of different worlds.* Cambridge: Harvard University Press.

Wu, D.H. (1981). Child abuse in Taiwan. In J.E. Korbin (Ed.), *Child abuse and neglect: Cross-cultural perspectives* (pp. 139–165). Los Angeles: University of California Press.

Yang, D.T. & Zhou, H. (1999). Rural-urban disparity and sectoral labour allocation in China. *The Journal of Development, 35*, 105–133.

Yu, R. (2002). On the reform of elementary school education in China. *Educational Exploration, 129*, 56–57.

Zhan, X., Sun, D., & Dong, Z. (2005). On adolescents' school adjustment in urban and rural China. *Journal of Shangdong Normal University, 203*, 144–147.

Zhang, W.W. (2000). *Transforming China: Economic reform and its political implications.* New York: St. Martin's Press.

Zhang, W., Wang, M., & Fuligni, A. (2006). Expectations for autonomy, beliefs about parental authority, and parent-adolescent conflict and cohesion. *Acta Psychologica Sinica, 38* (6), 868–876.

10

SOCIAL CHANGE AND PREMARITAL SEXUAL BEHAVIOR AND ATTITUDES IN VIETNAM

Rukmalie Jayakody, Jessica Heckert, and *Dang Nguyen Anh*

Dramatic changes have characterized Vietnam during the past several decades, including prolonged periods of war, socialist collectivization, political reunification, economic renovation, and an extensive opening to the outside world (Jayakody & Huy, 2008). While the economic consequences of these changes are well documented, the social ramifications have received little empirical attention. Despite the lack of empirical data, social observers and commentators, international organizations and the media have been quick to speculate on the resulting implications, particularly for Vietnam's adolescents and young adults. Despite recent fertility reductions, Vietnam has a young age structure, and young people between ages 14 and 25 are the largest demographic segment, comprising a quarter of the total population. This concentration of the population at younger age groups highlights the need to better understand the attitudes and behavior of this group, and the necessity for data-based, rather than speculation-based, assessments.

The recent social changes Vietnam has experienced, particularly its increased contact with the outside world, are believed to have resulted in changes in both attitudes and behavior regarding premarital sex. Although long considered a social taboo, and defined by the government as a 'social evil,' there is a widespread belief that younger generations are more accepting of premarital sex and have high rates of premarital sexual activity. The few empirical studies available, however, do not indicate that premarital sex is widespread in Vietnam (Mensch, Clark, & Dang Nyugen Anh, 2002). We use recently available, nationally representative data from the Survey and Assessment of Vietnamese Youth (SAVY) to examine the prevalence of premarital sexual activity and attitudes regarding the acceptability of premarital sex among adolescents and young adults aged 14 to 25. In assessing current behavior and attitudes towards premarital sex, we examine differences by geographic location and demographic characteristics. We also speculate on the potential implications of the mass media on the attitudes and behavior of adolescents and young adults.

Background

Explanations of social change

Dramatic family changes have occurred worldwide, and these changes have been extensive not only in their geographic scope but also in the dimensions affected. Of particular interest to demographers have been changes in sexual behavior and fertility, and explanations for these changes involve both structural and ideational perspectives. Structural explanations emphasize alterations in the cost-benefit calculus, attributed variously to shifts from agricultural to industrial to a service economy, the movement of populations from rural to urban areas, increases in income, changes in technology, increases in knowledge, and declines in disease and mortality. The fundamental argument of these theories is that changes in the social and economic circumstances and constraints – for example, industrialization and the expansion in education – have ramifications throughout society. On the other hand, other scholars argue that cost-benefit changes alone are insufficient to produce the observed changes in family behavior, and that other forces may also be at play (Caldwell, 1982; Cleland & Wilson, 1987; Freedman, 1979).

Along with structural changes, ideational dimensions have also been identified as important and central in shaping demographic behavior (Jayakody, Thornton, & Axinn, 2008). Ideation refers to new ways of thinking, and ideational change requires that individuals are in contact with ideas and information they had not previously encountered. Suggested mechanisms for spreading new ideas include educational institutions (Caldwell, 1982; Thornton & Fricke, 1987), increased migration, travel and tourism (Bongaarts & Watkins, 1996), gossip networks (Watkins & Danzi, 1995), and the mass media (Bongaarts & Watkins, 1996). Television is specifically designed to transmit new ideas and information and may be a particularly powerful source of ideational change. Television has been described as one of the most powerful idea disseminators, socializing agents, and public opinion molders in the contemporary world (Kottak, 1991), and television's power to change attitudes and behavior has long been assumed (Kottak, 1990; Westoff, 1999). Furthermore, new ideas transmitted through television often transcend traditional barriers of language and literacy. New models of social interaction and family behavior are introduced through television, and these new ideas are often labeled as modern and defined as good (Hornick, 2001).

Rather than being competing alternatives, structural and ideational explanations are inter-related and reinforcing (Jayakody et al., 2008). Ideational frameworks that specify approaches for experiencing and living with reality must take into account the economic and social systems bounding that reality. Similarly, ideational frameworks may modify those economic and social systems. Be it through structure or ideation or a combination of both, the dramatic changes experienced in Vietnam over the past few decades may have influenced premarital sexual attitudes and behavior in ways that may depart from traditional norms.

Social change in Vietnam

Vietnam is the second most populous country in Southeast Asia, with a population of 80.9 million and a per capita income around US$553 (General Statistics Office, 2003). The society is multi-ethnic with substantial ethno-cultural diversity. The majority group, the Kinh, comprise approximately 86 per cent of the population with 53 different ethnic minority groups making up the remaining 14 per cent. Ethnic minorities are those who have Vietnamese nationality and reside in Vietnam, but who do not share the identity, language, and other cultural characteristics with the Kinh (World Health Organization, 2003). Vietnam remains primarily an agricultural society; agriculture comprises the largest economic sector, accounting for about a quarter of the gross domestic product (Central Institute for Economic Management, 1999) and employs 63 per cent of the labor force. Reflecting this agricultural base, the population remains largely rural (in 2003 74 per cent of the population lived in rural areas) (General Statistics Office, 2005), although the pace of urbanization is increasing (National Committee for Population, 2003).

Vietnam has experienced dramatic social, economic, and political changes in its recent history. After nearly a century of foreign occupation, decades of war, and aggressive collectivization in the north, Vietnam was finally reunified in 1975. Following a decade of low agricultural output and economic stagnation, economic renovation policies were passed in 1986. These renovation policies called for a transition away from the collectivist structure to a free-market system, and were marked by an opening up of Vietnam to the rest of the world.

'Vietnam's development [since renovation] represents one of the more dramatic turnarounds in economic history' (Dollar & Litvack, 1998, p. 1). The success of renovation policies is well documented: the gross domestic product grew by nearly 9 per cent annually; inflation fell from 400 per cent in 1987 to 17 per cent by 1994; Vietnam went from being a rice importer to the second largest rice exporting country in the world; and there were substantial poverty and living standards improvements (Haughton, Haughton, & Phong, 2001; Lamb, 2002). The economic success of renovation policies are well illustrated by the dramatic drop in the share of the population living on less then $1 per day – while in 1981 58 per cent of Vietnam's population lived on less than $1 per day, by 2001 this had declined to only 3 per cent (*The Economist*, 2006).

Adolescents and the media

Along with structural explanations highlighting economic and political changes, another aspect of economic renovation policies often mentioned as leading to change is the increased presence of the foreign media. Market reforms have introduced new media, and the new images and ideas introduced through the media are believed to have contributed to increased sexual permissiveness, premarital sexual activity, sexually transmitted diseases, unintended pregnancy, and abortion (Ghuman, Loi, Huy, & Knodel, 2006). In fact, access to television has grown rapidly in Vietnam, with 79 per cent of urban households and 50 per cent of rural households owning a television.

Media messages, particularly those from the West, are thought to substantially change young people's attitudes. Given the developmental tasks required during adolescence, it may be that young people are particularly susceptible to media messages. For example, a core developmental task during adolescence is identity formation, and media messages may be particularly influential in two key areas: gender role identity and sexuality. The explicit images of television role models may influence adolescents as they absorb images of what it means to be a man or a woman (Steele & Brown, 1995). Television can also become an important source of sexual socialization, dramatically impacting adolescents' beliefs about sexual attractiveness, heterosexual interactions and relationships, sexual knowledge and behavior.

Some argue that television and movies serve as a sexual super peer providing information and models about sexuality (Brown, Halpern, & L'Engle, 2005; Strasburger & Wilson, 2002). New ideas about opposite sex relationships and the social models of adolescents on television may have important implications for adolescent sexuality. Adolescents are especially fascinated by depictions of male-female relationships, using television to learn sexual and romantic scripts (Brown, Childers, & Waszak, 1990). Television promotes certain sex roles and behavior, and depictions of adolescents on television provide models for attitude formation and behavior imitation (Chapin, 2000). Particularly in cultures where heterosexual interactions are limited and there is reticence about discussing sexual values and behavior, television can become the most accessible and compelling source for sexual information.

Premarital sexual activity and attitudes

There is the widespread belief in Vietnam that attitudes among the young have shifted dramatically away from the Confucian ideal of chastity before marriage and that more and more young people are engaging in premarital sexual activity. In fact, one reporter asserted that 'sex before marriage – "eating rice before the bell", as it is sometimes called – is now the norm' (McCarthy, 2000, p. 74). Sexual attitudes and activity are of substantial concern in a country facing increasing rates of HIV. About 50 per cent of HIV infections occur in young people, and 40 per cent of those living with HIV/AIDS are between the ages of 15 and 24 (The National Committee for AIDS Drug and Prostitution Prevention and Control, 2004). High rates of unplanned pregnancies and high rates of abortion further fuel public and governmental concern on young people's sexual activity. The perception of widespread sexual activity among young people was further disseminated and discussed during a recent scandal involving a young television star. Thuy Linh was the star of the very popular TV show *Vang Anh's Diaries*, where she played a high school girl that was modern and stylish, but also determined to uphold traditional virtues. A 16 minute video showing her and her former boyfriend in bed, both apparently aware that they were on camera, was released on the internet. The Vietnam state-owned television station VTV-3 promptly canceled the show after airing Thuy Linh's humiliating farewell, in which she acknowledged the mistakes she had made and apologized to her parents, teachers, friends and fans. Discussions surrounding this incident focused on how sex and gender roles in Vietnam are quickly changing as satellite TV and the internet bring Western influences to Vietnam. VietnamNet, a popular on-line newspaper, said the episode underscores 'the dark side of globalization' and warned people that a flood of foreign influences 'threaten Vietnam's cultural foundation' (Stocking, 2007).

Despite this public concern and speculation on rising rates of premarital sexual activity, little empirical research has documented the prevalence of premarital sexual activity and the attitudes that young people have towards this issue. Much of what is known comes from convenience samples of young people or from women interviewed at abortion clinics (Ghuman et al., 2006). Estimates from a larger, more representative sample are available from a survey of adolescents in six provinces, indicating that by age 22 about 29 per cent of unmarried men and about 16 per cent of unmarried women have had sex (Mensch et al., 2002). As the authors note, these proportions are much lower than those reported in the Philippines,

Thailand, and all 32 countries in Latin America and Sub-Saharan Africa in which Demographic and Health Survey data is collected (Mensch et al., 2002).[1] These figures are also lower than self-reported rates of premarital sex in China. For example, the 2000 Chinese Health and Family Survey, a nationally representative (excluding Tibet and Hong Kong) survey focusing on sexual behavior in contemporary China, reported that 30 per cent of women and 40 per cent of men had engaged in premarital sex by age 20 (Parish, Laumann, & Mojola, 2007).

Unfortunately, these prior Vietnamese studies fail to provide information on the country as a whole or how attitudes and behavior may differ by geographic locale or demographic characteristics. We use recently available, nationally representative data to examine the prevalence of premarital sex among Vietnamese youth and their attitudes towards premarital sex. This information is vital for assessing the accuracy of reports on a 'sexual revolution' in Vietnam. In examining differences, we are particularly interested in differences by urban status.

We hypothesize that attitudes and behavior regarding premarital sex will vary by urbanicity. Theoretical explanations of family change highlight the influence of urbanization as urban lifestyles and attitudes may differ from the traditional ideal, and the context and influence of globalization is heightened in urban areas. Urban areas may also offer young people more freedom to spend time alone together and to provide greater recreational activities aimed at the young. Furthermore, Vietnam's post-renovation economic growth provides evidence of increasing inequality by rural/urban residence. While renovation has clearly resulted in a dramatic poverty declines (for example, consumption poverty fell from 54 per cent in 1992–1993 to 37 per cent in 1997–1998 (World Bank, 1999)) and improvements in human development indicators (Justino & Litchfield, 2003), this economic growth success story masks rising economic disparities (Glewwe, Gragnolati, & Zaman, 2002; Minot, Baulch, & Epprecht, 2003; Nguyen & Popkin, 2003; World Bank, 1999). There are also substantial differences in poverty by rural/urban area, with urban areas having lower poverty rates and sharper poverty declines. While urban households enjoyed a 64 per cent poverty decline between 1992 and 1993 and again between 1997 and 1998, the decline for rural households was only half that (Justino & Litchfield, 2003). In fact, Liu's (2001) calculations indicate that increases in rural/urban inequality account for 76 per cent of the increase in total inequality between 1992 and 1993 and again between 1997 and 1998 (Liu, 2001). Differences between television ownership and access between rural and urban areas also exist. Since many speculate that Western television has played an important role in the supposed liberalization of attitudes towards sex, examining differences between rural and urban areas is important.

Data

The Survey Assessment of Vietnamese Youth (SAVY), a collaboration among the Vietnamese Ministry of Health, the Vietnam General Statistics Office, the World Health Organization, and the United Nation Children's Fund, was designed to provide information on the experiences and attitudes of Vietnamese youth. The survey sampled youth aged 14 to 25 (born between 1978 and 1989) and is a sub-sample of households in the 2002 Vietnam Living Standards Survey. The nationally representative sample covers the country's eight economic regions, and oversamples the largest cities, Hanoi and Ho Chi Minh City (formerly Saigon), to increase statistical power and allow for urban to rural comparisons. The sample does not include those living in special circumstances, such as barracks, re-education centers, social protection centers, factories, or dormitories.

To ensure interview quality, interviewers received extensive training and technical assistance from the supporting organizations. The questionnaire drew from previous questionnaires that were successful in the region and was field-tested with a diverse segment of young people. Each respondent was interviewed in a private place, and the interviewer was the same sex as the respondent. Many respondents were unfamiliar with questionnaires, and therefore the interviewer and the respondent sat side-by-side so that the respondent could observe the questionnaire and the coding process. Ethnic minority youth were interviewed using interpreters. The total interview process, including the self-administered portion, generally took between 60 and 80 minutes.

Married and unmarried respondents were asked slightly different questions about premarital sex. Married respondents were asked directly whether they ever had premarital sex and their age at first premarital sexual experience. Unmarried individuals were asked whether they had ever had sex with anyone, and if yes, the age at which they first had sex. The collection of accurate data on sexual experiences poses several challenges. Because premarital sex is considered socially taboo in Vietnam, respondents may be unwilling to provide information about their behavior. Furthermore, women may be particularly reticent about answering questions on premarital sex. In an attempt to avoid this problem, SAVY utilized a two-part questionnaire which included both an interviewer-administered portion and a self-administered portion. Information regarding sensitive issues, including sexual experiences and attitudes about premarital sex, was collected using the self-administered portion. After the interviewer was confident that the respondent understood the questionnaire and could correctly code responses, the respondent completed the self-administered portion and placed it in a ballot box to maintain privacy. The self-administered portion was completed with the help of the interviewer if the respondent was unable to complete it on his or her own.

In addition to behavior, we also examine attitudes towards premarital sex. SAVY includes several attitudinal questions, asking respondents whether or not premarital sex is acceptable under a variety of conditions: (1) Premarital sex is acceptable if both are willing; (2) Premarital sex is acceptable if they love each other; (3) Premarital sex is acceptable if they are about to marry; (4) Premarital sex is acceptable if both are mature; and (5) Premarital sex is acceptable if the woman can prevent pregnancy. For our multivariate examination of attitudes, we focus on a dichotomous measure of acceptability indicating whether respondents think premarital sex is acceptable if the two persons are willing.

We are particularly interested in potential differences between urban and non-urban areas. There are several urbanicity measures in SAVY for various ages: where the respondent was born, the area he/she was mostly between ages 8 to 14, and their current location. Depending on the aspect of premarital sex being examined, we use different measures. For premarital sexual activity, we rely on a measure of current residence, indicating whether or not the respondent currently resides in an urban area. Because attitudes are heavily influenced by conditions during which the respondent was growing up, we use a measure of whether or not they resided in an urban area for most of the time while growing up (age 8 to 14).

Results

Table 10.1 provides basic descriptive information on the SAVY sample. Our sample is split relatively evenly between males and females. Reflecting the agricultural nature of the country, almost 90 per cent of respondents did not grow up in urban areas and are not currently residing in urban areas. Strong educational differences are apparent. Although 61 per cent of non-urban men and 66 per cent of non-urban women have less than a secondary school education, for urban men and women these figures are 35 per cent and 28 per cent, respectively.

Behavior: Had premarital sex

We begin by using life table techniques to examine the risk of engaging in premarital sexual activity. Prior research using SAVY has presented a frequency distribution on those engaging in premarital sex by a particular age. However, when examining sub-group differences frequency distributions are less useful because the duration of risk for engaging in premarital sexual activity is heavily dependent on marriage age. Individuals that marry young

Table 10.1 Descriptive information

	Total	Male		Female	
		Urban	Other	Urban	Other
Unweighted sample size	7,584	738	3015	752	3079
Sex					
Male	50.0%				
Female	50.0%				
Urbanicity					
Urban area	11.1%				
Non-urban area	88.9%				
Age					
14 to 17	44.6%	37.6%	46.2%	39.1%	44.7%
28 to 21	33.3%	37.9%	32.8%	32.9%	33.2%
22 to 25	22.1%	24.6%	21.1%	28.1%	22.1%
Education					
Less than Secondary school	60.3%	34.5%	61.3%	28.3%	66.6%
Secondary school	30.9%	39.9%	31.8%	39.9%	27.9%
More than Secondary school	8.7%	26.1%	6.8%	31.8%	5.7%
Currently enrolled in school	43.1%	56.2%	45.4%	57.5%	37.4%
Kinh	85.7%	99.1%	84.5%	99.6%	83.5%
Region					
Red River Delta	25.7%	27.4%	25.1%	27.5%	25.9%
Mekong River Delta	19.8%	3.9%	22.2%	7.7%	21.0%
Other regions	54.4%	68.7%	52.7%	64.8%	53.0%
Age at marriage (among those married)	20.0	21.9	20.9	20.9	19.5
Age at first sex (among those with sexual experience)	19.7	19.6	20.0	20.5	19.4
Premarital sexual activity among married	22.2%	36.8%	36.7%	19.6%	14.8%
Partner was someone other than future spouse	6.0%	14.3%	16.1%	0.00%	1.1%
Premarital sexual activity among unmarried	4.9%	14.8%	7.3%	2.1%	0.9%
Contraceptive methods known	5.6	6.0	5.3	6.7	5.8

have a shorter risk duration for premarital sexual activity than individuals that marry at later ages. The life table calculates the probability that a person will have premarital sex at a given age, and removes them from the risk of premarital sex when they have premarital sex, marry, or reach the end of the study date.[2] Figure 10.1 is based on life table analysis and presents the cumulative proportion of individuals that have had premarital sex by age 18,

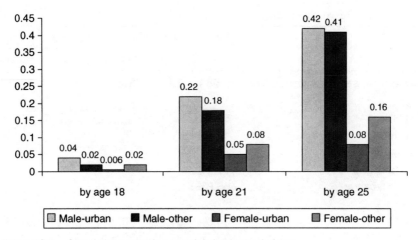

Figure 10.1   Cumulative proportion experiencing premarital sex.

by age 21, and by age 25. Estimates are presented separately by sex and whether they are currently living in an urban location (see Figure 10.1). Results indicate substantial differences by both sex and urban location. Results indicate that premarital sexual activity among individuals 18 and under is very rare, with less than 5 per cent of individuals aged 18 and younger experiencing premarital sexual activity. By age 21, about 22 per cent of men living in large urban centers had engaged in premarital sexual activity, compared to 18 per cent of men not living in large urban cities. By age 26, 42 per cent of men, regardless of location, had engaged in premarital sexual activity. Rates for women were substantially lower. While men in large urban cities had higher rates of premarital sexual activity, among women those in large urban areas had lower rates. By age 21, while about 5 per cent of women in large urban areas had premarital sex, among women not in large urban cities the corresponding proportion was 8 per cent. By age 25, 8 per cent of women in large urban cities reported premarital sexual activity, while for women not in large urban areas the proportion was double at 16 per cent.

Although these life table results provide important information on the probability of experiencing premarital sex and the cumulative proportion having had premarital sex, they treat individuals as a homogeneous group. That is, subgroup differences beyond sex and geographic area are not taken into account. In order to examine the impact of covariates on the probability of experiencing premarital sex, discrete time models for event history analyses are used . Rather than modeling the hazard rate directly, discrete-time event history models involve an approximation of the hazard, expressed as:

$$P_{it} = Pr[T_i = t | T_i \geq t, x_{it}].$$

Table 10.2 The risk of having premarital sex

	Odds ratio	B	S.E
Intercept		−2.86	0.08
Male	3.5	1.25***	0.04
Kinh	0.69	−0.37***	0.05
Less than Secondary school	1.50	0.40***	0.05
Mother's education	1.19	0.18**	0.05
Father's education	1.10	0.10	0.04
Attending school	.59	−0.54***	0.03
Ownership	1.04	0.05	0.06
Grew up and now living in urban area	1.39	0.33***	0.05

**p<.01; ***p < .001

This is the conditional probability that an event (premarital sex) will occur at time t to individual i, given that the event has not occurred prior to time t, where x_{it} is a vector of explanatory variables. The explanatory variables include both time constant and time varying covariates.

Event history analysis is concerned with the patterns and correlates of certain events. The time constant correlates we include are: mother's and father's education, measured as a dichotomous variable indicating whether they had an upper secondary school or higher education; whether they lived in an urban area for most of the time when they were aged 8 to 14; whether they had less than a secondary school education at the time of the survey; whether they are a member of the Kinh majority group; their sex; and an index of family ownership of items. The included time varying covariate is school attendance, indicating whether or not the individual was attending school during that time interval. The results are presented in Table 10.2. Results indicate that men are 3.5 times more likely to have premarital sex than are women. Individuals that spend most of their time in urban areas between ages 8 and 14 were 40 per cent more likely to engage in premarital sex. Education is also significantly associated with the risk of having premarital sex. Those with less than a secondary education are 50 per cent more likely to have premarital sex than those with higher levels of education. However, those that are currently attending school are 40 per cent less likely to have premarital sex.

Attitudes: The acceptability of premarital sex

Turning to attitudes on premarital sex (see Table 10.3), men were 2.6 times more likely than women to agree that premarital sex was acceptable as long as two people were willing. Large urban differences in attitudes were evident, with individuals that lived in urban areas while growing up

Table 10.3 Attitudes towards premarital sex if two people are willing: Binary logit model

	Odds ratio	B	S.E
Intercept		−2.35	0.23
Male	2.63	.97***	.05
Age	1.05	.05***	.01
Kinh	1.05	.05	.07
Completed Secondary school	1.05	.05	.07
Education past Secondary school	1.39	.12	.10
Mother's education	0.97	−.03	.07
Father's education	1.08	.08	.06
Attending school	0.76	−.28***	.04
Ownership	1.05	.04	.06
Grew up and now living in urban area	1.53	.44***	.08
Married	1.40	.34***	.06

**p<.01; ***p < .001

and currently live in urban areas being 1.5 times more likely to agree that premarital sex was acceptable. Figures 10.2 and 10.3 are presented to further illustrate some of the findings by calculating the predicted probability of saying premarital sex is acceptable if two people are willing. These predicted probabilities are based on the multivariate model presented in Table 10.3 and include all the variables in the model. As indicated by Table 10.3, there are significant differences in attitudes towards premarital sex by sex, urban area, marital status, and current school enrollment. Figure 10.2 focuses on differences by marital status, sex, and urban area. As illustrated, those who

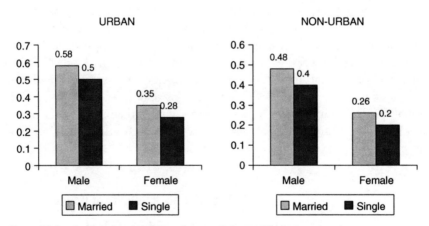

Figure 10.2 Predicted probabilities of premarital sex attitudes.
Note: Other variables in the model include age, mother's education, father's education, education level, ethnicity, ownership, and current enrollment status. The predicted probabilities are calculated holding these variables constant at their mean.

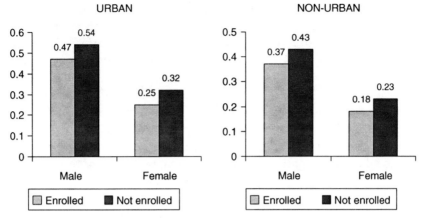

Figure 10.3 Predicted probabilities of premarital sex attitudes.
Note: Other variables in the model include age, mother's education, father's education, education level, ethnicity, ownership, and marital status. The predicted probabilities are calculated holding these variables constant at their mean.

are most accepting of premarital sex if both people are willing is urban, married men – 58 per cent of them said it was acceptable. Single, married, urban men reported lower levels of acceptability (35 per cent). Among women, almost half of married, urban women indicated acceptability of premarital sex (48 per cent). Rural, single women were the least likely to indicate that premarital sex was acceptable (20 per cent). Figure 10.3 focuses on differences by urban area, sex, and school enrollment status. Those indicating the highest degree of acceptability of premarital sex are urban men that are not currently enrolled (54 per cent); the lowest level of acceptability was reported by women in non-urban areas that are currently enrolled in school (18 per cent).

Discussion

Current public and media discussions suggest young people in Vietnam have rejected their grandparents' and parents' social norms and attitudes on premarital sex and have embarked on a sexual revolution. While social changes are occurring in Vietnam, it is important to understand the current status using empirical data. Premarital sex among adolescent and very young adults in Vietnam is quite low by comparative standards. By age 21, only 22 per cent of urban men and 18 per cent of non-urban men had engaged in premarital sex. Among women the proportions are even lower, at 5 per cent for urban women and 8 per cent for non-urban women.

The multivariate results highlight the differences in the risk of having premarital sex by key demographic variables. Controlling for all other variables in the model, the risk of having premarital sex is higher in urban areas. Young people in urban areas may have greater opportunities for premarital sex, either in the greater mobility and privacy afforded by urban areas or because they experience less supervision and monitoring by their parents.

Much discussion in Vietnam has centered on changing behavior and attitudes among adolescents and young adults in Vietnam regarding premarital sex. Public and media discussions depict premarital sex as widespread and argue that this represents a dramatic departure from the past. In particular, foreign influences, especially foreign television, is blamed for this perceived erosion in 'traditional' behavior. However, assessing change in Vietnam is difficult because of the lack of longitudinal data. It is not possible to evaluate whether the current findings on the rate of premarital sex represents a break from the past. In order to speculate on potential changes, we highlight prior findings on premarital sex from a survey specifically designed to assess family changes in Vietnam.

Using data from the Vietnam Surveys of Family Change (VSFC), we can assess trends in premarital sexual behavior in Vietnam's recent past from a representative sample. The VSFC was administered to married individuals who married during three different marriage cohorts. The first cohort, the war cohort, married between 1963 and 1971, representing the period during Vietnam's war for reunification. For the north, aggressive collectivization efforts and mass mobilization characterized this period. The reunification cohort married between 1977 and 1985, the early post-unification period when economic hardship and social upheaval was most severe and when a centrally planned economy was pervasive. The renovation cohort married between 1992 and 2000, the years when economic reforms and the opening up of Vietnam to global influences was well underway. Even though renovation policies were passed in 1986, it was not until the early 1990s that the implementation of the reform efforts brought noticeable change.

The results on reported premarital sexual activity are presented in Figure 10.4 and indicate increases in premarital sex among both men and women across the three cohorts examined. For example, among urban men, 19 per cent in the war cohort reported premarital sexual activity, compared to 26 per cent in the reunification cohort and 40 per cent in the renovation cohort. It is important to note that the VSFC data was based on already married individuals and so differs substantially from the SAVY sample. Despite these differences, the data on premarital sexual activity among urban men in the VSFC is not much different from rates of premarital sexual activity reported by urban men in SAVY by age 25 (see Figure 10.1). Therefore, it does appear that premarital sexual activity has increased. However, this increase is part of a long-term trend rather

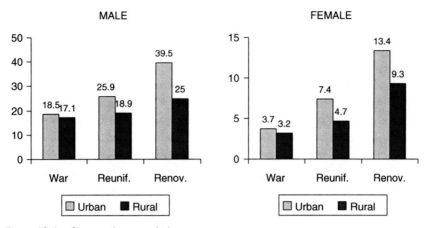

Figure 10.4 Changes in premarital sex.
Note: Data from the Vietnam surveys of family change.

than a recent development. The VSFC clearly show increases from the war to reunification cohort, with additional increases among the renovation cohort.

Just as there are behavioral differences, attitudinal differences in the acceptability of premarital sex are evident between respondents growing up in urban areas compared to those growing up in other areas. Both male and female respondents growing up in urban areas expressed more acceptability towards premarital sex. On the other hand, attitudes towards premarital sex are also relatively conservative with almost half of all respondents in all categories expressing disapproval. This information, combined with the data on behavior, does not provide support for the idea of a sexual revolution in Vietnam. While speculation on television's negative influences abound, it does not appear that adolescents and young adults in Vietnam have dramatically changed their attitudes and behavior.

Although public discourse in Vietnam has focused on the evils of television and the foreign messages being imported, television can also serve as an important source for information and education on reproductive and sexual health. Indeed, the Vietnam government has specific plans to use television to disseminate information, including information on HIV/AIDS and family planning, via television, and a recent policy decree called for all villages in Vietnam to have television access by 2015. When SAVY respondents were asked where they had heard about topics such as family planning, pregnancy and menstruation, gender and sexual relationships, and love and marriage, the overwhelming source for information was the mass media, and television in particular.

Clearly, there are both positive and negative aspects to television. The developmental tasks required in adolescents may lead to television's influence being particularly significant for this group. For example, identity formation is a key developmental task during adolescence, and researchers hypothesize that television may have a significant influence in gender role identity and sexual identity formation. Public concern focuses on the imported models of sexuality and gender relations depicted on television and its potential influence on young people. Television promotes certain sex roles and behavior, and depictions of adolescents on television provide models for attitude formation and behavior imitation (Chapin, 2000). Particularly in cultures where heterosexual interactions are limited and there is reticence about discussing sexual values and behavior, television can become the most accessible and compelling source of sexual information (Arnett, 1995).

Conclusion

Public and media discussions in Vietnam center on the dramatic changes in sexual behavior and attitudes among today's youth and imply that a sexual revolution is taking place. Data from SAVY, however, do not provide evidence for this view. Adolescents and young adults in Vietnam have relatively low levels of premarital sex and express generally conservative views towards it. Vietnam has experienced dramatic social changes over the past few decades, and young people today are growing up in a world very different from that in which their parents grew up. Concern and emphasis, however, would be better placed on ensuring that all young people are receiving adequate and accurate information on sexual and reproductive health. In particular, when available, television seems a ready source to provide this information.

The power of television should not be underestimated. As preparation for a larger study on the impacts of television, we conducted focus groups and semi-structured interviews in two, remote, rural villages. Because of rural electrification funds from the World Bank, one village received electricity five months prior to our visit. The other village had yet to be electrified. Topics in the electrified village focused on how electricity had changed their lives and community. Although a few older men noted how electricity had impacted agricultural production (i.e., using electricity to pump water into the fields), the majority stressed the introduction of television. While only 14 per cent of households owned a television five months after electrification, almost everyone in the village watched nightly, crowding into a house that contained a television. This is a 'captive' audience waiting for information that may be unavailable from other sources. As one 16-year-old girl explained, 'Television is very educational. It teaches us how to kiss and do things with boys.'

Notes

1 Comparable figures using the Vietnam Demographic and Health Survey are not possible because the Vietnam survey was limited to married respondents.
2 Life table techniques also make use of the full sample. A frequency on the proportion having sex by age 21, for example, is limited to those in the sample aged 21 and over.

References

Arnett, J.J. (1995). Adolescents' uses of media for self-socialization. *Journal of Youth and Adolescence, 24*(5), 519–533.
Bongaarts, J. & Watkins, S.C. (1996). Social interactions and contemporary fertility change. *Population and Development Review, 20,* 639–682.
Brown, J.D., Childers, K.M. & Waszak, C.S. (1990). Television and adolescent sexuality. *Journal of Adolescent Health Care, 11,* 62–70.
Brown, J.D., Halpern, C.T. & L'Engle, K.L. (2005). Mass media as sexual super peer for early maturing girls. *Journal of Adolescent Health, 36,* 420–427.
Caldwell, J.C. (1982). *Theory of fertility decline.* New York: Academic Press.
Central Institute for Economic Management (1999). *Vietnam's economy in 1998.* Hanoi: Education Publishing House.
Chapin, J.R. (2000). Adolescent sex and mass media: A developmental approach. *Adolescence, 35*(140), 799–811.
Cleland, J. & Wilson, C. (1987). Demand theories of the fertility transition: An iconoclastic view. *Population Studies, 41,* 5–30.
Dollar, D. & Litvack, J. (1998). Macroeconomic reform and poverty reduction in Vietnam. In D. Dollar, P. Glewwe, & J. Litvack (Eds), *Household welfare and Vietnam's transition* (pp. 1–26). Washington, DC: The World Bank.
Freedman, R. (1979). Theories of fertility decline: A reappraisal. *Social Forces, 58*(1), 1–17.
General Statistics Office (2003). *Data on social statistics in the early years of the 21st century.* Vietnam.
General Statistics Office (2005). Population and employment. 2005
Ghuman, S., Loi, V.M., Huy, V.T. & Knodel, J. (2006). Continuity and change in premarital sex in Vietnam. *Family planning perspectives, 32*(4), 166–174.
Glewwe, P., Gragnolati, M. & Zaman, H. (2002). Who gained from Vietnam's boom in the 1990s? *Economic development and cultural change, 50*(4), 773–792.
Haughton, D., Haughton, J. & Phong, N. (Eds), (2001). *Living standards during an economic boom: Vietnam 1993-1998.* Hanoi: Statistical Publishing House.
Hornick, R.C. (Ed.). (2001). *Public health communication: Evidence of behavior change.* Mahwah, NJ: Lawrence Earlbaum Associates.
Jayakody, R. & Huy, V.T. (2008). Social change and marriage in Vietnam: From socialist state to market reform. In R. Jayakody, A. Thornton, & W. Axinn (Eds), *International family change: Ideational perspectives* (pp. 199–222). New York: Lawrence Earlbaum Associates.
Jayakody, R., Thornton, A. & Axinn, W.G. (2008). Perspectives on international family change. In A. Thornton, R. Jayakody, & W.G. Axinn (Eds), *International family change: Ideational perspectives* (pp. 1–18). NJ: Lawrence Earlbaum Associates.

Justino, P. & Litchfield, J. (2003). Welfare in Vietnam during the 1990s: Poverty, inequality, and poverty dynamics. *Working paper, Poverty Research Unit at Sussex, Paper No. 8*, Sussex, United Kingdom.

Kottak, C.P. (1990). *Prime-time society: An anthropological analysis of television and culture*. Belmont, CA: Wadsworth Publishing Company.

Kottak, C.P. (1991). Television's impact on values and local life in Brazil. *Journal of Communication, 41*(1), 70–87.

Lamb, D. (2002). *Vietnam, now*. New York: Public Affairs.

Liu, A.Y.C. (2001). Markets, inequality and poverty in Vietnam. *Asian Economic Journal, 15*(2), 217–235.

McCarthy, T. (2000). The kids are all right. *Time Asia, 156*(7/8), 74–77.

Mensch, B., Clark, W.H. & Dang Nyugen Anh (2002). *Premarital sex in Vietnam: Is the current concern with adolescent reproductive health warranted?* (No. 163). New York: The Population Council.

Minot, N., Baulch, B. & Epprecht, M. (2003). *Poverty and inequality in Vietnam: Spatial patterns and geographic determinants*. Washington, DC, International Food Policy Research Institute and Institute for Development Studies.

National Committee for Population, F., and Children (2003). *Vietnam: Demographic and Health Survey 2002*. Hanoi: General Statistics Office.

Nguyen, T.M. & Popkin, B.M. (2003). Income and health dynamics in Vietnam: Poverty reduction, increased health inequality. *Population, 58*(2), 253–264.

Parish, W.L., Laumann, E.O. & Mojola, S.A. (2007). Sexual behavior in China: Trends and comparisons. *Population and Development Review, 33*(4), 729–756.

Steele, R. & Brown, J.D. (1995). Adolescent room culture: Studying media in the context of everyday life. *Journal of Youth and Adolescence, 24*(5), 535–550.

Stocking, B. (2007, October 10). Sex scandal snares young Vietnamese star. *USA Today*.

Strasburger, V.C. & Wilson, B.J. (2002). *Adolescents and the media*. Beverly Hills, CA: Sage.

The Economist (2006). Vietnam: Good morning at last. *The Economist, August 5th–11th*, 37–38.

The National Committee for AIDS Drug and Prostitution Prevention and Control (2004). *National strategy on HIV/AIDS prevention and control in Vietnam up to 2010 with a vision to 2020*. Hanoi.

Thornton, A. & Fricke, T.E. (1987). Social change and the family: Comparative perspectives from the West, China, and South Asia. *Sociological Forum, 2*(4), 746–778.

Watkins, S.C. & Danzi, A.D. (1995). Women's gossip and social change: Childbirth and fertility control among Italian and Jewish women in the U.S. *Gender and Society, 9*, 469–490.

Westoff, C.F. (1999). Mass communication and fertility. In R. Leete (Ed.), *Dynamics of values in fertility change* (pp. 237–251). New York: Oxford University Press.

World Bank (1999). *Vietnam attacking poverty*. Washington, DC: World Bank.

World Health Organization (2003). *Health and ethnic minorities in Vietnam*. Hanoi.

11

SOCIAL CHANGE AND TRANSITION EXPERIENCES AMONG YOUNG ADULTS IN BRITAIN

Ingrid Schoon

This chapter will address both conceptually and empirically recent debates about the transformation of the life course since the 1970s and early 1980s. It has been argued that lives are becoming less standardized and more individualized, less collectively patterned and more strongly influenced by individual decision making and choice. The terms destandardization and individualization are often used interchangeably. Here I will differentiate between destandardization as the demographic component of change, and individualization as the ideational component. Individualization is used as a more general term that encompasses destandardization and deinstitutionalization. It is argued that there cannot be a greater individualization of the life course without it becoming less standardized. Moreover, if the life course becomes more dependent on individual agency, this should lead to a greater destandardization and diversification of transition experiences. These assumptions are empirically tested, using data collected for two British birth cohorts born 12 years apart, in 1958 and 1970 respectively. Continuity and change in demographic experiences up to age 30 will be mapped, focusing on the timing and sequencing of work and family related transitions among young people in Britain. In particular I will examine the role of cognitive ability and motivation in shaping life course transitions in a changing socio-historical context, versus those of socio-demographic background and gender. The chapter will address issues of individual development in times of social change, and contribute to the debate of structural versus individual agency factors in shaping transition experiences.

Transitions in context

Across most Western societies the average age of primary employment, marriage and family formation has been pushed back from the early twenties to the late twenties and even the early thirties, as more education and skill development is required in response to the introduction of new technologies and changing labor market opportunities (Larson, 2002). It has been argued that since the 1970s transitions into adulthood have become destandardized, i.e. more variable and protracted, and less uniform (Beck, 1992; Buchmann, 1989; Giddens, 1991). There have also been observations of an increasing deinstitutionalization of life course transitions, in particular regarding family transitions, as reflected in the rise of non-marital unions and the decoupling of marriage and family formation (Bumpass & Lu, 2000; Coleman, 2000). Moreover, there are suggestions that an 'ideational shift' has taken place, characterized by changing social practices and the breakdown of many class, gender, and age-based constraints shaping demographic events (Lesthaeghe, 1995). It has been argued that individual biographies have become more removed from traditional life scripts and more dependent on individual agency (Buchmann, 1989). As individuals were freed from the traditional constraints of family, gender, and social structure they were able to exercise more agency in the construction of their biographies, leading to individualized biographies (Beck, 1992).

The assertion that individuals are now free to choose has been questioned, as there is persisting evidence of unequal access to educational and career opportunities (Bynner, 2006; Furlong & Cartmel, 1997; Schoon, 2007), as well as evidence of an increasing polarization into fast versus slow transitions (Jones, 2002; Ross et al., 2009). A distinction has opened up between those who take a slower route to adulthood involving longer education and delayed assumption of adult roles, and those who follow the traditional fast track transition, leaving school at minimum age, followed by early entry to the labor market and family formation. It appears that social change has affected all young people – but not all in the same way (Schoon & Silbereisen, 2009). There is a differentiation of transition pathways across different social groups in the population, and the preparation for adulthood has been elongated, especially for those who can afford to invest in their education. Questions about experiences of young people who do not obtain higher education and/or who marry and have their first child relatively early have not been posed or answered sufficiently, neither has the question of the importance of structural factors been systematically tested.

Structure and agency

From the debates cited above, it appears that the processes shaping individual development in times of social change are not yet fully understood, and that the effects of the correlated structural and individual level variables are difficult to entangle. In the following I will adopt assumptions formulated within life course theory to gain a better understanding of the interactions between developing individuals and a changing context. In life course theory it is argued that transition experiences and pathways through life are always embedded within a larger socio-historical and cultural context, and are shaped by complex interdependent relationships, including links to one's family of origin and individual agency processes (Elder, 1985). Structural characteristics such as socio-economic status at birth and parental education have been linked to variations in academic attainment and motivation, to educational and occupational opportunities later in life, as well as to the timing of partnership and family formation (Duncan & Brooks-Gunn, 1997; Schoon, 2006, 2008; Schoon & Parsons, 2002; Schoon, Martin, & Ross, 2007). Social changes and socio-historical influences often impact on the individual through the influence of such changes on their interpersonal contexts, such as the family environment (Conger & Elder, 1994; Elder & Conger, 2000). Yet, individuals are not passively exposed to these structural influences, and act upon their environment by making decisions and choices based on the alternatives and opportunities that they perceive are available to them (Schoon, 2007). The decisions made by individuals, within the particular constraints of their lives, can have important consequences for their future trajectories. For example, early school leaving might limit one's opportunities in the labor market, especially in the light of changing employment opportunities and increasing demand for a highly skilled labor force.

Another key structural factor that shapes transitions and the pacing of work and family related transitions is gender (Moen, 2001). The female life course has been described as more complex than that of males, and there is a persisting structural imbalance in the social pathways and biographical options available to women. This is largely because of the greater interdependence of family and work-related roles due to persisting gendered expectations ascribing women the main responsibilities for care and family tasks, rendering female participation in the labor market more interrupted and unstable than that of men. If women's life course is becoming less dependent on socio-demographic constraints, one would expect increasing deviation of this pattern.

Changes in transition experiences have been debated within the social sciences, yet there is still a lack of systematic empirical research on the structure of the life course, and how it has changed (Elder & Shanahan, 2007). The aim of this chapter is to move towards a more comprehensive understanding of individualization and destandardization of transitions into adult roles. The two concepts are generally used interchangeably and indiscriminately in the literature to describe the salient changes in life course patterns observed in recent years. Here I suggest to be more precise in the conceptualization of these two concepts, and to distinguish them from each other to indicate that they are tapping into different dimensions of influences on the life course. While individualization is considered to refer to the ideational component of change, destandardization reflects the demographic component. Individualization is considered to be the more general term that encompasses destandardization and deinstitutionalization. It is argued that pathways through the life course cannot become more individualized without becoming less standardized, i.e. less dependent on structural factors.

Laboratories for the study of human development are rare. The closest one can get is to compare experiences of individuals born in two different birth cohorts, which makes it possible to analyse transitions in times of social change, as the birth year locates cohort members within a specific historical time and related socio-historical changes. Within the Western world, major demographic changes in life course transitions have occurred, moving from a period of relative economic stability, a 'Golden Age' in the words of Eric Hobsbawm (Hobsbawm, 1995), to a period of increasing uncertainty and conflict. In the UK a major turning point was the winter of 1973/74 which brought the experience of the first oil crisis, accompanied by the fast disappearance of Britain's manufacturing industries (Halsey, 2000). These historic events place the two British cohorts at the pulse of events, enabling the comparison of a cohort born at the end of an economic boom period in 1978 to a cohort born in 1970, growing up during a major economic bust. Both cohorts provide information on socio-demographic background data as well as individual agency factors, such as ability and motivation, which enables the testing of the individualization hypothesis in context.

Has there been an increasing destandardization of life course patterns, as indicated by a reduced influence of social class and gender? And has there been an increasing individualization of the life course, as indicated by a greater importance of individual agency factors in shaping transition experiences and outcomes in the later born cohort? As mentioned before, individualization is used here as the more general term, encompassing the notion of destandardization. There cannot be a greater individualization of the life course without it becoming less standardized. Following the assumption of increasing individualization, one would expect that individual agency is becoming more important than structural factors in shaping transition experiences. Furthermore, increasing individualization in female careers might implicate that male and female careers become more similar, and less influenced by structural factors. In the following both assumptions will be assessed.

Individual agency is operationalized through indicators of cognitive ability and school motivation. Cognitive ability is understood as the ability to assess different available options and opportunities. School motivation, as assessed in the two cohorts, is understood as an indicator of individual striving. It has shown to predict the timing of school leaving age (Schoon, 2008) as well as timing of family formation and consequent educational and occupational attainment (Schoon et al., 2007). Unlike educational or occupational aspirations it is a more general indicator of individual agency and engagement in developmentally salient tasks.

Two British birth cohorts

The study is based on data collected for two British birth cohorts born in 1958 and 1970 respectively, following the lives of over 20,000 individuals from birth into the adult years (Ferri, Bynner, & Wadsworth, 2003; Schoon, 2006). Although born only 12 years apart, the two cohorts encountered a markedly different context for development. While the 1958 cohort was born at a time of extraordinary economic growth and social transformation, the 1970 cohort grew up during a time of increasing uncertainty and instability. Both cohorts experienced two successive major economic recession periods, lasting from the late 1970s until the mid-1990s, yet at different life stages. While most cohort members born in 1958 had completed their full-time education just before the onset of the recession period, the 1970 cohort reached minimum school leaving age right in the midst of it. Employment prospects were still relatively good when most of the 1958 cohort members left school at age 16, i.e. in 1974. Cohort members born in 1970, however, were directly hit by the increasing rates of unemployment at the time of compulsory school leaving age. Between 1991 and 1994 Britain witnessed a second period of economic decline. Since the mid-1990s, however, a period of recovery set in, coinciding with the 1958 cohort becoming more settled regarding their careers and family formation, and the 1970 cohort setting out in establishing their careers.

Have the changes outlined above influenced the transition into and assumption of adult roles? It has been argued that in a flourishing economy young people are more likely to enter the labor market early, to gain early financial independence and to form an adult identity (Bynner, 2001; Furlong & Cartmel, 1997). In recession economies and times of rapid structural change, on the other hand, young people are more likely to postpone the entry into adult roles (Reitzle, Vondracek, & Silbereisen, 1998). But have the social changes affected all young people in the same way? Drawing on the cohort data, assumptions regarding pathways adopted by young people in times of social change can be tested in a real-life context. If there is a greater destandardization of life course transitions, one would expect decreasing significance of socio-demographic background factors such as parental social status and gender in shaping transition experiences in the later born cohort. If there is a greater importance of individual agency processes, one would expect a greater role of individual characteristics, such as ability and motivation. In the following, differences in social structuring versus individual agency in shaping transition experiences will be assessed, focusing on educational and employment transitions as well as patterns of family formation.

Cohort changes in educational careers

Figure 11.1 shows the cumulative percentages of school leaving between ages 16 and 29 years. There has been an increase in further education, with more men and women in the later born cohort staying on in further education beyond age 16, the minimum school leaving age. However, the changes are less dramatic as one would expect, and by age 18 the majority of men and women in both cohorts have left education. In both cohorts men are more likely than women to leave full-time education at minimum school leaving age, yet after the age of 18 years, there are very small gender differences.

Has there been a reduction in the role of social background in shaping educational transitions, and an increase in individual agency factors?

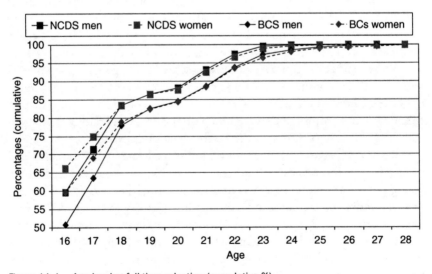

Figure 11.1   Age leaving full-time eduction (cumulative %).

To determine the relationship between family background, childhood cognitive ability and school motivation, a series of logistic regression models were run separately for both cohorts. The first model determines if there is a relationship between school leaving age and family social background. The second model adds the indicators for individual agency, i.e. childhood cognitive ability and school motivation, to test the independent contribution of structural versus individual factors in contributing to participation in further education. A description of the variables included in the model is given in the Appendix. Table 11.1 gives the odds ratios and 95 per cent confidence intervals for the variables included in the two models.

In both cohorts gender, family socio-economic status, and parental education are all significantly related to the cohort member's school leaving age (Model 1). Women are less likely to leave school at age 16 than men. Those leaving school at age 16 are more likely to come from less privileged family backgrounds, as characterized by lower social status and lower parental education. In the later born cohort the odds ratios for social family background are lower than in the 1958 cohort, suggesting a weakening role of parental social status and education in influencing educational transitions. The findings thus reflect the increasing participation in further education among young people, including those from less privileged backgrounds.

Model 2 adds the indicators for childhood cognitive ability and school motivation. Both variables had been z-standardized to ease cohort comparability. Introducing the two variables into the model lessens the magnitude of the effects of family social background, but family social status and parental education continue to be significant predictors of school leaving age in both cohorts. Interestingly, the addition of individual factor variables increases the proportion of explained variance by 19 per cent in the 1958 cohorts, yet only by 12 per cent in the 1970 cohort. This finding might suggest that the role of individual level variables in explaining variation in school leaving age has actually reduced for the later born cohort.

Cohort changes in employment and family careers

Evidence from the UK cohort studies suggests that young people from less privileged family backgrounds generally tend to make work and family related transitions earlier than their more privileged peers, with reduced career opportunities in later life (Bynner, 1998; Schoon et al., 2007). A distinction has opened up between those who take a slower route to adulthood involving longer education and delayed assumption of adult roles, and those who follow the traditional fast track transition leaving school at minimum age, followed by early entry to the labor market and family formation (Berrington, 2001; Bynner, 2005; Jones, 2002; Ross et al., 2009).

Table 11.1 Predicting leaving school at age 16 by parental social status, parental education, childhood cognitive ability, and school motivation (odds ratios and 05% Confidence Interval)

	NCDS				BCS70			
	Model 1		Model 2		Model 1		Model 2	
	Odds ratios	95% CI	Odds ratios	95% CI	Odds ratios	95% CI	Odds ratios	95% CI
Sex (Female)	.692*	(0.63–0.76)	.779*	(0.69–0.88)	.645*	(0.58–0.72)	.839#	(0.71–0.99)
RGSC prof/man (baseline)	1.000		1.000		1.000		1.000	
RGSC skilled	2.275*	(1.99–2.60)	1.898*	(1.60–2.26)	2.081*	(1.78–2.43)	1.789*	(1.40–2.26)
RGSC unskilled	4.375*	(3.70–5.18)	2.877*	(2.31–3.58)	3.115*	(2.58–3.76)	2.221*	(1.65–2.98)
Father's education	2.397*	(2.12–2.71)	1.885*	(1.61–2.21)	2.061*	(1.82–2.34)	1.595*	(1.31–1.94)
Mother's education	2.794*	(2.48–3.15)	2.204*	(1.89–2.57)	2.206*	(1.95–2.49)	1.824*	(1.51–2.20)
Cognitive ability			0.410*	(0.38–0.44)			0.536*	(0.49–0.59)
Motivation			0.452*	(0.42–0.49)			0.545*	(0.50–0.59)
R^2 (Nagelkerke)	.24		.43		.18		.30	

Note: *$p < .001$; #$p < 0.05$

Figure 11.2 shows the cumulative percentage of men in both cohorts making the step into full-time employment as well as parenthood by age. Men in the later born cohort are making the step into full-time employment and parenthood later than men born in 1958. We can also see that among men work and family transitions are relative independent from each other.

In the case of female careers, however, we can see that employment and parenthood histories are more closely linked than for men (see Figure 11.3). Women in the later born cohort enter employment and parenthood later than women born in 1958. Figures 11.2 and 11.3 show that by age 18 the majority of young people (men and women) are in paid employment, and that women become parents earlier in their lives than men.

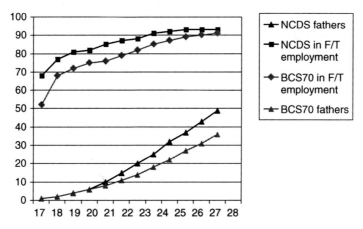

Figure 11.2   Employment & parenthood (men only).

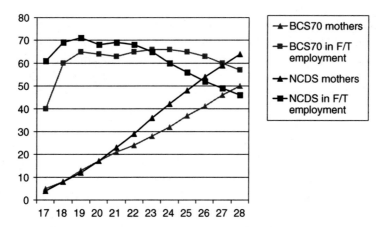

Figure 11.3   Employment & parenthood (women only).

The postponement of parenthood has not been as dramatic as one might have expected – the median age at first birth for women born in 1958 was 27 years, while for women born in 1970 it was 29 years. Around 1 in 10 of the women had become a teenage parent in both cohorts. Two-thirds of men and half of the women in the later born cohort did not have a child by age 29.

Entry into parenthood is strongly linked to social background and years of completed education. Figures 11.4 and 11.5 show the unadjusted odd ratios for cohort members delaying the step into parenthood by social background, as well as the odd ratios after adjusting for age leaving full-time education. Some delay in entry into parenthood is observed for all social groups, although the postponement of family formation is not fully explained by social class differences or increases in education. More educated men and women from relatively privileged families are most likely to delay the step into parenthood than the less educated. The experience of further education reduces social differentials but does not eliminate them. Neither does the social gradient disappear after the entry of cognitive ability and motivation into the model. The findings suggest persisting social differentiation in the experience of youth transitions, which contradicts the assumption of increasing destandardization. For men in the later born cohort, the social gradient has actually become steeper, while for women it has remained more or less the same. This finding might suggest a greater polarization of transition experiences among men.

Sequencing of employment careers

Has there been an increasing destandardization in the timing and sequencing of work transitions? Alternative trajectories are examined among young people leaving full-time education at age 16 versus those who stayed on in education. To capture the dynamics of multiple interlocking pathways and the sequencing of different transitions over time a sequence analysis was conducted. Sequence analysis offers an approach to examine combinations of sequences as a whole. In combination with cluster analysis it can be applied to provide summaries of typical patterns of sequences in the form of a typology. The specific technique used here is Optimal Matching Analysis (Abbott, 1995), which was applied to the economic activity data recorded for cohort members between ages 16 and 29 years. All economic history data was censored at age 29 to render the data comparable. Each individual's economic activity history is represented by a sequence consisting of 14 elements, recorded for the October of each year from 1974 to 1987 in NCDS, and from 1986 to 1999 in BCS70 (Martin, Schoon, & Ross, 2008). The original analysis was based on a pooled analysis of the cohort data.

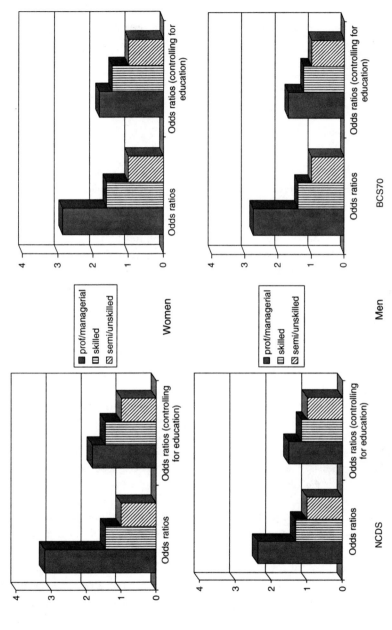

Figure 11.4 Odds ratios for predicting delay of parenthood after 29th birthday – relative to social class of origin (reference category: semi/unskilled).

Leaving school		16		17+
Economic career	NCDS %	BCS %	NCDS %	BCS %
Continuous ft employment	87.0	83.3	94.3	92.1
Interrupted career	.3	1.6	.4	1.6
Long term unemployed	9.3	6.3	1.2	1.0
Return to education	.4	1.8	2.3	2.5
Pt career	.5	1.4	1.4	2.0
Drop-out of labor market	2.2	4.4	.4	.6

Figure 11.5 Economic careers after leaving school NCDS/BCS70 (men only).

As reported by Martin and colleagues, the original aim of analysis was to proceed with the classification in such a way that small clusters, if they exist, can be found, and that the classification can be demonstrated to be reliable not just for a few large clusters, but for most of the cohort members. The original study identified 17 distinct groups, although some of them were rather small, comprising only about 1 per cent of the sample. Here the groupings are summarized as six distinct patterns:

- Cohort members who experienced continuous full-time employment after leaving education.
- Those with interrupted careers, characterized by a significant length of time (>1 year) spent in part-time employment or out of the labor market.
- Long-term unemployment (three years or more).
- Cohort members who returned to full-time education.
- Moving into part-time employment after some time working full-time.
- Dropping out of the labor force.

Findings from the sequence analysis suggest that there are no groundbreaking changes in transition experiences between ages 16 and 29. The majority of men and women are in continuous full-time employment after leaving school (except for women born in 1958 who left school at age 16). There are, however, changes in prevalences regarding minority pathways into full-time employment. The percentage of cohort members returning to full-time education has increased in the later born cohort, especially among men who left education at minimum age (Figure 11.5), and among women who left school after some further education (Figure 11.6). There has also been an increase in 'interrupted careers' and 'part-time careers' among men,

Leaving full-time education →	Leaving school	16		17+	
	Economic career	NCDS %	BCS %	NCDS %	BCS %
	Continuous ft employment	32.4	41.2	61.5	72.5
	Interrupted career	3.9	3.7	2.2	2.0
	Long term unemployed	2.6	2.1	.8	.6
	Return to education	.3	.8	.9	2.6
	Pt career	16.2	19.2	15.4	12.4
	Drop-out of labor market	44.4	31.7	18.9	9.5

Figure 11.6   Economic careers after leaving school NCDS/BCS70 (women only).

particularly among those who left school at age 16. Comparing the transition experiences of men who had left school at age 16 against those who stayed on in both cohorts we find those who leave school at age 16 are more likely to experience long spells of unemployment, and are more likely to drop out of the labor market completely. The findings thus suggest that a small but increased minority of men encountered problems in establishing themselves in the labor market.

Women generally have more diverse transition experiences than men (Figure 11.6), possibly reflecting the interdependence of work and family related roles. Compared to men they are less continuously attached to the labor market, and are more likely to drop out of paid employment completely, mostly to look after their children. An interesting finding however is that women in the later born cohort appear to be more attached to the labor market. This applies to women who left school at age 16, as well as to those who stayed on in further education. More women in the later born cohort are experiencing continuous full-time employment after leaving education, and are less likely to drop out of the labor force. Those with extended qualifications are generally more likely to be continuously employed after leaving school, while those leaving school at 16 are more likely to drop out of the labor market completely. The pathway characterized by return to education is generally more prevalent among women with further education, although among a relatively small group only. This pathway might be indicative of women who return to education after the birth of their children, but further research is needed to verify this speculation. Generally there are more men than women returning to full-time education.

Increasing individualization of employment transitions?

To what extent are the employment transitions shaped by socio-demographic factors and individual agency? To assess the relative impact of social versus individual influences on the transition experiences between ages 16 and 29, a nested series of multinominal regressions was conducted, entering social and individual level variables stepwise into the model (Table A.1 showing the results is given in the Appendix). In both cohorts the odds of entering an interrupted career compared to continuous full-time employment are lower for males than for females. None of the other factors reached significance. Including cognitive ability and school motivation into the model does not alter the significant gender differences, yet suggests that those with higher cognitive ability are less likely to experience an interrupted career. The effect is slightly stronger in NCDS than in BCS70 – a finding which does not support the assumption of increasing individualization.

The odds of experiencing long-term unemployment compared to continuous employment after leaving education are increased for men in both cohorts, as well as for those from non-professional family background, and those with a mother with minimum education only. Father's education is only important for cohort members in NCDS. Entering cognitive ability and motivation into the model removes the gender effect and reduces the influence of parental occupational status. Yet those cohort members who experience unemployment are significantly more likely to come from the most disadvantaged backgrounds than those who enter continuous full-time employment. They also score lower in the cognitive ability assessment and report lower school motivation. The influence of these two variables appears to be slightly stronger in the later born cohort, suggesting increasing importance of individual characteristics in avoiding unemployment.

Regarding return to education, we find no significant differences compared to those with continuous full-time employment, except in BCS70, where father's education appears to play an important role in influencing return to education. However, after entering cognitive ability and motivation into the model the significant influence of parental education in BCS70 is removed.

The odds of entering a part-time career compared to continuous full-time employment are increased for women in both cohorts, and for those cohort members with a father who left school at minimum school leaving age. In BCS70 we find an even stronger influence of social background in determining this pathway, with significant effects from parental occupational class and mother's education. After entering cognitive ability and school motivation into the model, the gender effect remains, yet the social background influences are reduced, especially in NCDS. In BCS70 cohort members in part-time careers, compared to those in continuous full-time employment, are more likely to have had a less educated mother. The effect of cognitive ability and motivation is of similar strength in both cohorts, which is not in accordance with the assumption of increasing individualization.

Dropping out of the labor market, compared to continuous full-time employment, is more likely among females, especially among those from more disadvantaged families and less educated parents. Including cognitive ability and motivation into the model reduces some of the social background effects, especially in BCS70, but does not eliminate them. Cohort members, especially women, from the most disadvantaged backgrounds and those with less educated mothers are most likely to drop out of the labor market completely. The effect of cognitive ability is of similar size in both cohorts, although school motivation seems to play a slightly more important role in the later born cohort.

The education-work-family nexus

What are the interlinkages between education and employment histories and family formation? And what is the role of structural versus individual variables in shaping these transitions. In the following I will first compare partnership and family arrangements of cohort members leaving school at age 16 versus those who are staying on in education after the age of 18. Second, patterns of living arrangements will be linked to demographic and individual agency factors, as well as to employment careers. Living arrangements of cohort members in their early thirties (at age 30 in BCS70 and age 33 in NCDS) were grouped into four categories, differentiating between those who have remained single with no children, who are living as a couple with no children, as a couple with children, and as single parents.

Figure 11.7 shows the patterns of living arrangements for men and women in their early thirties by school leaving age in both cohorts. For men and women in the 1958 cohort the predominant pattern is to live as a couple with children by the age of 33, especially among those who have left school at minimum age. In the 1970 cohort living as a couple with children is the predominant living arrangement among those men and women who left school at minimum age, while those with further education are more likely to postpone the step into parenthood.

In NCDS the great majority of men and women were married at the age of 33, while in BCS70 the rate of married couples by age 30 has nearly halved. Instead more men and women born in 1970 were living with partners to whom they were not married, reflecting the increasing popularity of cohabitation (Ferri & Smith, 2003). The BCS70 cohort features more childless couples than NCDS at a similar age (although it has to be kept

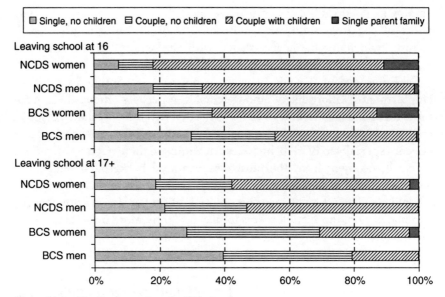

Figure 11.7   Family careers by school leaving age.

in mind that there is a three year age difference at point of assessment), especially among the more educated. The data suggests that the event of establishing a commitment to a partner is becoming more and more independent from the event of having a child. Of those women who do live with children, the proportion of single mothers is higher in BCS70 than in NCDS, especially among those with minimum education. There is also an increasing number of step-fathers.

The most obvious differences between the two cohorts are the greater proportion of childless singles and the smaller proportion of couples with children in BCS70. The dramatic increase of individuals without a partner is particularly evident among men and women with further education – but also among men in BCS70 who left school at minimum age. This latter finding might suggest a generally increasing preference for a 'single' life style, or increasing difficulties for young men who left school early to attract a partner.

Generally, the trends in patterns of partnership and family arrangements indicate an increasing instability and transitory nature of personal relationships. To appreciate fully the situation of many young people coming of age in the last decades of the twentieth century, the growing fragility of personal and emotional commitment has to be seen in conjunction with social background characteristics, individual agency factors, and increasing insecurity in the labor market. To assess the impact of structural and individual influences, as well as transition experiences between ages 16 and 29 on family and partnership status of cohort members in their early thirties, a nested series of multinominal regression was conducted (results are given in the Appendix, Table A.2).

In both cohorts the odds for staying single without children, compared to living as a couple with children, are higher for males than for females, and for those from relatively privileged backgrounds. In BCS70 the effect of the structural variables appears to be stronger than in NCDS. Adding cognitive ability and school motivation into the model reduces the impact of structural variables significantly in BCS70, but not in NCDS. While in NCDS cognitive ability and motivation are not significant in predicting being single, in BCS70 high levels of school motivation appear to be associated with remaining single by age 30. Adding the transition experiences eliminates the gender effect in NCDS but not in BCS70. In NCDS being single compared to living as a couple with children is less likely among relative disadvantaged cohort members, and less likely among those who dropped out of the labor force, who entered a part-time career, or experienced an interrupted career. In BCS70 being single compared to living as a couple with children is significantly more likely among men, among those with high school motivation, and those who returned to full-time education. It is less likely among those who dropped out of the labor force or entered a part-time career. These findings suggest that being single compared to living as a couple with children is based on different experiences in the two cohorts. While in NCDS social origin and lack of interruptions in one's employment career plays a crucial role, in BCS70 it might be more strongly associated with attempts to improve one's employment opportunities (and prospects for a relationship) after having left school with limited qualifications only.

Being partnered with no children compared to living as a couple with children is more likely among male cohort members from relatively privileged family background with educated parents. Cognitive ability and school motivation are significant predictors in both cohorts, reducing the effect of social background, especially in NCDS, although the influence of father's education remains significant in both cohorts. Controlling for transition experiences eliminates the gender effect in both cohorts, suggesting that living as a childless couple compared to living as a couple with children is more likely among cohort members with high cognitive ability from a relatively privileged background, especially in BCS70, who experienced little disruption in their employment careers. In BCS70 high school motivation as well as high cognitive ability school motivation play a significant role in shaping this pathway.

Single parenthood compared to living as a couple with children is more likely among women from a relatively disadvantaged social background. In both cohorts low school motivation plays a significant role in predicting this pathway, and in NCDS we also see a significant effect of cognitive ability. Controlling for employment histories suggest that in NCDS entry into single parenthood, a compared to living as a couple with children, is more likely among women with relative low cognitive ability and low school motivation, who experienced long-term unemployment and dropped out of the labor market completely. In BCS70 single parenthood, compared to living as a couple with children, is more likely among women with low school motivation, who experienced interrupted employment careers, long-term unemployment, and who dropped out of the labor market completely.

Discussion

Generally the findings provide mixed evidence in support of the assumption of increased individualization and destandardization of the life course. There has been an extended participation in further education, and a delay in entry into full-time employment and family formation. Yet transitions remain significantly shaped by social background and gender. Furthermore, there were only slight cohort changes regarding the sequencing of employment transitions. In both cohorts, most men and women spent most time between ages 16 and 29 in continuous employment after leaving school. What can be noted though, is that women generally have more varied employment careers than men, and are more likely to discontinue full-time work at some point, either to take up part-time work or by dropping out of the labor force altogether, most likely due to their parenting commitments. In the later born cohort women have become more attached to the labor market, while among men there is an increasing minority who are experiencing problems in establishing a full-time working career, especially among those who had left school early.

It could be argued that the life course of men and women has become more similar, in that women are becoming more attached to the labor market. However, despite increasing female labor force participation women's work careers have remained discontinuous, and women are generally more likely than men to experience interrupted careers, to work part-time, or drop out of the labor market completely. Thus, gender differences in transition experiences persist.

Furthermore, there are persisting differences by social background. Young people from less privileged families are more likely to leave school early, and to encounter problems in establishing themselves in the labor market. In three out of ten comparisons against those who experienced continuous full-time employment after leaving school individual factors showed a slightly stronger effect in the later born cohort: low cognitive ability was more strongly associated with the experience of long-term unemployment, and low school motivation was more strongly associated with unemployment as well as dropping out of the labor market. Yet, in all other comparisons individual factors had a similar or even slightly stronger effect in the earlier born cohort. The findings suggest that non-normative life course patterns, such as part-time careers or dropping out of the labor market, are followed by an increasing minority of men in the 1970 cohort, and that young people born in 1958 might have had more opportunities to realize their individual capabilities than those born 12 years earlier. These findings might thus suggest evidence of 'involuntary' individualization, of being condemned to pursue and experience trajectories that are not collectively well-trodden pathways, and not necessarily the result of one's own choice (Buchmann, 1989; Shanahan, 2000).

Regarding partnership and family arrangements the findings suggest increasing the instability and transitory nature of personal relationships. There has been a decoupling of partnership and family formation, with an increasing number of young people living as a couple without children, and a dramatic rise of young people, especially men, living as singles in their early 30s. Individual level factors, in particular school motivation, play an increasing role in shaping family arrangements. Compared to those living as a couple with children, young people with high levels of school motivation are more likely to remain childless, living either as a single or as a couple, and are less likely to become a single parent. The significant role of school motivation in influencing the timing of family formation, but also of education and employment transitions, has been highlighted in previous studies (Schoon, 2008; Schoon et al., 2007).

Taken together the findings suggest that destandardization of life course transitions has been less extensive than it is generally discussed in the literature, especially regarding education and employment careers. The greatest changes are observed in the increasing individualization of private lives and living arrangements, especially among women. A similar conclusion was drawn by Brückner and Mayer, who examined intra-cohort variations in the timing of education, employment, and family transitions of West German men and women born between 1919 and 1971, using data from the German Life History Study (GLHS) (Brückner & Mayer, 2005). These findings highlight the need to put theories regarding the impact of social change on individual lives to the test, and not to rely on armchair speculations only. Assumptions about a changing life course can have serious implications, especially as they are influencing the thinking of policy makers who are shaping the institutionalized context of transitions. We have only started to gain a better understanding of the mechanisms and processes that produce life course patterns in a changing socio-historical context. In interpreting the findings reported here it has to taken into consideration that the measures used were restricted to those collected in the cohort studies. What is needed to develop the field further is a clearer conceptualization and operationalization of key concepts, such as individualization and destandardization, and the use of empirical evidence generated from multiple longitudinal studies, following the lives of individuals born in different cohorts.

Acknowledgments

The analysis and writing of this chapter was supported by grants from the UK Economic and Social Research Council (ESRC): L32625306, RES-225-25-2001, and RES-594-28-0001. Data from the Cohort Studies were supplied by the ESRC Data Archive. Those who carried out the original collection of the data bear no responsibility for its further analysis and interpretation.

Bibliography

Abbott, A. (1995). Sequence analysis. New methods for old ideas. *Annual Review of Sociology, 21*, 93–113.

Arnett, J.J. (2000). Emerging adulthood. A theory of development from the late teens to the late twenties. *American Psychologist, 55*(5), 469–480.

Arnett, J.J. (2006). Emerging adulthood in Europe: A response to Bynner. *Journal of Youth Studies, 9*, 111–123.

Beck, U. (1992). *Risk society. Towards a new modernity*. London: Sage.

Bond, R. & Saunders, P. (1999). Routes of success: influences on the occupational attainment of young British males. *British Journal of Sociology, 50*(2), 217–249.

Breen, R. & Goldthorpe, J.H. (1999a). Class inequality and meritocracy: a critique of Saunders and an alternative analysis. *British Journal of Sociology, 50*(1), 1–27.

Breen, R. & Goldthorpe, J.H. (1999b). Class, mobility, and merit: The experience of two British birth cohorts. *European Sociological Review, 17*, 81–101.

Breen, R. & Goldthorpe, J.H. (2001). Class, mobility and merit. The experience of two British birth cohorts. *European Sociological Review, 17*(2), 81–101.

Breen, R. & Goldthorpe, J.H. (2002). Merit, mobility, and method: Another reply to Saunders. *British Journal of Sociology, 53*, 575–582.

Buchmann, M. (1989). *The script of life in modern society: entry into adulthood in a changing world*. Chicago: Chicago University Press.

Brückner, H. & Mayer, K.U. (2005). De-standardization of the life course: What does it mean? And if it means anything, whether it actually took place? In R. Macmillan (Ed.), *The structure of the life course: Standardized? Individualized? Differentiated?* (pp. 27–54). Amsterdam: Elsevier.

Buchmann, M. (1989). *The script of life in modern society: Entry into adulthood in a changing world*. Chicago: Chicago University Press.

Bumpass, L.L. & Lu, H.H. (2000). Trends in cohabitation and implications for children's family contexts in the United States. *Population Studies, 54*, 29–41.

Bynner, J. (2001). British youth transitions in comparative perspective. *Journal of Youth Studies, 4*(1), 5–23.

Bynner, J. (2006). Rethinking the youth phase of the life-course: The case for emerging adulthood? *Journal of Youth Studies, 9*, 367–384.

Coleman, D. (2000). Population and family. In A.H. Halsey & J. Webb (Eds), *Twentieth century British social trends* (pp. 27–93). London: Macmillan.

Conger, R.D. & Elder, G.H. (1994). *Families in troubled times: Adapting to change in rural America*. New York: Aldine De Gruyter.

Duncan, G.J. & Brooks-Gunn, J. (1997). *Consequences of growing up poor*. New York: Russell Sage Foundation Press.

Elder, G.H. (Ed.) (1985). *Life course dynamics: Trajectories and transitions*. Ithaca, NY: Cornell University Press.

Elder, G.H. & Shanahan, M.J. (2007). The life course and human development. In *The handbook of child psychology (6th Ed.)*. New York: Wiley.

Elder, G.H., Jr. & Conger, R.D. (2000). *Children of the land: Adversity and success in rural America*. Chicago: University of Chicago Press.

Ferri, E., Bynner, J., & Wadsworth, M. (2003). *Changing Britain, changing lives: three generations at the turn of the century*. London: Institute of Education.

Ferri, E. & Smith, K. (2003). Partnership and parenthood. In E. Ferri, J. Bynner & M. Wadsworth (Eds), *Changing Britain, changing lives: three generations at the turn of the century* (pp. 105–132). London: Institute of Education.

Furlong, A. & Cartmel, F. (1997). *Young people and social change*. Buckingham: Open University Press.

Giddens, A. (1991). *Modernity and self-identity: self and society in the late modern age*. Cambridge: Polity Press.

Halsey, A.H. (2000). Introduction: Twentieth-century Britain. In A.H. Halsey & J. Webb (Eds), *Twentieth-century British social trends* (pp. 1–23). London: Macmillan Press.

Hobsbawm, E.J. (1995). *Age of extremes: The short twentieth century, 1914–1991*. London: Abacus.

Jones, G. (2002). *The youth divide: diverging paths to adulthood*. York: Joseph Rowntree Foundation.

Lesthaeghe, R. (1995). The second demographic transition in western countries: An interpretation. In K.O. Mason & A.-M. Jenson (Eds), *Gender and family change in industrialised countries* (pp. 17–62). Oxford: Clarenden Press.

Martin, P., Schoon, I., & Ross, A. (2007). Beyond transitions. Applying optimal matching analysis to life course research. *International Journal of Social Research Methodology*, 1–21.

Martin, P., Schoon, I. & Ross, A. (2008). Diverse sequences, ideal types. Applying optimal matching analysis to life course research. *International Journal of Social Research Methodology*, 11, 179–199.

Modell, J. (1989). *Into one's own: From youth to adulthood in the United States, 1920–1975*. Berkeley: University of California Press.

Moen, P. (2001). The gendered life course. In L. George & R.H. Binstock (Eds), *Handbook of aging and the social sciences (5th Ed.)*. (pp. 179–196). San Diego: Academic Press.

Reitzle, M., Vondracek, F.W., & Silbereisen, R.K. (1998). Timing of school-to-work transitions: A developmental-contextual perspective. *International Journal of Behavioral Development*, 22, 7–28.

Ross, A., Schoon, I., Martin, P., & Sacker, A. (2009). Family and nonfamily role configurations in two British cohorts. *Journal of Marriage and the Family*, 71(1), 1–14.

Schoon, I. (2006). *Risk and resilience. Adaptations in changing times*. Cambridge: Cambridge University Press.

Schoon, I. (2007). Adaptations in changing times: Agency in context. *International Journal of Psychology.*

Schoon, I. (2008). A transgenerational model of status attainment: the potential mediating role of school motivation and education. *National Institute Economic Review.*

Schoon, I., Martin, P., & Ross, A. (2007). Career transitions in times of social change. His and her story. *Journal of Vocational Behavior, 70,* 78–96.

Schoon, I. & Parsons, S. (2002). Teenage aspirations for future careers and occupational outcomes. *Journal of Vocational Behavior, 60*(2), 262–288.

Schoon, I. & Silbereisen, R.K. (Eds) (2009). *Transitions from School to Work: Globalisation, Individualisation, and Patterns of Diversity.* New York: Cambridge University Press.

Shanahan, M.J. (2000). Pathways to adulthood in changing societies: Variability and mechanisms in life course perspective. *Annual Review of Sociology, 26,* 667–692.

Shanahan, M.J. & Elder, G.H. (2006). *History, human agency and the life course.* Lincoln, NE: University of Nebraska Press.

Appendix

Parental social status was measured by the Registrar General's measure of parental social class (RGSC), which is defined according to job status and the associated education or prestige (OPCS, 1980). It is assessed by the current or last held job of the father. Where there was no father present, the RGSC of the mother was noted. Here RGSC is coded on a three-point scale: I professional/ managerial; II skilled; III semi/unskilled occupations. Class I represents the highest level of prestige or skill and class III the lowest. *Parental education* indicates whether the mother or the father have left school at minimum school leaving age or later.

Childhood cognitive ability was assessed differently in the two cohorts. In NCDS a general ability test has been completed by cohort members at age 11, comprising the assessment of verbal and non-verbal skills. Scores from this test correlate strongly with scores on an IQ-type test used for secondary school selection ($r = 0.93$), suggesting that the test can serve as a good proxy for IQ scores (Douglas, 1967). In BCS70 cohort members completed a modified version of the British Ability Scales (BAS), which, like the assessment in NCDS, can serve as a measure for childhood IQ (Elliott, Murray, & Pearson, 1978). In BCS70 the assessment involved the administration of four sub-scales: word definitions and word similarities which were used to measure verbal ability, and recall of digits and matrices which were used to measure non-verbal ability. For both cohorts a principal components analysis (PCA) was carried out for each of the verbal and non-verbal subtests in order to establish the presence of a general cognitive ability factor (g). In both cohorts the examination of the scree slope suggested the presence of a single component. The first principal component scores were saved for each subject as an indicator of each person's general

Table A.1 Multinominal regression to predict transition experiences of cohort members (reference category is continuous full-time employment)

	Interrupted career		Long-term unemployed		Return to education		Part-time career		Drop out	
	NCDS	BCS	NCDS	BCS	NCDS	BCS	NCDS	BCS	NCDS	BCS
Socio-Demographics										
Sex (male)	0.39*	0.40*	1.52#	1.80*	0.79	0.79	0.03*	0.07*	0.02*	0.10*
RGSC: skilled	1.62	1.11	2.37*	2.05#	0.71	0.78	1.11	0.88	1.93*	1.47#
semi/unskilled	1.44	1.44	3.94*	4.07*	0.52	0.93	1.33	1.38#	2.75*	2.34*
Father's education	1.39	1.22	1.75#	1.17	1.20	1.47#	1.33#	1.28#	1.64*	1.88*
Mother's education	1.55	1.47	1.94#	1.64#	0.68	1.18	1.14	1.37#	1.63*	1.89*
Controlling for IQ and motivation										
Sex (male)	0.36*	0.40#	1.11	1.73	0.81	0.72	0.02*	0.06*	0.02*	0.06*
RGSC: skilled	1.31	2.16	1.73	1.02	0.67	0.63	1.01	0.86	1.76*	1.11
semi/unskilled	0.95	2.18	2.42*	3.48#	0.57	0.99	1.17	1.35	2.11*	2.08*
Father's education	1.08	0.89	1.48	1.03	1.15	0.91	1.15	1.12	1.29#	1.39
Mother's education	1.21	1.09	1.41	1.23	1.09	0.87	1.09	1.37#	1.38#	1.75*
Cognitive ability	0.55*	0.67#	0.62*	0.48*	1.32	1.07	0.76*	0.76*	0.65*	0.64*
School motivation	0.83	0.81	0.70*	0.60#	1.34	0.84	0.85#	0.85#	0.78*	0.66*

Note: Table A.1. shows the odds ratios for the sociodemographic and individual agency factors in predicting entry into an interrupted career, long-term unemployment, return to education, part-time career, or dropping out of the labor market in comparison to engaging in continuous full-time employment after leaving school (which is the baseline category).
*p<0.001; #p<0.05

Table A.2 Multinominal regression predicting living and family arrangements of cohort members by their early 30's (reference category is being partnered with children)

	Single (no children)		Partnered (no children)		Single with children	
	NCDS	BCS	NCDS	BCS	NCDS	BCS
Socio-Demographics						
Sex (male)	2.13*	2.41*	1.50*	1.34*	0.13*	0.08*
RGSC: skilled	0.75#	0.89	0.86	0.85#	1.28	1.24
semi/unskilled	0.70#	0.71*	0.79#	0.68*	1.53#	1.50#
Father's education	0.76#	0.73*	0.70*	0.67*	1.17	1.28
Mother's education	0.90	0.67*	0.81#	0.70*	1.31	1.11
Controlling for IQ and motivation						
Sex (male)	2.02*	2.53*	1.59*	1.44*	0.12*	0.08*
RGSC: skilled	0.75#	1.06	0.85	0.96	1.23	1.41
semi/unskilled	0.69#	0.75	0.92	0.69#	1.46	1.23
Father's education	0.73#	0.84	0.76#	0.72*	0.96	1.04
Mother's education	0.90	0.78#	0.89	0.89	1.11	1.51
Cognitive ability	0.98	1.09	1.23*	1.27*	0.71*	0.89
School motivation	0.97	1.17*	1.08#	1.20*	0.79*	0.66*

Controlling for IQ, motivation, and transition experiences

Sex (male)	0.85	1.53*	0.77	0.85	0.15*	0.08*
RGSC: skilled	0.72#	1.05	0.94	0.94	1.20	1.45
semi/unskilled	0.72#	0.85	1.06	0.72#	1.27	1.23
Father's education	0.76#	0.87	0.79#	0.72*	1.01	0.97
Mother's education	0.96	0.82	0.96	0.98	1.11	1.31
Cognitive ability	0.91	1.01	1.13#	1.14#	0.77*	0.93
School Motivation	0.96	1.13#	1.04	1.13#	0.78*	0.70*
Out of labor force	0.09*	0.12*	0.03*	0.03*	1.49#	1.90#
Part-time career	0.14*	0.14*	0.16*	0.11*	1.43	1.23
Return to education	0.65	2.31#	1.63	1.01	1.36	–
Long-term unemployment	1.37	1.15	0.77	0.28#	2.28#	4.56#
Interrupted career	0.32*	0.66	0.11*	0.64	0.87	5.89*
Encontinuous ft employment (ref category)						

Note: Table shows the odds ratios for the sociodemographic and individual agency factors, as well as for the transition experiences predicting being single with no children, living as a couple without children, and being a single parent. Living as a couple with children was used as the baseline category.
*$p<0.001$; #$p<0.05$

cognitive ability (g). Statistically, the first principal component is a linear combination of the original test scores, maximizing the total explained variance. By reducing a data set from a group of interrelated variables into a smaller set of factors, PCA achieves parsimony by explaining the maximum amount of variance in a correlation matrix using the smallest number of explanatory concepts. For ease of interpretation, the principal component scores were z-standardized within each cohort.

Academic motivation was assessed in both cohorts at age 16. Cohort members completed a five-item academic motivation scale. Although item wordings were identical in both cohorts (school is largely a waste of time; I do not like school; etc.), response categories were not. Items were measured on a five-point Likert scale in NCDS, and a three-point Likert scale in BCS70. Item analysis of the five-item scale suggests good internal consistency within each cohort, with coefficient alpha = 0.77 in NCDS and 0.76 in BCS70. For the path estimation, the scale score was z-standardized to ensure comparability of coefficients across cohorts. A high score indicates positive school motivation and a low score school disengagement.

12

POLITICAL ELITES AS AN AGENT OF SOCIAL CHANGE: THE POLISH PERSPECTIVE

Jacek Wasilewski

The aim of this chapter is to present a summary view from the elite theory perspective on the transformation of the political and economic system in East-Central Europe, especially in Poland, in order to show political elites as major agents of social change.

What does the *elite theory perspective* mean in the context of transformations of political regimes? The contemporary elitist approach to the subject is precisely defined. John Higley, who is the leading representative of this belief, expresses it best:

> The composition and functioning of political elites is, we contend, the most important determinant of the type of regime that exists in a country. There are, of course, other determinants of regimes, but none is as critical as the configuration of elites. (Dogan & Higley, 1998: 20).

The 'configuration of elites' is described by elite differentiation, which means a degree of social and organizational heterogeneity of elites, as well as by elite unity consisting of two dimensions: the normative dimension and the interactive one.

> The normative dimension is the extent of shared beliefs and values, as well as more specific norms – most of them informal and uncodified – about political access, competition, and restrained partisanship. The interactive dimension is the extent of inclusive channels and networks through which elite persons and groups obtain relatively assured access to key decision-making centers. (Higley & Lengyel, 2000: 2).

A model picture of the opposing types of elites contrasts divided elites with consensual elites. Divided elites are characterized by narrow differentiation. This means that they are relatively homogeneous, and they represent similar environments and organizations. Another feature of divided elites is weak unity. Interactions between competing elites are limited, if any, and common normative base does not exist, as the elites subscribe to distinct values and norms, and they have different views on rules of the political game. As far as consensual elites are concerned, they are characterized by a wide differentiation, which means they represent various social segments, and by strong unity, that is a far-reaching agreement concerning elementary values and rules of political rivalry.

The key statement says that the configuration of elites is the main factor which decides the nature of a political regime. Divided elites, which are typically arranged in two hostile camps clinging to their own values and rules of political rivalry, cannot 'produce' stable democracy. They are typical for various kinds of authoritarianism. On the other hand, the formation of consensual elites is a necessary condition of stable and consolidated democracy. Obviously, consensual elites differ from each other in their ideological, political and economic programs, in their priorities and ways to achieve them, as well as in many other, often essential, issues. Still, they share the main values such as freedom, democracy or human rights, and they share the same set of principles which rule the political game. Generally speaking, it is the set of democratic principles.

The assumption about a determining influence of the configuration of elites on the shape of a political regime is preceded by some more general premises formed by such classics as Gaetano Mosca, Vilfredo Pareto and Robert Michels.

The first premise concerns elite universalism. It states that there are no societies without elites, because the main principles of social organization require leading groups, leaders and organizers; in other words, they require elites. According to elite theorists, a society which is not differentiated in terms of power distribution could not exist.[1]

The second premise speaks about elite autonomy. Elites encounter some limits, they cannot do whatever they want. Nevertheless, the limits of their autonomy are widely defined. If they are staying within these limits, in practice they answer 'before God and history' (Field & Higley, 1980). It also concerns democratic systems. Elitism rejects a naive conviction of Abraham Lincoln about 'government of the people, by the people, for the people.' The people never rule, as elites always wield power. This does not mean that the masses neither take part in the selection of elites via voting procedures, nor influence elites, nor determine – directly or indirectly – an extensive range of elite autonomy. Commonly shared values which are deeply rooted in the masses define borders of elite autonomy. Elites always require the support of non-elites, which means that 'political arguments of elites must generally conform to the orientations and attitudes of the non-elites to whom they are addressed' (Field & Higley, 1980: 19). If, for example, the masses are deeply religious, elites cannot lead openly anti-religious policies, as they would lose their power.

The radical political change in Central and Eastern Europe at the turn of the 80s and the 90s encouraged a discussion on the role of elites and the masses in the transformation of regimes. A definitely predominant view claims that the role of elites in the downfall of communism and its transition to a new political system (either democratic or not, yet different from the previous one), is crucial or at least very important. Obviously, such a view is held by scholars who are identified with the elitist approach. However, researchers who are not associated with elitism (Karl & Schmitter, 1991; Linz & Stepan, 1996; Offe, 1991; Hankiss, 1990) also emphasize the leading role of elites in East-Central European revolutions.

Taking into consideration the fact that during the domination of the Soviet model of post-totalitarianism (Linz & Stepan, 1996: 42–51) in Eastern Europe in the 1980s there were no conditions for independent political activity of the masses, a relatively minor role of the non-elites is understandable.[2] The mass social movement of Solidarity in Poland was an exception.

Diversity of Eastern European transitions

I use the term *transition* in its theoretical meaning given by 'transition school' which was launched by the famous book *Transitions from Authoritarian Rule* (1986) edited by O'Donnell, Schmitter, & Whitehead. *Transition* denotes a period of a political vacuum, which lasts from the downfall of an old regime to the establishment of a new one. Although old rules are still in force, they are no longer valid and obeyed. There are no new rules yet. Transition is the time of struggle for the new rules. It ends at the moment the rules are set and accepted by the main actors. This means that transition is over when the first stage of institution-building is completed. It takes relatively little time, as it usually lasts months, rarely lasts more than 2–3 years. Generally, it is assumed that the acceptance of a law code setting the fundamentals of a new system (constitution) or founding elections mean the end of transition.

The meaning of transformation is not so unambiguous and theoretical. In Poland and in the majority of the former Soviet bloc countries, the term transformation is used to describe a much longer period of time than in the case of transition. It encompasses further stages of new institution-building, improvement of mutual relations between those institutions, development of their efficiency, and introduction of citizens to new operational rules. In the countries which have transformed from authoritarianism (communism) to democracy the imprecise term 'transformation' is closer to a comparatively imprecise term 'consolidation of democracy.' According to Phillippe Schmitter (1992: 424) consolidation of democracy is:

> the process of transforming the accidental arrangements, prudential norms, and contingent solutions that emerged during the transition into relations of cooperation and competition that are reliably known, regularly practiced, and voluntarily accepted by those persons or collectivities that participate in democratic governance.

When is the transformation/consolidation over? It is not easy to answer this question. East European researchers tend to prolong the transformation period *ad infinitum*. Adam Przeworski proposes a sensible, in my opinion, criterion:

> Democracy is consolidated when under given political and economic conditions a particular system of institutions becomes the only game in town, when no one can imagine acting outside the democratic institutions, when all the losers want to do is to try again within the same institutions under which they have just lost. Democracy is consolidated when it becomes self-enforcing, that is, when all the relevant political forces find it best to continue to submit their interests and values to the uncertain interplay of the institutions (1991: 26).

Przeworski's institutional point of view orders one to treat today's East-Central European countries as 'normal' democracies, because there are no serious political forces which would question the rule that 'democracy is the only game in town.' I agree with John Mueller who, in the mid-1990s, postulated to analyse young East-Central European democracies by means of the devices used to analyse other countries with a democratic political system and capitalist economy, instead of treating those young democracies as two-headed freaks:

> The time of fundamental change is substantially over: further developments will take place in environments which are essentially democratic and capitalistic. The societies may become more or less efficient, humane, responsive, productive, corrupt, civil, or effective, but these changes will probably have to come about within (or despite) the present political and economic framework, not through further institutional transformation. In consequence, it might be sensible now to decrease the talk of 'transition' and to put a quiet, dignified end to the new field of transitology (1996: 103).

Obviously, the legacy of communism is a burden to Eastern European democracies, and it has a significant influence on their appearance today. After all, history, especially recent history, somehow shapes the present everywhere. Has the Nazi past not left its stamp on German democracy, the fascist past on Italian democracy, Francism and the Civil War on Spanish democracy? Would British democracy and economy be what they are without the British Empire?

In order to analyse Eastern European processes of transition from communism and transformation to democracy in the context of elite theory, we need to move back to the second half of the twentieth century, especially to the final decade of communism. At that time the way of getting out of communism (in literature depicted as 'mode of transition'), together with the shape of new elites and their role in forming the new order, was defined to a large extent.

The European Soviet bloc countries were considerably differentiated. American Sovietologists did not usually notice this when looking across the Atlantic Ocean directly at the Kremlin. According to the view which they imposed, all satellite states copy the same Soviet model with some minor local modifications. Although such conviction was arguable in Stalin's time, after 1956 it was difficult to defend it any more, and in the last two decades of communism in Eastern Europe it was overtly false. There may have been just one model (until Gorbatchev), but only on paper, because in reality there were profound differences within bloc countries. According to the *path dependency* paradigm the differences explain, to a large extent, for dissimilar modes of transition and the configuration of elites during the transformation period (Ekiert, 1999).

The Western media paid attention to spectacular actions of tiny groups of dissidents, usually intellectuals, who operated during the declining period of communism in most of the bloc countries: in the Soviet Union (e.g. Sacharow), in Czechoslovakia (Havel and *Charter 77*), and occasionally in GDR, Bulgaria or Romania. In practice, this influenced neither the political system, nor the communist elite, nor the non-elites. The masses remained passive and treated dissidents as enemies or madmen deserving of compassion.

The situation in Poland and in Hungary was different. A strong faction of technocrats and modernizers within the party's leadership is a distinctive feature of the Hungarian exit from communism. This was connected with a radical de-ideologization of the Hungarian party: in the 1980s nobody believed in the communist ideals, and even the leaders of the Communist Party did not hide this fact.[3] In 1987 the party modernizers forced Janos Kadar, who had governed for 30 years, to resign. They deepened economic reforms, increasing the role of the market, and liberalizing the political system. It opened a new political opportunity structure. Dissidents' groups re-organized themselves, forming independent associations and proto-parties. Thus the new elite became institutionalized as the political opposition, challenging the old communist elite (Hankiss, 1990; Bruszt, 1991; Szelenyi, Szelenyi, Kovach, 1995). Nevertheless, often the political and ideological distance between the modernized communist elite and the new elite was not substantial.

The endogenic character of *transition* is crucial to understanding the Hungarian road to democracy. The old elites were its main actor. To a large extent, hampered by the communist doctrine yoke, they decided to loosen it. Then the new elites came to the fore and threw off the communist yoke definitively. Throughout the period of liberalization preceding *transition* the masses remained immobilized, except for sporadic rallies and anti-government manifestations in Budapest.

The Hungarian example points to another important factor which needs to be included. It is the change which took place in the final period of communist rule within the inner core of the old elites. In many countries of the region the generation of leaders shaped by struggle for power and Stalinism left the stage, and was replaced by a generation of younger leaders, who were better educated, less orthodox, technocratic and more open to the West. Such changes were most advanced in Hungary, then in Poland. In the Soviet Union they were initiated by Gorbatchev. However, in GDR, Czechoslovakia, Bulgaria and Romania they took place on a small scale, if at all. It is an important explanation of the distinct modes of transition.

The Polish case is even more different. The changes within the communist elite were significant[4] although they did not go as far as in Hungary. Undeniably, Solidarity and unprecedented mobilization of the masses are the crucial difference compared to other countries. Apparently, Solidarity, whose legal activity lasted merely 16 months, was the only legal, secular[5] organization which was not subordinate to the party-state control during the European history of communism. This went against the iron law of communism. That is why the martial law was imposed and, for a short time, as it soon turned out, the party-state restored its monopoly over the public life of the country.

Thanks to the Solidarity mass movement,[6] it was only in Poland that a counter-elite to the ruling communist elite was formed and became institutionalized. The counter-elite covered the entire country, from Gdańsk, its cradle, to small towns and villages, as branches of Solidarity were everywhere. The counter-elite was institutionalized in the form of a universal social movement which was not united around a particular political program, but around universal values such as truth, freedom, dignity, Europe, and faith. Solidarity, thereby the solidarity counter-elite, were considerably weakened by the martial law, and were driven underground. It lost its mass character, but still survived. It maintained its ability to act, and in 1988 came to the surface once again.

We may talk about the beginning of transition from communism in Poland and Hungary in 1988, but hardly anything changed in other East-Central European countries at that time. The general profile of the region at the beginning of transition is presented in Table 12.1.

Table 12.1 Profile of the region

	Old elite	New elite	The masses / civil society
Poland	Tries to escape from defeat. Is divided into conservatives (hard-liners) who seek help in tough policy towards Solidarity, and liberals (soft-liners) who seek help in negotiating with Solidarity its support for limited economic and political reforms.	Institutionalized in the universal social movement which encompasses the whole country. The social base of the new elite is heterogeneous. It includes intellectuals from democratic opposition and Solidarity activists from all social groups. Strongly represented are leaders with industrial workers' background.	The masses are scarcely mobilized. They are rather observers than participants. Short-lived strike mobilization in some industrial centers. Civil society organizations begin to reactivate their activity from 1980–81 under the auspices of Solidarity.
Hungary	Dominated by technocrats aiming at further liberalization, or even democratization of the system. Reforming the country they try to stay in power. De facto, at the end of 1988 the old elite agreed to political pluralism, competitive politics, and market economy.	Institutionalized in the form of pluralistic political organizations (proto-parties, clubs and associations) operating in Budapest. The social base of the new elite includes intellectuals, professionals, students and former dissidents.	The masses are scarcely mobilized. They are rather observers than participants. Quick development of the civil society organizations which transform into political society organizations (they politicize their programs and place themselves in pluralistic public space).
Other countries of the region	Relative monolith hostile towards modernization and devoted to communist orthodoxy. First weak signs of the inner-party opposition appear in 1989, after June elections in Poland.	Does not exist or is limited to narrow groups of dissidents. Lack of institutionalization.	Demobilized masses. Civil society does not exist or is limited to narrow groups gathered around dissidents.

Significant differences in the configuration of elites, numbers and institutionalization of the rising new elites, as well as in the attitudes of the masses towards the weakening regime, must have been reflected in the way of exiting from communism. To a large degree, these differences determined the composition and configuration of political elites of the post-communist period.

Elite settlement

A crucial phase of the Polish *transition* began in autumn 1988, when moderate reformers within the old regime, gathered around General Jaruzelski, decided to initiate talks with leaders of the democratic opposition, headed by Lech Walesa. It was the beginning of the idea of the Round Table, which met during the first months of 1989 (February–April).

Entering into negotiations with the political opponent was not easy for either side. Firstly, it was necessary to convince the radicals in their own ranks that sitting at the Table could be beneficial. Both Jaruzelski and Walesa had big problems with this. Radicals of both sides (hard-liners in the party and anti-communist extremists in Solidarity) were considerable forces. The masses were also rather reluctant to the idea: the party masses on the one hand (the party still numbered over 2 million), the social masses on the other.

To a large extent, the Polish situation met the conditions described in the classic work of Burton and Higley (1987) on elite settlement as a way of changing the political regime. Neither side was strong enough to eliminate the rival, nor was the prolonged political deadlock worked to the advantage of any of them. Both sides had strong leaders of great esteem (Walesa and Jaruzelski) who were able to impose on their camps rather unpopular conciliatory solutions, and later they could force obedience to the arrangements.

In the light of elitist theorists, the key feature of transition from authoritarianism to democracy through elite settlement is a higher probability than in the case of other modes of transition of a successful consolidation of a new democratic regime. To a large extent, the inclusive character of transition (all significant political actors, including representatives of old elites, are actively engaged in the transformation) guarantees a successful installation of a new system, because there are no influential political forces which would sabotage the changes. Everybody is interested in the success of regime change.

Apart from 'elite settlement,' such mode of transition from communism and entering the initial phase of democracy-building is also called 'negotiated transition,' 'pacted transition,' 'negotiated revolution' (see Bruszt, 1991;

Karl & Schmitter, 1991; Linz & Stepan, 1996). Radical opponents of this way of exiting from communism still talk about 'elite conspiracy' and 'elite betrayal.'

We will not focus on the well-known political consequences of the Round Table and negotiating transformation to democracy. We will look at the elites and their creative role.

The heterogeneous character of the Solidarity movement is a basic issue necessary to understand the configuration of Polish political elites throughout the whole period since 1989. Solidarity was launched as a trade union which, apart from typical employees' requests, defended fundamental values shared by the whole population. Yet, it soon became normatively and socially diversified. It was unavoidable, because the movement included people coming from all social groups and mirrored a complex composition of Polish society.

During its legal activity between autumn of 1980 and December of 1981 Solidarity attracted various groups, social organizations, and local/regional initiatives, which thus gained a powerful patron and defender. By joining the Solidarity movement, these groups, organizations, and initiatives got the chance to operate officially and to be heard. Everybody hid under the Solidarity wing, from political radicals and daydreamers, through religious and ideological fundamentalists, various cultural, ethnic, trade and economic associations, to newly launched social movements and émigré organizations.[7] Solidarity was unable to control effectively its inner hyper-variety. It weakened the movement, caused inner conflicts and created new confrontational grounds with the communist regime. It gave the authorities reasons to accuse the movement of extremism, lack of responsibility, stimulating political and economic disturbances.

Another important reason for the strong inner diversification of the movement were new, mainly economic, interests. It soon turned out that universal values welded Solidarity as long as the movement represented the whole of society *vis-à-vis* the unaccepted power holders. Conflicting group interests began to dominate when it became more and more obvious that the new order would be pluralistic and capitalist. Members of the movement realized that sharing of universal values (such as truth, dignity, solidarity, etc.) did not have to mean common economic interests.

At this stage, an important difference between the Polish and Hungarian pacted transition is clearly visible. In Hungary, group interests were defined and institutionalized in a political dimension (in the form of proto-parties and political clubs) *before transition*. In Poland it occurred *during transition*, mainly in 1990, when the outwardly homogeneous Solidarity movement, being under pressure of conflicting interests, disintegrated itself and split into factions which then unwillingly began to institutionalize into political parties. Disorder on the Solidarity side facilitated the communist elite (now social-democratic), which was recovering from defeat and reintegrating itself, to regain its poise.

The Polish party system was created with a considerable delay in comparison to Hungary. Besides, group and personal animosities were a more important criterion of party formation than differing political programs and policy preferences.

Transformation of the regime through elite settlement means that elites have obtained considerable autonomy and relative independence from their non-elite supporters. Elites got *carte blanche* to negotiate/design a new political system. Neither party masses nor Solidarity masses controlled their representatives who negotiated at the Round Table.[8] We may say that whatever had been arranged at the Round Table, it would have been put into practice. It is the peak moment of elite creationism: in effect, they created the foundation of a new political system on their own, and those fundaments have survived with some later modifications until now. Elites turned out to be the main agent of change in the majority of the former Soviet bloc countries.

Three tasks of elites

During the long-lasting and arduous transformation process of the political regime from communism to democracy, elites and societies of East-Central Europe had to confront three phases and three huge tasks.

The first phase and the first task were to form a general vision of the change and to define one's own collective identity. Following Claus Offe (1991: 869), both elites and masses had to answer the question 'who are *we*?' The task was performed by the *breakthrough* or *transition* elite. That was the elite of spiritual leaders, visionaries and missionaries who outlined a picture of a better future and mobilized the masses around it. In Poland these were such figures as Lech Walesa, Tadeusz Mazowiecki, and Jacek Kuron. In other countries these were Borys Jelcyn, Vaclav Havel, Vladimir Meciar, Vitautas Landsbergis.

The transition elite appeals to emotions: to patriotism, honor, dignity and social justice. It uses cultural, national or religious symbols, thus it appeals to *symbolic politics*. Its legitimacy does not depend on policy making. Rather, it is based on readiness for changes and on identification with changes, on restoration of the values which have been devaluated and eliminated by the communist system, yet which are strongly rooted in the collective identity and considered correct and desirable. In other words, breakthrough elite legitimization has predominantly a moral character.

The breakthrough elite answers the question 'who are *we*?' The question was not critically important in Poland and Hungary, because the Poles and

Hungarians have a strong feeling of their own national collective identity, and they do not have to be told who they are. However, in some other countries, e.g. Yugoslavia, Czechoslovakia, the disintegrating Soviet Union, these were the matters of the utmost importance. The breakthrough elites in those countries provided a solution to the problem. 'We are Serbs, heirs of the Great Serbia and it is our duty to bring its glory back,' said Slobodan Milosevic. Vaclav Klaus declared that Czechs would be doing better without civilizationally backward Slovaks. In the republics of the Soviet Unions local elites defined their new collective identity in terms of nationalism. Although nationalism turned out to be a very strong factor, it did not appear from nowhere. It was the transition elites who reactivated it and made it a key element in the process of changes. Obviously, in all of these cases, the masses had to be ready somehow to accept the projects of elites. Yet, elites had the decisive voice. We can easily imagine the Czechs and Slovaks not carrying out the velvet divorce. In Yugoslavia Tito's integrating ideology was widespread enough for the masses, should they be appropriately motivated and mobilized by the elites, to opt for keeping the Yugoslavian federation, perhaps in a different shape. I could quote many more similar scenarios.

The breakthrough elite pictures best a general feature of political elites: their autonomy. The choices made by breakthrough elites in the initial phase of transition set in motion an irreversible sequence of events whose effects we may observe even today. For example, in 1990 Walesa made a decision on a popular election of President, and that introduced to Polish political system elements of a semi-presidential system, which have lasted until now, in spite of the 1997 changes of the Constitution, weakening presidential power.

Karl and Schmitter (1991) rightly note that during the transition period 'normal' limits of elite power, which lie in the social and economic structure and in political institutions, are suspended. Elites have freedom to choose basic institutions of a new order, because to a large extent they are freed from class, political or cultural restrictions. They are the real architects of a new political system.

The second phase and second task is an implementation of the general visions and development of the institutions outlined by the breakthrough elites in the first phase. *Politics of reform* replace symbolic politics. *Institution-builders* elite replace the breakthrough elite. The fundaments of a new political system having already been prepared, now it is time to build new storeys and to make practical choices based on specialist knowledge. The inspiring vision has to be translated into routine operating procedures. Visionaries and missionaries have fulfilled their tasks, now it is time for technologists and craftsmen. The consolidation of the new order and arduous effort began so that the new machines, the democratic machine and market machine, could work efficiently and reliably. The main figures of the second phase were Leszek Balcerowicz in Poland and Vaclav Klaus in Czechoslovakia.

The elite of technologists and craftsmen of democracy and market put new rules into practice and work in a more difficult environment than the breakthrough elite. The autonomy of their undertakings is smaller. New interests are being revealed and the suspension of structural and institutional limits, which was described by Karl and Schmitter, is almost over. The common interests of elites and the masses in the first phase were based on the unification of the society *against* something (generally: against the communist power), not *for* something. Nowadays, detailed repair programs and institutional solutions are being introduced. For some people they are advantageous, for others they are not. There are conflicts of interests, which translates into political conflicts. The time of an exceptional unity of society is over. Organizations which represent distinct collective interests, especially economic interests connected with privatization and capitalist class formation, enter the arena. In Poland it additionally gains a moral dimension. Social forces being the basis of Solidarity and the driving force behind the changes, that is industrial working class, became losers of the transition. It caused a widespread feeling of injustice: we, who participated actively in the downfall of communism, who risked and made sacrifices, we now observe our plants being closed, our welfare benefits being limited, and we witness poverty and unemployment instead of reward.

The elite of institution-builders is under constant pressure from interest groups and vigorously protesting masses, and at the same time must continue reforms. The moral legitimacy of the breakthrough elite does not matter any more. Legitimization of the institution-builders is based upon the same factors which counted in the old system, like economic efficiency and guarantee of **welfare benefits**.

The third phase is the consolidation of a new political system (democracy) and economic system (capitalism). The task of *consolidation* elites is to improve the already existing democratic and market mechanisms and to cause democratic rules and procedures to become habitual ways of solving political conflicts. Politics of reforms is unimportant, because the reforming phase is practically finished. *Distributing politics* comes to the fore. The legitimization of the consolidation elite depends on successful stimulation of economic growth (elites are to be growth-inducers), on pragmatism, on stability and predictability of its politics. In Poland Aleksander Kwasniewski was considered a typical representative of consolidation elites.

The consolidation elite is no longer deeply engaged in conflicts from the final period of communism and transition era. It is more pragmatic, less ideological, and less focused on the moral and symbolic aspects of politics.

At this phase younger politicians, who in the 1980s were too young to play important roles in public life, are entering the political arena. They do not treat politics as a mission, moral crusade, or patriotic obligation. They treat it as a career path which will allow them to achieve a high status.

The autonomy of consolidation elite is being constantly narrowed. Group interests are well crystallized and institutionalized within the political system through competing parties. This means that 'normal' limits of the elite autonomy, which were suspended in the first and to some extent in the second phases, are now working in full.

Old and new elites

'Circulation or reproduction?' was the question that fascinated elite researchers at the beginning of transformation. Was the old (communist) elite reproduced in a new political and economic configuration? Or maybe, as Vilfredo Pareto maintained, a circulation of elites took place, which means that the old elite lost its power and was replaced by the new one. The issue was often considered in terms of conversion of the old political capital into new economic capital (Hankiss, 1990; Staniszkis, 1991; Eyal, Szelenyi, Townsley, 1998). According to this hypothesis the communist nomenclature converted its political assets from the old regime into economic assets in the new regime. Put simply, thanks to its privileged political position in communism it gained a privileged economic position in capitalism.

An important question concerning the status of the old elite in the new system still gives rise to many controversies. That is why it is worth devoting some time to explain this complicated issue.

Undoubtedly, a radical circulation of elites did not occur in any of the former socialist bloc countries (*Theory and Society*, 1995; Wasilewski, 1998). To some extent, by means of two distinct mechanisms, old elites kept their high positions everywhere.

In the countries where transition took place through elite settlement (Poland and Hungary) the reform-minded part of the communist elite were (together with the oppositional elite) the leading actors of regime change. They were signatories of the pact which guaranteed them participation in public life under the same conditions as others (Hungary) or even under privileged conditions (Poland in 1989). The presence of the representatives of the old regime in the new elite results from the logic of transition through settlement. The old elites could miss the chance which resulted from negotiations (for example they could lose founding elections entirely and vanish from political arena); however, as we know, this did not happen in any of the countries.

In other countries transition through settlement did not take place, because there were hardly any oppositional elites: communist elites had no partner to negotiate with. Apart from Czechoslovakia, the nomenclature, divided into factions from liberal factions to orthodox ones, was the only real political force. Therefore, the central part of the new elite had to be made up of reform-minded communist activists together with a few oppositionists and emigrants from the West. That happened in Bulgaria, Romania, as well as in Russia and Ukraine. In the former Yugoslavia communists-nationalists played the central role.

The question about how many former communist leaders succeeded to survive in elite positions after regime change, carried with it a quietly accepted assumption: the more representatives of the *ancient regime* keep their political, administrative and business positions, so much the worse for democracy and the market economy. It was feared that former communists who then declared themselves as social democrats would sabotage democratic and market changes and aim at restitution of the former political system. Taking into consideration the fact that East-Central European societies had an almost half-century-long experience of the communist system, the fear of re-communization, which was widely spread across the region in the early 1990s, is entirely understandable.

The fear turned out to be in vain. Post-communists adjusted to capitalist and democratic rules successfully and very quickly.[9] They did not sabotage democracy and capitalism. On the contrary, they used the new possibilities as much as they could. Apparently, they were possibly the prime winners of transformation (Wasilewski, 2004).

How can we explain the seemingly surprising transformation of old elites? The answer lies in the mentioned changes which took place within the ruling elites during the final period of communism (Wasilewski, Wnuk-Lipiński, 1995). At that time, young, educated activists fascinated with the West began to wield power. They mouthed communist platitudes at party meetings, but deep down they were tired of the communist backwardness from which they tried to free themselves. Apparently, they were the winners of transition. At the Round Table they successfully negotiated security for the former personnel. Besides, starting talks with the opposition they got rid of hard-liners from their ranks, mainly those advanced in years, who withdrew from active public life, as they did not agree on any pacts with enemies of socialism.[10]

The hypothesis on conversion of the old political capital into new economic capital described accurately the processes which took place at the end of the 1980s and the first half of the 1990s. It needs to be added that first of all such conversion was done by party economic staff, mainly higher managers in socialist economy. The proportion of the former party-administrative apparatus in capitalist business was lower

(Wasilewski, 1998). Having a high post in the party was not enough to successfully convert the old political capital into new economic capital. One needed to be strategically located in the network of social relations and to have know-how. The high-ranked managerial staff of socialist economy met the requirements best. They had political support (otherwise, they could not have taken up high posts in economy), they were experienced in managing economic processes and human resources; finally they had numerous connections within the financial sector and easy access to foreign partners. They carried these key resources over to the new system, which allowed them to retain high social positions in democratic and capitalist environment.

Disruption of elite continuity

In Poland governing elites have changed many times since 1989, but the developmental logic presented above was preserved till 2005. More or less successfully, the elites fulfilled three tasks connected with transition: institution-building and consolidation of democracy and the market economy. Elite continuity was disrupted in 2005 when the Kaczynski brothers took office. How can this be explained?

There is a political force active in Polish public life from the beginning of transition which considered the negotiated transformation to democracy to be a huge mistake and a source of all failures. They treat the political stage and even the whole public arena as a simple dichotomy: 'us' versus 'them.' Thus they recreate the division from the martial law period when 'us' meant the majority of society and 'them' meant the communist power holders. Although the Kaczynski brothers themselves took part in the Round Table talks, they adopted this kind of view at the beginning of the 1990s and after several years, in 2005, they managed to take office. It shows the significance of elites as an agent of social changes.

At the end of the 1980s in East-Central Europe and at the beginning of the 1990s in Eastern Europe (Soviet republics) elites defined the collective identity ('who are *we?*') and that was the key feature of transition (or breakthrough) elite. The Kaczynski brothers and their supporters tried to do exactly the same at the beginning of the twenty-first century. To some extent, ignoring everything that had happened in Poland for several years, they moved political discourse and political actions back to the transition stadium. However, their definition of 'us' differs from the one which appeared at the turn of the 1980s and 1990s. Now 'us' stands for real Polish patriots, honest Catholics who care about their families, sovereignty and national tradition. 'Them' are not only communists, post-communists, and hostile intelligence agencies and/or secret services, but also liberals of all splinter groups, cosmopolitans and decadents who mindlessly imitate the West together with all its deviations. 'Them' means even affluent people, because they surely did not gain their high material standard honestly. The whole political, economic, and social system formed after 1989 is captured by forces which are hostile to the Polish nation. That is why it should be annihilated so that a new political system, the Fourth Republic, could be built in its place.

The Kaczynski brothers made an attempt to extract and recreate social divisions which seemed to have been overcome long time ago. Why was the attempt successful, to some degree at least?

The example of the Kaczynski brothers shows the considerable significance of elites in the process of initiation and implementation of social changes. Simultaneously, it shows the limits of their autonomy. Among the Polish masses there has always been some mental potential which could be easily mobilized by the Kaczynski brothers. The post-communists who governed between 2001 and 2005 enabled the Kaczynski brothers to successfully point to an oversimplified contrast between bad communists and their henchmen with good, honest (i.e. poor) patriots. The media uncovered a wave of corruptive and criminal acts involving the power holders of all tiers. It created a critical social atmosphere towards post-communist establishment and propelled many voters to the Kaczynski brothers. It would not have happened if the elite had not defined and given the conflict a name (in other words had not defined political discourse) and had not skilfully mobilized the disappointed masses. This is a classic mechanism of elites operation.

Notes

1. Higley and Burton (2006: 6–7) express it as follows: ... the preference is for a minimalist definition that equates elite status with the holding of strategic positions in large organizations and powerful sociopolitical movements. [...] ... elites are seen as arising from the functional imperatives of such organizations and movements. [...] To survive and prosper they [organizations and movements] need hierarchical system of communications, though decisions flow from those who make them to those who implement them. And they require hierarchical systems of rewards and punishments to ensure that decisions are obeyed. If we call the persons who command these hierarchical systems elites, we can say that organizations and movements beyond some minimum size and complexity necessarily create elites.
2. It needs to be emphasized that the thesis on 'leading,' 'determining' or 'key' role of the elites in the Eastern European transitions does not mean that the elites overthrew communism on their own, with a passive attitude of the masses. As far as I know, even the most radical supporters of elite paradigm do not defend such a statement. The thesis maintains that elites were the initiator and the main

actor in the spectacle, yet even the most outstanding actor is unable to carry through the whole process by himself. Elitists agree that elites would not have achieved so much without the support of the masses.

3   For example, Imre Pozsgay, a member of the Politburo of the Hungarian Communist Party, at the conference held in Germany in May 1989, said: In the socialist countries of East-Central Europe there are two conflicting and controversial approaches to the problem of reform, the problem of dealing with this crisis. One view [...] says that this state-socialist or Stalinist model can be adapted to the times, corrected and improved by a series of small rationalisation measures. The other view maintains that the system cannot be rationalised. The Stalinist model is not reformable; what is needed is to get rid of it. Only by abolishing this model and by creating a new democratic socialist model will it be possible to solve this problem. Hungarian efforts are going in this second direction but not, of course, without conflict and not without inner contradictions. Continuing, he said that Hungary is in the process of beginning to construct a market economy, and that without democracy there can be no *socialism*. See: Weilmann, Brunner, Tokes 1991: 191–202.

4   They took place in three stages. The first stage was in the 1970s, when Gierek got rid of Gomulka's orthodox staff and replaced them with younger technocrats. The second stage took place between 1980 and 1981 when, influenced by Solidarity liberalization, supporters of democratization of communism took many leading posts in the party (most of them were fired after imposition of martial law). The third stage took place in 1985–88, when the party tried to regain the initiative by co-opting into the elite virtually everyone who enjoyed any public recognition, provided that candidates declared loyalty towards the communist constitution.

5   The Catholic Church in Poland has never been fully controlled by the communist party. Obviously, it was influenced by the party-state in many ways (e.g. through secret police informers within clergy) and dependent on government's decisions, but in contrast to churches in other communist countries it preserved its autonomy.

6   In the peak period it numbered more than nine million members.

7   This is why Solidarity movement, and similar movements in other countries, as Civic Forum or Society Against Violence, are called 'umbrella organizations.'

8   The situation in Hungary was different, because final talks were preceded by 'the oppositional round table,' during which various oppositional organizations agreed that free elections are an indisputable condition necessary for any agreement with the government.

9   Victories of post-communist parties in parliamentary elections in Lithuania in 1992, in Poland in 1993 and in Hungary in 1994 show this clearly.

10 For example, 27 per cent out of over 800 communist officials interviewed in 1993 in Hungary, and 25 per cent out of almost 900 interviewed the same year in Poland, were retired (Wasilewski, 1998).

References

Bruszt, Laszlo (1991). The negotiated revolution of Hungary. W. Gyorgy Szoboszlai (Ed.), *Democracy and political transformation*. Budapest: Hungarian Political Science Association, pp. 213–225.

Burton, Michael G. & Higley, John (1987). Elite settlements. *American Sociological Review*, 52, 295–307.

Dogan, M. & Higley, J. (1998). *Elites, crises, and the origins of the regimes*. Lanham: Rowman and Littlefield.

Ekiert, G. (1999). Patterns of postcommunist transitions in Eastern Europe. In J. Miklaszewska (Ed.), *Democracy in Central Europe 1989-1999*. Krakow: Meritum, pp. 13–40.

Eyal, G., Szeleyi, I., & Townslay, E. (1998). *Making capitalism without capitalists. The new ruling elites in Eastern Europe*. London: Verso.

Field, L.G. & Higley, J. (1980). *Elitism*. London: Routledge & Kegan Paul.

Hankiss, E. (1990). *East European alternatives*. Oxford: Clarendon Press.

Higley, J. & Lengyel, G. (2000). (Eds), *Elites after state socialism. Theories and analysis*. Boulder, CO., Rowman & Littlefield.

Higley, J. & Burton, M. (2006). *Elite foundations of liberal democracy*. Boulder, CO., Rowman & Littlefield.

Karl, T.L. & Schmitter, P.C. (1991). Modes of transition in Latin America, Southern and Eastern Europe. *International Social Science Journal*, 128, 269–284.

Linz, J.J. & Stepan, A. (1996). *Problems of democratic transition and consolidation*. Baltimore, Johns Hopkins University Press.

Mueller, J. (1996). Democracy, capitalism, and the end of transition. In M. Mandelbaum (Ed.), *Postcommunism: Four perspectives*. New York: A Council of Foreign Relations Book, pp. 102–167.

O'Donnell, G., Schmitter, P.C. & Whitehead, L. (Eds), (1986). *Transitions from authoritarian rule: Tentative conclusions about uncertain democracies*. Baltimore: Johns Hopkins University Press.

Offe, C. (1991). Capitalism by democratic design? Democratic theory facing the triple transition in East Central Europe. *Social Research*, 58(4).

Przeworski, A. (1991). *Democracy and the market*. Cambridge: Cambridge University Press.

Schmitter, P. (1992). The consolidation of democracy and representation of social groups. *American Behavioral Scientist*, 35, 422–449.

Staniszkis, J. (1991). *The dynamics of the breakthrough in Eastern Europe*. Berkeley: University of California Press.

Szelenyi, S., Szelenyi, I., & Kovach, I. (1995). The making of the Hungarian postcommunist elite: Circulation in politics, reproduction in economy. *Theory and Society*, 24(5), 697–722.

Theory and Society (1995) 24(5). Special issue on circulation vs reproduction of elites during the postcommunist transformation of Eastern Europe. I. Szelenyi, D. Treiman, & E. Wnuk-Lipinski (Eds).

Wasilewski, J. (1998). Hungary, Poland, and Russia: The fate of nomenklatura elites. In M. Dogan, & J. Higley (Eds), *Elites, crises, and the origins of regimes*. Boulder, CO: Rowman & Littlefield, pp. 147–168.

Wasilewski, J. (2004). Die ehemaligen kommunistischen Eliten in demokratischen Polen: Sind sie noch interessant?, w: *Alte Eliten in jungen Demokratien*? Bohlau Verlag, Koln Weimar Wien, pp. 177–193.

Wasilewski, J. & Wnuk-Lipiński, E. (1995). Poland: Winding road from the communist to the post-Solidarity elites. *Theory and Society*, 24(5), 669–696.

Weilmann, P.R., Brunner, G., & Tokes, R.L. (Eds) (1991). *Upheaval against the plan. Eastern Europe on the eve of the storm*. Oxford: Berg.

INDEX

Adolescence, adolescents, 8, 10, 15, 62, 110, 132, 135, 136, 144, 151, 209, 215, 216, 221, 222, 227, 228, 230, 231, 240–242
Agency, 16, 21, 50, 51, 53, 55, 73–76, 78, 79, 92, 149, 153, 157, 169, 170, 172, 178, 187, 246
Aspirations, 2, 3, 16, 17, 34, 63, 73, 136, 157–160, 170–173, 176, 178, 186, 187, 249
Attitudes, 11, 19, 20, 34, 41, 53, 82–84, 86–92, 96, 210, 211, 213, 214, 218, 219, 221, 227–234, 237–242, 272, 278

British Birth Cohort Studies, 20, 249

Capitalism, 3, 4, 20, 40, 190, 191, 195–197, 199, 202, 203, 282–284
Career, 7, 14, 16, 21, 103, 104, 111–118, 127, 130, 131, 134–138, 141, 148–158, 160, 248, 250, 251, 253, 254, 256–259, 261–263, 267, 269
  development, 103, 127, 131
Challenge/Response, 11, 13, 18, 32, 38, 46
  model of, 5, 31, 32–37, 169–174
Change
  cultural, 50, 53, 54, 74, 82–85, 89, 92–95, 102, 209, 218, 222
  economic, 9, 14, 20, 24, 103, 104, 126, 210
  social, *see* Social Change
  political, 6, 11, 21, 129, 209, 229, 230, 273
Childrearing,
  beliefs, 210, 212, 219
  practices, 212–214, 218, 219, 221
China, 2–4, 9, 17–20, 24, 37, 190, 191, 201–207, 210–222, 232

changing society, 210, 212, 221
  urban-rural differences, 218–221
Civic engagement, 47, 128, 129, 138, 139, 145
Cognitive ability, 245, 249, 251, 252, 254, 258, 259, 261, 262, 266–270
Cohort comparisons, 20, 21, 75, 110, 125, 159, 214, 215, 217, 240, 241, 245, 248–251, 253, 254, 256–264, 266, 270
Conflicts, 32, 34, 44, 45, 60, 64, 211, 279, 282
Confucianism, 211, 231
Control Striving, primary and secondary, 16, 149, 150–151, 159
Coping, 6–9, 12, 14, 24, 43, 47, 51, 57, 59, 125–129, 134, 140, 141, 144, 167, 170, 171, 174, 186, 188
  institutional, 18, 167, 168
Cross-cultural/Cross-national,
  differences 204, 205, 213–214, 215, 217
  research, 190, 193

Democracy, transition to, 273, 275, 276, 278, 279, 282–286
Demographic,
  change, 82, 168, 169, 171, 173–176, 178–182, 184, 186, 188, 245, 248
  characteristics, 228, 229, 232
Destandardization, 245, 248, 250, 254, 262–264
Developmental,
  assets, 64–65
  regulation, 15, 16, 23, 149, 150, 156
  tasks, 14, 127, 131, 138, 150, 230, 241

Eastern Europe, 2, 17, 21, 31, 108, 111, 201, 209, 273–275, 285, 286

Economic growth, 20, 22, 232, 249, 282
Educational
  expectations, 160
  transition, 246, 250, 251, 257, 258, 262, 263
Elder, Glen, 1, 4, 5, 8, 17, 24, 51, 73–75, 92, 126, 170, 171, 174, 209, 247, 248
Elite,
  autonomy, 272, 280–283, 286
  settlement, 22, 278, 280, 283
  theory, 271, 275
Employment/Unemployment, 1, 2, 11, 14, 15, 20, 21, 39–42, 47, 78, 80, 81, 84, 86, 87, 103–118, 126, 127, 132–136, 138, 140–143, 153, 155–158, 160, 174, 175, 181, 182, 185–187, 197, 198, 210, 246, 247, 249–251, 253, 254, 256–259, 261–263, 267, 269; *see also* Work
  part time, 86, 108, 110, 114, 127, 130, 131, 153, 181, 182, 256, 258, 261, 262, 263, 267, 269
  precarious, 11, 14, 40, 110, 114, 155
Ethnic minorities, 229, 233

Family, 1, 8, 10, 12–15, 19–21, 23, 36, 53, 60, 77, 79–85, 91, 93, 105, 107, 108, 109, 111, 113–115, 119, 126, 127, 129–141, 143, 144, 149, 150, 153–156, 209–213, 219, 221, 222, 228, 232, 237, 240, 241, 245–247, 251, 253, 257–261, 263, 268
  change, 212, 228, 232, 240, 241
  formation, 8, 12, 14, 104, 111, 112, 127, 246, 247, 249–251, 254, 259, 262, 263
  social status, 247, 250, 251, 252, 266
Flexible goal adjustment, 51, 54, 55, 57, 59, 60

Gender, 7, 21, 81, 107, 111, 130, 133, 192, 198, 202, 203, 231, 241, 242, 245–248, 250, 251, 258, 261, 262
  role identity, 230, 242
Geographic locale, 228, 232, 236
Germany, 2–6, 8, 9, 15–17, 24, 25, 37, 42, 43, 47, 101, 105–107, 109, 110, 126, 130, 132, 133, 139, 144, 154, 155, 157, 158, 160, 167, 168, 172–179, 182, 185, 188, 210, 287
  East/GDR, 3, 14, 17, 23, 32, 36–41, 129, 168–170, 172–179, 181, 184–187, 275, 276
  reunification, 24, 32; *see also* Germany, unification
  unification, 5, 11, 125, 129, 134; *see also* Germany, reunification
GLOBALIFE, 4, 13, 101, 102, 104, 108–110, 112–119, 152–155
Globalization, 1–4, 6–9, 12–16, 22–24, 50, 101–108, 110–119, 125–127, 129, 132, 148–150, 152, 153, 155–158, 160, 231, 232

Habitus, 33, 34, 36, 37, 41, 76, 157
HIV, 231, 241

Ideational dimensions, 228
Identity formation, 230, 242
Individual,
  adaptation, 2–7, 9, 12, 23, 25
  agency, 10, 21, 55, 148–150, 154–156, 160, 245–251, 258–260, 267, 269
Individualization, 21, 112, 118, 127, 129, 148, 210, 245, 248, 258, 259, 262–264

Japan, 190, 192–195, 202, 207

Labor market, 5, 21, 39–41, 47, 75, 102, 104–108, 110–118, 125, 133, 134, 138, 141, 151, 153, 155, 156, 158, 173, 182, 183, 185–187, 246, 247, 249, 251, 256, 257, 259, 260, 262, 263, 267
Life Course, 5, 10, 13, 14, 21, 50–55, 63, 64, 73–89, 91–95, 101, 102, 104, 105, 107, 108, 111, 113, 116, 118, 119, 126, 127, 148–154, 157, 158, 160, 169, 245–248, 250, 262, 263
Life management, 12, 50–55, 59, 62–66
Lifespan,
  development, 148–152, 158
  theory of control, 136, 148, 149
Longitudinal research, 104, 119
Low fertility, 168, 176

Market reforms, 230
Media, Mass, 228, 241
Media, New, 230
Micro-macro linkage, 101
Modelling of social ruptures, 32
Modernity, 10, 50, 53, 148, 167
Motivation, 16, 21, 51, 53, 57, 64, 137, 148, 149, 151, 152, 156–158, 185, 245, 247–252, 254, 258, 259, 261–263, 266–270
Municipalities, 3, 9, 10, 17, 169, 174–178, 180, 182, 184, 185, 187, 188

Planful competence, 51, 62, 110
Poland, 3, 4, 9, 17, 18, 105, 108, 109, 154, 168–170, 172–176, 178–182, 184–188, 190–198, 201–207, 271, 273, 275–277, 279, 280, 282, 283, 285, 287
  new elites, 275, 276, 278,
  old elites, 276, 278, 283, 284,
Political,
  transformation, 2–4, 7, 8, 10, 15–18, 20, 22
  transition, 1, 3, 8, 12, 16, 17, 20
Psychosocial outcomes, 5, 7, 8, 10, 24, 129, 138
Public,
  opinion, 95, 228
  sector, 107, 108, 181, 182, 184–187

Recession, 20, 126, 249
Regional moderation, 140–143
Relationships, same-sex, 74, 82–84, 86–90; *see also* Sexuality
Renovation policies, 229, 230, 240
Rural, 9, 19, 20, 209, 211, 212, 218–221, 228–230, 232, 233, 239, 241, 242

School leaving, 21, 247, 249–251, 258–260, 266
Scripts, 12, 80, 230, 246
Self-continuity, 52
Sequence analysis, 254, 256
Sexual,
  behavior, premarital, 227–242
  knowledge, 230
  socialization, 230

Sexuality, 20, 82, 85, 230
  Homo-, 13, 82–84, 89
  Hetero-, 82, 86
Social,
  change, 1, 2, 4–7, 9–13, 15–17, 19–25, 31–35, 40, 43–47, 55, 73–76, 78–82, 85, 86, 92–95, 103, 104, 125–130, 132, 135–141, 143, 144, 148, 149, 152, 156, 157, 160, 167, 168, 170, 190, 191, 195, 196, 198–200, 206, 209, 210, 218, 222, 227–229, 239, 242, 245–250, 263, 271, 285, 286
  conceptual model of, 5–9
  inequality, 118, 151–154, 156, 192
  structure and personality, 18, 190, 191, 193, 195–197, 199–203, 205, 206
  theory, 46, 76, 94
  types of, 2–4
Societal canalization, 151, 152, 155
Society, 3, 6, 7, 11, 18, 22, 25, 32, 33, 35, 37, 41, 42, 46, 47, 79, 83, 86, 92, 93, 103, 125, 148–152, 155, 160, 168, 171, 172, 187, 190, 191, 193, 196, 201, 209, 210, 211, 213, 215, 217, 221, 222, 228, 229, 272, 277, 279, 282, 283, 285, 287
Socioemotional functioning, 209, 210, 212, 215, 218, 219, 221, 222
Stability-flexibility dilemma, 54, 55, 62
Stress, 4, 64, 125, 127, 132, 144, 220
Structural perspectives, 228, 229, 230
Structure, 1, 11, 17–19, 31, 32, 38, 43, 51, 55, 59, 73–76, 78, 81, 82, 92, 127, 148, 149, 151, 160, 167, 170, 178–180, 186, 187, 190, 191, 193–203, 205, 206, 212, 227, 229, 246, 247, 275, 281
Subjective well-being, 131, 138, 143, 160
Survey, 47, 83, 95, 130, 132, 190, 198, 206, 227, 231–233, 237, 240, 243

Television, 228, 230–232, 240–242
Tenacious goal pursuit, 54, 55, 57, 59
Transformation, 2–4, 6–8, 10, 12, 15, 17–24, 32, 37, 38, 41, 42, 45, 47, 82, 109, 111, 115, 126, 132, 134, 144, 152, 160, 167–173, 175, 178,

179, 181, 186–188, 191, 195, 197–203, 209, 212, 221, 245, 249, 271, 273–275, 278–280, 283–285
processes, 3, 5, 16, 31, 32, 34, 37, 38, 39, 44–46, 171, 173, 181, 196, 275, 280
theory, 32, 45, 46
Transition, 1–3, 5, 6, 8, 10, 12, 14, 16, 17, 20–23, 51, 61, 63, 75, 81, 86, 102, 104, 108, 109, 111, 119, 136, 150–152, 155, 158, 160, 167, 190, 191, 195, 197, 201–203, 205–207, 217, 218, 229, 245–251, 253, 254, 256–263, 267, 269, 273–276, 278–286
school-to-college, 155, 156, 158–160
school-to-work, 16, 20, 106, 127, 155, 156, 158–160

Ukraine, 2–4, 17, 18, 190, 191, 195–207, 284
Uncertainty, 3, 4, 7, 8, 12, 19, 21, 22, 24, 40, 51, 52, 54, 63–65, 103–107, 111, 112, 118, 141, 153, 156, 157, 167, 196, 206, 248, 249

Unemployment, 1, 2, 8, 15, 20, 41, 106, 108, 110, 113, 114, 117, 126, 132, 134, 140–143, 153, 210, 249, 256–258, 262, 267, 269, 282
Urban, 9, 18–20, 195, 199, 201, 203, 209–212, 217–221, 228–230, 232–241, 279

Vietnam, 2, 3, 9, 17, 20, 227, 229–233, 239–243

Welfare state regimes, 102–105, 107–111, 118, 119
Work, 5, 8, 11, 12, 14, 15, 18, 21, 23, 51, 52, 65, 77, 79, 80, 83–86, 92, 93, 105, 110, 112, 114–117, 126, 127, 130–141, 143, 144, 150, 156, 158–160, 184, 185, 191, 194, 196–198, 200, 203–206, 245, 247, 251, 253, 254, 257, 262; *see also* Employment

Youth, 14, 36, 53, 104, 106, 110, 111, 155, 156, 158–160, 185, 219, 227, 232, 233, 242, 254